THE NEW TESTAME

A NEW TRANS

THE NEW TESTAMENT

A NEW TRANSLATION

VOLUME ONE

The Gospels and the Acts of the Apostles

By WILLIAM BARCLAY

COLLINS
ST JAMES'S PLACE LONDON
1968

Printed in Great Britain
Collins Clear-Type Press
London and Glasgow

Foreword

In making this translation I have had two aims in view. The first was to try to make the New Testament intelligible to the man who is not a technical scholar. The technical New Testament scholar does not need a new translation made for him; he is well able to make his own; and anyone whose business it is to teach the New Testament could have done what I have done—and could very probably have done it better. The second was to try to make a translation which did not need a commentary to explain it. I am well aware that this second aim is an impossibility, for biblical words and manners and customs, the biblical environment, the biblical ideas and categories of thought need explanation. But I have tried in so far as it was possible to make the New Testament speak for itself.

The man who attempts to translate the New Testament all by himself cannot but remember Luther's charge against Jerome. Luther's criticism, as W. Schwarz reminds us in his *Principles and Problems of Biblical Translation*, was that Jerome did his rendering alone, without help, and thus lost the promise: 'For where two or three are gathered together in my name, there am I in the midst of them' (Matthew 18.20). But it was my very great privilege to have some small part in the translation of the New English Bible, although not in the New Testament part of it, and to have had over many years a share in the work of the 'Translator's Translation', the Diglot, of the British and Foreign Bible Society. And there I learned far more about translation than ever I contributed. So even if the translation and the responsibility for it are mine, there are debts and there was a fellowship.

It was not until my own translation was well-nigh completed that there appeared the Greek New Testament of the United Bible Societies edited by Kurt Aland, Matthew Black, Bruce M. Metzger and Allen Wikgren. I had begun by using the second edition of the British and Foreign Bible Society's Greek Testament. But I revised the translation in the light of the newer text, which surely must become the standard New Testament Greek text.

A word of explanation is necessary with regard to the printing layout of the Sermon on the Mount in Matthew chapters 5 to 7, and in the parallel passages such as Luke 6.20-49. The material is arranged in apparently broken lines for three reasons.

i. In the ancient manuscripts the material was sometimes arranged in sense-lines in order to make the public reading of it easier. The lines indicate the phrasing which in reading makes the material easiest to follow and to understand.

ii. The lining is used to show how Jesus, so to speak, built up a saying.

Yours is this bliss,
when men shall heap their insults on you,
  and persecute you,
    and tell every wicked kind of lie about you
    for my sake (Matthew 5.11).

The first line is the general principle. Then each of the next three lines lays down a separate instance—insult, persecution, slander—in which the general principle is true. Each indentation of the margin marks a new instance in which the general principle is true.

iii. Hebrew poetry does not rhyme; it is built up on a series of parallels, and often the series is quite elaborate. A good example is in Matthew 7.24-27, where each one of the first ten lines has its exact parallel in each of the second ten lines. A shorter example is in Matthew 5.45.

If you do that,
you will be like your Father in heaven,
  for he makes his sun to rise,
    on the bad and on the good alike,
  and he sends the rain
    on saint and sinner.

The last four lines have the clear pattern a b a b.

It is to try to reproduce these characteristics of the form of the original Greek that the lay-out I have used has been chosen.

No one ever made a translation without the haunting sense of how much better it might have been, and of the imperfections of this translation no one is more conscious than I am. I can but pray that in spite of its inadequacy it may shed for some readers a clearer light on the book which is the word of God to men.

The University of Glasgow,
April, 1968

WILLIAM BARCLAY

Contents

General Introduction to the Gospels

In Revelation 4.7 we read of the four living creatures who were around the throne of God. One was like a lion, another like an ox, another like a man, and another like an eagle. As early as the second century these four living creatures were taken to be the emblems and symbols of the four Gospels, and to this day they are very often thus used in stained-glass windows. Different writers assigned them differently to each of the four Gospels; but the allocation which seems most fitting is that made by Augustine in his book *On the Agreement of the Gospels* (1.6). Augustine takes the man to represent Mark; the lion to represent Matthew; the ox to represent Luke; and the eagle to represent John.

The man represents Mark, because Mark has the simplest and the most human picture of Jesus. The lion represents Matthew, because Matthew is concerned to show us Jesus as the Lion of Judah, the promised Messiah. The ox represents Luke, because the ox is the animal of sacrifice, and Luke shows us Jesus in his all-embracing love as the sacrifice, not for any chosen nation, but for all mankind. The eagle represents John, because of all birds the eagle flies highest, and it is said that of all living creatures the eagle alone can look straight into the blaze of the sun, and not be dazzled. So John's thought climbs highest of all, and John sees furthest of all into the eternities.

So we may think of Mark as the simplest Gospel; of Matthew as the Messianic Gospel; of Luke as the universal Gospel; and of John as the profoundest Gospel.

Introduction to Mark

It is generally agreed that Mark is the earliest Gospel, and that it was written in Rome about A.D. 65. There is a very old tradition that Mark contains the preaching material which Peter was in the habit of using. Peter, the Galilean fisherman, was unable to write it down for himself, and Mark, acting as his interpreter, wrote it down for him.

There is in Mark what has been called 'an incomparable touch of reality'. Mark has many little incidental touches which read as if they went back to an eye-witness of the scene which is being described. When Mark is telling the stories of Jesus and the children, only he tells us that Jesus took the children *in the crook of his arm* (Mark 9.36; Matthew 18.2; Luke 9.47; Mark 10.16; Matthew 19.15; Luke 18.16). In the story of the Gerasene demoniac only Mark tells us that the man was always crying out and bruising himself with stones (Mark 5.5). In the story of the storm at sea only Mark tells us that Jesus was in the stern of the boat sleeping on a rower's cushion (Mark 4.38).

Far oftener than any other Gospel Mark has the habit of giving Jesus' words in the original Aramaic (3.17; 5.41; 7.11; 7.34; 14.36; 15.22). It looks as if Peter, when he told these stories, could not help hearing again the voice of Jesus speaking these words, not in Greek, but in his native tongue.

Mark was written before the days when theology had thrown a curtain of too much reverence around the events of the Gospels. When Mark tells the story of the ambitious request of James and John for the chief places in Jesus' kingdom, he does not hesitate to say that it was James and John themselves who made the request (10.35-45), but when Matthew tells the story, he does not wish to record anything that might bring discredit on an apostle, so he says that their mother made the request for them (Matthew 20.20-28). When Mark tells the story of Jesus' rejection by the people of Nazareth, he ends it by saying that Jesus could do no mighty works there (6.5); but when Matthew tells the story he says that Jesus did not do many mighty works there because of their unbelief (Matthew 13.58), because he does not like to say that Jesus was unable to do anything.

This is not to say that in Mark there is not deep reverence and great thought; but it is to say that in this the first of the Gospels we come nearest of all to a simple account of the man Jesus in the days of his flesh, the man who was also the Son of God.

MARK'S VERSION
of the Story of the Good News

Chapter 1

THIS is the beginning of the story of how Jesus Christ, the Son of
God, brought the Good News to men. 2It all began as the passage
in Isaiah the prophet said it would:

> 'See! I am sending my messenger ahead of you,
> and he will prepare your road.
> He will be like a voice shouting in the wilderness:
> 3Get ready the road by which the Lord will come,
> straighten the paths by which he will travel.'

4This came true when John the Baptizer emerged in the wilderness,
announcing a baptism, which was a sign of the repentance which
leads to the forgiveness of sins. 5People from all over Judaea flocked
out to him, and so did all the people of Jerusalem, and a continuous
stream of them were baptized by him in the River Jordan, while they
confessed their sins.

6John was dressed in clothes made of camel's hair; he wore a
leather belt round his waist; and his food consisted of locusts and
wild honey. 7This was his message: 'The One who is stronger than I
is coming after me. I am not fit to stoop down and to untie the strap
of his sandals. 8I have baptized you with water; he will baptize you
with the Holy Spirit.'

9It was then that Jesus came from Nazareth in Galilee, and was
baptized by John in the Jordan. 10At the very moment when he was
coming up out of the water, Jesus saw the heavens opening, and the
Spirit coming down like a dove upon himself. 11A voice came from
heaven. 'You are my Son,' it said, 'the Beloved and Only One, and on
you my favour rests.'

12No sooner had Jesus had this experience than the Spirit compelled

him to go out into the desert. 13He was in the desert for forty days,
and all the time he was undergoing the ordeal of temptation by
Satan. His companions were the wild animals, and the angels were
helping him.

14After John had been committed to prison, Jesus came into Galilee
proclaiming God's Good News. 15'The appointed time has come,'
he said. 'The Kingdom of God is almost here. Repent, and believe
that the Good News is true.'

16When Jesus was walking along the shore of the Lake of Galilee, he
saw Simon and Andrew, Simon's brother, casting their nets into the
sea, for they were fishermen. 17'Follow me!' he said to them. 'I will
make you into fishermen who catch men!' 18There and then they left
their nets and became his followers. 19He went on a little farther, and
saw James, Zebedee's son, and his brother, John. They were in the boat
servicing their nets. 20There and then he called them, and they left
their father Zebedee in the boat with the hired servants, and took the
decision to leave home and to become his followers.

21Jesus and his disciples went into Capernaum, and, as soon as the
Sabbath came round, he went into the synagogue, and began to teach.
22They were astonished at the way he taught, for he taught them like
a teacher who needed no authority other than his own, and not like
the experts in the Law. 23No sooner had Jesus entered the synagogue
than a man there with an unclean spirit shouted: 24'What business
have you with us, Jesus of Nazareth? Have you come to destroy us?
I know who you are! You are God's Holy One!' 25Jesus reprimanded
the spirit. 'Silence!' he said. 'Come out of him!' 26The unclean spirit
threw the man into a convulsion, and shrieked, and came out of him.
27They were all astonished. 'What is this?' they kept on asking. 'A new
kind of teaching! A teaching with the accent of authority! When he
gives his orders to the unclean spirits, even they obey him!' 28And in
no time the story of what Jesus had done spread everywhere, all over
the surrounding district of Galilee.

29They went straight out of the synagogue, with James and John,
into the home of Simon and Andrew. 30Simon's mother-in-law was
confined to bed with an attack of fever. They lost no time in telling
Jesus about her. 31He went in to her, gripped her hand, and lifted her
up. The fever left her, and she began to serve them with their meal.

32When evening came, and when the sun had set, they kept on

bringing to Jesus all who were ill and demon-possessed. 33Everyone
in the town gathered at the door. 34He healed many who were ill
with many different kinds of diseases, and ejected many demons. He
would not allow the demons to speak, for they knew who he was.

35Very early in the morning, long before the night had gone, Jesus
left the town and went away to a lonely place. He was praying there.
36Simon and his friends tracked him down. 37'They are all looking
for you,' they said, when they had found him. 38He said to them: 'Let
us move on somewhere else to the nearby villages. I want to proclaim
my message there too, for that is what I came to do.' 39So he went all
over Galilee, proclaiming his message in their synagogues, and
ejecting demons.

40A leper came to him, urgently appealing for help. 'If you want to
cure me,' he said, kneeling before Jesus, 'you can.' 41Jesus was heart-
sorry for him. He reached out his hand and touched him. 'I do,' he
said. 'Be cured!' 42Then and there the leprosy left him, and he was
cured. 43Jesus at once sent him away with a stern warning. 44'See to
it,' he said, 'that you don't tell anyone anything about this. But go
and show yourself to the priest, and take to him the offering for your
cleansing which Moses prescribed, to prove to them that you really
are cured.' 45But he went off and told everyone, and spread the story
everywhere. The result was that Jesus could no longer appear in any
town, but had to stay outside in the lonely places, and even then
people kept coming to him from all over.

Chapter 2

WHEN Jesus returned to Capernaum some days later, the news
went round that he was at home there. 2Such crowds gathered
that there was no room, not even round the door. 3While he was
speaking to them, a party of people came to him, bringing a paralysed
man carried by four men. 4When they could not carry the man in to
him, because the crowd was so dense, they removed part of the roof
of the house in which Jesus was; and, when they had dug their way
through, they let down the stretcher on which the paralysed man was
lying. 5When Jesus saw their faith, he said to the paralysed man: 'Child,
your sins are forgiven.' 6There was a group of experts in the Law
sitting there. Their minds immediately began to ask: 'How can this

fellow speak like this? 7This is an insult to God! Can anyone but God
forgive sins?' 8Jesus was at once inwardly aware of what was going on
in their minds. 'What put questions like that into your heads?' he
said. 9'Which is easier—to say to this paralysed man, "Your sins are
forgiven", or to say, "Get up! Lift your stretcher and walk?" 10Just
to show you that the Son of Man actually has authority on earth to
forgive sins'—with this he said to the paralysed man—11'I tell you,
Get up! Lift your stretcher, and away you go home!' 12On the spot, in
front of them all, the man got up, lifted his stretcher, and went off.
This left them in such a state of astonishment that they kept on
praising God. 'Never,' they kept on saying, 'have we seen anything
like this.'

13Jesus went out again and walked along the seashore. The people
all crowded to him, and he continued to teach them. 14As he was
walking along, he saw Levi, Alphaeus' son, sitting in the office in
which he collected the customs duties. 'Follow me!' Jesus said to him.
He rose from his seat and followed him.

15Jesus was sitting at a meal in Levi's house. Many tax-collectors
and people with whom no respectable Jew would have had anything
to do were guests along with him and his disciples, for there were
many people like that who were eager for Jesus' company. 16When
the experts in the Law, who belong to the school of the Pharisees, saw
that he was eating with disreputable characters and tax-collectors,
they said to his disciples: 'Why does he eat with tax-collectors and
with people with whom no respectable Jew would have anything to
do?' 17Jesus heard what they were saying. 'It is not those who are well
who need a doctor,' he said, 'but those who are ill. I did not come to
bring an invitation to those who are good but to sinners.'

18John's disciples were in the habit of fasting, and so were the
Pharisees. Some people came to Jesus and said: 'Why do John's dis-
ciples and the disciples of the Pharisees fast, while your disciples do
not fast?' 19'Obviously,' Jesus said to them, 'the bridegroom's closest
friends cannot fast so long as he is with them. So long as they have
the bridegroom they cannot fast. 20But the time will come when
the bridegroom will be taken from them, and then, when that time
comes, they will fast.

21'No one,' Jesus went on, 'sews a patch of unshrunk cloth on an
old coat. If he does, the patch that was meant to fill the hole tears
the cloth apart—the new from the old—and the tear becomes worse.

22No one puts new fermenting wine into old wineskins that have lost
their elasticity. If he does, the wine will burst the wineskins, and the
wine and the wineskins will both be lost. No! New wineskins for new
wine!'

23Jesus was walking through the cornfields on a Sabbath day. His
disciples, as they walked along, began to pluck the ears of corn. 24The
Pharisees said to him: 'Why are they doing what may not legally be
done on the Sabbath?' 25'Have you never read,' he said to them,
'what David did, when he and his friends were hungry and needed
food? 26Don't you know the story of how he went into the house of
God, when Abiathar was High Priest, and ate the sacred loaves, which
are placed in the presence of God, and which legally only the priests
may eat, and gave them to his companions as well? 27The Sabbath,'
he said to them, 'was made for the sake of man, and not man for the
sake of the Sabbath. 28So the Son of Man's authority extends over
the Sabbath too.'

Chapter 3

JESUS went into the synagogue again, and there was a man there
whose hand was withered. 2They were watching Jesus closely to see
if he would heal on the Sabbath, for they wanted to find something
which they could use as a charge against him. 3Jesus said to the man
with the withered hand: 'Get up, and stand where everyone can see
you! 4Whether is it permitted,' he said to them, 'to help or to hurt
on the Sabbath, to save life or to kill?' They remained silent. 5His gaze
swept round them, and there was anger in his eyes, for he was sad-
dened by the imperviousness of their hearts. 'Stretch out your hand!'
he said to the man. He stretched it out, and his hand was restored to
health.

6Thereupon the Pharisees went out and began to concoct a scheme
with Herod's supporters to kill Jesus.

7Jesus withdrew to the lakeside with his disciples, and crowds of
people from Galilee followed him. The crowds flocked to him also
from Judaea 8and from Jerusalem and from Idumaea and from Trans-
jordan and from the neighbourhood of Tyre and Sidon. They came
because the story of his deeds was common knowledge. 9The crowd
was so dense that he told his disciples to keep a boat ready to avoid

being crushed by the crowd, 10for he performed many cures, and the
result was that all who were suffering from the scourges of disease
rushed forward to touch him. 11Whenever the unclean spirits saw
him, they flung themselves down at his feet. 'You are the Son of
God,' they kept shouting. 12But he strictly ordered them not to sur-
round him with publicity.

13Jesus went up to the hill country, and there he called to his
service the men of his choice. They left their homes and their jobs
and came to him. 14He appointed twelve, because he wanted them to
be with him, and he planned to send them out to proclaim his
message, 15and to have power to eject the demons. 16He chose Simon
to whom he gave the new name Peter; 17and James Zebedee's son, and
his brother John, to whom he gave the new name Boanerges, which
means Sons of Thunder; 18and Andrew and Philip and Bartholo-
mew and Matthew and Thomas, and James Alphaeus' son, and Thad-
daeus, and Simon the Nationalist, 19and Judas Iscariot, who was the
man who betrayed him.

20Jesus went into a house, and once again such a crowd gathered
that it was impossible for them even to eat a meal. 21When his own
family heard what was going on, they left home to come and forcibly
restrain him. 'He has taken leave of his senses,' they said.

22The experts in the Law, who had come down from Jerusalem,
said: 'He has Beelzebul as his ally. It is by the help of the prince of
demons that he ejects the demons.' 23Jesus called them to him, and
used these illustrations to answer them. 'How,' he said, 'can Satan
eject Satan? 24If a kingdom is split against itself, it cannot survive.
25If a household is split against itself, it will not be able to survive.
26So, if Satan is attacking himself, and if he is split against himself, he
cannot survive—he is finished. 27The fact is that no one can go into a
strong man's house and plunder his goods, unless he first ties up the
strong man. Then indeed, he will be able to plunder his house.
28This is the truth I tell you,' Jesus went on. 'Men will be forgiven
for everything, for all their sins and their insults to God. 29But if any-
one insults the Holy Spirit, he will never be forgiven for ever. He is
guilty of a sin that not even eternity can wipe out.' 30Jesus said this
because they were saying that he had an unclean spirit.

31Jesus' mother and brothers came and stood outside. They sent in
a message to him to ask him to come out and see them. 32A crowd of

people were sitting round him. 'Look!' they said to him. 'Your
mother and your brothers and your sisters are outside asking for you.'
33'Who is my mother?' Jesus answered. 'Who are my brothers?'
34His gaze swept round the circle of people sitting round him. 'See!'
he said. 'My mother and my brothers! 35Anyone who obeys God's
will is my brother and sister and mother!'

Chapter 4

JESUS was again teaching by the lakeside, and a very large crowd
gathered round him. There was such a crowd that he got into a
boat and sat in it on the lake, while the whole crowd stood on the
land facing the lake. 2Much of his teaching was in the form of parables,
and this is what he said to them as he taught.

3'Listen! Look! A sower went out to sow his seed. 4As he sowed,
some seed fell by the side of the road, and the birds came and snapped
it up. 5Some seed fell on ground where there was only a thin skin of
earth over the rock. It sprang up immediately, because the soil was
so shallow. 6But, when the sun rose, it was scorched, and it withered,
because it had no root. 7Other seed fell among thorn-bushes, and the
thorn-bushes shot up and choked the life out of the seed, and it
produced no crop. 8Other seeds fell on good ground, and, as they
sprang up and grew, they produced a good crop, yielding up to thirty
and sixty and a hundred times as much as had been sown. 9If a man
has ears,' said Jesus, 'let him use them!'

10When Jesus was alone, the Twelve and his other friends asked him
about the meaning of the parables. 11'You,' he said, 'have received the
privilege of knowing the meaning of the Kingdom of God, a secret
which only a disciple can understand, but to those who are not
disciples everything has to be expounded by means of parables, 12so
that

"They may certainly see,
and yet not perceive the meaning of what they see;
and so that they may certainly hear,
and yet not understand the meaning of what they hear,
in case at any time they should turn to me,
and have their sins forgiven."

13You do not know the meaning of this parable?' Jesus said to them.
'Then how will you understand the meaning of all the parables? 14It
is the word that the sower sows. 15The picture of the seed that was
sown by the side of the road represents the people who hear the
word, but no sooner have they heard it, than Satan snatches away the
word that was sown into them like seed. 16In the same way the picture
of the seed that was sown on the ground which was only a thin skin
of earth over the rock represents the people who immediately and
enthusiastically welcome the word, whenever they hear it; 17but
they have no inner root, and they are at the mercy of the moment.
And so, when trouble or persecution comes because of the word,
they at once stumble and collapse. 18Then there are those who are
represented by the picture of the seed that fell among the thorn-
bushes. These are the people who hear the word, 19but the worry of
this present world, and the deceptive seduction of wealth, and the
desire for other things, get into them at the same time, and choke the
life out of the word, and it never gets a chance to produce a crop.
20The picture of the seed that was sown on the good ground repre-
sents the people who hear the word, and who really make it part of
their lives, and produce a crop, some thirty, some sixty, some a
hundred times as much as they received.'

21'Surely,' Jesus said to them, 'a lamp is not brought into the room
to be put under a bowl or under the bed? Surely a lamp is brought
into the room to be placed on its stand? 22If anything is hidden, it is
only in order that it should be revealed; and if anything is secret, it is
only that it should be brought out into the open. 23If a man has ears,
let him use them!'

24'Pay attention to what you are hearing,' Jesus said to them.
'What you get depends on what you give—only more so. 25For, if a
man already has, more will be given to him, and if a man has not, even
what he has will be taken from him.'

26'This,' said Jesus, 'is what the situation in the Kingdom of God is
like. It is like what happens when a man sows seed on the ground.
27He wakens in the morning and he goes to sleep at night. The seed
sprouts and grows—he does not know how. 28With no help from
anyone the ground produces its crop, first the shoot, then the ear,
then the ripe grain in the ear. 29And, as soon as the crop is ready for

it, he sends out the sickle, for the time to reap the harvest has come.'

30'How,' said Jesus, 'will we find something with which to compare
the Kingdom of God, or what picture can we use to represent it?
It is like a grain of mustard seed. 31When mustard seed is sown on the
ground, it is the smallest of all seeds which are sown on the ground.
32But when it is sown, it keeps on growing, until it becomes the
biggest of all kitchen herbs, and produces branches so big that the
birds nest in its shade.'

33Jesus talked to them in many parables like these, in so far as they
were capable of receiving his message. 34He never spoke to them
without using parables, but in private he explained the meaning of
everything to his disciples.

35Late on that day Jesus said to them: 'Let us cross over to the other
side of the lake.' 36So they left the crowd, and took him with them
without disembarking. Other boats accompanied them. 37A violent
squall of wind swept down on them, and the waves broke over the
boat with such force that it was on the point of being completely
swamped. 38Jesus was sleeping on a cushion in the stern of the boat.
They woke him up. 'Master,' they said, 'we're drowning. Can't you do
something about it?' 39He woke up and reprimanded the wind, and
said to the waters: 'Silence! Quiet!' The wind dropped, and there
was a complete calm. 40'Why are you such cowards?' he said to them.
'Can you not trust me even yet?' 41They were awe-struck. 'Who can
this be?' they said. 'Even the wind and the waters obey him!'

Chapter 5

JESUS and his disciples crossed over to the other side of the lake to
the district of the Gerasenes. 2No sooner had he disembarked from
the boat than there met him out of the tombs a man with an unclean
spirit. 3This man had his home among the tombs. He had reached
such a pitch of madness that it was no longer possible to bind him
with a chain, 4for he had often been bound with fetters and chains,
but he had wrenched the chains apart and had smashed the fetters in
pieces. No one was able to tame him. 5Night and day amongst the
tombs and on the hills he never stopped shrieking and gashing
himself with stones. 6When he saw Jesus in the distance, he ran and
knelt in front of him. 7'What business have you got with me, Son of

the Most High God?' he shouted at the top of his voice. 'For God's
sake don't torture me!' 8He said this because Jesus had been ordering
the unclean spirit to come out of him. 9'What is your name?' Jesus
asked him. 'My name is Regiment,' he said, 'for we are many.' 10Re-
peatedly he pleaded with Jesus not to send them out of the country.

11A large herd of pigs was grazing on the hillside. 12'Send us into
the pigs,' they pleaded with him. 'Let us go into them.' 13Jesus allowed
them to do as they asked. So the unclean spirits left the man and
went into the pigs, and the herd—there were about two thousand of
them—stampeded down the cliff into the lake, and were drowned
in the sea. 14The herdsmen fled, and told the story both in the town
and all over the countryside. So the people came to see what had
actually happened. 15They came to Jesus and found the demon-
possessed man sitting fully clothed and in his senses—that very man
who had had the regiment of devils—and they were terrified. 16Those
who had seen what had taken place told them what had happened to
the demon-possessed man and the whole story of the pigs; 17and
they begged Jesus to get out of their neighbourhood. 18When Jesus
was getting on board the boat, the man who had been demon-
possessed pleaded to be allowed to stay with him, 19but Jesus would
not allow him. 'Go back,' he said, 'to your own home and your own
friends, and tell them the story of all that the Lord has done for you,
and how he took pity on you.' 20So he went back and told all over the
Ten Towns the story of all that Jesus had done for him, and everyone
was astonished at the tale.

21When Jesus had made the return voyage in the boat to the other
side, crowds of people gathered to meet him. 22Before he had got any
farther than the shore, one of the presidents of the local synagogue,
Jairus by name, came to him. As soon as he saw Jesus, he threw him-
self at his feet 23with an urgent appeal. 'My little daughter,' he said, 'is
at death's door. Please come and lay your hands on her. Please come
and cure her and save her life.' 24Jesus went with him. Crowds of
people were following him, and they were jostling in on him on all
sides.

25There was a woman who for twelve years had suffered from a
haemorrhage. 26She had undergone many different kinds of treat-
ment at the hands of many doctors. She had spent her last penny
trying to find a cure. It had done her no good at all. Indeed her
trouble grew worse and worse. 27She had heard the stories about

Jesus. She came up behind him in the crowd and touched his cloak,
28for she said to herself: 'If I touch even his clothes, I will be cured.'
29There and then her flow of blood was staunched, and she felt in her
body that she was cured of the trouble which had been her scourge
for so long. 30Jesus was aware that his power had gone out of him.
Immediately he swung round in the crowd. 'Who touched my
clothes?' he said. 31The disciples said to him: 'Don't you see the
crowd jostling you on every side? What's the sense in asking who
touched you?' 32But Jesus continued to search the crowd with his
eyes to discover who had done it. 33The woman was so scared that
she was still shaking. She knew what had happened to her. So she
came and threw herself at Jesus' feet, and told him the whole truth.
34'Daughter,' he said, 'your faith has cured you. Go and God bless
you! Go and enjoy your new health, free from the trouble that was
your scourge.'

35While Jesus was still speaking, messengers came from the presi-
dent's house. 'Your daughter has died,' they said. 'Why trouble the
Teacher any further?' 36Jesus heard the message, but he disregarded
it. 'Don't be afraid,' he said to the president. 'Keep on trusting!' 37He
allowed no one to come with him except Peter, James and John,
James's brother. 38They arrived at the president's house. Jesus saw the
uproar. He saw them weeping and wailing unrestrainedly. 39He went
in. 'Why all this uproar? Why these tears?' he said. 'The child is not
dead—she's sleeping.' 40They laughed at him. He put them all out.
He took with him the child's father and mother and his own men
and went into the room where the child was. 41He gripped the
child's hand. 'Talitha kum,' he said to her, which means, 'Little girl!
I tell you, Get up!' 42There and then the little girl got up and began
to walk about. She was about twelve years old. They were suddenly
and completely amazed. 43He gave them very definite instructions
that no one should be told about this, and he told them to give the
child something to eat.

Chapter 6

JESUS left there and went to his own native place, and his disciples
accompanied him. 2When the Sabbath came round he taught in the
synagogue. The general reaction of his hearers was complete astonish-
ment. 'Where did he get these things he is teaching?' they said.

'What wisdom is this that has been given to him? How can he perform
such miracles? 3Isn't this the carpenter, Mary's son, the brother of
James and Joses and Judas and Simon? Aren't his sisters here with
us?' They were shocked and resentful that someone they knew so well
should speak and act like that. 4Jesus said to them: 'The only place in
which a prophet has no honour is his own native place, and among
his own relations and in his own family.' 5He could not do any
miracles there. All he could do was to lay his hands on a few sick
people and cure them. 6He was amazed at their unwillingness to
believe.

Jesus made a teaching tour of the villages. 7He summoned the
Twelve and sent them out in twos. He gave them authority to deal
with unclean spirits. 8He gave them orders to take nothing for the
road except a staff. They were not to take any bread, or a beggar's
knapsack, or any money in their money-belts. 9They were to wear
sandals. 'And,' he said to them, 'you must not wear two shirts.
10Wherever you enter a house,' he went on, 'stay there until you leave
that place. 11And if any place refuses you a welcome or a hearing,
shake the last speck of its dust from your feet, as you would do if
you were leaving a heathen town, to make them see the seriousness
of what they have done.' 12So they went out with a summons to
repent, and, 13everywhere they went, they ejected many demons,
and anointed many sick people with oil, and cured them.

14King Herod heard of what was going on, for the name of Jesus was
widely known. Some people were saying: 'John the Baptizer has
come back to life. That is why he possesses these miraculous powers.'
15Others said: 'He is Elijah.' Others said: 'He is a prophet, like one of
the great prophets.' 16When Herod heard what was going on, he said:
'This is John whom I beheaded come back to life.' 17Herod himself
had sent and arrested John, and had imprisoned him in chains,
because of the affair of Herodias, his brother's wife. The trouble had
arisen because Herod had married her, 18for John had told Herod that
he had no right to marry his brother's wife. 19Herodias nourished a
grudge against John, and would have liked to kill him, but she was
unable to succeed in her purpose, 20because Herod was afraid of
John, for he well knew that John was a good and holy man, and he
did his best to protect him. When Herod listened to John, he did not
know what to do, and yet he found a certain pleasure in listening to
him. 21But a day came when Herodias got her chance, when Herod

on his birthday gave a banquet for his courtiers and commanders
and for the leading men of Galilee. 22On that occasion Herodias'
daughter came in and danced for them. Herod and his guests were
delighted with her performance. The king said to the girl: 'Ask me for
anything, and I will give you it.' 23He pledged his oath to her: 'I will
give you whatever you ask for, up to half of my kingdom.' 24She
went out and said to her mother: 'What will I ask for?' 'John the
Baptizer's head,' her mother said. 25She at once went in and hurried
to the king, and made her request. 'I want you,' she said, 'to give me
John the Baptizer's head on a dish.' 26The king was very distressed,
but because he had given her his sworn promise in front of his guests,
he would not break his word to her. 27So there and then he de-
spatched a soldier of the guard with orders to bring John's head.
The soldier went and beheaded John in prison, 28and brought his
head on a dish, and gave it to the girl, and the girl gave it to her
mother. 29When John's disciples heard what had happened, they
came and took away his body, and laid it in a tomb.

30The apostles returned to Jesus and told him all about what they
had done and taught. 31'Come away by yourselves into a lonely
place,' he said, 'and rest for a little while.' For so many people were
continually coming and going that they did not even get time to eat
an uninterrupted meal. 32So they went away in the boat to a lonely
place where they hoped they could be by themselves. 33But many
saw them go and recognized them, and hurried there on foot from
all the towns, and went on ahead of them. 34So when Jesus dis-
embarked he saw a great crowd, and he was heart-sorry for them,
because they were sheep who had no shepherd, and he taught them
many things.

35By this time it was late in the day. So the disciples came to Jesus.
'This place is a desert,' they said, 'and it is late in the day. 36Send them
away to the farms and the villages round about to buy themselves
something to eat.' 37'You,' Jesus answered, 'must give them some-
thing to eat.' 'Are we,' they said to him, 'going to spend a year's
wages buying bread to give them a meal?' 38'How many loaves have
you?' Jesus said. 'Go and find out.' 'Five,' they said when they had
checked up, 'and two fishes.' 39He ordered them all to sit down in
groups on the green grass. 40So they sat down in sections of hundreds
and fifties. 41Jesus took the five loaves and the two fishes. He looked
up to heaven and said the blessing. Then he broke the loaves into

pieces, and gave them to the disciples to serve to the people, and he
shared out the two fishes among them all as well. 42They ate until
they could eat no more, and 43they collected enough broken pieces
of bread and scraps of fish to fill twelve baskets. 44Those who ate the
loaves numbered five thousand men.

45Jesus immediately made his disciples get into the boat and go on
ahead to the other side to Bethsaida, while he himself dismissed the
crowd. 46When he had taken leave of them, he went away up to the
hill country to pray. 47When evening came, the boat was half way
across the lake, and Jesus was alone on the land. 48He saw that they
were being buffeted by the storm as they rowed, for the wind was
dead against them. About three o'clock in the morning he came to
them, walking on the water, and it looked as though he meant to
walk past them. 49When they saw him walking on the water, they
thought he was a ghost, and they cried out in terror, 50for they all
saw him, and they were distracted with fear. At once he spoke to
them. 'Courage!' he said. 'It is I! Don't be afraid.' 51Then he got into
the boat with them, and the wind sank to rest. They were astonished,
52for they did not understand about the loaves, because their minds
were dully uncomprehending.

53When they had crossed over, they landed at Gennesaret, and
moored the boat there. 54When they had disembarked from the boat,
the people at once recognized Jesus. 55They hurried all over the
countryside, and from all over they carried the sick on stretchers to
where they heard that he was. 56And wherever he came into villages
or towns or country places, they laid the sick in the market-places,
and kept pleading with him to be allowed to touch even the tassel of
his cloak; and everyone who touched it was cured.

Chapter 7

A GROUP of Pharisees and experts in the Law came down from
Jerusalem to meet Jesus. 2They saw that some of his disciples ate
food with hands which were ceremonially unclean, that is, with
hands which had not been washed in the way which the ceremonial
law prescribes, 3for the Pharisees and indeed all the orthodox Jews do
not eat unless they first wash their hands as meticulously as the Law
prescribes, for they strictly observe the tradition of the elders. 4When

they come in from business, they do not eat until they have carried
out the ritual washing of themselves with water. There are many
other traditions which they observe, traditions connected with the
ritual washing of cups and pots and utensils of bronze. 5So the
Pharisees and experts in the Law asked Jesus: 'Why do your disciples
not behave as the traditional law of the elders prescribes? Why do
they eat food with hands which are ceremonially unclean?' 6Jesus said
to them: 'Isaiah well described the insincerity of your religion in his
prophecies in the passage which says:

"This people honours me with their lips,
but their heart is far from me.
7It is a futile worship which they offer me,
for they teach as divine commandments
man-made rules and regulations."

8You abandon the commandment of God, while you carefully ob-
serve man-made traditions. 9You are experts,' he went on to say to
them, 'in finding a way to cancel the commandment of God in order
to preserve your man-made traditions. 10Moses said: "Honour your
father and your mother," and, "The man who curses his father or
mother must certainly be put to death," 11but you say that if a man
says to his father or mother: "This money that I might have con-
tributed to your support is Korban" (that is, a gift dedicated to the
service of God and usable for no other purpose), 12he can, so far as
you are concerned, no longer be allowed to give any help to his father
or mother. 13You thereby use your humanly transmitted tradition
to render null and void the word of God. And this is only one of
many such things that you do.'

14Again he invited the crowd to listen to him. 'Listen to me, all of
you,' he said, 'and try to understand. 15Nothing which enters a man
from outside can defile him. On the contrary, it is what comes out
of a man that defiles him.'*

17When he had left the crowd and had gone indoors, the disciples
asked him what this difficult saying meant. 18'Are even you not able
to understand?' he said to them. 'Do you not realize that anything
which goes into a man from outside cannot defile him, 19because it
goes, not into his heart, but into his stomach, and is then evacuated
into the drain by natural processes?' (By this statement he in effect

*Here some manuscripts insert verse 16:
If a man has ears to hear, let him hear.

declared all foods to be clean.) 20 'It is what comes out of a man that
defiles him, 21 for it is from within, from the heart, that there emerge
evil thoughts, fornication, theft, murder, 22 adultery, the desire to
possess what a man has no right even to desire, wickedness, deceitful
trickery, shameless immorality, jealousy, slander, arrogance, folly.
23 All these wicked things come from inside, and it is they which de-
file a man.'

24 Jesus left there and went away into the districts of Tyre. He went
into a house because he did not want anyone to know that he was
there, but his presence could not remain concealed. 25 As soon as she
had heard that he was there, a woman whose daughter had an un-
clean spirit came and threw herself at his feet. 26 This woman was a
Greek by birth, a Syro-Phoenician. Persistently she asked him to eject
the demon from her daughter. 27 'You must first allow the children
to eat their fill,' he said, 'for it is not proper to take the food which
belongs to the children and to fling it to the pet dogs.' 28 'True, sir,'
she said, 'but the pet dogs below the table eat their share of the
crumbs that the children drop!' 29 'Because of this answer,' Jesus said
to her, 'go! The demon has gone out of your daughter!' 30 So she went
home, and found the child lying in bed, and the demon gone.

31 Jesus left the district of Tyre, and went by way of Sidon to the
Lake of Galilee. On the way he went through the district of the Ten
Towns. 32 They brought to him a deaf man who had also a bad
impediment in his speech, and begged him to lay his hand on him.
33 Jesus took the man away from the crowd because he wanted to be
alone with him. He put his fingers into his ears, and spat and touched
his tongue with the spittle. 34 He looked up to heaven, and took a
deep breath. 'Ephphatha!' he said to him, which means: 'Be opened!'
35 The man's hearing returned, and then and there the impediment
in his speech was removed, and he spoke clearly. 36 Jesus instructed
them not to tell anyone; but the more he so instructed them, the
more eagerly they broadcast the story to everyone. 37 They were com-
pletely astonished. 'He has done everything well!' they said. 'The deaf
get back their hearing, and the dumb their speech!'

Chapter 8

THERE was at that time another occasion when there was a great
crowd with Jesus, and when they had nothing to eat. He sum-
moned his disciples. 2'I am heart-sorry for the crowd,' he said, 'for
they have stayed with me for three days now, and they have nothing
to eat. 3If I send them away home without a meal, they will collapse
on the road, and some of them have come a long way.' 4'Where
could anyone find food here in a desert to satisfy them?' his disciples
answered. 5'How many loaves have you?' he asked them. 'Seven,'
they said. 6He ordered the crowd to sit down on the ground. He took
the seven loaves and gave thanks for them. Then he broke them into
pieces and gave them to the disciples to serve to the crowd. They
served them to them. 7They had a few little fishes as well. Jesus said
the blessing for them and told them to serve them to the crowd too.
8They ate until they could eat no more. They gathered up the broken
pieces that were left over, and there were seven hamperfuls of them.
9There were about four thousand people there. He sent them away
10and immediately got into the boat with his disciples and went to the
district of Dalmanutha.

11The Pharisees came and tried to involve Jesus in an argument.
They were trying to subject him to a test by demanding that he should
produce some visible divine action from heaven. 12Jesus sighed deeply.
'Why,' he said, 'are the people of today always looking for some
visible action of God? This is the truth I tell you, no such action will
be given to them.' 13So he left them, and got into the boat, and went
away to the other side.

14It so happened that the disciples had forgotten to bring any loaves
with them, and they had only one loaf with them in the boat. 15Jesus
proceeded to give them a warning. 'Watch what you are doing,' he
said. 'Be on your guard against the evil influence of the Pharisees and
against the evil influence of Herod.' 16They kept talking to each other
about having no loaves. 17Jesus knew what they were arguing about.
'Why do you keep on talking about having no loaves?' he said to them.
'Do you not even yet understand, and do you not even yet see the
meaning of things? Are your minds so completely impervious to the
truth? 18You have eyes—can you not see? You have ears—can you

not hear? Don't you remember the time 19when I broke the five loaves
into pieces and shared them out among the five thousand people?
Don't you remember how many basketfuls of fragments you col-
lected?' 'Twelve,' they said. 20'Don't you remember,' he said, 'the
time when I divided the seven loaves among the four thousand
people? Don't you remember how many hamperfuls of fragments
you collected?' 'Seven,' they said. 21'Do you still not understand?' he
said to them.

22They went to Bethsaida. A blind man was brought to Jesus with
the earnest request that Jesus should touch him. 23Jesus took the
blind man by the hand and led him out of the village. He spat into
his eyes and laid his hands on him. 'Do you see anything?' he asked
him. 24The man's sight began to come back. 'I see men,' he said. 'I
see them walking about, and they look like trees.' 25Jesus laid his hands
on his eyes again. The man saw clearly; his sight was completely
restored; and he was able to see everything plainly. 26Jesus sent him
away home. 'Don't even go into the village,' he told him.

27Jesus and his disciples went away to the villages of Caesarea
Philippi, and on the way Jesus put a question to his disciples. 'Who
are people saying that I am?' he asked them. 28'Some,' they said, 'are
saying John the Baptizer. Others, Elijah. Others, one of the prophets.'
29'And you,' he asked them, 'who do you say I am?' 'You are the
Messiah,' said Peter. 30Jesus sternly insisted that they must not tell
anyone about him.

31He now began to teach them that the Son of Man must undergo
many sufferings, and that he must be rejected by the chief priests and
the experts in the Law, and that he must be killed, and that after three
days he must rise again. 32He kept telling them this very plainly and
very definitely. Peter caught hold of him and sternly forbade him to
talk like that. 33Jesus swung round and looked at his disciples. 'Get
out of my sight, Satan!' he said sternly to Peter. 'Your ideas are not
God's but man's.'

34Jesus called both the crowd and his disciples to him. 'If anyone,'
he said, 'wishes to walk in my steps, he must once and for all say No
to himself; he must decide to take up his cross; and he must keep on
following me. 35Anyone who wishes to keep his life safe will lose it,
but anyone who is prepared to lose his life for my sake and for the
sake of the Good News will save it. 36What good will it do a man to

gain the whole world, if in so doing he forfeits his own life? 37For
what could a man give that would be an equal exchange for his life?
38If anyone is ashamed of me and my words in this apostate and sinful
age in which we live, the Son of Man will be ashamed of him, when he
comes with the glory of his Father and with the holy angels.'

Chapter 9

'I TELL you truly,' Jesus said to them, 'that there are some of those
who are standing here who will not experience death until they
see the arrival in power of the Kingdom of God.'

2About a week later Jesus took with him Peter and James and John,
and brought them up into a high mountain alone, all by themselves.
He was transformed before their very eyes. 3His clothes became
glistening, intensely white, with a whiteness with which no earthly
laundering could whiten them. 4Elijah appeared to them, along with
Moses. These two were talking with Jesus. 5'Rabbi,' Peter said to Jesus,
'it's a wonderful thing for us that we are here. Let us make three
shelters, one for you, one for Moses and one for Elijah.' 6He did not
know what to say, for they were terrified. 7There came a cloud,
enveloping them, and out of the cloud there came a voice: 'This is
my Son, the beloved and only One. Listen to him!' 8And suddenly,
when they looked round, they no longer saw anyone with them,
except Jesus.

9On the way down from the mountain Jesus gave them strict
injunctions not to tell to anyone the story of what they had seen,
until the Son of Man had risen from the dead. 10They could not stop
thinking of this saying of his, and they discussed with each other
what to rise from the dead could mean. 11They put a question to
Jesus. 'Why,' they said, 'do the experts in the Law say that Elijah must
first come?' 12'It is quite true,' he said to them, 'that Elijah is to come
first, and is to set everything in order. But what does scripture say
about the Son of Man? It says that he must go through many suffer-
ings, and that he must be treated with utter contempt. 13But, to re-
turn to your question, I tell you that the fact is that Elijah has come,
and they did what they liked to him, as scripture said they would.'

14When they came to the other disciples, they saw a large crowd

round them, and the experts in the Law engaged in an argument with
them. 15The crowd were all astonished to see Jesus, and, as soon
as he came in sight, they ran up to him, and welcomed him. 16'What
are you arguing about with my disciples?' he asked. 17'Teacher,' a man
in the crowd answered, 'I brought my son to you, because he has a
spirit that makes him dumb. 18And, whenever he has a seizure, the
spirit tears him, and he foams at the mouth and grinds his teeth, and
the boy is wasting away. And I asked your disciples to eject the spirit,
and they could not.' 19'This modern generation has no faith,' Jesus
said. 'How long have I to be with you? How long must I endure you?
Bring him to me.' 20So they brought the boy to Jesus. When the spirit
saw Jesus, it immediately threw the boy into a convulsion, and he
collapsed on the ground, and rolled about, foaming at the mouth.
21'How long has he been like this?' Jesus asked the father. 'Since he
was a child,' the father said, 22'and it often throws him into the fire
and into the water, for it is out to kill him. If you can do anything,
take pity on us and help us.' 23Jesus said: ' "If you can do anything,"
you say—everything is possible for the man who has faith.' 24Im-
mediately the father cried out: 'I do have faith. Help me, if I haven't
enough!' 25When Jesus saw a crowd running up, he spoke to the
unclean spirit with stern authority. 'Deaf and dumb spirit,' he said,
'it is I who order you—come out of him and never enter him again!'
26The spirit shrieked and violently convulsed the boy, and came out
of him. The boy was left so like a corpse that most of them said: 'He's
dead.' 27Jesus gripped the boy by the hand and lifted him up, and the
boy stood up. 28When Jesus had gone indoors and when they were by
themselves, the disciples asked him: 'Why were we not able to eject
it?' 29'This kind,' he said to them, 'can only be driven out through
prayer.'

30They left there and were travelling through Galilee, but Jesus did
not wish his presence to be known, 31for he was trying to teach his
disciples about what was going to happen. 'The Son of Man,' he said
to them repeatedly, 'is to be handed over into the power of men, and
they will kill him, and three days after he has been killed, he will rise
again.' 32But they did not understand what he was saying, and they
were afraid to ask him what he meant.

33They came to Capernaum, and, when Jesus was in the house, he
asked his disciples: 'What were you arguing about on the road?'
34They remained silent, because on the road they had been arguing

with each other about which of them was greatest. 35Jesus sat down
and called the Twelve to him. 'The man who wishes to be first,' he
said, 'must be the last of all and the servant of all.' 36He took a little
child and made him stand where they could all see him. Then he took
him up in the crook of his arm and said to them: 37'To welcome a
little child like this in my name is to welcome me; and to welcome
me is to welcome not me but him who sent me.'

38'Teacher,' John said to Jesus, 'we saw a man ejecting demons by
the use of your name, and we tried to stop him because he is not a
follower of yours like us.' 39'Don't try to stop him,' Jesus said. 'A man
cannot do a miracle in my name and then immediately go on to
slander me. 40For the man who is not our opponent is our supporter.'

41'If anyone gives you a cup of water to drink for my sake because
you belong to the Messiah, I tell you truly, he will not be unrewarded.'

42'If anyone does anything to cause one of these little ones who believe in me to sin, it would be better for him to have a huge millstone
hung round his neck and to be thrown into the sea.'

43Jesus went on to say: 'If your hand becomes a cause of sin to you,
cut it off. It is better that you should enter into life maimed than that
you should go to hell with two hands to the fire that can never be
quenched.* 45If your foot becomes a cause of sin to you, cut it off. It
is better that you should enter into life a cripple than that you
should be flung into hell with two feet.* 47If your eye becomes a
cause of sin to you, throw it away. It is better that you should enter
into the Kingdom of God with one eye than that you should be
thrown into hell with two eyes, 48where the destructive worm never
dies and the fire is never put out.

49'Every man's life must be a sacrifice to God, and the salt of the
sacrifice is the purifying fire of affliction.

50'Salt is good, but if the salt has lost its saltness, with what can you
give it back its flavour?

'Have a heart seasoned with the salt of purity, and then you will be
able to live at peace with one another.'

*Verses 44 and 46, which are the same as verse 48, are omitted by the best manuscripts.

Chapter 10

JESUS moved on from there, and went into the districts of Judaea
and of the country on the far side of the Jordan. Once again crowds
of people flocked to him and again, as his custom was, he continued
to teach them.

2A group of Pharisees came to him with what they intended to be a
test question. 'Is a man permitted to divorce his wife?' they asked.
3'What was the regulation which Moses prescribed for you?' Jesus
said. 4'Moses,' they said, 'allowed a man to draw up a deed of divorce
and to send his wife away.' 5Jesus said to them: 'Moses would never
have prescribed any such regulation, if it had not been for the fact that
your hearts are quite impervious to the real commandment of God.
6From the beginning of creation God made mankind male and fe-
male. 7For this reason a man will leave his father and mother and will
be joined inseparably to his wife, 8and the two will become so com-
pletely one that they will no longer be two persons but one. 9What
God has united man must not separate.' 10In the house the disciples
again questioned him about this. 11'If,' he said to them, 'a man divor-
ces his wife and marries another woman, he is guilty of adultery
against her; 12and if she divorces her husband and marries another
man, she commits adultery.'

13Little children were brought to Jesus for him to touch them, but
the disciples warned off those who were trying to bring them.
14When Jesus saw what the disciples were doing, he was vexed.
'Let the little children come to me,' he said, 'and don't try to stop
them, for it is to such as they are that the Kingdom of God belongs.
15I tell you truly, if a man does not receive the Kingdom of God like
a little child, he will certainly not get into it.' 16And he took them
up in the crook of his arm, and laid his hands on them, and blessed
them.

17As Jesus was going out of the house on to the road, a man came
running to him, and knelt in front of him. 'Good teacher,' the man
said, 'what am I to do to get this eternal life that God has promised?'
18'Why call me good?' Jesus said to him. 'No one is good except God.
19You know the commandments, Do not kill. Do not commit

adultery, Do not steal, Do not tell lies about anyone, Do not cheat
anyone, Honour your father and mother.' 20 'Teacher,' the man said
to Jesus, 'I have obeyed all these since I was a child.' 21 Jesus looked at
him and loved him. 'One thing is missing in your life,' he said. 'Go,
sell everything you have, give the proceeds to the poor, and you will
have treasure in heaven. Then come! Follow me!' 22 When he heard
Jesus saying this, a look of the deepest gloom came over the man's
face, and he went sadly away, for he was very wealthy.

23 Jesus' eyes swept over the company. 'With what difficulty,' he
said to his disciples, 'will the wealthy get into the Kingdom of God!'
24 His disciples were very surprised to hear this. 'Children,' said Jesus
again, 'how difficult it is to get into the Kingdom of God! 25 It is easier
for a camel to go through the eye of a needle than for a rich man to
get into the Kingdom of God.' 26 They were utterly astonished. 'Who,
then,' they said to each other, 'can be saved?' 27 Jesus looked at them.
'With men,' he said, 'it may be impossible, but not with God, for
everything is possible with God.'

28 Peter said to Jesus: 'We have left everything to become your
followers.' 29 'I tell you truly,' Jesus said to him, 'there is no man who
has left a house or brothers or sisters or mother or father or children
or estates for my sake and for the sake of the Good News 30 who will
not now in this present world get them back a hundred times over—
houses and brothers and sisters and mothers and children and estates,
yes, and persecution too—and in the world to come eternal life.
31 But many who are first will be last, and the last will be first.'

32 They were on their way up to Jerusalem, and Jesus was walking
ahead of them. They were in a state of bewildered astonishment. They
went with him, but they were frightened. Once again he took the
Twelve aside, and talked to them about what was going to happen
to him. 33 'We are going up to Jerusalem,' he said, 'and the Son of
Man will be handed over to the chief priests and to the experts in
the Law. They will condemn him to death, and they will hand him
over to the Romans. 34 They will mock him and spit on him and flog
him and kill him, and after three days he will rise again.'

35 James and John, Zebedee's two sons, came to Jesus. 'Teacher,'
they said, 'we want you to do for us whatever we ask you.' 36 'What do
you want me to do for you?' Jesus said. 37 They said to him: 'Give us
the right to sit one on your right hand and one on your left in your
glory.' 38 'You do not know what you are asking,' Jesus said. 'Can you

pass through the bitter experience through which I must pass? Can
you be submerged in the sea of troubles in which I must be sub-
merged?' 39'We can,' they said. Jesus said to them: 'You will pass
through the bitter experience through which I must pass. You will
be submerged in the sea of troubles in which I must be submerged.
40But the right to sit on my right and left hand is not mine to give you.
That is reserved for those for whom it has been prepared.'

41When the ten heard this, they were annoyed with James and John.
42Jesus called them to him. 'You know,' he said, 'that those who have
the prestige of ruling the Gentiles lord it over them, and that in their
society the mark of greatness is the exercise of authority; 43but in your
society the situation is very different. With you, if anyone wishes to
be great, he must be your servant; 44and with you, if anyone wishes
to hold the first place, he must be everyone's slave. 45Yes, indeed!
For the Son of Man did not come to be served but to serve, and to give
his life a ransom for many.'

46They came to Jericho, and, as Jesus was leaving Jericho accom-
panied by his disciples and a large crowd of people, Bartimaeus, the
son of Timaeus, a blind beggar, was sitting at the roadside. 47When he
heard that it was Jesus of Nazareth who was passing, he shouted:
'Son of David! Jesus! Take pity on me!' 48Many sharply told him to be
quiet, but he kept shouting all the more: 'Son of David! Take pity on
me!' 49Jesus stopped. 'Call him!' he said. They called the blind man.
'Keep your heart up!' they said. 'Get up! He's calling you!' 50Barti-
maeus threw off his cloak, leapt to his feet and went to Jesus. 51'What
do you want me to do for you?' Jesus said. 'Master,' the blind man
said, 'the one thing I want is to see again!' 52'Go!' said Jesus. 'Your
faith has cured you.' There and then his sight returned, and he fol-
lowed Jesus along the road.

Chapter 11

WHEN they were nearing Jerusalem, at Bethphage and Bethany,
near the Hill of Olives, Jesus sent on two of his disciples. 2'Go into
the village opposite you,' he said, 'and, as soon as you enter it, you
will find a tethered colt which no one has ever ridden. Untie it and
bring it to me. 3And, if anyone says to you: "Why are you doing this?"
say: "The Master needs it; and he will return it very soon."' 4So they

went off, and they found a colt tethered at a door, outside on the
open street, and they untied it. 5Some of the bystanders said to them:
'What are you doing untying this colt?' 6They told them what Jesus
had told them to say, and the bystanders made no effort to stop them.
7They brought the colt to Jesus; they put their cloaks on it; and he
mounted it. 8Many of the people spread their cloaks on the road;
others cut down leafy branches from the fields and spread them on it.
9Those who were going on ahead and those who were following
behind kept shouting:

'God save the people!
God bless him who comes in the name of the Lord!
10God bless the kingdom of our father David, which is
now on the way!
O send your salvation from the heights of heaven!'

11So Jesus entered Jerusalem. He went into the Temple precincts and
surveyed the scene, and then, since it was late in the day, he went out
to Bethany with his disciples.

12On the next day, when they had left Bethany, Jesus felt hungry.
13In the distance he saw a fig tree in full leaf. He went up to it to see if
he could find any fruit on it; but, when he reached it, he found noth-
ing but leaves, for it was not yet the season for figs. 14'May no one ever
again eat figs from you!' he said. His disciples were listening.

15So they came to Jerusalem. Jesus went into the Temple precincts,
and proceeded to drive out those who were selling and buying there,
and to upset the tables of the money-changers and the seats of the
pigeon-sellers. 16And he would not allow anyone to use the Temple
court as a short-cut between the shops and their houses. 17He began
to teach them. 'Does not scripture say,' he said, ' "My house must be
regarded as a house of prayer for all nations"? But you have made
it a brigands' den.' 18The chief priests and the experts in the Law
heard about this, and they tried to find a way to kill Jesus, for
they were afraid of him, because the crowd were all astonished at his
teaching.

19When evening came, they left the city. 20In the morning on their
way into the city they passed the fig tree, and they noticed that it was
withered root and branch. 21Peter remembered the incident of the
previous day. 'Look, Rabbi!' he said. 'The fig tree you cursed is

withered!' 22'Have faith in God,' Jesus answered. 23'I tell you truly, if
anyone were to say to this hill: "Be picked up and flung into the sea,"
if there are no doubts in his mind, but if he really believes that what
he is saying will happen, what he asks will be done. 24That is why I
tell you that you must believe that you have as good as received
everything for which you pray and ask, and then you will receive it.
25And, whenever you stand praying, if you have anything against
anyone, forgive it, for it is then that your Father in heaven will for-
give your sins.'*

27Once again they came to Jerusalem. When Jesus was walking in
the Temple precincts, the chief priests and the experts in the Law and
the elders came to him. 28'What right have you to act as you are do-
ing?' they asked him. 'Or, who gave you this right to do so?' 29'I will
put one question to you,' Jesus said. 'Answer it, and I will tell you
what right I have to act like this. 30Was the source of the baptism
which John administered divine or human? Answer me!' 31They
began to argue with each other. 'If,' they said, 'we say, "Divine," he
will say: "Why then did you not believe in him?" 32On the other
hand, suppose we say, "Human" '—they were afraid of the people,
for everyone was quite sure that John was genuinely a prophet. 33So
they answered Jesus: 'We do not know.' Jesus said to them: 'No more
am I going to tell you what right I have to act as I do.'

Chapter 12

JESUS went on to speak to them in parables. 'A man,' he said,
'planted a vineyard, and surrounded it with a hedge, and had a pit
dug in which the juice could be extracted from the grapes, and built a
watch-tower. He then let it out to tenants and went abroad. 2At the
proper time he sent a servant to the tenants to collect from the
tenants his due share of the crop of the vineyard. 3They took the
servant and beat him up and sent him away empty-handed. 4Again
he sent another servant to them. They knocked him on the head and
shamefully maltreated him. 5He sent still another. They killed him.
He sent many others. They beat up some of them and killed others.
6He had still one person to send, a beloved and only son. Last of all
he sent him. "They will treat my son with respect," he said. 7But these

* Some manuscripts here add verse 26: *'But if you refuse to forgive, your Father in heaven will not forgive your sins either.'*

tenants said to each other: "This is the heir. Come on! Let's kill him!
Then the estate will be ours!" 8So they seized him and killed him, and
threw his body out of the vineyard. 9What will the owner of the
vineyard do? He will come and wipe out these tenants, and give the
vineyard to others. 10Have you never read this passage of scripture?

"The stone which the builders rejected,
this has become the headstone of the corner.
11This is the action of the Lord,
and it is marvellous in our eyes." '

12They tried to find a way to arrest Jesus, but they were afraid of the
crowd, for they were well aware that Jesus had directed this parable
against them. So they left him and went away.

13A group of the Pharisees and of Herod's supporters were sent to
set a verbal trap for Jesus. 14'Teacher,' they came and said to him, 'we
know that you speak the truth, and that it makes no difference to you
who or what anyone is. Man-made prestige means nothing to you,
and you really do teach the life that God wishes us to live. Is it right
for us to pay the poll-tax to Caesar, or not? Are we to pay it, or are we
not to pay it?' 15Jesus was well aware that they were not asking for
information but that they were out to make trouble for him. 'Why
are you trying to catch me out?' he said. 'Bring me a shilling and let
me see it.' 16They brought him one. 'Whose portrait and whose
inscription is this?' he said. 'Caesar's,' they answered. 17Jesus said to
them: 'Pay to Caesar what belongs to Caesar, and to God what belongs
to God.' They were astonished at the way in which he had parried
their question.

18A group of Sadducees came and put a question to him. They
belong to the school of thought which denies that there is any resur-
rection from the dead. They put a question to him. 19'Teacher,' they
said, 'Moses prescribed a regulation in the Law for us that, if a man's
brother dies, and leaves a wife behind him, but leaves no child, his
brother should marry the wife, and raise a family for his brother.
20There were seven brothers. The first married a wife, and, when he
died, he left no family. 21The second married her and died, leaving no
family. The third did the same. 22The whole seven left no family.
Last of all the woman died. 23When they rise from the dead at the
resurrection, whose wife will she be, for she was married in succession
to the whole seven?' 24'Surely you are on the wrong track altogether,'

Jesus said to them, 'and it is because you do not know either the mean-
ing of the scriptures or the power of God. 25When men and women
rise from the dead, they neither marry nor are married, but are like the
angels in heaven. 26As for the fact that the dead are raised, have you
not read in the Book of Moses in the passage about the bush how
God said to him: "I am the God of Abraham and the God of Isaac and
the God of Jacob"? 27He is not the God of the dead but of the living.
You are on the wrong track altogether.'

28One of the experts in the Law came to Jesus. He had listened to the
course of the discussion between Jesus and the Sadducees, and he had
seen how well Jesus had met their arguments. So he put a question to
Jesus: 'Which is the commandment which takes priority of all the
others?' 29Jesus answered: 'The commandment which takes priority
over all the others is, "Hear, O Israel, the Lord our God is the only
Lord 30and you must love the Lord your God with your whole heart
and your whole soul, and your whole mind and with all your
strength." 31The second commandment is this: "You must love your
neighbour as yourself." These are the two commandments which
take priority over all the others.' 32'Well said, Teacher!' answered the
expert in the Law. 'You spoke the truth when you said that God is
one, and there is no other but him; 33and that for a man to love him
with his whole heart and his whole intelligence and with all his
strength, and to love his neighbour as himself, far outweighs all
burnt-offerings and sacrifices.' 34Jesus saw that he had answered
wisely. 'You are not far from the Kingdom of God,' he said to him.
And no one dared to ask him any more questions.

35Jesus was teaching in the Temple precincts. 'How,' he said, 'can
the experts in the Law say that the Messiah is David's son? 36David
himself, moved by the Holy Spirit, said:

> "The Lord said to my Lord,
> Sit at my right hand
> until I give you the victory over your enemies."

37David calls him Lord—how can he be David's son?'

The thronging crowd listened to Jesus gladly.

38In his teaching Jesus said: 'Be on your guard against the experts
in the Law, for they like to walk about in long flowing robes; they like
to be deferentially greeted as they move through the market-places;
39they like the front seats in the synagogue and the top places at ban-

quets. 40They greedily extract the last penny from credulous widows,
and then with their long prayers they try to give an impression of
exceptional piety. They will receive all the heavier a sentence.'

41Jesus sat down opposite the Temple treasury. He was watching
how the crowds of people put their money into the treasury. Many
wealthy people put in large contributions. 42A poor widow came and
dropped in two little copper coins, which were together worth half a
farthing. 43Jesus summoned his disciples and said to them: 'I tell you
truly, this poor widow has put in more than all the others who put
money into the treasury put together. 44They all have more than they
need, and it was out of their surplus that they made their contrib-
utions. She has far less than she needs, and it was out of her want that
she put in every farthing she possessed, all that she had to live on.'

Chapter 13

As Jesus was leaving the Temple, one of his disciples said to him:
'Teacher! Look! What a size these stones and buildings are!'
2'You see these huge buildings?' Jesus said. 'Not one stone of them will
be left standing on another. There is not a building here which will
not be utterly demolished.'

3When Jesus was sitting on the Hill of Olives, opposite the Temple
buildings, Peter and James and John and Andrew privately asked him:
4'Tell us, when will these events take place? What will be the sign that
the time has come when all these events are actually going to hap-
pen?' 5Jesus said to them: 'You must be careful that no one misleads
you. 6Many will come claiming to be my representatives. They will
say: "I am he," and they will mislead many. 7Don't get into a panic
when you hear of wars and reports of wars. These things must hap-
pen, but it is not yet the end. 8For nation will attack nation, and
kingdom will attack kingdom. There will be earthquakes here and
there. There will be outbreaks of famine. These events are the
beginning of the birth-pangs of the new age.

9'You must be continually on your guard. They will hand you over
to the councils; you will be flogged in synagogues; you will have to
stand your trial before governors and kings for my sake. This will be
an opportunity for you to show them what you believe. 10And first

the Good News must be proclaimed to all nations. 11When they
bring you to trial and hand you over to the authorities, do not worry
beforehand about what you are to say, but say whatever is given you
to say at the moment, for it is not you who are the speakers; it is the
Holy Spirit. 12Brother will hand over brother to death; father will
hand over child; children will attack their parents and murder them.
13You will be universally hated because of your connection with me.
But the man who sees things through to the end will be saved.

14'When you see the desolating abomination standing where it has
no right to be' (let the reader mark this well), 'then those who are in
Judaea must flee to the hills. 15Anyone who happens to be on the
housetop must not even come down and go into his house to take
something out of it. 16Anyone who is at work in the field must not
turn back to pick up his coat. 17It will be a tragic day for women who
are carrying children in the womb or feeding them at the breast.
18Pray that it may not be winter time when all this happens. 19For
these days will mean suffering such as has never happened since the
beginning, when God created the world, to this present day, and such
as will never happen again. 20And if the Lord had not cut short the
period during which the suffering lasted, no human being could
survive. But for the sake of the elect whom he had chosen, he has cut
it short.

21'If at that time anyone says to you: "Look! Here is the Messiah!
Look! There he is!" do not believe him. 22False Messiahs and false
prophets will emerge, and, by performing miracles and wonders, will
try everything possible to mislead God's chosen ones. 23But you must
be on your guard. I have forewarned you about these things before
they happen.

24'At that time, after the period of suffering,

> "The sun will be darkened,
> and the moon will not give its light,
> 25the stars will fall from the sky,
> and the powers in the heavens will be shaken."

26Then they will see the Son of Man coming on the clouds with great
power and glory. 27Then he will send out his angels, and they will
gather in God's chosen ones from the four points of the compass,
from the limits of the earth to the limits of the sky.

28'Learn the lesson which the fig tree offers you. When the sap rises
in its branches, and when it produces its leaves, you know that

summer is near. 29So when you see these events happening, you too
must realize that he is near, standing at the very door. 30I tell you
truly, all these things will happen within the life-time of this genera-
tion. 31Heaven and earth will cease to be, but my words will never
cease to be.

32'No one knows about that day or hour, not even the angels in
heaven, not even the Son—no one except the Father.

33'Be on your guard. Be sleeplessly on the watch! For you do not
know when the crucial moment will come. 34You are in a situation
like that which arises when a man leaves home and goes abroad, after
putting his servants in full charge of his affairs, and assigning to each
his task, and after issuing orders to the doorkeeper to be always on
the watch. 35So then you must be always on the watch, for you do
not know when the master of the house is coming, late in the
evening, at midnight, at dawn, or early in the morning. 36You must
watch all the time in case he comes all unexpectedly and finds
you asleep. 37What I say to you, I say to everyone—Be always on the
watch!'

Chapter 14

IT was now two days before the Passover and the Festival of Un-
leavened Bread. The chief priests and the experts in the Law were
trying to work out some stratagem which would enable them to arrest
and to kill Jesus. 2Their problem was that they could not arrest him
during the festival without serious danger of a popular riot.

3When Jesus was in Bethany as the guest of Simon the leper, as he
sat at table, a woman came in with an alabaster phial of very expensive
pure spikenard perfumed oil. She broke the alabaster phial, and
poured the perfume over his head. 4Some of the guests were annoyed
at what she had done. They said angrily to her: 'What is the point of
wasting the perfume like this? 5This perfume could have been sold
for more than fifteen pounds—a year's wages—and the money could
have been used to help the poor.' And they snarled their reproaches
at her. 6But Jesus said: 'Let her alone! Why distress her? It is a lovely
thing that she has done to me. 7You have the poor with you always,
and you can do something for them any time you like, but you do not
have me always. 8She has done all that she had it in her power to do.

She has anointed my body in advance for burial. 9I tell you truly,
wherever the Good News is proclaimed all over the world, what she
has done will be told too, and she will always be remembered.'

10Judas Iscariot, one of the Twelve, went to the chief priests with
an offer to deliver Jesus into their hands. 11They were delighted
when they heard his proposal, and promised to pay him well; and
Judas began to look for a good opportunity to deliver Jesus into their
hands.

12On the first day of the Festival of Unleavened Bread, the day on
which it was the custom to kill and to sacrifice the Passover lamb,
Jesus' disciples said to him: 'Where do you wish us to go and make the
necessary preparations for you to eat the Passover meal?' 13So he
despatched two of his disciples. 'Go into the city,' he said, 'and a man
carrying an earthenware water-jar will meet you. Follow him, 14and
say to the owner of whatever house he goes into: "The teacher says:
'Where is my guest-room where I am to eat the Passover meal with
my disciples?' " 15He will show you a big upstairs room, with every-
thing ready, and with the couches spread with rugs. There make all
the necessary preparations for us.' 16So the disciples went off into the
city, and found everything exactly as Jesus had told them. And they
made all the necessary preparations for the Passover.

17In the evening Jesus went to the room with the Twelve. 18When
they had taken their places at the table, during the meal, Jesus said:
'I tell you truly, one of you will betray me, one who is eating with me.'
19They were all distressed, and one by one they said to him: 'Surely it
can't be me?' 20'It is one of the Twelve,' Jesus said, 'one who is dipping
his bread in the dish with me. 21For the Son of Man goes out on the
road that scripture says he must go, but tragic is the fate of that man
through whom the Son of Man is betrayed! Better for that man if
he had never been born!'

22During the meal Jesus took a loaf and said a blessing over it. He
broke it into pieces and gave it to them. 'Take it,' he said, 'this means
my body.' 23Then he took a cup, and gave thanks to God, and gave it
to them, and they all drank from it. 24'This means my life-blood,' he
said, 'through which the new relationship between man and God is
made possible, the blood which is being shed for the sake of many.
25I tell you truly, I shall not drink again of the fruit of the vine until
the time comes when I drink it new in the Kingdom of God.' 26When

they had sung the psalm of praise, they went out to the Hill of Olives.

27Jesus said to them: 'There is not one of you whose courage will
stand the test, for scripture says: "I will smite the shepherd and the
sheep will be scattered." 28But after I have risen, I will go on ahead of
you into Galilee.' 29Peter said to him: 'Even if everyone else's courage
fails, mine will not.' 30'I tell you truly,' Jesus said to him, 'today,
this very night, before the cock crows twice, you will disown me three
times.' 31Peter strenuously insisted: 'If I have to die with you, I will
never disown you.' And they all said the same.

32They went to a place called Gethsemane. Jesus said to his disciples:
'Sit here, while I pray.' 33He took with him Peter and James and John.
The increasing realization of what lay ahead came to him with such a
sense of overwhelming shock that he was distraught in mind. 34'My
soul is grief-stricken with a grief like death,' he said to them. 'Wait
here, and stay awake.' 35He went a little farther on, and threw himself
on the ground, and prayed again and again that, if it was possible, he
might not have to face this terrible crisis. 36'Dear Father,' he said,
'everything is possible to you. Save me from having to go through this
bitter ordeal. But not what I will, but what you will.' 37He came and
found them sleeping. 'Simon,' he said to Peter, 'are you asleep?
Were you not able to stay awake for one hour? 38Stay awake and pray,
for you may well have to face an ordeal of temptation. I know that
you mean well and that you want to do the right thing, but human
nature is frail.' 39He went away again and prayed in the same words.
40Again he came back and found them sleeping, for they could not
keep their eyes open, and they did not know what to say for them-
selves. 41He came a third time. 'Sleep on now,' he said to them, 'and
take your rest. He has had his pay! The crisis is here! The Son of Man is
betrayed into the hands of sinful men! 42Up! On your way! The traitor
is coming!'

43Just as he was saying this, Judas, one of the Twelve, arrived,
accompanied by a mob armed with swords and cudgels, sent from the
chief priests and the experts in the Law and the elders. 44The traitor
had given them a prearranged signal. 'The man I shall kiss is the man
you want,' he said. 'Hold him and make sure of his arrest!' 45As soon
as Judas arrived, he went up to Jesus and said to him: 'Rabbi!' and
kissed him lovingly. 46They seized Jesus and held him. 47One of those
who were standing beside Jesus drew his sword, and struck the High
Priest's servant, and cut off his ear. 48Jesus said to them: 'Have you

come out with swords and cudgels to arrest me as if you were out to
arrest a brigand? 49I was with you daily, teaching in the Temple
precincts, and you made no attempt to arrest me. But this has hap-
pened this way that what the scriptures say should come true.' 50And
they all abandoned him and ran away.

51A young man was following Jesus, wearing nothing but a linen
sheet over his naked body. They tried to catch him, 52but he left the
sheet in their hands and fled naked.

53They took Jesus away to the High Priest, and all the chief priests
and the elders and the experts in the Law assembled. 54Peter followed
him at a distance, right into the courtyard of the High Priest's house.
He was sitting there with the High Priest's attendants. He was warming
himself at the fire.

55The chief priests and the whole council made repeated attempts
to find evidence against Jesus, which would justify them in putting
him to death, but they could find none. 56There were many who were
quite prepared to perjure themselves, but their evidence did not
agree. 57Some men came forward and falsely alleged in evidence
against him: 58'We heard him say: "I will demolish this Temple
made with hands, and in three days I will build another not made
with hands." ' 59But not even so did their evidence agree. 60Then the
High Priest rose in the middle of the council. 'Have you nothing to
say in answer?' he asked Jesus. 'What are these allegations that these
witnesses are making against you?' 61But Jesus remained silent and
made no reply. Once again the High Priest questioned him. 'Are you
the Messiah, the Son of the Blessed One?' he asked. 62Jesus said:
'I am, and you will see the Son of Man seated at the right hand of
Almighty God, and coming with the clouds of heaven.' 63The High
Priest ripped his clothes in horror. 'What further witnesses do we
need?' he said. 64'You have heard his blasphemous claim. What is
your verdict?' They all condemned Jesus as guilty of a crime for
which the penalty was death. 65Some of them spat on him, and
blindfolded him, and punched him with their clenched fists. 'Pro-
phesy!' they said to him. And the guards slapped him across the face,
as they took him into custody.

66While Peter was below in the courtyard, one of the High Priest's
maidservants came up to him. 67She saw him warming himself and
looked at him closely. 'You too were with the Nazarene, Jesus,' she

said. 68He denied it. 'I don't know him,' he said, 'and I don't under-
stand what you're talking about.' He went outside into the forecourt.
69The maidservant saw him, and again she said to the bystanders:
'This man is one of them.' 70Again he repeatedly denied it. Shortly
afterwards the bystanders again said to Peter: 'You certainly are one
of them, for you are a Galilean.' 71Peter swore that he was telling the
truth, and called down curses on himself if he was not. 'I do not know
this man you are talking about,' he said. 72Just then the cock crew the
second time, and Peter remembered how Jesus had said to him:
'Before the cock crows twice you will disown me three times.' He
flung himself out and wept.

Chapter 15

FIRST thing in the morning the chief priests and the elders and the
experts in the Law and the whole Sanhedrin prepared a plan of
action. They put Jesus in chains and took him away and handed him
over to Pilate. 2Pilate put the question to him: 'Are you the King of
the Jews?' Jesus answered: 'If you like to put it so.' 3The chief priests
brought many charges against him. 4Once again Pilate questioned
him. 'Have you nothing to say in answer?' he said. 'Look how many
charges they are making against you.' 5But to Pilate's astonishment
Jesus made no answer.

6It was Pilate's custom at the festival to release for them any one
prisoner for whom they asked. 7There was a man named Barabbas in
detention, along with the rebels who had committed murder in the
recent revolt. 8The crowd came and asked Pilate to observe his usual
custom. 9Pilate answered: 'Do you wish me to release the King of the
Jews for you?' 10For he was well aware that it was malicious ill will
which had prompted the chief priests to hand Jesus over to him. 11But
the chief priests incited the mob to demand that he should release
Barabbas to them rather than Jesus. 12Once again Pilate asked them:
'What am I to do with the man you call King of the Jews?' 13'Crucify
him!' they shouted back. 14'Why?' Pilate said. 'What crime has he
committed?' But they shouted all the more insistently: 'Crucify
him!' 15It was Pilate's desire to satisfy the mob, so he released Barabbas
for them. He had Jesus flogged, and handed him over to be crucified.

16The soldiers led Jesus away, and took him inside the courtyard,

that is, into the governor's headquarters. They summoned the whole
company to come. 17They dressed him in a purple robe, and they
plaited a crown of thorns and put it on him. 18Then they began to
salute him: 'Hail, King of the Jews!' 19Repeatedly they struck him on
the head with a cane, and spat on him, and knelt down and offered
him a mocking homage. 20When they had finished their horseplay,
they took off the purple robe, and dressed him in his own clothes,
and led him out to crucify him.

21A man called Simon of Cyrene was passing, on his way into the
city from the country. He was the father of Alexander and Rufus.
They forcibly commandeered him to carry Jesus' cross. 22So they
brought Jesus to the place called Golgotha, which means the Place of
a Skull. 23They tried to give him wine drugged with myrrh, but he
refused to take it. 24So they crucified him. They shared out his
clothes between them by drawing lots for them, to see who should
take what. 25It was nine o'clock in the morning when they crucified
him. 26On the placard stating the charge against him was written:
'The King of the Jews.' 27They crucified two brigands along with him,
one on his right and one on his left.*

29The passers-by tossed their heads at him and hurled their insults
at him. 'Aha!' they said. 'You are the man who was going to demo-
lish the Temple and build it in three days! 30Come down from the
cross and save yourself!' 31So the chief priests and the experts in the
Law jested with each other. 'He saved others,' they said. 'He cannot
save himself. 32Let us see the Messiah, the King of Israel, coming
down from the cross here and now, if he wants to make us believe
in him!' And those who were hanging on their crosses with him flung
their taunts at him.

33When it was twelve o'clock midday, darkness came over the whole
country, and it lasted until three o'clock in the afternoon. 34At three
o'clock in the afternoon Jesus shouted at the top of his voice: 'Eloi,
Eloi, lama sabachthani?' which means: 'My God, my God, why have
you abandoned me?' 35When some of the bystanders heard this, they
said: 'Look! He is calling for Elijah!' 36One of them ran and soaked a
sponge in vinegar, and offered it to him to drink. 'Wait!' he said.
'Let's see if Elijah is coming to take him down.' 37Jesus gave a great
shout and died. 38And the curtain of the Temple which veiled the

*Here some manuscripts insert verse 28: *So the passage of scripture which says, 'He was reckoned with the transgressors' came true.*

Holy of Holies was ripped from top to bottom. 39When the company
commander, who was standing facing him, saw how Jesus had died,
he said: 'This man was indeed a son of God!'

40Some women were looking on from a distance. Among them
were Mary from Magdala, and Mary the mother of James the Little
and of Joses, and Salome. 41They had attached themselves to Jesus
when he was in Galilee, and had attended to his needs there; and there
were many other women who had come up with him to Jerusalem.

42It was already late in the day, and, since it was the Day of Prepara-
tion, that is, the day before the Sabbath, 43Joseph of Arimathaea, who
was a well-respected member of the Sanhedrin, and who was himself
waiting for the Kingdom of God, greatly daring, went to Pilate and
asked for Jesus' body. 44Pilate wondered if it could be the case that
Jesus had died so soon. So he sent for the company commander and
asked if Jesus had been dead for long. 45When he had ascertained from
the commander that he was dead, he allowed Joseph to have the
body. 46Joseph brought linen, and took Jesus' body down from the
cross, and wrapped it in the linen, and laid it in a tomb which had
been hewn out of the rock. And he rolled a stone against the door
of the tomb. 47Mary of Magdala and Mary the mother of Joses were
watching where the body of Jesus was laid.

There is more than one ending to Mark's Gospel in the ancient manuscripts. All the manuscripts agree down to 16.8. It is after that that the variation comes. i. In the best and most ancient manuscripts the Gospel ends at 16.8. ii. In the great majority of the later manuscripts there is the longer ending which finishes at 16.20, and which is the ending in the Authorised Version. iii. In certain manuscripts there is an alternative shorter ending. iv. In one important manuscript there is additional material following 16.14. In this translation all the various endings are given.

Chapter 16

WHEN the Sabbath had ended, Mary of Magdala, and Mary the
mother of James, and Salome bought perfumed oils to go and
anoint Jesus' body. 2Very early on the Sunday morning they came to
the tomb, just after sunrise. 3They were saying to each other: 'Who
will roll the stone away from the door of the tomb for us?' 4They
looked up and saw that the stone, for all its immense size, had been
rolled away. 5They went into the tomb, and they were very surprised

to see a young man sitting there, on the right-hand side, dressed in a
white robe. 6 'There is no need to be so surprised,' he said to them.
'You are looking for Jesus of Nazareth who was crucified. He has
risen! He is not here! Look! There is the place where they laid him.
7 Go, and tell his disciples and Peter that he is going on ahead of you to
Galilee. You will see him there as he told you you would.' 8 They
came out of the tomb and fled, for they were reduced to a state of
trembling bewilderment; and they did not tell anyone about their
experience, for they were afraid.

THE LONGER ENDING

9 When Jesus had risen from the dead early on Sunday morning, he
appeared first of all to Mary of Magdala, out of whom he had ejected
seven demons. 10 She went and told the story to those who had been
with Jesus, and who were in mourning and tears. 11 When they were
told that Jesus was alive, and had been seen by her, they refused to
believe it. 12 After that, he appeared in another form to two of them,
when they were walking on their way to the country. 13 They went
back and told the news to the others, but they did not believe them
either. 14 Later he appeared to the eleven themselves, as they were
sitting at a meal, and he reprimanded them for their refusal to believe
and for the stubbornness of their hearts, because they had refused to
believe those who had seen him after he had risen.

15 'Go all over the world,' he said to them, 'and proclaim the Good
News to the whole of creation. 16 He who believes and is baptized will
be saved but he who refuses to believe will be condemned.

17 'These are the visible demonstrations of the action of God which
will accompany the life of those who believe. By using my name they
will eject demons. They will speak in strange languages. 18 They will
lift snakes in their bare hands. Even if they drink any deadly poison,
it will not hurt them. They will place their hands on the sick and
they will be cured.'

19 After he had spoken to them, the Lord Jesus was taken up into
heaven, and took his seat at the right hand of God. 20 They went and
preached everywhere, and all the time the Lord worked with them,
and confirmed their message by visible demonstrations of his power.

THE SHORTER ENDING FOLLOWING 16.8

They gave to Peter and his friends a brief account of all the instructions they had received. After that, Jesus through them sent out from east to west the holy and imperishable proclamation of eternal salvation.

THE ADDITIONAL MATERIAL FOLLOWING 16.14

They defended themselves by saying: 'This lawless and faithless generation is under the domination of Satan, who does not allow those who are subject to the unclean spirits to understand the truth and power of God. Therefore, reveal your righteousness now.' So they said to Christ, and Christ said to them: 'The limit set for the years of the power of Satan has been finally reached, but other terrible things are near. And I was delivered to death for the sake of those who had sinned, that they might turn to the truth, and no longer go on sinning, so that they might enter into the promised possession of the spiritual and incorruptible glory of righteousness, which is in heaven.'

Introduction to Matthew

MATTHEW's Gospel was written about twenty years after Mark's Gospel, between A.D. 80 and 90, and it has two great characteristics.

Matthew's Gospel is the most Jewish of the Gospels. It is the Gospel which is most conscious of the unbreakable link between the old and the new. Matthew wished to convince the Jews that Jesus was the Messiah for whom they had so long prayed and hoped. He knew that to a Jew the surest proof of that claim would be to demonstrate that Jesus fulfilled the prophecies of the Old Testament prophets about the Messiah. That is why again and again Matthew says that Jesus did or said something in order that something that some prophet said might come true (1.22; 2.15,17,23; 4.14; 8.17; 12.17; 13.35; 21.4; 26.56; 27.9). Matthew is above all concerned to prove to the Jews that in Jesus the prophecies are fulfilled, and that therefore in Jesus the Messiah has come.

Matthew's Gospel is above all the teaching Gospel. Matthew has a habit of collecting Jesus' teaching in great blocks. He takes certain subjects, and he collects together what Jesus said about them, thus bringing together in an orderly pattern things which are scattered all over the other Gospels. In the Old Testament there are five books of the Law, the Pentateuch as they are called, the first five books of the Old Testament. So Matthew presents us with five great blocks of Jesus' teaching, as if in them he was giving us the new law which supersedes the old law. The five great blocks are:

1. The Sermon on the Mount, or, The Law of the Kingdom (5-7).
2. The Charge to the Twelve, or, The Ambassadors of the Kingdom (10).
3. The Chapter of Parables, or, the Parables of the Kingdom (13).
4. The Discourse about Greatness and Forgiveness, or, the Personal Relationships of the Members of the Kingdom (18).
5. The Discourses about the Future, or, the Coming of the Kingdom (24,25).

Matthew's Gospel could well be called the first handbook of the teaching of Jesus.

Matthew's Gospel has one further characteristic. It is the Gospel of the Church. It is the only Gospel which uses the word Church (16.18; 18.15-17). It has much to say about Church practices. It tells of the right way to fast, to give alms and to pray (6.1-18). It lays down the Christian rule for marriage and divorce (5.27-28; 19.3-9). It gives the authority for baptism (28.19,20). It assures the smallest company of worshipping Christians of the presence of their Lord (18.20). It has indeed been suggested that Matthew's Gospel is deliberately constructed in such a way that it can be read through section by section at the meetings of the Church.

Without Matthew our knowledge of the teaching of Jesus would be very much poorer than it is.

MATTHEW'S VERSION
of the Story of the Good News

Chapter 1

THIS is the family tree of Jesus Christ, the Son of David, the son of
Abraham.
2 Abraham was the father of Isaac, Isaac was the father of Jacob,
Jacob was the father of Judah and his brothers, 3 Judah was the father
of Perez and Zerah, whose mother was Tamar, Perez was the father of
Hezron, Hezron was the father of Aram, 4 Aram was the father of
Aminadab, Aminadab was the father of Naasson, Naasson was the
father of Salmon, 5 Salmon was the father of Boaz, whose mother was
Rahab, Boaz was the father of Obed, whose mother was Ruth, Obed
was the father of Jesse, 6 Jesse was the father of King David.

David was the father of Solomon, whose mother was Uriah's wife,
7 Solomon was the father of Rehoboam, Rehoboam was the father of
Abijah, Abijah was the father of Asa, 8 Asa was the father of Jehosha-
phat, Jehoshaphat was the father of Joram, Joram was the father of
Uzziah, 9 Uzziah was the father of Jotham, Jotham was the father of
Ahaz, Ahaz was the father of Hezekiah, 10 Hezekiah was the father of
Manasseh, Manasseh was the father of Amos, Amos was the father of
Josiah, 11 Josiah was the father of Jechoniah and his brothers, in the
days of the exile in Babylon.

12 After the exile in Babylon, Jechoniah was the father of Shealtiel,
Shealtiel was the father of Zerubbabel, 13 Zerubbabel was the father of
Abiud, Abiud was the father of Eliakim, Eliakim was the father of
Azor, 14 Azor was the father of Zadok, Zadok was the father of Achim,
Achim was the father of Eliud, 15 Eliud was the father of Eleazar,
Eleazar was the father of Matthan, Matthan was the father of Jacob,
16 Jacob was the father of Joseph, the husband of Mary, and Mary was
the mother of Jesus, called Messiah.

17 From Abraham to David there were in all fourteen generations;

from David to the exile in Babylon there were also fourteen genera-
tions; from the exile in Babylon to the coming of the Messiah there
were also fourteen generations.

18This was the way in which the birth of Jesus took place. Mary his
mother was pledged to be married to Joseph, but, before they became
man and wife, it was discovered that she was going to have a child, as
a result of the action of the Holy Spirit. 19Although Joseph, her in-
tended husband, was a man who strictly kept the Law, he had no
desire publicly to humiliate her, so he wished to divorce her secretly.
20While he was planning to do this, an angel of the Lord appeared to
him in a dream. 'Joseph, son of David,' the angel said, 'do not hesitate
to marry Mary, for it is as a result of the action of the Holy Spirit that
she is going to have a child. 21She will have a son, and you must call
him by the name Jesus, for it is he who will save his people from their
sins.' 22All this happened that the statement made by the Lord
through the prophet might come true:

23'The virgin shall conceive and have a child,
and they shall give him the name Emmanuel,'

for that name means, 'God is with us.' 24So Joseph woke from sleep
and carried out the instructions of the angel of the Lord. He married
Mary, 25but he did not have any intercourse with her, until she had
had her son. And he called him by the name Jesus.

Chapter 2

WHEN Jesus had been born in Bethlehem in Judaea, in the time of
King Herod, there came to Jerusalem from the East scholars who
were students of the stars. 2'Where,' they asked, 'is the newly born
King of the Jews? We are looking for him, because we have seen his
star rise, and we have come to do homage to him.' 3When King Herod
heard about this he was alarmed, and all Jerusalem shared his alarm.
4So he called a meeting of the chief priests and the experts in the Law,
and tried to find out from them where the Messiah was to be born.
5'In Bethlehem in Judaea,' they told him, 'for scripture through the
prophet says:

6"And you Bethlehem, in land of Judah,
are by no means the least of the leaders of Judah,
for from you there shall emerge
the leader who will be the shepherd of my people Israel." '

7Then Herod secretly sent for the scholars from the East, and care-
fully questioned them about the date when the star had appeared.
8He sent them to Bethlehem. 'Go,' he said, 'and make every effort to
trace the child. And, when you have found him, send word to me, for
I too wish to go and do homage to him.' 9When they heard what the
king had to say, they set out, and the star, which they had seen when
it first rose, led them on, until it came and stopped where the little
child was. 10And very great was their rejoicing when they saw the
star. 11They went into the house and they saw the little child with
Mary his mother, and they knelt down and did him homage. They
unpacked their treasures, and offered him gifts, gold, frankincense
and myrrh. 12Because a message from God came to them in a dream,
warning them not to go back to Herod, they returned to their own
country by another way.

13When they had gone, an angel of the Lord appeared in a dream to
Joseph. 'Up!' he said. 'Take the little child and his mother and make
your escape to Egypt, and stay there until I tell you. Herod is about to
institute a search for the little child, for he is out to kill him.' 14So
Joseph set out, and took the little child and his mother by night and
left for Egypt. 15He remained there till the death of Herod. This hap-
pened that the statement made by the Lord through the prophet
might come true: 'Out of Egypt I have called my son.'
16Herod was very angry when he saw that he had been tricked by
the scholars from the East. So he sent and had all the boy children in
Bethlehem and in all the nearby districts killed. He had every child of
two years and under killed. This, he reckoned, would be the age of
the child about whose birth he had learned in his enquiries from the
scholars from the East. 17At the time that statement made through
Jeremiah the prophet came true:

18'A voice was heard in Ramah,
weeping and great lamentation,
Rachel weeping for her children,
and refusing to be comforted,
for they were no more.'

19When Herod died, an angel of the Lord appeared in a dream to
Joseph in Egypt. 20'Up!' he said. 'Take the little child and his mother,
and go into the land of Israel, for those who wanted to kill the child
are dead.' 21So he set out and took the child and his mother, and went
into the land of Israel.

22When he heard that Archelaus was reigning in Judaea instead of
his father Herod, he was afraid to return there. So, after he had
received a message from God in a dream, he went away to the district
of Galilee, 23and went and settled in a town called Nazareth. This
happened so that the statement made through the prophets might
come true: 'He shall be called a Nazarene.'

Chapter 3

It was at that time that John the Baptizer appeared on the scene,
preaching in the Judaean desert. 2'Repent,' he preached, 'for the
Kingdom of God is almost here.' 3It was he who was spoken of by
Isaiah the prophet, when he said:

> 'The voice of one shouting in the wilderness,
> "Get ready the road by which the Lord will come,
> straighten the paths by which he will travel." '

4John's coat was made of camel's hair, and he wore a leather belt
round his waist. His food consisted of locusts and wild honey. 5People
from Jerusalem and from all over Judaea and from all over the
Jordan valley flocked out to him. 6And a continuous stream of them
were baptized in the River Jordan, while they confessed their sins.

7When John saw the Pharisees and Sadducees coming in large
numbers to be baptized, he said to them: 'Brood of vipers! Who put it
into your heads to flee from the coming wrath? 8Prove the sincerity
of your repentance by your life and conduct. 9Don't get the idea that
you can say to yourselves: "We have Abraham as our father." For I
tell you, God can produce children for Abraham from these stones.
10Even now the axe is poised at the root of the trees. Every tree which
does not produce good fruit is going to be cut down and flung into
the fire. 11I baptize you with water to make you repent. He who is
coming after me is stronger than I am. I am not fit to carry his sandals.
He will baptize you with the Holy Spirit and with fire. 12He is going to
winnow the chaff from the corn, and he will clear every speck of

rubbish from his threshing-floor. His corn he will gather into the
store-house; the chaff he will burn with fire that nothing can put
out.'
13At that time Jesus came from Galilee to the Jordan to be baptized
by John. 14John tried to stop him. 'I need to be baptized by you,' he
said, 'and are you coming to me?' 15'For the present,' Jesus answered,
'let it be so, for the right thing for us to do is to do everything a good
man ought to do.' Then John let him have his way. 16No sooner had
Jesus been baptized and come out of the water, than the heavens
were opened, and John saw the Spirit coming down like a dove and
settling on him. 17And there came a voice from heaven. 'This is my
Son, the Beloved and Only One,' the voice said, 'and on him my
favour rests.'

Chapter 4

JESUS was then taken into the desert by the Spirit to undergo the
ordeal of temptation by the Devil. 2After he had deliberately gone
without food for forty days and forty nights, he was attacked by the
pangs of hunger. 3So the tempter came and said to him: 'If you really
are the Son of God, tell these stones to become loaves of bread.'
4Jesus answered, 'Scripture says: "It takes more than bread to keep a
man alive; man's life depends on every word that God speaks."'
5Then the Devil took him to the holy city, and placed him on the
highest spire of the Temple. 6'If you really are the Son of God,' he
said to him, 'fling yourself down, for scripture says: "He will give his
angels orders to protect you, and they will carry you in their arms to
ensure that you will never strike your foot against a stone."' 7Jesus
said to him, 'Again, scripture says: "You must not try to see how far
you can go with the Lord your God."' 8The Devil took him to a very
high mountain, and showed him all the kingdoms of this world and
their splendour. 9'I will give you all these,' he said to him, 'if you kneel
down and worship me.' 10Then Jesus said to him, 'Begone, Satan!
For scripture says: "You must worship the Lord your God, and you
must serve him only."' 11Then the Devil left him, and angels came
to his help.

12When Jesus heard that John had been committed to prison, he
withdrew to Galilee. 13He left Nazareth and went and made his

home in Capernaum, a town on the lakeside, in the territory of Zeb-
ulun and Naphtali. 14He did this so that the statement made through
the prophet Isaiah might come true:

15'Land of Zebulun and land of Naphtali!
Road of the sea beyond Jordan,
Heathen Galilee!
16The people who sat in darkness
have seen a great light,
and a light has arisen for those
who sat in the land and the shadow of death.'

17From that time on Jesus began to proclaim his message. 'Repent,'
he said, 'for the Kingdom of Heaven is almost here.'

18When Jesus was walking along the shore of the Lake of Galilee, he
saw two brothers, Simon, who is called Peter, and his brother Andrew,
casting a net into the lake, for they were fishermen. 19'Follow me,' he
said to them, 'and I will make you fishermen who catch men!'
20There and then they left their nets and became his followers.
21He went on from there and saw other two brothers, James, Zebe-
dee's son, and his brother John. They were in the boat with Zebedee
their father, servicing their nets. He called them. 22There and then
they left the boat and their father, and became his followers.

23Jesus made a circular tour of the whole of Galilee, teaching in
their synagogues, and proclaiming the Good News of the Kingdom
and healing all kinds of illness and all kinds of sickness among the
people. 24Reports of what he was doing spread all over Syria. So they
brought to him all those who were ill, in the grip of the most varied
diseases and pains, those who were possessed by demons, epileptics
and paralysed people, and he cured them. 25And huge crowds from
Galilee and from the Ten Towns and from Jerusalem and from
Judaea and from Transjordan followed him.

Chapter 5

WHEN Jesus saw the crowds, he went up the hill. He sat down to
teach, and his disciples came to listen to him. 2He opened his
mind and his heart to them, and this was the substance of his teach-
ing.

3 'O the bliss of those who realize
the destitution of their own lives,
for the blessings of the Kingdom of Heaven
are theirs here and now.
4 O the bliss of those whose sorrow is sore,
for they shall find courage and comfort.
5 O the bliss of those whose strength is in their gentleness,
for they shall enter into possession of the earth.
6 O the bliss of those who hunger and thirst
for all that sets them right with God,
for they shall be satisfied to the full.
7 O the bliss of those who treat others with mercy,
for they shall be treated with mercy.
8 O the bliss of those who are pure in heart,
for they shall see God.
9 O the bliss of those who make men friends with each other,
for they shall be ranked as the sons of God.
10 O the bliss of those who are persecuted
for their loyalty to God's way of life,
for the blessings of the Kingdom of Heaven
are theirs here and now.
11 Yours is this bliss,
when men shall heap their insults on you,
and persecute you,
and tell every wicked kind of lie about you
for my sake.
12 When that happens,
rejoice and exult in it,
for you will receive a rich reward in heaven,
for it was thus that they persecuted
the prophets who lived before you.

13 'You are the salt of the earth.
If the salt has lost its taste,
what can ever give it its saltness back again?
If that happens, you can do nothing with it
but throw it out for people to tramp on.

14 'You are the light of the world.
A town situated on a hilltop
cannot be hid.

15A lamp is not lit to be put under a bowl.
It is lit to be put on a lampstand,
and then it shines for everyone in the house
to see it.
16Just so, your light must shine
for everyone to see, so that,
when they see the lovely things you do,
it may make them want to praise
your Father who is in heaven.

17'You must never suppose that
I have come to destroy the Law and the Prophets;
I did not come to destroy them;
I came to fulfil them.
18This is the truth I tell you,
so long as heaven and earth shall last,
not the smallest letter,
not the smallest part of a letter of the Law
will cease to be valid.
It will remain until history comes to an end.

19'So then, anyone who tries to weaken
the authority of one of these commandments,
even if it is the least of them,
will have the lowest rank in the Kingdom of Heaven,
but anyone who obeys them,
and teaches others to obey them,
will have high rank in the Kingdom of Heaven.
20I tell you, you will certainly not get into
the Kingdom of Heaven,
unless your loyalty to the Law
surpasses that of the experts in the Law
and of the Pharisees.

21'You know very well that
"You must not kill"
is an ancient law;
and, if anyone kills,
he is liable to the judgment of the law-courts.

22 But I tell you that
anyone who is angry with his fellow man*
will have to stand his trial;
anyone who calls his fellow man a brainless idiot
will have to stand his trial in the supreme court;
anyone who calls his fellow man a wicked fool
is liable to be condemned to hell-fire.
23 If, then, you are bringing your gift to the altar,
and, when you are standing there,
you remember that your fellow man has a grievance against you,
24 leave your gift there in front of the altar,
and go and make peace with your brother,
and then come and offer your gift.

25 'Settle your difference quickly
with the man who is going to prosecute you,
while you are still on the road to the court with him.
If you do not,
the prosecutor may well hand you over to the judge,
and the judge may well hand you over to the court officer,
and you may well be thrown into prison.
26 I tell you, if that happens,
you will certainly not be released,
until you have paid the last farthing in full.

27 'You know that the Law states,
"You must not commit adultery."
28 But I tell you,
if anyone looks at a woman in such a way
as deliberately to awaken within himself
the forbidden desire for her,
he has already committed adultery with her in intention.

29 'If your right eye becomes a cause of sin to you,
tear it out, and throw it away,
for it is better that one part of your body
should be destroyed
than that your whole body
should be flung into hell.

*Some manuscripts add here *without a cause*.

30 If your right hand becomes a cause of sin to you,
cut it off, and throw it away,
for it is better for you that one part of your body
should be destroyed
than that your whole body
should go to hell.

31 'The Law states that,
if a man divorces his wife,
he must give her an official certificate of divorce.
32 But I tell you that
if a man divorces his wife
for any reason other than infidelity,
he makes her commit adultery;
and if anyone marries a woman who has been divorced,
he commits adultery.

33 'To take another example,
you know very well that it is an ancient law
that you must not take an oath in God's name
with no intention of keeping it,
but you must discharge the obligation of your oaths
in full to the Lord.
34 But I tell you,
do not take an oath at all,
neither by heaven,
for heaven is the throne of God;
35 nor by earth,
for earth is his footstool;
nor by Jerusalem,
for Jerusalem is the city of the Great King;
36 nor by your head,
for you cannot make one hair white or black.
37 In your speaking,
when you mean yes, say yes—nothing more;
when you mean no, say no—nothing more.
Anything which goes beyond that
has been prompted by the Evil One.

38 'You know that the Law states,
"An eye in exchange for an eye,
and a tooth in exchange for a tooth."

39 But I tell you
not to resist evil, but,
if anyone slaps you on the right cheek,
let him slap you on the other as well;
40 if anyone wishes to obtain judgment against you
for possession of your shirt,
let him have your coat as well.
41 And if a Roman officer commandeers you
to act as a baggage-porter for one mile,
go two miles.
42 If anyone asks you for anything,
give it to him,
and do not refuse anyone
who wishes to borrow from you.

43 'You know that the Law states that
you must love your neighbour
and hate your enemy.
44 But I tell you,
love your enemies,
and pray for those who persecute you.
45 If you do that,
you will be like your Father in heaven,
for he makes his sun to rise,
on the bad and on the good alike,
and he sends the rain
on saint and sinner.
46 What reward can you expect,
if you love those who love you?
Do not even the renegade tax-collectors do that?
47 Is there anything special about it,
if you greet only your friends?
Do not even the heathen do that?
48 You must be perfect
as your heavenly Father is perfect.'

Chapter 6

'TAKE care
not to make a public performance
of your goodness,
with the intention of letting everyone see
how good you are.
If you do,
you can expect no reward
from your Father who is in heaven.
2When you are going to perform an act of charity,
do not announce yourself
with a fanfare of trumpets,
as those whose religion consists
in ostentatious play-acting do
in the synagogues and on the streets,
to win popular applause.
I tell you truly, they have all the reward
they will ever get.
3But when you perform an act of charity,
your left hand must not know
what your right hand is doing.
4Your aim must be to keep your charitable giving secret.
And your Father who sees what is done in secret
will give you your reward in full.

5'When you are saying your prayers
you must not be like those whose religion consists
in ostentatious play-acting.
They love to say their prayers,
standing in the synagogue
and at the street corners.
Their idea is to be seen praying
by as many people as possible.
I tell you truly, they have all the reward
they will ever get.
6But when you say your prayers,
you must go into your private room,
and shut the door,

and say your prayers to your Father
who is in secret.
And your Father who sees what is done in secret
will give you your reward in full.
7When you say your prayers,
don't pile up meaningless phrases,
as the heathen do.
Their idea is that God will hear their prayers
because of their length.
8Don't become like them, you don't need to;
your Father knows what you need,
before you ask him.
9So, when you pray, pray like this:
Our Father in heaven,
May your name be held in reverence,
10May your Kingdom come,
May your will be done,
as in heaven, so on earth.
11Give us today our bread for the coming day.
12Forgive us for our failures in our duty to you,
as we have forgiven those who have failed
in their duty to us.
13Do not submit us to any time of testing,
but rescue us from the Evil One.★
14For if you forgive your fellow men
for the wrongs they have done to you,
your Father will forgive you;
15but if you do not forgive your fellow men,
then your Father will not forgive you either
for the wrongs you have done to him.

16'When you are fasting,
don't put on a gloomy face
as those whose religion consists
in ostentatious play-acting do.
They deliberately disfigure their faces,
so that no one will be able to fail to see
that they are fasting.

★ Some manuscripts add here, *For the Kingdom and the power and the glory are yours for ever. Amen.*

I tell you truly, they have all the reward
they will ever get.
17 But when you are engaged in fasting,
anoint your head and wash your face,
18 so that you may look to men
as if you were not fasting at all,
although your Father who is in secret will see it.
And your Father who sees what is done in secret
will give you your reward in full.

19 'Do not amass for yourselves treasures on earth,
where the moth eats them away,
and the rust corrodes them,
and thieves break in and steal.
20 Amass for yourselves treasures in heaven,
where the moth cannot eat them away,
and the rust does not corrode them,
and thieves do not break in and steal.
21 For your heart is bound to be
where your treasure is.
22 The eye is the body's lamp.
So then, if your eye is sound and generous,
your whole body will be full of light;
23 but if your eye is diseased and grudging,
your whole body will be full of darkness.
If the light that ought to be in you
has turned to darkness,
what a terrible darkness that darkness is!

24 'No one can be a slave to two owners,
for he will either hate the one and love the other,
or he will be devoted to one and despise the other.
You cannot be the servant both of the God of heaven
and of the god of this world's wealth.

25 'That is why I tell you,
Stop worrying about what you are going to eat and drink
to keep you alive;
stop worrying about the clothes you are going to wear
to keep your body warm.
Surely there is more to life than food,
and more to the body than clothes?

26Look at the birds of the sky.
See how they do not sow or reap
or collect things into storehouses.
And yet your heavenly Father gives them their food.
Are you not much more valuable than they?
27Can any of you add half a yard to his height
by worrying about it?
28And why worry about clothes?
Learn a lesson from the way
in which the wild lilies grow.
They do not toil or spin.
29But I tell you,
that not even Solomon in all his splendour
was robed like one of these.
30You have so little faith.
If God clothes like that the wild flowers
which have one brief day,
and which tomorrow are used
to make a fire to heat an oven,
can you not depend on him far more
to clothe you?
31So then, make up your mind to stop worrying,
and to stop saying,
"What are we going to eat?"
or, "What are we going to drink?"
or, "What are we going to wear?"
32These are the kind of things
which the people who don't know God
keep thinking about.
Your heavenly Father knows you need all these things.
33Make the Kingdom of God,
and life in loyalty to him,
the object of all your endeavour,
and you will get all these other things as well.
34So then, make up your mind
to stop worrying about tomorrow.
Tomorrow will worry about itself.
The day's trouble is quite enough for the day.'

Chapter 7

'DON'T make a habit of judging others,
  if you do not want to be judged yourselves.
2For the verdict which you pass on others
  will be the verdict that is passed on you.
You will get in exactly the same proportion
  as you give.
3Why do you see the speck of dust
  in your fellow man's eye,
and never notice the plank
  that is in your own eye?
4Or, how can you say to your fellow man:
  "Let me take the speck of dust
  out of your eye,"
while all the time there is a plank
  in your own eye?
5Your trouble is that you completely fail
  to practise what you preach.
Begin by taking the plank
  out of your own eye.
Then you will be able to see clearly
to take the speck of dust
  out of your fellow man's eye.

6'Never give to dogs what is sacred,
  and never offer your pearls to pigs.
If you do, they may well trample on them with their feet,
  and turn on you,
  and tear you in pieces.

7'Keep on asking,
  and you will get;
keep on seeking,
  and you will find;
keep on knocking,
  and the door will be opened for you.

8 For everyone who keeps on asking
gets what he asks for;
he who keeps on seeking,
finds;
if a man keeps on knocking,
the door will be opened.
9 Is any of you likely to give his son a stone,
if he asks for a loaf?
10 Is he likely to give him a snake,
if he asks for a fish?
11 If then, evil and ungenerous as you are,
you know how to give your children good gifts,
how much more can you depend on your Father in heaven,
to give good things to those who ask him for them?

12 'In everything you must treat others
as you would want them to treat you.
This is a summary of the message
of the Law and the Prophets.

13 'Go in by the narrow gate.
There is plenty of room to go through
the gate that leads to ruin;
it is no trouble to travel that road;
and there are crowds who go through it.
14 The gate that leads to life is narrow;
the road is beset with troubles;
and there are few who find it.

15 'Be continually on your guard
against false prophets,
for they come disguised as sheep
but they are really rapacious wolves.
16 You will recognize them by their conduct.
Obviously, you cannot gather
grapes from thorn bushes,
or figs from thistles.
17 Every good tree
produces fine fruit
but every rotten tree
produces bad fruit

18 It is not possible
for a good tree
to bear bad fruit,
or for a rotten tree
to bear fine fruit.
19 If a tree does not produce fine fruit,
it is cut down and thrown into the fire.
20 As with trees, so with men—
you can tell what kind of men they are
by the conduct they produce.

21 'It is not everyone who says to me, "Lord, Lord"
who will get into the Kingdom of Heaven.
It is the man who does the will
of my Father who is in heaven.
22 On the great day there will be many who will say to me,
"Lord, Lord, didn't we prophesy in your name?
Didn't we eject devils in your name?
Didn't we perform miracles in your name?"
23 When that happens, I will tell them straight:
"You are complete strangers to me!
Out of my sight!
Your deeds were sins!"

24 'So then, if anyone listens to these words of mine,
and obeys them,
he will be like a man of sound sense
who built his house
with its foundations laid on rock.
25 The rains lashed down,
and the rivers swelled,
and the winds blew and battered that house,
but it did not collapse,
for its foundations were laid on rock.
26 But if anyone listens to these words of mine,
and does not obey them,
he will be like a senseless man
who built his house
with its foundations laid on sand.
27 The rains lashed down,
and the rivers swelled,

and the winds blew and buffeted that house,
and it collapsed,
and its ruin was complete.'

28When Jesus finished speaking, the crowds were astonished at the
way he taught, 29for he taught as one who needed no authority be-
yond his own, and not like the experts in the Law.

Chapter 8

WHEN Jesus came down from the hill, great crowds of people
followed him. 2A leper came and knelt at his feet. 'Sir,' he said,
'if you want to cure me, you can.' 3Jesus reached out his hand and
touched him. 'I do,' he said. 'Be cured.' There and then his leprosy
was cured. 4'See to it,' Jesus said to him, 'that you do not tell anyone
about this, but go and show yourself to the priest, and take to him the
gift which Moses prescribed, to prove to them that you really are
cured.'

5When Jesus came into Capernaum, a centurion came up to him
with an urgent appeal. 6'Sir,' he said, 'my servant is lying at home
paralysed and in terrible pain.' 7'I will come and cure him,' Jesus said.
8'Sir,' answered the centurion, 'I am not fit to have you come into my
house. All I ask you to do is to say the word, and my servant will be
cured. 9For I too know what it is to be under authority, and I have
soldiers under my command. I am used to saying to one, "Go" and
he goes, and to another, "Come here" and he comes, and to my
slave, "Do this" and he does it.' 10Jesus was astonished to hear this.
'I tell you truly,' he said to those who were following him, 'I have not
found anyone in Israel with a faith like this. 11I tell you that many
will come from the east and the west and will be fellow-guests with
Abraham and Isaac and Jacob in the Kingdom of Heaven, 12but those
who were born to be members of the Kingdom will be flung out into
the outer darkness, where there will be tears and agony. 13Go,'
Jesus said to the centurion. 'Because you have a faith like this, your
prayer is granted.' And the servant was cured at that very hour.

14When Jesus went into Peter's house, he saw Peter's mother-in-law
lying in bed with an attack of fever. 15So he touched her hand and the

fever left her, and she got up and began to serve him with his
meal.

16When evening came, they brought many demon-possessed
people to him, and he ejected the spirits with a word, and cured all
those who were ill. 17This happened that the statement made through
the prophet Isaiah might come true: 'He took upon himself our
weaknesses and carried the burden of our diseases.'

18When Jesus saw the crowds on all sides, he gave orders to his
disciples to go away across to the other side of the lake. 19An expert
in the Law came up to him. 'Teacher,' he said, 'I will follow you
wherever you go.' 20Jesus said to him: 'The foxes have lairs and the
birds of the sky have nests, but the Son of Man has nowhere to lay
his head.' 21Another man, one of his disciples, said to him: 'Sir, let me
go and bury my father first.' 22'Follow me,' said Jesus, 'and let the dead
bury their dead.'

23He embarked on the boat, and his disciples accompanied him.
24Such a violent storm blew up on the lake that the boat was en-
gulfed in the waves. Jesus was sleeping. 25They came and wakened
him. 'Master,' they said, 'save us! We're drowning!' 26'Why are you
such cowards?' he said to them. 'You have so little faith!' Then he got
up and reprimanded the winds and the sea, and there was a complete
calm. 27The men were astonished. 'What kind of man is this,' they
said, 'for even the winds and the waters obey him?'

28When Jesus had crossed to the other side of the lake, to the
territory of the Gadarenes, two demon-possessed men met him on
their way out of the tombs. They were so fierce that no one was able
to pass along that road. 29They shouted at the top of their voices:
'What business have you with us, you Son of God? Have you come
here to torture us before the proper time?' 30Some distance away a
large herd of pigs was feeding. 31The demons pleaded with Jesus: 'If
you eject us from these men, send us into the herd of pigs.' 32'Begone!'
he said to them. They came out of the men and went into the pigs,
and the whole herd stampeded down the cliff and died in the waters
of the lake. 33The herdsmen fled. They went away into the town and
related the whole story, and told of what had happened to the
demon-possessed men. 34The whole town came out to meet Jesus,
and, when they saw him, they begged him to get out of their district.

Chapter 9

JESUS got into a boat, and crossed over to the other side of the lake,
and came to his own town. 2They brought to him a paralysed man,
lying on a bed. When Jesus saw their faith, he said to the paralysed
man: 'Courage, child. Your sins are forgiven.' 3Some of the experts
in the Law said to themselves: 'This fellow is insulting God!' 4Jesus
knew what was going on in their minds. 'What put such mistaken
ideas into your heads?' he said. 5'Which is easier—to say, "Your sins
are forgiven," or to say, "Get up and walk"? 6But just to show you
that the Son of Man actually has authority on earth to forgive sins'—
then he said to the paralysed man—'Up! Lift your bed! And away you
go home!' 7He got up and went off home. 8When the crowds saw this,
they were moved to awe, and they praised God that he had given
power like this to men.

9As Jesus was walking along from there, he saw a man called
Matthew, sitting in the office where he collected the customs duties.
'Follow me!' he said. And Matthew rose from his seat and followed
him.

10Jesus was sitting at a meal in the house, and many tax-collectors
and people with whom no respectable Jew would have had anything
to do came to be guests along with Jesus and his disciples. 11When the
Pharisees saw this, they said to the disciples: 'Why does your Teacher
eat with tax-collectors and with people with whom no respectable
Jew would have anything to do?' 12Jesus heard this. 'It is not those
who are well who need a doctor,' he said, 'but those who are ill. 13Go
and learn the meaning of the saying, "It is mercy I want, not sacrifice."
For I did not come to bring an invitation to those who are good but to
those who are sinners.'

14John's disciples approached Jesus. 'Why,' they said, 'do we and the
Pharisees make a habit of fasting, while your disciples do not?' 15Jesus
said to them: 'Obviously, the bridegroom's closest friends cannot be
in a state of mourning when the bridegroom is with them. But there
will come a time when the bridegroom will be taken away from them,
and then they will fast.

16'No one,' Jesus went on, 'sews a patch of unshrunk cloth on an
old coat, for, if he does, the patch that was meant to fill the hole tears

the coat apart, and the tear becomes worse than ever. 17No more do
people pour new fermenting wine into old wineskins that have lost
their elasticity. If they do, the skins burst, and the wine is spilled, and
the skins are destroyed. New wine is put into new wineskins, and both
are preserved.'

18While Jesus was speaking, a man who was president of the local
synagogue came and knelt in front of him. 'My daughter has just
died,' he said, 'but come and lay your hand on her and she will live.'
19Jesus started out to go with him, and the disciples went too.
20A woman who had had a haemorrhage for twelve years came up
behind Jesus and touched the tassel of his cloak. 21She said to herself:
'If I touch only his cloak, I will be cured.' 22Jesus turned and saw her.
'Courage, daughter!' he said. 'Your faith has made you well!' There
and then the woman was cured.
23When Jesus reached the president's house, he saw the flute-
players, and the crowd in an uproar. 24'Get out of here!' he said. 'The
girl is not dead. She is sleeping.' They laughed at him. 25When the
crowd had been put out, he went in. He gripped her by the hand, and
the girl got up. 26The story of this spread all over the country.

27As Jesus was passing on from there, two blind men followed him
shouting. 'Take pity on us, son of David!' they said. 28When he had
gone indoors, the blind men approached him. Jesus said to them:
'Do you really believe that I can do this?' 'Yes, sir,' they said. 29He
touched their eyes. 'Let your prayer be answered in proportion to your
faith,' he said. 30Their sight was restored. Jesus sternly ordered them:
'See that no one gets to know about this.' 31But they went and spread
the story all over that district.

32As they were leaving there, a dumb man who was demon-pos-
sessed was brought to Jesus. 33When the demon had been ejected
from him, the dumb man regained the power of speech. The crowds
were amazed. 'Nothing like this,' they said, 'was ever seen in Israel.'
34But the Pharisees said: 'He ejects the demons by the power of the
prince of the demons.'

35Jesus made a tour of all the towns and villages, teaching in their
synagogues, and proclaiming the Good News of the Kingdom, and
healing every disease and every sickness. 36When he saw the crowds he

was heart-sorry for them, for they were bewildered and dejected, like
sheep who had no shepherd. 37‘There is a rich harvest,’ he said to the
disciples, ‘but there are few workers. 38So you must pray to the Lord
of the harvest to send out workers to gather in his harvest.’

Chapter 10

JESUS summoned his twelve disciples and gave them such authority
over unclean spirits that they were able to eject them, and to cure
every disease and every sickness.

2These are the names of the twelve apostles: first, Simon, who is
called Peter, and his brother Andrew; James, Zebedee’s son, and his
brother John; 3Philip and Bartholomew; Thomas and Matthew, the
tax-collector; James, Alphaeus’ son, and Thaddaeus; 4Simon, the
Nationalist, and Judas Iscariot, the man who betrayed him.

5Jesus sent out these twelve, and these were his marching orders
to them: ‘You must not go off on any road that leads to Gentile
territory; you must not go into any Samaritan town; 6it is rather to
the sheep of the family of Israel who have gone lost that you must go.
7As you go, make this proclamation: “The Kingdom of Heaven
is almost here.” 8Cure the sick, raise the dead to life, cleanse the
lepers, eject the demons. You paid nothing to get, accept nothing
to give.

9‘Do not lay in a stock of gold or silver or copper coins in your
money-belts. 10Do not take a beggar’s knapsack for the road, nor two
shirts, nor shoes, nor a staff. The workman deserves his keep.

11‘Whenever you enter a town or village, look for someone who
deserves the presence of my messengers, and stay there until you
leave it. 12When you go into a house, give your greeting to it. 13If the
house deserves it, let your prayer for God’s blessing rest upon it. If it
does not deserve it, let your prayer for God’s blessing return to you.
14If anyone refuses you a welcome or a hearing, as you leave that
house or town, shake the last speck of its dust from your feet, as if you
were leaving a heathen town. 15I tell you truly, it will be easier for the
land of Sodom and Gomorrah on the day of judgment than for that
town.

16‘I am sending you out like sheep among wolves. You must there-
fore show yourselves to be as wise as serpents and as pure as doves.
17You must be constantly on your guard. They will hand you over to

the councils; they will flog you in the synagogues;
18you will be brought before governors and kings for my sake, but you must regard that as an opportunity to demonstrate to them and to the Gentiles your loyalty to me.
19When they hand you over, do not worry about how you are to speak, or about what you are to say. What you are to say will be given you at that time,
20for it is not you who are the speakers; the speaker is the Spirit of your Father, speaking in and through you.

21'Brother will hand over brother to death, and father will hand over child. Children will attack their parents and murder them.
22You will be universally hated because of your connection with me. But the man who sees things through to the end will be saved.
23When they persecute you in one town, make your escape to another. I tell you truly, you will not complete your circuit of the towns of Israel before the Son of Man shall come.

24'A scholar cannot hope to escape what his teacher has to suffer, nor a slave what his owner has to suffer.
25The scholar must be content to undergo the same experience as his teacher, and the slave as his owner. If they called the head of the house a child of the Devil, it is only to be expected that they will do the same to the members of the household.

26'Don't be afraid of them. What is veiled must be unveiled, and what is hidden must be made known.
27What I tell you in the darkness, speak in the full light of day; broadcast from the housetops what is whispered in your ear.

28'Don't be afraid of those who can kill the body but who cannot kill the soul. The one you must fear is the One who is able to destroy both body and soul in hell.

29'Everyone knows that two sparrows can be bought for one farthing, and yet death does not come to one of them without your Father knowing about it.
30Even the hairs of your head have all been counted.
31So, then, don't be afraid. You are more valuable than a whole collection of sparrows.

32'If anyone publicly acknowledges his loyalty to me in front of his fellow men, I will do the same for him in front of my Father who is in heaven.
33If anyone disowns me in front of his fellow men I will disown him in front of my Father who is in heaven.

34'You must not suppose that the result of my coming will be peace for the world. The result of my coming will not be peace but a sword.
35My coming is bound to result in a cleavage between a man and his

father, between a daughter and her mother, between a daughter-in-
law and her mother-in-law. 36A man's enemies will be his own kith
and kin.

37'If a man loves his father and mother more than he loves me, he
is not fit to belong to me. If a man loves his son or daughter more
than he loves me, he is not fit to belong to me. 38If a man does not
take up his cross and follow in my footsteps, he is not fit to belong
to me. 39To find your life is to lose it, and to lose it for my sake is to
find it.

40'To welcome you is to welcome me; to welcome me is to welcome
him who sent me. 41The man who recognizes a prophet and wel-
comes him as such will receive the same reward as a prophet. The
man who recognizes a good man and welcomes him as such will
receive the same reward as a good man. 42If anyone recognizes one
of these little ones as a disciple of mine, and gives him even a cup
of cold water, he can be sure of his reward.'

Chapter 11

WHEN Jesus had completed his instructions to the twelve disciples,
he moved on from there to continue teaching and proclaiming
his message in their towns.

2When news of the things that the Messiah was doing reached
John in prison, he sent his disciples to ask him: 3'Are you the One
who is to come, or are we to go on waiting and hoping for some-
one else?' 4'Go,' answered Jesus, 'and tell John the story of all you are
hearing and seeing. 5Blind men are seeing again; lame men are
walking; lepers are being cleansed; deaf men are hearing; dead men
are being raised to life; poor men are hearing the Good News. 6And
happy is the man who does not find himself antagonized by me.'

7As John's disciples were leaving, Jesus spoke to the crowds about
John. 'What did you go out to the desert to see?' he said. 'Was it to
see what you can see any day there—the long grass swaying in the
wind? 8If it was not that, what was it you went out to see? Was it to see
a man dressed in dainty and delicate clothes? The people who wear
dainty and delicate clothes live in kings' palaces. 9If it was not that,
what was it you went out to see? Was it to see a prophet? Yes, indeed,

it was, and, I tell you, more than a prophet. 10This is the man of whom
scripture says:

"Look! I am sending my messenger ahead of you,
And he will go on in advance to prepare your road for you."

11I tell you truly, that among mortal men no greater figure than John
the Baptizer has ever emerged in history. All the same, the least in
the Kingdom of Heaven is greater than he. 12It was in the days of John
the Baptizer that a situation first arose—a situation which still exists—
in which the Kingdom of Heaven is stormed, and in which those who
are eager to storm their way into it clutch at it. 13For up to John all
the prophets and the whole Law told of the things which were
destined to happen. 14But, if you are prepared to accept it, John is
Elijah who was destined to come. 15If you have ears to hear, then
hear.'

16'With what can I compare the people of today? They are like
children sitting in the market-place, calling to their companions and
saying:

17"When we played you a happy tune,
you did not dance;
when we wailed you a sad lament,
you did not mourn."

18For John came living the life of an ascetic, and they say: "The man
is demon-possessed!" 19The Son of Man came enjoying life like a
normal person, and they say: "A glutton and a drunkard! The friend
of renegade tax-collectors and of people with whom no respectable
Jew would have anything to do!" But God's wisdom is vindicated by
its results.'

20It was then that Jesus reproached the towns in which very many
of his miracles had been performed, because they refused to repent.
21'Tragic will be your fate, Chorazin! Tragic will be your fate, Beth-
saida! For, if the miracles which have been done in you had been done
in Tyre and Sidon, they would long ago have repented in sackcloth
and ashes. 22But I tell you, Tyre and Sidon will get off more lightly in
the day of judgment than you. 23And you, Capernaum—do you
think you are going to be exalted as high as heaven? You will go down
to the depths of hell. For, if the miracles which have been done in you
had been done in Sodom, it would still be standing today. 24But I tell

you, the land of Sodom will get off more lightly in the day of judg-
ment than you!'

25It was then that Jesus said: 'I thank you, Father, Lord of heaven
and earth, that you have hidden these things from the wise and
clever and that you have revealed them to those who are as simple as
little children. 26Yes, indeed, Father, I thank you, for this is what you
chose to do.'

27'All things have been entrusted to me by my Father. No one
really knows the Son except the Father, and no one really knows the
Father except the Son, and those to whom the Son chooses to make
him known.'

28'Come to me, all you who are tired and bent beneath your
burdens, and I will give you rest. 29Take my yoke on your shoulders,
and let me teach you, for I am gentle and humble in heart, and you
will find rest for your souls, 30for my yoke is kindly and my load is
light.'

Chapter 12

IT was then that Jesus went for a walk through the cornfields on
the Sabbath day. The disciples felt hungry and began to pluck the
ears of corn and eat them. 2The Pharisees saw this. 'Look!' they said.
'Your disciples are doing what it is not permitted by the Law to do on
the Sabbath day.' 3'Have you not read,' he said to them, 'what David
did when he and his friends were hungry? 4Do you not know the story
of how he went into the house of God and ate the sacred loaves which
are placed in the presence of God, although he and his friends had no
right to eat them, because only the priests are permitted to eat them?
5Or, have you not read in the Law how the work of the priests in the
Temple compels them to break the Sabbath law, and thus to profane
the Sabbath, and yet they remain blameless? 6I tell you that some-
thing greater than the Temple is here. 7If you had known the meaning
of the saying, "It is mercy I want, not sacrifice," you would not have
condemned those who are blameless, 8for the Son of Man's authority
extends over the Sabbath.'

9He moved on from there, and went into their synagogue. 10There

was a man there with a withered hand. In an attempt to find some-
thing which they could use as a charge against him, they asked him:
'Is it permitted to heal on the Sabbath day?' 11'If one of you has a
sheep,' he said, 'and the sheep falls into a hole in the ground on the
Sabbath day, will he not take a grip of it and lift it out? 12Surely you
will admit that a man is more valuable than a sheep? Obviously, there
is no law to stop a man doing good on the Sabbath day.' 13Then he
said to the man: 'Stretch out your hand!' He stretched it out, and it
was restored, healthy as the other. 14The Pharisees went away and
concocted a scheme to kill him.

15Jesus was well aware of what they were doing, so he withdrew
from there. Large numbers of people followed him, and he healed
them all. 16He strictly ordered them not to surround him with
publicity. 17All this happened that the statement made through the
prophet Isaiah might come true:

18'Behold, my servant whom I have chosen!
My Beloved and Only One in whom my soul
has found delight!
I will put my Spirit upon him,
and he will announce to the nations that the time
of judgment has come.
19He will not be a loud-mouthed man of strife,
nor will anyone hear his voice in the streets.
20He will not break a crushed reed,
and he will not extinguish a dimly-burning wick,
until he makes his judgment victorious;
21and in his name shall the Gentiles place their hope.'

22It was after that that a demon-possessed man who was blind and
dumb was brought to Jesus, and he cured him so effectively that the
dumb man was able to speak and see. 23The crowds were all aston-
ished. 'Can this be the Son of David?' they said.

24But when the Pharisees heard of this, they said: 'The only way in
which this fellow ejects demons is by the help of Beelzebul, the
prince of the demons.' 25Jesus knew what they were thinking. 'Every
kingdom,' he said, 'which is split within itself is on the way to being
laid waste. No city or household which is split within itself can sur-
vive. 26If Satan is ejecting Satan, he is split within himself. How then
can his kingdom survive? 27Further, if I eject demons by the help of

Beelzebul, by whose help do your own disciples eject them? Ask
them what they think of this argument of yours. 28If I eject demons
by the help of the Spirit of God, then the Kingdom of God has reached
you here and now. 29To put it in another way, how can anyone enter
the house of a strong man and plunder his goods, unless he first ties
up the strong man? Then indeed he will be able to plunder his
house.

30'If a man is not my ally,' Jesus went on, 'he is my enemy, and if a
man is not helping my work he is undoing it. 31That is why I tell you
that men will be forgiven for every sin and every insult to God, but
they will not be forgiven for insulting the Spirit. 32If any man
speaks a word against the Son of Man, he will be forgiven for it, but
if anyone speaks a word against the Holy Spirit, he will not be forgiven
for it, either in this world or in the world to come. You must make
up your minds. 33If the tree is good, the fruit must be good, and if the
tree is bad, the fruit must be bad, for you can only tell what kind of
tree a tree is by its fruit.

34'You brood of vipers! How can you say anything good when you
are evil? A man's words are nothing other than the overflow of what
is in his heart. 35A good man brings good things out of his good
treasure-house; an evil man brings evil things out of his evil treasure-
house. 36I tell you that on the day of judgment men will have
to answer for every careless word they shall speak. 37For by your
words you will be acquitted, and by your words you will be con-
demned.'

38Some of the experts in the Law and the Pharisees then said to
Jesus: 'Teacher, we would like you to provide us with some visible
action of God which will prove your claims.' 39Jesus answered: 'This
age which demands some visible action of God is an evil and apostate
age, and the only such action that will be given to it is the action of
God which was seen in the case of the prophet Jonah. 40For as Jonah
was inside the sea-monster for three days and three nights, so the Son
of Man will be in the heart of the earth for three days and three
nights. 41When the day of judgment comes, the people of Nineveh
will rise from the dead at the same time as the people of today and
will condemn them, for they repented at the preaching of Jonah, and
there is a greater event than Jonah here. 42When the day of judgment
comes, the Queen of the South will rise from the dead at the same
time as the people of today, and will condemn them, for she came

from the ends of the earth to listen to the wisdom of Solomon, and
there is a greater event than Solomon here.'

43'When an unclean spirit goes out of a man, it roams through
waterless places, looking for rest, and finds none. 44Then it says: "I
will go back to the house which used to be mine and which I left."
So it comes and finds the house empty, swept and in perfect order.
45Then it goes and brings back along with it seven other spirits worse
than itself, and they go in and make their home there. So the last
state of that man becomes worse than the first. So it will be with the
men of this evil age.'

46While Jesus was speaking to the crowds, his mother and brothers
stood outside, wanting to speak to him. 47Someone said to him:
'Look! Your mother and brothers are standing outside, wanting to
speak to you.' 48He answered the man who told him: 'Who is my
mother? Who are my brothers?' 49He pointed to his disciples. 'See!'
he said. 'My mother and my brothers! 50Anyone who does the will
of my Father in heaven is my brother and sister and mother.'

Chapter 13

On that day Jesus went out of the house and sat by the lake-side.
2Such crowds gathered to listen to him that he got into a boat
and sat in it, while the crowd all stood on the shore. 3He used par-
ables to tell them many things.

'Look!' he said. 'A sower went out to sow his seed. 4As he sowed,
some seeds fell by the side of the road, and the birds came and snapped
them up. 5Others fell on ground where there was only a thin skin of
earth over the rock, and, because the soil was so shallow, they sprang
up immediately, 6but when the sun rose they were scorched, and they
withered, because they had no root. 7Some fell among thorn-bushes,
and the thorn-bushes shot up and choked the life out of them.
8Others fell on good ground, and produced a crop, some a hundred
times, some sixty times, some thirty times as much as had been sown.
9If a man has ears, let him hear.'

10The disciples came to Jesus and asked him: 'What is your reason
for speaking to them in parables?' 11'You,' he said, 'have received the
privilege of knowing the secrets of the Kingdom of Heaven, secrets

which only a disciple can understand, but to them that privilege has
not been given. 12For, if anyone already has, he will continue to re-
ceive more and more until he has enough and more than enough;
but, if anyone has not, even what he has will be taken away from him.
13The reason why I speak to them in parables is that, although they
see, they do not see, and, although they hear, they do not hear,
nor do they understand. 14In them Isaiah's prophecy has come
true:

"You will certainly hear,
but you will certainly not understand
the meaning of what you hear;
you will certainly see,
but you will certainly not perceive
the meaning of what you see.
15The mind of this people has become lazily shut,
and their ears have become hard of hearing,
and they have deliberately obscured their own sight,
lest at any time they should see with their eyes,
and hear with their ears,
and understand with their minds,
and turn and find their cure in me."

16Happy are your eyes, because they are seeing, and your ears, because
they are hearing. 17I tell you truly, many a prophet and many a good
man longed to see the events which you are seeing, and did not see
them, and to hear the words which you are hearing, and did not hear
them.'

18'Listen, then, to the meaning of the parable of the sower. 19If
anyone hears the message of God's Kingdom, and does not really
understand it, the Evil One comes and snatches away what was sown
in such a man's heart. This kind of person is represented by the
picture of the seed sown on the side of the road. 20The picture of the
seed which was sown on the ground which was only a thin skin of
earth over the rock represents the man who hears the word and who
immediately receives it enthusiastically. 21But he has no inner root,
and is at the mercy of the moment, and so, when trouble or per-
secution comes, he at once stumbles and collapses. 22The picture of
the seed which was sown among the thorn-bushes represents the man
who hears the word, but the worry of this world and the deceptive

seduction of wealth choke the life out of the word, and it never gets
a chance to produce a crop. 23The picture of the seed which was sown
on the good ground represents the man who hears the word and
understands it. He indeed bears a crop which produces sometimes a
hundred times, sometimes sixty times, sometimes thirty times as
much as he received.'

24Jesus gave them another parable to think about. 'What happens
in the Kingdom of Heaven,' he said, 'is like what happened when a
man sowed good seed in his field. 25When everyone was asleep, his
enemy came and sowed darnel among the corn, and went away.
26When the blade sprouted, and when it began to produce its crop,
then the darnel appeared. 27The servants of the master of the house
came to him. "Sir," they said, "didn't you sow good seed in your
field? How did the darnel get into it?" 28"This is the work of an
enemy," he said. "Do you want us to go and gather the darnel?" the
servants asked him. 29"No," he said. "If you gather the darnel, the
danger is that you may tear up the corn by the roots at the same
time. 30Let them both grow together, until the harvest time. At the
harvest time I will give instructions to the reapers, first to gather the
darnel and tie it up in bundles for burning, and then to gather the
corn and to store it in my granary." '

31Jesus gave them another parable to think about. 'The Kingdom
of Heaven,' he said, 'is like a grain of mustard seed, which a man took
and sowed in his field. 32It is the smallest of all seeds, but when it has
reached full growth, it becomes the biggest of all kitchen herbs, and
grows into a tree big enough for the birds of the sky to come and nest
among its branches.'

33He told them another parable. 'The Kingdom of Heaven works
like a piece of leaven,' he said, 'which a woman took and inserted into
three pecks of flour, with the result that it was all leavened.'

34Jesus said all this to the crowds in parables, and it was his practice
to say nothing to them without a parable. 35He followed this method
so that the statement made through the prophet might come true:

> 'I will speak in parables;
> I will utter things which have been veiled in secrecy
> since the world was created.'

36Jesus left the crowds and went into the house. His disciples came

to him. 'Tell us,' they said, 'the meaning of the parable of the darnel
in the field.' 37 'The sower of the good seed,' Jesus answered, 'stands
for the Son of Man. 38 The field stands for the world. The good seed
stands for the children of the Kingdom. The darnel stands for the
children of the Evil One. 39 The enemy who sowed them stands for
the Devil. The harvest stands for the end of the world as we know it.
The reapers stand for the angels. 40 The collecting of the darnel and
the burning of it in the fire is a picture of what is going to happen at
the end of the world. 41 The Son of Man will send his angels, to weed
out of the Kingdom all those who are a cause of sin to others, and all
who act lawlessly, 42 and to throw them into the blazing furnace.
There will be tears and agony there. 43 But the good shall shine like
the sun in their Father's Kingdom. If a man has ears, let him hear.'

44 Jesus went on: 'The Kingdom of Heaven is like a treasure which
lay hidden in a field. A man discovered it and kept his discovery
secret. He was so glad that he went off and sold everything he pos-
sessed, and bought the field.'

45 'To take another illustration, what happens in the Kingdom of
Heaven is like what happened to a trader who was searching for
lovely pearls. 46 When he found one pearl of supreme value, he went
and sold everything that he had and bought it.'

47 'To take another illustration, what happens in the Kingdom of
Heaven is like what happened when a net was cast into the sea. It
collected all kinds of things. 48 When it was full, they hauled it up on
to the shore. Then they sat down and picked out the good things
and put them into containers, and flung away the useless things.
49 This is what will happen at the end of the world. The angels will
come and separate the evil from the good, 50 and they will throw
them into the blazing furnace. There will be tears and agony
there.'

51 'Have you understood all that I have been saying to you?' Jesus
asked. 'Yes,' they said. 52 'That,' he said, 'is why, if an expert in the
Law has been instructed in the meaning of the Kingdom, he is like a
householder, who brings out of his treasure-store things both new
and old.'

53 When Jesus had finished these parables, he left there. 54 He went

to his own native place, and began to teach them in their synagogue.
His teaching left them astonished. 'Where did this man get this
wisdom?' they said. 'How can he do these miracles? 55Isn't he the
carpenter's son? Isn't his mother Mary, and aren't his brothers James
and Joses and Simon and Judas? 56Aren't his sisters all here with us?
Where did he get all this?' 57They were shocked at him. Jesus said to
them: 'The only place in which a prophet has no honour is in his own
native town and among his own family.' 58He did not do many
miracles there because of their refusal to believe.

Chapter 14

It was at that time that the reports which were circulating about
Jesus reached the ears of Herod the tetrarch. 2'This is John the
Baptizer,' he said to his servants. 'He has come back to life. That is why
he possesses these miraculous powers.' 3Herod thought this because
he had arrested John the Baptizer, and had imprisoned him in chains
because of the affair of Herodias, his brother Philip's wife. 4The trouble
had arisen because John had told him that he had no right to marry
her. 5Herod would have liked to kill John, but he was afraid of the
crowd, for they regarded John as a prophet. 6On the occasion of
Herod's birthday celebrations Herodias' daughter danced in public
and delighted Herod. 7So he pledged himself on oath to give her any-
thing she asked. 8Urged by her mother, she said: 'Give me here and
now the head of John the Baptizer on a dish.' 9The king was distressed,
but, because he had given his sworn promise in front of his guests, he
ordered her request to be granted. 10So he sent and had John beheaded
in prison. 11His head was brought in on a dish and given to the girl,
and she took it to her mother. 12John's disciples came and took his
body away and buried it, and they came and told Jesus what had
happened.

13When Jesus heard what had happened, he withdrew from there,
and sailed in a boat to a desert place where he could be alone by
himself; but when the crowds learned of this, they followed him
from the towns on foot. 14When he disembarked, he saw a great
crowd, and he was heart-sorry for them, and cured their sick. 15Late
on in the day the disciples came to him. 'This place is a desert,' they
said, 'and it is now past the time for the evening meal. Send the

crowd away into the villages to buy themselves food.' 16'There is no
necessity for them to go away,' Jesus said. 'You must give them
something to eat.' 17'All that we have here,' they said to him, 'is five
loaves and two fishes.' 18'Bring them to me,' Jesus said. 19So he
ordered the crowd to sit down on the grass. He took the five
loaves and the two fishes. He looked up to heaven and said the
blessing. He broke the loaves into pieces and gave them to the dis-
ciples, and the disciples gave them to the crowds. 20They all ate until
they could eat no more. They collected twelve basketfuls of pieces of
bread that were left over. 21Those who ate numbered about five
thousand men, not counting women and children.

22Jesus immediately made his disciples get into the boat and go on
ahead to the other side, while he stayed to dismiss the crowds.
23When he had dismissed the crowds, he went up the hill by himself
to pray. When evening came he was there alone. 24The boat by this
time was a good distance from land. It was being buffeted by the
waves, for the wind was dead against them. 25About three o'clock in
the morning he came to them, walking on the lake. 26When the dis-
ciples saw him walking on the lake, they were terrified. 'It is a ghost,'
they said, and they cried out in fear. 27Jesus immediately spoke to
them. 'Courage!' he said. 'It is I. Don't be afraid!' 28'Master,' Peter
answered, 'if it really is you, give me an order to come to you on the
water.' 29Jesus said: 'Come!' Peter got out of the boat and walked on
the water, and began to go to Jesus. 30But when he saw the wind, he
was afraid. He began to sink below the water. 'Master,' he shouted.
'Save me!' 31Jesus stretched out his hand and gripped him. 'You have
so little faith!' he said. 'Why did you begin to doubt?' 32When they
got on board the boat, the wind sank to rest. 33The men in the boat
knelt in reverence in front of Jesus. 'Beyond a doubt,' they said, 'you
are the Son of God.'

34When they had crossed over, they landed at Gennesaret. 35When
the people of that place recognized Jesus, they sent all over the
countryside, and brought in to him everyone who was ill. 36They
begged to be allowed to do no more than touch the tassel of his cloak.
All who touched it were completely cured.

Chapter 15

IT was then that a deputation of experts in the Law and Pharisees
came from Jerusalem to interview Jesus. 2'Why,' they said, 'do your
disciples break the traditional law of the elders? They do so in that
they do not give their hands the prescribed washings when they eat a
meal.' 3Jesus answered: 'Why do you too disobey the commandment
of God for the sake of your traditional law? 4God said: "Honour your
father and your mother," and, "The man who curses his father or
mother must certainly die." 5But you say: "If a man says to his father
or mother: 'The money I might have contributed to your support is
a gift dedicated to God, and usable for no other purpose,' 6then he
must not honour his father." For the sake of your traditional
law you have cancelled the word of God. 7Your fault is that you
do not practise what you preach. Isaiah well described you in his
prophecy:

> 8"This people honour me with their lips,
> but their heart is far from me.
> 9It is a futile worship which they offer me,
> for they teach as divine commands man-made rules
> and regulations." '

10Jesus invited the crowds to listen to him. 'Listen,' he said, 'and
understand. 11It is not what goes into a man's mouth that defiles him.
On the contrary, it is what comes out of a man's mouth that defiles
him.' 12His disciples then came and said to him: 'Do you know that,
when the Pharisees heard what you said, they were shocked by it?'
13'Every plant,' he answered, 'which my heavenly Father did not
plant will be uprooted. 14Let them alone! They are blind leaders of
the blind. If the blind lead the blind, both of them will fall into a
hole in the road.' 15'Tell us,' Peter said to him, 'what this difficult
saying means.' 16'Are even you still unable to understand?' Jesus said.
17'Do you not realize that everything that goes into a man's mouth
goes into his stomach, and is evacuated into the drain by natural
processes? 18But what comes out of his mouth comes from his heart,
and it is that which defiles a man. 19For from the heart come evil
thoughts, murder, adultery, fornication, theft, lies about other
people, slander. 20These are the things which really defile a man. To

eat with hands which have not been washed as the ritual law prescribes does not defile a man.'

21 Jesus left there and withdrew to the districts of Tyre and Sidon.
22 A Canaanite woman from these parts came to him. 'Take pity on
me, sir, Son of David,' she kept shouting. 'My daughter is possessed
by a demon and is very ill.' 23 Jesus did not answer her at all. His
disciples came and asked him: 'Send her away. She won't stop following us and shouting at us.' 24 Jesus said: 'It is only to the lost sheep of
the family of Israel that I have been sent.' 25 She came and knelt in
front of him in entreaty. 'Sir,' she said, 'help me.' 26 'It is not proper,'
Jesus answered, 'to take the bread which belongs to the children, and
to fling it to the pet dogs.' 27 'True, sir,' she said, 'but the pet dogs do
eat their share of the crumbs which fall from their master's table.'
28 At that Jesus answered: 'You have great faith. Let your wish be
granted.' From that moment her daughter was cured.

29 Jesus left there and went along the coast of the lake of Galilee.
He climbed the hill and sat there, 30 and the crowds flocked to him,
bringing those who were lame and blind, crippled and deaf, and
suffering from many other diseases. They laid them at his feet, and
he cured them. 31 His power to heal left the crowd amazed, when they
saw the dumb speaking, the crippled restored to fitness, the lame
walking, and the blind seeing, and they praised the God of Israel.

32 Jesus called the disciples to him. 'I am heart-sorry for the crowd,'
he said, 'for they have stayed with me for three days now, and they
have nothing to eat. I don't want to send them away without a meal,
because I don't want them to collapse on the road.' 33 'Where could
we find loaves enough in a desert place to satisfy a crowd like this?'
the disciples asked him. 34 'How many loaves have you?' Jesus said to
them. 'Seven,' they said, 'and a few little fishes.' 35 Jesus ordered the
crowd to sit down on the ground. 36 He took the seven loaves and the
fishes. He gave thanks for them, and broke them into pieces, and gave
them to the disciples, and the disciples gave them to the crowds.
37 They all ate until they could eat no more. They gathered up what
was left of the broken pieces of bread, and there was enough to fill
seven hampers. 38 Those who ate numbered four thousand men, not
counting women and children. 39 When Jesus had sent the crowds
away, he got into the boat, and went to the district of Magadan.

Chapter 16

THE Pharisees and Sadducees came to interview Jesus. They tried
to submit him to a test by asking him to show them some visible
divine action from heaven. 2He answered: 'In the evening, you say:
"The sky is red. The weather will be good." 3Early in the morning,
you say: "The sky is red and threatening. The weather will be stormy
today." You know how to read the weather signs in the sky. Can you
not read the signs of the times? 4It is a wicked and apostate generation
which wants to see some visible action of God. The same action as
God showed in Jonah is the only divine action which will be given to
it.' He went away and left them.

5When the disciples arrived at the other side, they discovered that
they had forgotten to bring any loaves with them. 6'Watch what you
are doing,' Jesus said to them. 'Beware! Be on your guard against the
leaven of the Pharisees and Sadducees.' 7They kept on talking among
themselves about bringing no loaves. 8Jesus knew what they were
arguing about. 'You have so little faith,' he said. 'Why do you keep on
talking about having no loaves? 9Do you not even yet understand?
Don't you remember the five loaves and the five thousand, and how
many basketfuls you collected? 10Don't you remember the seven
loaves and the four thousand, and how many hamperfuls you
collected? 11Why can't you understand that it was not about loaves
that I spoke to you? Be on your guard against the leaven of the
Pharisees and Sadducees.' 12Then they understood that he was not
telling them to beware of leaven in the sense of leaven that is in
loaves, but in the sense of the evil influence of the teaching of the
Pharisees and Sadducees.

13When Jesus had come to the districts of Caesarea Philippi, he put
a question to his disciples. 'Who are people saying that the Son of
Man is?' he asked. 14They said: 'Some are saying, John the Baptizer;
others, Elijah; others, Jeremiah, or one of the prophets.' 15'And you,'
he said to them, 'who do you say that I am?' 16Simon Peter answered:
'You are the Messiah, the Son of the living God!' 17'You are indeed
blessed, Simon Barjona,' Jesus said, 'for it was no human being who
revealed this to you; it was my Father who is in heaven. 18I tell you,
you are Peter—the man whose name means a rock—and on this rock

I will erect my Church, and the powers of death will be helpless to
harm it. 19I will give you the keys of the Kingdom of Heaven, and
whatever you forbid on earth will be forbidden in heaven, and what-
ever you allow on earth will be allowed in heaven.' 20Jesus gave
strict orders to his disciples not to tell anyone that he was the Messiah.

21From then on Jesus began to show his disciples that he must go
to Jerusalem, and that he must undergo many sufferings at the hands
of the elders and the chief priests and the experts in the Law, and that
he must be killed, and that he must be raised to life again on the third
day. 22Peter caught hold of him, and sternly forbade him to talk like
that. 'God forbid, Master!' he said. 'This must never happen to you!'
23Jesus swung round. 'Get out of my sight, Satan!' he said to Peter.
'You're doing your best to trip me up! Your ideas are not God's, but
man's!'

24Jesus went on to say to his disciples: 'If anyone wishes to walk in
my steps, he must once and for all say No to himself; he must
decide to take up his cross, and he must keep on following me.
25Anyone who wishes to keep his life safe will lose it, but anyone who
is prepared to lose his life for my sake will find it. 26What good will it
do to a man to gain the whole world, if in so doing he forfeits his own
life? What could a man give that would be an equal exchange for his
life? 27For the Son of Man will come with his angels in his Father's
glory, and he will settle accounts with each man on the basis of how
each man has lived. 28I tell you truly, there are some of those who are
standing here who will not experience death until they see the Son
of Man coming in his Kingdom.'

Chapter 17

ABOUT a week later Jesus took with him Peter and James and John,
James's brother, and brought them up into a high mountain
alone. 2He was transformed before their very eyes. His face shone like
the sun, and his clothes became as white as the light. 3Moses and
Elijah appeared to them, talking to Jesus. 4'Master,' Peter said to Jesus,
'it is a wonderful thing for us to be here. Would you like me to make
three shelters here, one for you, one for Moses, and one for Elijah?'
5While he was still speaking, a shining cloud enveloped them, and out
of the cloud a voice said: 'This is my Son, the Beloved and Only One,

on whom my favour rests. Listen to him!' 6When the disciples heard
this, they flung themselves face down on the ground, for they were
terrified. 7Jesus came and touched them. 'Up!' he said. 'Don't be
afraid!' 8And when they looked up, the only person they could see
was Jesus, all by himself.

9On the way down from the mountain Jesus gave them strict orders
not to tell anyone what they had seen, until the Son of Man had been
raised from the dead.

10The disciples put a question to him. 'Why,' they asked, 'do the
experts in the Law say that Elijah must come first?' 11'It is quite true,'
Jesus answered, 'that Elijah is to come and is to set everything in order.
12But the fact is, Elijah has already come, and, so far from recognizing
him, they did what they liked to him. In exactly the same way the
Son of Man is going to suffer at their hands.' 13Then the disciples
understood that it was about John the Baptizer that Jesus had been
speaking to them.

14When they reached the crowd, a man came to Jesus and knelt at
his feet. 15'Sir,' he said, 'take pity on my son. He is an epileptic, and he
is very ill. He often falls into the fire and into the water. 16And I
brought him to your disciples, and they were quite unable to cure
him.' 17'This modern generation has no faith,' Jesus answered. 'There
is a fatal perversity about it. How long have I to be with you? How
long must I endure you? Bring him here to me!' 18Then Jesus spoke
to him with a stern authority, and the demon came out of him, and
there and then the boy was cured. 19Afterwards when they were alone,
the disciples came to Jesus. 'Why were we unable to eject the demon?'
they asked him. 20'Because,' he said, 'you have so little faith. I tell you
truly, if you have faith as big as a mustard seed, you will say to this
mountain: "Move from here to there," and it will remove itself.
There will be nothing that you cannot do.'*

22When they were moving about in Galilee together, Jesus said to
them: 'The Son of Man is going to be handed over into the power of
men, 23and they will kill him, and on the third day he will be raised
to life again.' And they were very distressed.

24When they arrived in Capernaum, the collectors of the Temple
tax approached Peter. 'Does your teacher not pay the half-crown

* Some manuscripts here add verse 21, *This kind comes out only by prayer and fasting.*

Temple tax?' they asked. 25'Yes, he does,' said Peter. When Peter came
into the house, before he could even mention the matter, Jesus said
to him: 'Tell me your opinion, Simon—who do earthly kings collect
tolls and taxes from? Is it from their own family or from strangers?'
26'From strangers,' Peter said. 'So then,' Jesus said, 'their own family
are exempt. 27All the same, we do not want to give offence to anyone.
So go to the lake. Throw in a hook. Take the first fish that comes up.
Open its mouth and you will find a five-shilling piece. Take it and give
it to the collectors for me and for you.'

Chapter 18

THE disciples came to Jesus at that time. 'Who,' they said, 'is the
greatest in the Kingdom of Heaven?' 2Jesus called a little child,
and made him stand where they could all see him. 3'I tell you truly,'
he said, 'unless you change the whole direction of your lives, and
become like little children, you will certainly not get into the King-
dom of Heaven at all. 4It is the man who thinks as little of his import-
ance as this little child, who is the greatest in the Kingdom of Heaven.
5'To welcome a little child like this in my name is to welcome me.
6It would be better for a man to have a huge millstone hung round
his neck and to be drowned in the deepest part of the sea than to do
anything to cause one of these little ones who believe in me to sin.
7'The tragedy of the world is the existence of the things which make
men sin! True, things which make men sin must come, but tragic is
the fate of the man who is responsible for the coming of such a
thing!
8'If your hand or your foot becomes a cause of sin to you, cut it off
and throw it away. It is better for you to enter into life maimed or
crippled than to be thrown into eternal fire with two hands or two
feet. 9If your eye becomes a cause of sin to you, tear it out and throw
it away. It is better for you to enter into life with one eye than to be
thrown into hell-fire with two eyes.
10'Be very careful never to think of one of these little ones as of no
importance. I tell you that in heaven their guardian angels always
have the right of access to the presence of my Father who is in
heaven.'*

*Some manuscripts insert here verse 11, *For the Son of Man came to save the lost.*

12‘What do you think? If a man has a hundred sheep, and if one of
them has wandered away, will he not leave the ninety-nine on the
hillside, and go and search for the wandering one? 13And, if he finds
it, I tell you truly, he rejoices more over it than over the ninety-nine
which never wandered away. 14Just so, your Father in heaven doesn't
want one of these little ones to be lost.’

15‘If your fellow man wrongs you, go, and with no one but him and
you there, try to persuade him to admit his fault. If he listens to you,
you have gained a friend. 16If he refuses to listen to you, take one or
two other people with you, and go and see him, so that everything
that is said may be confirmed by the evidence of two or three wit-
nesses. 17If he refuses to listen to them, report the whole trouble to
the church. And, if he refuses to listen even to the church, then he
must be regarded as no better than a heathen and a renegade tax-
collector.’

18‘I tell you truly, all that you forbid on earth will be forbidden in
heaven, and all that you allow on earth will be allowed in heaven.’

19‘Still further, I tell you truly, if two of you on earth agree about
anything for which you are praying, they will receive it from my
Father who is in heaven. 20For, where two or three have met in my
name, I too am there with them.’

21Peter came to Jesus. ‘Master,’ he said to him, ‘how often ought I to
forgive my fellow man, if he goes on wronging me? As many as seven
times?’ 22‘I tell you,’ Jesus said to him, ‘not as many as seven times,
but as many as seventy times seven. 23That is why what happens in
the Kingdom of Heaven can be compared with the situation which
arose when a king wished to settle accounts with his servants. 24When
he began to settle up, one debtor was brought in who owed him two
and a half million pounds. 25He was quite unable to pay. So his master
gave orders for him to be sold, along with his wife and children and
everything he had, and the money to be paid over. 26The servant
threw himself on his knees at his master's feet. “Give me time,” he
said, “and I will pay you everything in full.” 27The servant's master
was heart-sorry for the man, and let him go free, and remitted the
debt. 28That same servant went out and met one of his fellow-
servants who owed him five pounds. He seized him by the throat.
“Pay your debt!” he said. 29His fellow-servant threw himself at his
feet. “Give me time,” he begged, “and I will pay you in full.” 30He

refused, and went and had him thrown into prison, until he should
pay the debt in full. 31When his fellow-servants saw what had hap-
pened, they were very distressed. So they went to their master and
informed him of all that had happened. 32The master sent for the
servant. "You utter scoundrel!" he said. "I remitted that whole debt
of yours, because you pleaded with me to do so. 33Surely you should
have had the same pity for your fellow-servant as I had for you."
34The master was furious, and handed him over to the torturers
until he should repay the whole debt in full. 35My heavenly Father
will do the same to you, if you do not, each one of you, genuinely
forgive your fellow man.'

Chapter 19

WHEN Jesus had finished what he had to say on this occasion, he
left Galilee, and went to that part of Judaea which lies on the far
side of the Jordan. 2Great crowds followed him, and he healed them
there.

3The Pharisees came to him with what they intended to be a test
question. 'Is a man permitted,' they asked, 'to divorce his wife for any
reason he likes?' 4'Have you not read,' he answered, 'that in the
beginning the Creator made mankind male and female? 5And that
he said: "For this reason a man will leave his father and mother, and
will be joined inseparably to his wife; 6and they two shall become so
completely one that they shall be no longer two persons but one"?
What God has united man must not separate.' 7They said to him:
'Why did Moses prescribe a regulation allowing a man to give his wife
a deed of divorce, and so to send her away?' 8'Moses would never have
allowed you to divorce your wives,' Jesus said, 'if it had not been that
your hearts are quite impervious to the real commandment of God.
That was not the original intention. 9I tell you, anyone who divorces
his wife for any reason other than infidelity and marries another
woman commits adultery.'* 10His disciples said to him: 'If that is the
only ground on which a man may divorce his wife, then it is better
not to marry at all!' 11'This principle,' he said to them, 'is not practic-
able for everyone. It is only practicable for those whom God has

*Some manuscripts add here, *And anyone who marries a divorced woman commits adultery.*

enabled to accept it. 12There are some who have been born incapable
of marriage. There are some who by the action of men have been
made incapable of marriage. There are some who have voluntarily
made marriage impossible for themselves for the sake of the Kingdom
of Heaven. Let the man who is able to accept this principle accept
it.'

13Little children were brought to Jesus for him to lay his hands on
them and to say a prayer over them, but the disciples warned them
off. 14Jesus said: 'Let the little children come to me, and don't try to
stop them. It is to such as they are that the Kingdom of Heaven
belongs.' 15So he laid his hands on them, and then he moved on from
there.

16A man came to Jesus. 'Teacher,' he said, 'what must I do to make
myself good enough to possess eternal life?' 17'Why do you ask me
about what is good?' Jesus said to him. 'One and One alone is good.
If you want to get into life, obey the commandments.' 18'What
commandments?' he said. Jesus said: 'The commandments which say:
You must not kill, You must not commit adultery, You must not
steal, You must not tell lies about anyone, 19Honour your father and
your mother, and, You must love your neighbour as yourself.' 20'I
have obeyed all these,' the young man said to him. 'What is still miss-
ing in me?' 21'If you really want to be perfect,' Jesus said to him, 'go
and sell everything you have and give the proceeds to the poor, and
you will have treasure in heaven. Then come! Follow me!' 22When
the young man heard Jesus say this, he went sadly away, for he was
very wealthy.

23'I tell you truly,' Jesus said to his disciples, 'it is very difficult for a
rich man to get into the Kingdom of Heaven. 24I repeat, it is easier for
a camel to go through the eye of a needle than it is for a rich man to
get into the Kingdom of God.' 25The disciples were astonished to hear
this. 'Who then can be saved?' they said. 26Jesus looked at them.
'With men this may be impossible,' he said, 'but everything is possible
with God.'

27Peter said to him: 'We have left everything to become your
followers. What will we get for this?' 28'I tell you truly,' Jesus said to
them, 'at the rebirth of the world, when the Son of Man takes his seat
upon his glorious throne, you who chose to follow me will sit on
twelve thrones, as the judges of the twelve tribes of Israel. 29Anyone

who has left houses or brothers or sisters or father or mother or
children or estates for my sake will get them back a hundred times
over, and will receive the promised gift of eternal life. 30But many
who are first will be last, and the last will be first.'

Chapter 20

'THE situation in the Kingdom of Heaven is like the situation in the
following story. There was a householder who went out first
thing in the morning to engage workmen to work in his vineyard.
2He came to an agreement with the workmen to work for a normal
day's wage, and sent them to his vineyard. 3He went out again about
nine o'clock in the morning, and saw other men standing in the
market-place unemployed. 4"Go to my vineyard along with the other
men," he said to them, "and I will pay you whatever is a fair wage."
5So they went off to the vineyard. He went out again about twelve
o'clock midday and about three o'clock in the afternoon, and did the
same. 6He went out about five o'clock in the evening and found others
standing there. "Why have you stood here all day unemployed?" he
said to them. 7"Because no one engaged us," they said. "Go to my
vineyard as well as the other men," he said. 8When evening came, the
owner of the vineyard said to his foreman: "Call the workers and give
them their pay. Start with the last ones and go on to the first."
9When those who had started work at five o'clock in the evening
came, they each received a normal full day's wage. 10When those who
had been engaged first came, they expected to get more. But they too
received a normal day's wage. 11When they got their pay, they began
to grumble at the way in which the householder had treated them.
12"The men who came last," they said, "worked for one hour, and
you have treated them the same as us, and we have done a whole day's
work, and in a wind like a furnace too." 13"Friend," he said to one of
them, "I am not doing you any wrong. Did you not agree with me to
work for the usual day's wage? 14Take what is due to you, and go. It is
my wish to give the last man the same as I gave you. 15Have I not
a perfect right to do what I like with my own money? Are you going
to be mean, because I am generous?" 16Just so, the last will be first,
and the first will be last.'

17When Jesus was on his way up to Jerusalem, he took the Twelve

aside by themselves, and spoke to them as they walked along the road.
18'We are on our way up to Jerusalem,' he said, 'and the Son of Man
will be handed over to the chief priests and to the experts in the Law;
they will condemn him to death; 19they will hand him over to the
Gentiles to mock and to flog and to crucify; and on the third day he
will be raised to life again.'

20It was then the mother of Zebedee's sons came to him with her
sons. She knelt before him and asked him to give her a special favour.
21'What is it you want?' he said to her. 'I want my two sons,' she said,
'to sit one on your right hand and one on your left in your Kingdom.'
22'You do not know what you are asking for,' Jesus said. 'Can you pass
through the bitter experience through which I must pass?' 'We can,'
they said. 23He said to them: 'You will pass through the same ex-
perience as I must go through, but to sit on my right hand and on
my left is not in my power to give you. That is reserved for those
for whom it has been prepared by my Father.'

24When the ten heard about this, they were annoyed with the two
brothers. 25Jesus called them to him. 'You know,' he said, 'that the
leaders of the Gentiles lord it over them, and that in their society the
mark of greatness is the exercise of authority. 26But in your society
the situation is very different. With you, if anyone wishes to be great,
he must be your servant; 27and with you, if anyone wishes to hold the
first place, he must be everyone's slave, 28just as the Son of Man did
not come to be served but to serve, and to give his life as a ransom for
many.'

29They were leaving Jericho followed by a large crowd. 30There
were two blind men sitting at the roadside. When they heard that
Jesus was passing, they shouted: 'Master! Take pity on us! Son of
David!' 31The crowd sharply told them to be quiet, but they shouted
all the louder: 'Master! Take pity on us! Son of David!' 32Jesus stop-
ped and called them. 'What do you want me to do for you?' he said.
33'Sir,' they said to him, 'the only thing we want is to be able to see.'
34Jesus was heart-sorry for them. He touched their eyes, and there and
then their sight returned, and they followed him.

Chapter 21

WHEN they were near Jerusalem, and when they had reached
Bethphage, at the Hill of Olives, Jesus sent on two of his dis-
ciples. 2'Go into the village opposite you,' he said, 'and you will at
once find a tethered donkey, and a foal with her. Untie them and
bring them to me. 3If anyone says anything to you, you will say:
"The Master needs them," and he will send them at once.' 4This hap-
pened so that the statement made through the prophet might come
true:

> 5'Say to the daughter of Sion:
> "Look! Your king is coming to you,
> gentle, and riding on an ass,
> and on a colt, the foal of a beast of burden." '

6The disciples went off and carried out Jesus' instructions. 7They
brought the donkey and the foal. They put their cloaks on them, and
Jesus mounted them. 8The huge crowd spread their cloaks on the
road, while others cut down branches from the trees, and spread
them on the road. 9The crowds who were going on ahead and the
crowds who were following behind kept shouting:

> 'God save David's Son!
> God bless him who comes in the name of the Lord!
> O send your salvation from the heights of heaven!'

10When Jesus entered Jerusalem, the whole city seethed with excite-
ment. 'Who is this?' they said. 11The crowds said: 'This is the prophet
Jesus from Nazareth in Galilee.'

12Jesus went into the Temple precincts, and drove out all who were
selling and buying there, and upset the tables of the money-changers,
and the seats of the pigeon-sellers. 13'Scripture says,' he said to them,
' "My house must be regarded as a house of prayer," but you are
making it a brigands' den.'

14The blind and the lame came to him in the Temple precincts and
he cured them. 15When the chief priests and the experts in the Law
saw the astonishing things that Jesus did, and when they heard the
children shouting in the Temple precincts: 'God save David's Son!'

they were enraged. 16'Do you hear what the children are saying?'
they said to him. 'I do,' Jesus said to them. 'Have you never read:
"Out of the mouths of babes and sucklings you have brought perfect
praise"?' 17So he left there, and went out of the city to Bethany, and
spent the night there.

18When Jesus was on his way back to the city early in the morning,
he felt hungry. 19He saw a fig tree at the roadside. He went up to it,
and found nothing but leaves on it. 'May no fruit ever grow again on
you,' he said. And there and then the fig tree withered. 20The disciples
were astonished to see what had happened. 'How did the fig tree
wither on the spot?' they said. 21'I tell you truly,' Jesus answered, 'if
you have unquestioning faith, you will be able to do not only what
was done to the fig tree, but even if you were to say to this hill: "Be
picked up and flung into the sea," it will happen. 22You will receive
everything you ask in prayer, if you ask in faith.'

23Jesus went into the Temple precincts. As he was teaching there,
the chief priests and the elders of the people approached him. 'What
right have you to act as you are doing,' they said, 'and who gave you
the right to do so?' 24'I will ask you one question,' Jesus answered,
'and, if you tell me the answer to it, I will tell you what right I have
to act like this. 25What was the source of the baptism that John
administered? Was it divine or human?' They began to argue with each
other. 'If,' they said, 'we say, "Divine," he will say: "Why then did you
not believe in him?" 26On the other hand, we are afraid to say,
"Human," because of the crowd, because they all regard John as a
prophet.' 27So they answered Jesus: 'We do not know.' So Jesus said
to them: 'No more am I going to tell you what right I have to act as I
do.'

28'What do you think?' Jesus went on. 'There was a man who had
two sons. He went to the first son and said: "Son, go and work in my
vineyard today." 29He answered: "I will not." But he afterwards
changed his mind and went. 30So the father went to the second and
said the same to him. He said: "Certainly, sir." But he didn't go.
31Which of these two really obeyed his father?' 'The first,' they said.
'I tell you truly,' Jesus said to them, 'the tax-collectors and the
prostitutes are going to go into the Kingdom of Heaven before you.
32For John came to you, and showed you how to live as God wants
you to live, and you refused to believe him. But the tax-collectors and

the prostitutes did believe him. And, even when you saw the effect
of his preaching on them, you still did not change your mind and
believe him.'

33'Listen to another parable. There was a householder who planted
a vineyard. He surrounded it with a hedge, and dug out a pit in which
the juice could be extracted from the grapes, and built a watch-
tower. He then let it out to tenants and went abroad. 34When the
fruit season arrived, he sent his servants to the tenants to receive his
due share of the crop. 35The tenants took the servants, and beat one
up, and killed another, and stoned another. 36Again he sent other
servants, more than the first lot he had sent, and they treated them in
the same way. 37He then sent his son to them. "They will treat my
son with respect," he said. 38But, when the tenants saw the son, they
said to themselves: "This is the heir. Come on! Let's kill him! And
let us seize his estate!" 39So they took him, and threw him out of the
vineyard and killed him. 40When the owner of the vineyard comes,
what will he do to these tenants?' 41They said, 'He will see to it that
these bad men come to a bad end, and he will let out the vineyard to
other tenants, who will pay him his full share of the crops when it
is due.' 42Jesus said to them: 'Have you never read in the scriptures:

> "The stone which the builders rejected,
> this has become the headstone of the corner.
> This is the action of God,
> and it is marvellous in our eyes"?

43I tell you, that is why the Kingdom of God will be taken from you,
and given to a nation whose conduct befits it. 44Anyone who falls
against this stone will be shattered, and it will crush anyone it falls
upon.'

45When the chief priests and Pharisees heard Jesus' parables, they
were well aware that he was speaking about them. 46They tried to find
a way to arrest him, but they were afraid of the crowds, for they re-
garded him as a prophet.

Chapter 22

ONCE again Jesus spoke to them in parables. 2‘The situation in the
Kingdom of Heaven,’ he said, ‘is like the situation which arose
when a king gave a wedding banquet for his son. 3He sent out his
servants to tell the guests, who had already received their invitations
to the banquet, to come, and they refused to come. 4He sent out a
second lot of servants. “Tell those who have been invited,” he said,
“that I have completed the preparations for the dinner I am giving.
My oxen and specially fattened calves have been killed. Everything is
ready. Come to the wedding banquet.” 5They completely disregarded
the invitation, and went off, one to his farm and another to his
business. 6The others seized the servants, and wantonly ill-treated
them, and killed them. 7The king was furious and sent his troops and
wiped out those murderers, and burned their town. 8Then he said
to the servants: “The wedding banquet is all ready, but those who
received invitations to it did not deserve them. 9Go out to the open
roads and invite everyone you meet to the banquet.” 10So the servants
went out to the roads and collected everyone they met, good and bad
alike, and so the room where the wedding banquet was to be held
was filled with guests.

11‘When the king came in to look at the guests, he saw a man there
who was not dressed in wedding clothes. 12“Friend,” he said to him,
“why have you come like this, without wedding clothes?” The man
had nothing to say. 13Then the king said to the attendants: “Tie him
up, hand and foot, and fling him out into the outer darkness.” There
will be tears and agony there. 14For many are invited but few are
chosen.’

15The Pharisees went and concocted a scheme to lay a verbal trap
for Jesus. 16They sent their disciples to him along with Herod’s
supporters. ‘Teacher,’ they said to him, ‘we know that you speak the
truth, and that you really do teach the life that God wishes us to live.
We know that it makes no difference to you who or what anyone is,
and that man-made prestige means nothing to you. 17Well, then, tell
us, what is your opinion—is it right for us to pay the poll-tax to
Caesar, or is it not?’ 18Jesus was well aware of their malicious motives.
‘You are not out for information,’ he said to them, ‘you are out to

make trouble in your two-faced maliciousness. 19Show me the coin
with which the poll-tax is paid.' They brought him a silver piece.
20'Whose portrait and whose inscription is this?' he asked. 21'Caesar's,'
they said. 'Well, then,' he said to them, 'pay to Caesar what belongs
to Caesar, and to God what belongs to God.' 22When they heard that
answer, they were astonished, and went away and left him.

23On the same day a group of Sadducees approached Jesus. It is
their contention that there is no such thing as a resurrection from
the dead. So they put a question to Jesus. 24'Teacher,' they said,
'Moses said that, if a man dies childless, his brother must marry his
wife, and raise a family for his brother. 25There were amongst us
seven brothers. The first married and died, and, since he died child-
less, he left his wife to his brother. 26The same happened with the
second, and with the third, and with the whole seven. 27After them
all, the woman died. 28Well then, at the resurrection, of which of the
seven will she be the wife, for they all had her as a wife?' 29Jesus said
to them: 'You are on the wrong track altogether, because you do not
know either the meaning of the scriptures or the power of God.
30At the resurrection men and women neither marry nor are married,
but are like angels in heaven. 31As for the resurrection of the dead,
have you never read what God said to you, when he said: 32"I am
the God of Abraham and the God of Isaac and the God of Jacob"?
He is not the God of the dead, but of the living.' 33When the crowds
heard this answer, they were astonished at his teaching.

34When the Pharisees heard that Jesus had silenced the Sadducees,
they came in a body. 35One of them, a legal expert, put a question to
Jesus as a test. 36'Teacher,' he said, 'which is the greatest command-
ment in the Law?' 37Jesus said to him: 'You must love the Lord your
God with your whole heart and your whole soul and your whole
mind. 38This is the first and greatest commandment. 39And there is
a second one like it: You must love your neighbour as yourself.
40On these two commandments the whole message of the Law and
of the Prophets depends.'

41When a group of the Pharisees had come to him, Jesus put a
question to them. 42'What is your opinion about the Messiah?' he
said. 'Whose son is he?' 'David's,' they answered. 43'How, then,' he
said to them, 'does David, moved by the Spirit, call him Lord? For he
says:

44"The Lord said to my Lord,
Sit at my right hand,
until I give you the victory over your enemies."

45If then David calls him Lord, how can he be his son?' 46No one was
able to give Jesus any answer; and from then on no one dared to ask
him any more questions.

Chapter 23

JESUS spoke to the crowds and to his disciples. 2'The experts in the
Law and the Pharisees,' he said, 'have inherited the authority of
Moses. 3Their instructions you must carry out, but you must not
copy their actions, for their practice is very different from their
profession. 4They take heavy burdens, and strap them on to men's
shoulders, but they themselves will not lift a finger to help to move
them.

5'Their every action is designed for self-display. They wear out-
size prayer-boxes, and exaggerate the size of the tassels on their robes.
6They like the top places at banquets and the front seats in the syna-
gogues. 7They like to be deferentially greeted as they move through
the market-places, and to be called Rabbi by ordinary people. 8You
must not let anyone call you Rabbi. There is One who is your teacher,
and you are all brothers. 9You must not call any man on earth father.
There is One who is your Father, and he is in heaven. 10You must not
let anyone call you leaders. There is One who is your leader, I mean
the Messiah. 11Your top-ranking man must be your servant. 12If a
man exalts himself, he will be humbled; and, if he humbles himself,
he will be exalted.'

13'Tragic will be the fate of you experts in the Law and you Pharisees
with your façade of ostentatious piety! You shut the door of the
Kingdom of Heaven in men's faces. You will not go in yourselves, and
you will not allow those who are trying to get in to go in.*

15'Tragic will be the fate of you experts in the Law and you Pharisees

*Some manuscripts insert here verse 14, *Tragic will be the fate of you experts in the law and you Pharisees with your façade of ostentatious piety! For you greedily extract the last penny from credulous widows, and then with your long prayers try to give an impression of exceptional piety. You will receive all the heavier a sentence.*

with your façade of ostentatious piety! You roam sea and land to
make one convert, and, when he has become a convert, you make
him twice as much hell-begotten as yourselves.

16 'Tragic will be your fate, for you are blind guides! You say: "If a
man swears by the Temple, there is no necessity to keep the oath, but,
if a man swears by the gold of the Temple, he is bound to keep it."
17 You are senseless and blind! Which is greater—the gold, or the
Temple which makes the gold sacred? 18 You say: "If a man swears by
the altar, there is no necessity to keep the oath, but, if a man swears
by the gift that is on it, he is bound to keep it." 19 You are blind!
Which is greater—the gift, or the altar which makes the gift sacred?
20 If a man swears by the altar, he swears by it and by all that is on
it. 21 If a man swears by the Temple, he swears by it, and by him
whose home it is. 22 If a man swears by heaven, he swears by the
throne of God, and by him who sits on it.

23 'Tragic will be the fate of you experts in the Law and you Pharisees
with your façade of ostentatious piety! For you meticulously pay the
tenth part of your crop of mint and dill and cummin to the Temple,
and you completely neglect the more important demands of the
Law—justice, mercy and loyalty. You ought to have kept the second
without neglecting the first. 24 You are blind guides, you who care-
fully filter a midge out of your drink and then swallow a camel!

25 'Tragic will be the fate of you experts in the Law and you Pharisees
with your façade of ostentatious piety! For you carefully clean the
outside of the cup and the plate while you leave the inside full to
overflowing with greed and unbridled self-indulgence. 26 You blind
Pharisee! First clean the inside of the cup, and then outside and inside
will both be clean.

27 'Tragic will be the fate of you experts in the Law and you Pharisees
with your façade of ostentatious piety! For you are like white-washed
tombs, which look beautiful from the outside, but which are full of
dead men's bones and all kinds of filth. 28 So you too, as far as external
appearances go, seem to people to be carefully obeying the Law, but
you are really putting on an act, for inside you are full of disobedience
to the Law.

29 'Tragic will be the fate of you experts in the Law and you Pharisees
with your façade of ostentatious piety! You build tombs for the
prophets and erect lovely memorials to good men, 30 and you say:
"If we had lived in the days of our ancestors, we would not have been
partners with them in the murder of the prophets." 31 By your very

statement you provide evidence that you yourselves are the descend-
ants of those who killed the prophets. 32Carry on! Equal your fathers
in their sins! 33You serpents! You brood of vipers! How can you
escape being condemned to hell?

34'Let me tell you why I send you prophets and sages and experts in
the Law. Some of them you will kill and crucify. Some of them you
will flog in your synagogues, and hunt from town to town. 35The
reason is that there may rest on you the responsibility for the murder
of every good man from the murder of the good Abel to the murder
of Zachariah, Barachiah's son, between the Temple and the altar.
36I tell you, retribution for all this will descend upon the people of
today.'

37'O Jerusalem, Jerusalem! Killer of the prophets! Stoner of those
who were sent to you by God! How often I have wanted to gather
your children together as a bird gathers her nestlings under the shel-
ter of her wings—and you refused! 38God no longer has his home
among you, 39for, I tell you, you will not see me again until you say:
"God bless him who comes as the representative of the Lord." '

Chapter 24

WHEN Jesus had come out of the Temple precincts, and when he was walking away, his disciples came to tell him to look at the
Temple buildings. 2'You see all these?' he said. 'I tell you truly that
not one stone of them will be left standing on another here. There is
not a building here which will not be utterly demolished.'

3When he was sitting on the Hill of Olives, his disciples came to him
privately. 'Tell us,' they said, 'when these events will take place, and
what will be the sign of your coming and of the end of this world.'

4'You must be careful that no one misleads you,' Jesus answered.
5'For many will come claiming that they are my representatives.
They will claim to be the Messiah, and they will mislead many. 6You
will hear of wars and reports of wars. See that you don't get into a
panic, for these things must happen, but it is not yet the end. 7Nation
will attack nation, and kingdom will attack kingdom. There will be
outbreaks of famine and earthquakes here and there. 8All these
events are the beginning of the birth-pangs of the new age.

9'You will have much to suffer at the hands of men at that time.

They will kill you, and because of your connection with me you will
be hated in every country. 10At that time the faith of many
will collapse; they will betray each other and they will hate each
other. 11Many false prophets will emerge, and they will mislead
many. 12Lawlessness will flourish increasingly, and it will be char-
acteristic of that time that men's love for each other will grow
cold. 13But the man who sees things through to the end will be
saved.

14'This Good News of the Kingdom will be proclaimed all over the
inhabited world, so that all nations may be confronted with the truth,
and after that the end will come.

15'When you see the desolating abomination, of which the prophet
Daniel spoke, standing in the Holy Place' (let the reader mark this
well) 16'then those who are in Judaea must flee to the hills. 17Anyone
who happens to be on the housetop must not go down to take his
possessions out of his house. 18Anyone who is at work in the field
must not turn back to pick up his coat. 19It will be a tragic day for
women who are carrying children in the womb or feeding them at
the breast. 20Pray that you may not have to flee in winter or on the
Sabbath, 21for at that time there will be suffering so great that nothing
like it has happened from the beginning of the world to this present
day, or will ever happen again. 22Unless this period had been cut short,
no human being could survive. But this period will be cut short for
the sake of God's chosen ones.

23'If at that time anyone says to you: "Look! Here is the Messiah!"
or "There he is!" do not believe him. 24False Messiahs and false
prophets will emerge, and will perform such miracles and wonders,
that, if possible, they will mislead even God's chosen ones. 25I have
forewarned you about these things before they happen. 26If they say
to you: "See! Here he is out in the wilderness!" do not go out. If they
say: "See! Here he is in the secret rooms!" do not believe it. 27For, as
the lightning flashes across the whole sky from east to west, so will
be the coming of the Son of Man. 28Where the carrion is, there the
vultures will gather.

29'Immediately after the period of suffering of that time,

"The sun will be darkened,
and the moon will not give its light;
the stars will fall from the sky,
and the powers in the heavens will be shaken."

30Then the sign of the Son of Man will appear in the sky, and then
every nation will lament, when they see the Son of Man coming in
the clouds of the sky with great power and glory. 31With a blast on
the trumpet he will send out his angels, and they will gather in his
chosen ones from the four points of the compass, from the limits of
heaven to the furthest bounds of the universe.'

32'Learn the lesson which the fig tree offers you. When the sap
rises in its branches, and when it produces its leaves, you know that
summer is near. 33So, when you see all these events happening, you
must realize that he is near, standing at the very door. 34I tell
you truly, all these events will happen within the lifetime of this
generation. 35Heaven and earth will cease to be, but my words
will never cease to be. 36No one knows about that day or hour, not
even the angels in heaven, not even the Son, no one except the
Father.'

37'What happened in the time of Noah will happen again at the
coming of the Son of Man. 38As in the days before the flood they spent
their time eating and drinking, marrying and being married, right up
to the day when Noah went into the ark, 39and just as they did not
realize what was happening until the flood came and swept them all
away, so it will be at the coming of the Son of Man. 40At that time
two men will be working in the field; one will be taken and the other
will be left. 41Two women will be grinding corn at the mill; one will
be taken and the other will be left.'

42'Be sleeplessly on the watch, for you do not know the day when
your Lord is coming. 43It is obvious that, if the householder had
known at what hour of the night the thief was going to come, he
would have been awake, and would not have allowed his house to be
broken into. 44The reason why you too must be ready is that the Son
of Man is coming at an hour when you do not expect him.

45'Suppose there is a dependable and sensible servant whose master
put him in charge of the household staff, with instructions to issue
them with their food at the right time. 46That servant is a happy man,
if his master, when he comes, finds him engaged on that very task.
47I tell you truly, his master will put him in charge of all his property.
48But, if a bad servant says to himself: "I need not expect my master
for a long time yet," 49and if he begins to beat his fellow-servants, and

to eat and drink with drunkards, 50the master of that servant will
come on a day when he is not expecting him—he doesn't know at
what hour to expect him—51and he will cut him in pieces, and will
assign to him the same fate as the fate of those whose religion is only a
pretence. There will be tears and agony there.'

Chapter 25

'WHAT will happen in the Kingdom of Heaven is like what hap-
pened to ten bridesmaids, who took their lamps and went out
to meet the bridegroom. 2Five of them were foolish and five were
sensible. 3The foolish ones brought their lamps, but they did not
bring any oil with them. 4The sensible ones took oil in jars along with
their lamps. 5When the bridegroom was a long time in coming, they
grew drowsy. They were all asleep, 6when in the middle of the night
there was a shout: "Here comes the bridegroom! Out you go and
meet him!" 7At this all the girls woke up and trimmed their lamps.
8The foolish ones said to the sensible ones: "Our lamps have gone out.
Give us some of your oil." 9"We can't do that," the sensible ones
answered, "because then there might not be enough oil for us and for
you. You had better go to those who sell oil, and buy some for your-
selves." 10While they were away buying it, the bridegroom arrived.
The bridesmaids who were ready went in to the banquet with him,
and the door was shut. 11Later on the other girls arrived. "Sir!" they
said, "Sir! Open the door for us!" 12"I tell you truly," he said, "I don't
know who you are!" 13So, then, be sleeplessly on the watch, because
you do not know the day or the hour.'

14'What will happen in the Kingdom of Heaven is like what hap-
pened when a man went on a journey abroad. He called his servants
and handed over his property to them. 15He gave twelve hundred
and fifty pounds to one, five hundred to another, and two hundred
and fifty to a third. He gave each man a sum proportionate to his
ability, and went abroad. 16The man who had been given the twelve
hundred and fifty pounds lost no time in going and trading with the
money, and made a profit of another twelve hundred and fifty
pounds. 17In the same way the man who had been given the five
hundred pounds made a profit of another five hundred pounds.
18But the man who had been given the two hundred and fifty pounds

went away and dug a hole in the ground, and hid his master's money
in it.

19 'After a long time the master of these servants returned and
settled accounts with them. 20 The man who had been given the
twelve hundred and fifty pounds came up with another twelve
hundred and fifty pounds. "Master," he said, "You handed over
twelve hundred and fifty pounds to me. I have made a profiit of
another twelve hundred and fifty pounds." 21 "Well done!" his
master said to him. "You have shown yourself a good and trust-
worthy servant. Because you have shown that I could depend on you
to do a small job well, I will give you a big job to do. Come and share
your master's joy." 22 The man who had been given the five hundred
pounds came up. "Sir," he said, "you handed over five hundred
pounds to me. I have made a profit of another five hundred pounds."
23 "Well done!" his master said to him. "You have shown yourself to
be a good and trustworthy servant. Because you have shown that I
could depend on you to do a small job well, I will give you a big job
to do. Come and share your master's joy."

24 'The man who had been given the two hundred and fifty pounds
came up. "Sir," he said, "I am well aware that you are a shrewd and
ruthless business man. I know that you have a habit of letting some-
one else do the work and of then taking the profits. I know you often
step in and appropriate the results of some enterprise which you did
not initiate. 25 So I went and hid your two hundred and fifty pounds
in a hole in the ground, because I was afraid to take the risk of doing
anything with it. Here you are! Your money is safe!" 26 "You lazy
good-for-nothing!" his master answered. "You knew very well that
I have a habit of letting other people do the work and of then taking
the profits. You knew very well that I often step in and appropriate
the results of some enterprise which I did not initiate. 27 That is all the
more reason why you ought to have lodged my money with the
bankers, and then, when I came home, I would have got my money
back with interest. 28 Take the two hundred and fifty pounds from
him, and give it to the man who has two thousand five hundred
pounds. 29 For, if any man has much, he will be given still more, but,
if any man has nothing, he will lose even what he has. 30 Fling the
useless servant out into the outer darkness. There will be tears and
agony there." '

31 'When the Son of Man comes in his glory, accompanied by all the

angels, he will take his seat on his glorious throne. 32The people of
every nation will be assembled before him, and he will separate them
into two groups, in the same way as a shepherd separates the sheep
from the goats. 33He will place the sheep on the right hand and the
goats on the left. 34Then the king will say to those on the right: "You
have earned my Father's blessing. Come and take possession of the
kingdom, which has been prepared for you since the creation of the
world. 35For, when I was hungry, you gave me food to eat; when I
was thirsty, you gave me water to drink; when I was a stranger, you
took me into your home circle; 36when I was naked, you clothed me;
when I was ill, you came to visit me; when I was in prison, you came
to see me." 37Then the good people will answer: "Sir, when did we
see you hungry and feed you, or thirsty and give you water to drink?
38When did we see you a stranger and take you into our home circle,
or naked and clothe you? 39When did we see you ill or in prison and
come to visit you?" 40The king will answer: "The truth is that every
time you did these things for one of my brothers, even for the least of
them, you did them for me." 41Then he will say to those on the left:
"God's curse is on you! Begone to the eternal fire which has been
prepared for the devil and his angels! 42For, when I was hungry, you
did not give me food to eat; when I was thirsty, you did not give me
water to drink; 43when I was a stranger, you did not take me into your
home circle; when I was naked, you did not clothe me; when I was
ill and in prison, you did not come to visit me." 44At that they will
answer: "Sir, when did we see you hungry or thirsty or a stranger or
naked or ill or in prison, and fail to give you help?" 45Then he will
answer: "The truth is that every time you failed to do these things for
one of these, even for the least of them, you failed to do them for me."
46These will go away to eternal punishment, but the good will go to
eternal life.'

Chapter 26

WHEN Jesus had finished all he had to say on this occasion, he said
to his disciples: 2'You know that in two days' time it will be the
Passover, and the Son of Man is going to be handed over to be cruci-
fied.' 3It was then that the chief priests and the elders of the people
met in the palace of the High Priest, whose name was Caiaphas, 4and

discussed how to arrest Jesus by some stratagem, and so to kill him.
5Their problem was that they could not arrest him during the festival,
because they could not take the risk of a popular riot breaking out
among the people.

6When Jesus was in Bethany as the guest of Simon the leper, 7a
woman came up to him with an alabaster phial of very expensive
perfume, which she poured over his head as he sat at table. 8The
sight of her action annoyed the disciples. 'What is the point of this
waste?' they said. 9'This could have been sold for a large sum of
money, and the proceeds could have been used to help the poor.'
10Jesus knew what they were saying. 'Why are you distressing the
woman?' he said. 'She has done a lovely thing to me. 11You have the
poor with you always, but you do not have me always. 12By pouring
this perfume over my body, she has by her action prepared me for
my burial. 13I tell you truly, wherever this Good News is proclaimed
all over the world, what she has done will be told too, so that she
will always be remembered.'

14It was at this time that one of the Twelve, called Judas Iscariot,
went to the chief priests. 15'What are you prepared to give me,' he
said, 'if I deliver him into your hands?' They settled with him for five
pounds. 16From then on Judas was always looking for a good oppor-
tunity to deliver Jesus into their hands.

17On the first day of the Festival of Unleavened Bread Jesus' disciples
came and said to him: 'Where do you wish us to make the necessary
preparations for you to eat the Passover meal?' 18Jesus said to them:
'Go into the city to so-and-so, and tell him: "The teacher says: 'My
hour of crisis will not be long now. I am going to celebrate the Pass-
over festival at your house with my disciples.'"' 19The disciples
carried out Jesus' instructions, and made all the necessary prepara-
tions for the Passover.

20When evening came, Jesus took his place at the table with his
twelve disciples. 21During the meal he said to them: 'I tell you truly,
one of you will betray me.' 22They were very distressed, and each of
them said to him: 'Master, surely it can't be me?' 23Jesus answered:
'It is one who has dipped his bread with me in the dish who is going to
betray me. 24The Son of Man goes out on the road the scripture says
he must go. But tragic is the fate of the man by whom the Son of
Man is betrayed! It would have been better for that man, if he had

never been born!' 25Judas, who was busy trying to betray him, said:
'Master, surely it can't be me?' Jesus said to him: 'You have said it
yourself!'

26During the meal Jesus took a loaf. He said the blessing over it, and
broke it into pieces, and gave it to his disciples. 'Take! Eat!' he said.
'This means my body.' 27He took a cup, and gave thanks to God. He
gave it to them and said: 'All of you drink it. 28This means my life-
blood, through which the new relationship between man and God
is made possible, the blood which is being shed for many, that their
sins may be forgiven. 29I tell you, I shall not drink of this fruit
of the vine, until the time comes when I drink it new with you in my
Father's kingdom.'

30When they had sung the psalm of praise, they went out to the
Hill of Olives. 31Then Jesus said to them: 'There is not one of you
whose courage will stand the test of what is going to happen to me
tonight, for scripture says: "I will smite the shepherd, and the sheep
of the flock will be scattered." 32But, after I have risen, I will go on
ahead of you into Galilee.' 33Peter answered: 'Even if everyone else's
courage fails because of what is going to happen to you, mine never
will.' 34'I tell you truly,' Jesus said to him, 'that this very night, before
the cock crows, you will disown me three times.' 35'Even if I have
to die with you,' Peter said to him, 'I will never disown you.' And
all the disciples said the same.

36Then Jesus went with them to a place called Gethsemane. 'Sit
here while I go over there and pray,' he said to his disciples. 37He took
with him Peter and Zebedee's two sons, and he began to be distressed
and distraught in mind. 38'My soul is grief-stricken with a grief like
death,' he said to them. 'Wait here and share my vigil.' 39He went a
little farther, and flung himself face down on the ground in prayer.
'My Father,' he said, 'if it is possible, don't let this bitter ordeal come
to me. But not what I will, but what you will.' 40He came to his
disciples and found them sleeping. He said to Peter: 'So the three of
you could not keep vigil with me for one hour? 41Sleeplessly watch
and pray, for you may well all have to face your ordeal of temptation.
I know that you mean well and that you want to do the right thing,
but human nature is frail.' 42He went away a second time and prayed
again. 'My Father,' he said, 'if there is no escape from this situation,
unless I go through it to the bitter end, your will be done.' 43He came

back again, and again he found them sleeping, for they could not keep
their eyes open. 44Again he went away and left them, and again a
third time he prayed the same prayer. 45Then he came to his disciples
and said to them: 'Are you still lying there sleeping? The hour has
come for the Son of Man to be delivered into the hands of sinful men.
46Up! On your way! The traitor is coming!'

47Just as he was saying this, Judas, one of the Twelve, arrived,
accompanied by a mob armed with swords and cudgels, sent by the
chief priests and elders of the people. 48The traitor had given them a
signal. 'The man I shall kiss is the man you want,' he said. 'Hold him!'
49He went straight up to Jesus and said: 'Greetings, Rabbi!' and kissed
him lovingly. 50'Comrade,' Jesus said, 'get on with what you came to
do!' Then they came up to Jesus and seized and held him. 51One of
Jesus' friends reached out and drew his sword, and struck the High
Priest's servant, and cut off his ear. 52'Put your sword back in its place,'
Jesus said. 'All who draw the sword will die by the sword. 53Do you
think that I cannot appeal to my Father and he will here and now
provide me with twelve regiments of angels? 54But, if I were to do this,
how could the scriptures, which say things must be so, come true?'
55At the same time Jesus said to the mob: 'Have you come out with
swords and cudgels to arrest me, as if you were out to arrest a brigand?
I sat teaching in the Temple precincts every day, and you made no
attempt to arrest me. 56All this has happened that the writings of the
prophets should come true.' It was then that all the disciples aban-
doned him and ran away.

57Those who had arrested Jesus took him to the house of Caiaphas
the High Priest, where the experts in the Law and the elders had
assembled. 58Peter followed him at a distance, right into the court-
yard of the High Priest's house. He went in and sat down with the
attendants to see the end.

59The chief priests and the whole Sanhedrin made repeated at-
tempts to find fabricated evidence against Jesus, which could be used
to justify them in putting him to death. 60Many witnesses who were
prepared to perjure themselves came forward, but the court was un-
able to find any evidence upon which it could legitimately proceed.
At last two witnesses came forward 61and said: 'This man said: "I can
demolish God's Temple, and in three days I can rebuild it."' 62The
High Priest stood up and said to Jesus: 'Have you no answer to these

allegations which these witnesses are making against you?' 63Jesus
remained silent. The High Priest said to him: 'I call on you to tell us
on oath, in the name of the living God—are you the Messiah, the Son
of God?' 64'If you like to say so,' Jesus said. 'But I tell you, from now
on you will see the Son of Man sitting at the right hand of Almighty
God, and coming on the clouds of heaven.' 65At that the High Priest
ripped his clothes in horror. 'This statement is blasphemy,' he said.
'What further witnesses do we need? You have actually here and now
heard his blasphemous claim. 66What is your verdict?' They answered:
'He is guilty of a crime for which the penalty is death.' 67Then they
spat in his face, and punched him with their clenched fists. Some of
them slapped him across the face. 68'Prophesy to us, Messiah,' they
said. 'Who struck you?'

69Peter was sitting outside in the courtyard. One of the maid-
servants came up to him. 'You too were with Jesus the Galilaean,' she
said. 70He denied it in front of them all. 'I have no idea what you're
talking about,' he said. 71He went out to the gateway. Another maid-
servant saw him. She said to the people there: 'This man was with
Jesus the Nazarene.' 72Again he denied it. 'I swear I do not know the
man,' he said. 73Shortly afterwards the bystanders came up to Peter
and said to him: 'You certainly are one of them. Indeed you are.
Your Galilaean accent makes it obvious.' 74Peter swore he was telling
the truth, and called down curses on himself if he was not. 'I do not
know the man,' he said. 75Just then the cock crew, and Peter remem-
bered how Jesus had said: 'Before the cock crows, you will disown me
three times.' And he went out and wept bitterly.

Chapter 27

WHEN morning came, all the chief priests and elders of the people
laid their plans to make sure that Jesus would be put to death.
2So they put him in chains and took him away and handed him over
to Pilate, the Roman governor.

3When Judas, who had betrayed him, saw that Jesus had been
condemned, he realized the horror of what he had done. He took the
five pounds back to the chief priests and elders. 4'I sinned,' he said,
'when I betrayed to death a man who is completely innocent.' 'That

has nothing to do with us,' they said. 'That's your look-out!' 5He
flung the money into the Temple and went out and went away and
hanged himself. 6The chief priests took the money. 'It is not right,'
they said, 'to put this into the treasury, for it is the price of a man's
life.' 7So, after conferring about the matter, they bought the Potter's
Field with it, to serve as a burying-ground for strangers. 8That is why
to this day that field is called the Bloody Field. 9Then the statement
made through the prophet Jeremiah came true: 'They took the five
pounds, the price of him on whom a price had been set by the sons
of Israel, 10and they paid for the Potter's Field with them, as the Lord
had instructed me.'

11Jesus was brought before the governor, and, as he stood there, the
governor put the question to him. 'Are you the King of the Jews?' he
asked. Jesus said: 'If you like to put it so.' 12Jesus made no reply to the
accusations of the chief priests and elders. 13Pilate said to him: 'Do
you not hear all the evidence they are alleging against you?' 14But to
Pilate's surprise Jesus did not answer even one single word.

15At the festival it was the governor's custom to release any one
prisoner whom the crowd chose. 16At that time a notorious prisoner
called Jesus Barabbas was under arrest. 17When they had assembled,
Pilate said to them: 'Whom do you wish me to release for you, Jesus
Barabbas, or Jesus called the Messiah?' 18He was well aware that it
was malicious ill-will which had prompted them to hand Jesus over
to him.

19When he was presiding over his court, his wife sent a message to
him. 'Have nothing to do with this innocent man,' she said, 'for today
I have had the most disturbing dream about him.' 20But the chief
priests and the elders persuaded the crowds to ask for the release of
Barabbas and the death of Jesus. 21'Which of the two do you wish me
to release for you?' the governor asked. 'Barabbas,' they said. 22'What
am I to do with Jesus called the Messiah?' said Pilate. 'To the cross
with him!' they all said. 23'Why? What crime has he committed?'
Pilate asked. They kept on shrieking the more insistently: 'To the
cross with him!' 24When Pilate saw that nothing was any use, and that
there was every prospect of a riot, he took water and publicly washed
his hands. 'I am not responsible for this man's death,' he said. 'The
responsibility is yours.' 25The whole people answered: 'Let the re-
sponsibility for his death be on us and on our children.' 26Then

Pilate released Barabbas for them, and he had Jesus flogged, and
handed him over to be crucified.

27Then the governor's soldiers took Jesus to their headquarters.
They collected the whole company. 28They stripped him of his
clothes, and dressed him in a scarlet cloak. 29They plaited a crown of
thorns and placed it on his head. They put a cane in his right hand
and knelt mockingly before him. 'Hail, King of the Jews!' they said.
30They spat on him. They took the cane and hit him across the head
with it. 31When they had finished their horseplay, they took the cloak
off, and dressed him in his own clothes, and took him away to crucify
him.

32On the way out they came on a man from Cyrene called Simon,
and they forcibly commandeered him to carry Jesus' cross.

33When they came to a place called Golgotha, which means the
Place of a Skull, 34they offered Jesus drugged wine mixed with gall to
drink. He tasted it and refused to drink it. 35When they had crucified
him, they shared out his clothes between them by drawing lots for
them; 36and they sat there and kept watch on him. 37Above his head
they placed a written copy of the charge against him: 'This is Jesus,
the King of the Jews.' 38Two brigands were crucified at the same time
as he was, one on his right and one on his left.

39The passers-by tossed their heads at him and hurled their insults
at him. 40'You are the man who was going to demolish the Temple
and rebuild it in three days,' they said. 'If you really are God's Son,
save yourself, and come down from the cross.' 41The chief priests too
joined in the mockery with the experts in the Law and the elders.
42'He saved others,' they said. 'He cannot save himself! He is the King
of Israel! Let him come down from the cross here and now, and we
will believe his claims! 43He trusted in God! He claimed to be God's
Son! Let God rescue him now—if he wants him!' 44The brigands who
were crucified with him flung the same taunts at him.

45From twelve o'clock midday until three o'clock in the afternoon
there was darkness over the whole land. 46About three o'clock in the
afternoon Jesus gave a great shout: 'Eli, Eli, lama sabachthani?' which
means: 'My God, my God, why have you abandoned me?' 47When
some of the bystanders heard this, they said: 'He is calling Elijah!'
48One of them at once ran and took a sponge and soaked it in vinegar

and put it on a cane, and offered it to him to drink. 49The others said:
'Wait! Let us see if Elijah is coming to save him.'* 50Jesus again shouted
at the top of his voice, and died.

51The curtain of the Temple which veiled the Holy of Holies was
ripped from top to bottom, and the ground was shaken and the
rocks were split. 52The tombs were burst open, and the bodies of many
of the people of God who slept in death were raised to life. 53They
came out of their tombs, and after his resurrection they went into the
holy city, and appeared to many. 54When the company commander
and his men who were watching Jesus saw the earthquake and the
things which were happening, they were awe-stricken. 'Beyond a
doubt,' they said, 'this man was indeed a son of God.'

55There were many women looking on from a distance. They had
followed Jesus from Galilee, attending to his needs. 56Among them
were Mary from Magdala, and Mary the mother of James and Joseph,
and the mother of Zebedee's sons.

57When evening came, a wealthy man from Arimathaea called
Joseph, who had himself been a disciple of Jesus, 58went to Pilate and
asked for Jesus' body. Pilate gave orders for it to be given to him.
59Joseph took Jesus' body away, and wrapped it in clean linen, 60and
placed it in his new tomb, which had been hewn out of the rock. He
rolled a huge stone up to the doorway of the tomb, and went away.
61Mary of Magdala was there with the other Mary, sitting opposite
the tomb.

62On the next day, the day after the Day of Preparation, the Phari-
sees went in a body to Pilate. 63'Sir,' they said, 'we remember that,
while he was alive, that impostor claimed that after three days he
would rise from the dead. 64In view of this, please issue orders for
special security measures to be taken in regard to the tomb for the
next three days, to prevent his disciples coming and stealing his body
and telling the people that he has risen from the dead. If that happens
the deception will go from bad to worse.' 65Pilate said to them: 'You
can have a military guard. Go and take all possible security measures.'
66They went and secured the tomb by affixing a seal to the stone as
well as posting a military guard.

*Other manuscripts add here, *Another took a spear and pierced his side, and water and blood came out.*

Chapter 28

LATE on the Sabbath, just as the day was breaking on the Sunday,
Mary from Magdala and the other Mary came to look at the tomb.
2There was a great earthquake, for the angel of the Lord came down
from heaven, and came and rolled away the stone, and sat on it.
3His face shone like lightning, and his clothes were as white as snow.
4The guards were shaken with fear, and lay like dead men. 5The
angel said to the women: 'Do not be afraid. I know that you are
looking for Jesus who was crucified. 6He is not here, for he has risen,
as he said he would. Come! See for yourselves the place where his
body lay. 7Hurry and tell his disciples that he has risen from the dead,
and that he is going on ahead of you into Galilee. You will meet him
there. That is the message I have for you.' 8They hurried away from
the tomb in mingled awe and great joy, and ran to tell the news to
the disciples. 9Suddenly Jesus was standing in their path. 'Joy be with
you,' he said. They went up to him, and clasped his feet, and knelt
before him. 10Then Jesus said to them: 'Don't be afraid. Go and tell
my brothers to leave for Galilee. They will see me there.'

11While the women were on their way, some of the military guard
went into the city, and told the chief priests the news of what had
happened. 12When they had met and conferred with the elders, they
gave the soldiers a considerable sum of money. 13'You must say,' they
said, 'that his disciples came at night and stole his body, while you were
sleeping, 14and, if the governor gets to know about this, we will make
it all right with him, and we will see to it that you have nothing to
worry about.' 15They took the money, and carried out their instruc-
tions, and this story is still current in Jewish circles.

16The eleven disciples made their way to Galilee, to the mountain
to which Jesus had instructed them to go. 17When they saw him, they
worshipped him, but some were not sure. 18Jesus came to them and
said: 'All authority in heaven and on earth has been given to me.
19You must therefore go and make the people of all nations my
disciples. You must baptize them in the name of the Father and of the
Son and of the Holy Spirit, 20and you must teach them to obey all
the commands I have given you. And there is not a day when I will
not be with you to the end of time.'

Introduction to Luke

LUKE's Gospel was written between A.D. 80 and 90. There must always be for us a very special interest about Luke's Gospel, because Luke is the only writer in the New Testament who was a Gentile and not a Jew. This can even be seen in Luke's Greek. The preface to his gospel (1.1-4) is written on the model of the Greek classical writers and is in the best Greek in the New Testament.

One characteristic of Luke's Gospel stands out very clearly. Luke is the universal gospel. Matthew traces the genealogy of Jesus back to Abraham, the father and founder of the Jewish nation (Matthew 1.2), but Luke traces it right back to Adam, the father of the human race (3.38). All the Gospel writers quote Isaiah 40.3 in connection with John the Baptist, the forerunner of Jesus. Matthew (3.3), Mark (1.2,3) and John (1.23) all have:

> The voice of one crying in the wilderness:
> Prepare the way of the Lord,
> make his paths straight.

Only Luke (3.4-6) continues the quotation:

> Every valley shall be filled,
> and every mountain and hill shall be brought low,
> and the crooked shall be made straight,
> and the rough ways shall be made smooth,
> and all flesh shall see the salvation of God.

Right from the beginning Luke sees Jesus in terms of the world.

In this universal sweep the Samaritans are included. The one grateful leper is a Samaritan (17.11-19), and the hero of the parable is a Samaritan (10.30-37). The Gentiles are included. The aged Symeon sees in the child Jesus a light for revelation to the Gentiles (2.32). The faith of the Gentile centurion surpasses any faith in Israel (7.1-10). The poor are included. It is to the poor that the Gospel is preached (4.18; 7.22), and it is the poor who are blessed (6.20-25). In the parable of the rich man and Lazarus it is godly poverty which is in heaven and selfish wealth which is in hell (16.19-31). Even the disreputable, the outcast and the sinner are included. It is precisely the lost things that

God loves to find (15). Luke is concerned to show the universal embrace of the love of God.

Women have a very special place in Luke's Gospel. It is there that we meet Anna the prophetess (2.36-38); the widow of Nain (7.11-17); the woman who was a sinner but whose love was great (7.35-50); Martha and Mary (10.38-41); the weeping daughters of Jerusalem (23.27-31). In those days the place of women in society was very low, and we see in Luke the beginning of Christian chivalry to women.

Prayer has a very special place in Luke's Gospel. There are seven occasions when only Luke shows us Jesus at prayer (3.21; 5.16; 6.12; 9.18; 9.29; 11.1; 23.46); and it is in Luke that we find the two prayer parables of the friend at midnight and the unjust judge (11.5-8; 18.1-8).

Luke's Gospel is the Gospel of praise. The phrase *praising God* occurs oftener in the writings of Luke, the Gospel and Acts, than in all the rest of the New Testament put together.

Renan, the famous French scholar, called Luke's Gospel the most beautiful book in the world, and certainly no book gives such a picture of the universal love of God in Jesus Christ.

LUKE'S VERSION
of the Story of the Good News

Chapter 1

THERE have been many who attempted the task of drawing up an
account of the events on which our faith is based. 2They have
transmitted the story in the form in which it was handed down to
us by those who were the original eye-witnesses of the events, and
who were given the task of spreading the Christian message. 3I, too,
therefore, have made up my mind to carry out a careful investigation
of the history of all these events, and to write to you, Theophilus,
your Excellency, an orderly account of them, 4because I want you to
have in your mind a full and reliable knowledge of the things about
which you may well have been misinformed.

5In the time of Herod, the King of Judaea, there was a priest called
Zacharias, who belonged to the Abia section of the priests. He had a
wife called Elisabeth who like himself was a direct descendant of
Aaron. 6They were both good people in God's sight, for they lived in
blameless obedience to all the commandments and ordinances of the
Lord. 7They were childless, because Elisabeth had been unable to have
a child, and by this time they were both far advanced in years. 8When
Zacharias was performing his priestly offices before God, during the
week when his section was on duty, 9it fell to him by lot, in the nor-
mal priestly arrangements, to enter the Lord's Temple to burn in-
cense. 10The assembled people were praying outside at the hour
when the incense was being offered. 11The angel of the Lord appeared
to him, standing on the right of the altar of incense. 12When Zacharias
saw him, he was alarmed and afraid. 13'Don't be afraid, Zacharias,'
the angel said to him, 'for your prayer has been heard. Your wife
Elisabeth will bear you a son, and you must give him the name John.
14His birth will bring a thrill of joy to you and happiness to many.
15God will give him a great task to do. He must never drink wine or

strong drink, and from the day of his birth he will be filled with the
Holy Spirit. 16He will be the means whereby many of the sons of
Israel turn to the Lord their God. 17God means him to be the fore-
runner, and the spirit and the power of Elijah will be his. It will be
his task to reconcile fathers and children, to persuade the disobedient
to accept the wisdom of the good, and to make ready a people pre-
pared for the Lord.' 18Zacharias said to the angel: 'How shall I know
that this is really going to happen, for I am an old man and my wife is
far advanced in years?' 19'I am Gabriel,' the angel answered. 'I stand
in God's presence awaiting his command, and I have been sent to
speak to you and to bring you this good news. 20You will be silent,
and you will not be able to speak, until this happens, because you did
not believe my words, and my words are such that in their own due
time they will come true.'

21The people were waiting for Zacharias, and they were surprised
that he was lingering so long in the Temple. 22When he came out, he
was unable to speak to them, and they realized that he had seen a
vision in the Temple. He made signs to them, but he remained speech-
less. 23When his period of Temple duty was completed, he returned
home. 24After this time his wife Elisabeth conceived a child, and for
five months she did not see anyone. 25'The Lord has done this for me,'
she said, 'and now in his kindness to me he has taken away the thing
that was always a public humiliation to me.'

26In Elisabeth's sixth month the angel Gabriel was sent by God to a
town in Galilee called Nazareth, 27to a girl who was pledged to marry
a man called Joseph, who was a direct descendant of David. The girl's
name was Mary. 28He went in to her and said: 'Joy be with you! You
are specially dear to God! The Lord is with you!' 29She was deeply
moved at what he said, and wondered what a greeting like this could
mean. 30'Don't be afraid, Mary,' the angel said to her. 'God has chosen
you for a very precious privilege. 31You will conceive, and you will
have a son, and you must give him the name Jesus. 32He will be great;
his title will be the Son of the Most High. The Lord will give him the
throne of David his ancestor. 33He will reign over the house of Jacob
for ever, and his reign will never come to an end.' 34Mary said to the
angel: 'How can this happen when I have no husband?' 35The angel
answered: 'The Holy Spirit will come upon you, and the power of
the Most High will overshadow you. That is why the holy child who
will be born will be called Son of God. 36Elisabeth, your kinswoman,

has also conceived a son in her old age. They said that she could
never have a child. But now she is in her sixth month, 37for there is
nothing impossible to God.' 38Mary said: 'I am the Lord's servant.
Whatever you say, I accept.' And the angel went away and left
her.

39At that time Mary set out and went as fast as she could to a town
of Judah in the hill country. 40She went into Zacharias' house and
greeted Elisabeth. 41When Elisabeth heard Mary's greeting, the baby
stirred in her womb. Elisabeth was filled with the Holy Spirit, 42and
burst into speech. 'You are the most blessed of women,' she said, 'and
blessed is the child you will bear. 43Why have I received this privilege
that the mother of my Lord should come to me? 44For, when I heard
your greeting, the baby in my womb leaped for joy. 45Blessed is she
who has believed that the message she received from the Lord will
come true.'

46Mary said:
'My soul tells of the greatness of God,
47and my spirit thrills in God my Saviour,
48because he has looked kindly on his servant,
even though my place in life is humble.
From now on those of all time to come will call me blessed,
49for the Mighty One has done great things for me,
and holy is his name.
50His mercy is from age to age
to those who reverence him.
51He has done mighty deeds with his right arm.
He has scattered the proud with their arrogant plans.
52He has thrown down the mighty from their seats of power.
He has exalted the humble,
53He has filled those who are hungry with good things.
and those who are rich he has sent empty away.
54He has come to the aid of Israel his servant.
55He has kept the promise that he made to our fathers,
the promise never to forget his mercy to Abraham,
and to his descendants for ever.'

56Mary stayed with Elisabeth for about three months, and then
returned to her own home.

57When the time for her baby to be born came, Elisabeth gave birth

to a son. 58When her neighbours and relations heard of God's great
kindness to her, they shared in her joy. 59On the eighth day they went
to have the child circumcised, and it was their intention to call him
Zacharias after his father. 60But his mother said: 'No! He is to be
called John.' 61They said to her: 'There is no one in your family circle
who is called by that name.' 62They asked his father by signs what he
wished him to be called. 63He asked for a writing-tablet and wrote:
'John is his name.' They were all very surprised. 64There and then he
recovered his powers of speech, and he was able to talk again, and he
began to praise God. 65The neighbours regarded these events with
awe, and the story was the talk of the whole hill country of Judaea.
66No one who heard it could forget it. 'What will this child turn out
to be?' they said. 'For indeed it is to the action of God that he owes
his existence.'

67His father Zacharias was filled with the Holy Spirit. With prophetic inspiration he said:

68'Blessed be the Lord, the God of Israel,
for he has kindly cared for his people,
and has rescued them from their bondage.
69From the family of David his servant,
he has raised up a champion to save us,
70as long ago through the words of the holy prophets
he said he would, when he promised
71to deliver us from our enemies
and from the power of those who hate us,
72to fulfil the promise of mercy which he made to our fathers,
and to remember his holy covenant.
73It was his sworn promise to Abraham our father
74that he would rescue us from the power of our enemies,
and enable us to serve him with nothing to fear,
75in holiness and goodness all our lives.
76And you, child, shall be called the prophet of the Most High,
for you will be the Lord's forerunner,
to prepare the roads by which he will travel,
77for it will be your task to tell his people
how they may be saved and have their sins forgiven,
78through the deep compassion of our God
which has graciously sent heaven's dawn to break upon us,

79to shine on those who sit in darkness and in the shadow of death,
and to direct our steps in the road that leads to peace.'

80So the child grew physically and developed spiritually; and he lived
in the desert places until he publicly emerged upon the scene of
Israel's history.

Chapter 2

AT that time a decree was issued by Caesar Augustus that a census
should be taken of the whole inhabited world. 2This was the
first census, and it took place when Quirinius was governor of Syria.
3Everyone went to his own native town to be registered. 4So Joseph
went up from Galilee, from the town of Nazareth, to Judaea, to
David's town, which is called Bethlehem, 5to register himself, along
with Mary, who was pledged to marry him, and who was expecting a
child. 6When they were there, the time for her to have her baby
came, 7and she gave birth to a son, her first child, and wrapped him
in swaddling clothes, and laid him in a manger, because there was no
room for them inside the village guest-house.

8In that district there were shepherds out in the fields, guarding
their flock by night. 9An angel of the Lord appeared to them, and the
glory of the Lord shone round them, and they were terrified. 10'Don't
be afraid,' the angel said to them, 'for I am bringing you good news of
great joy, a joy in which all peoples will share. 11For today there has
been born to you in David's town a saviour who is the Messiah, the
Lord. 12This is how you will recognize him. You will find a baby,
wrapped in swaddling clothes, lying in a manger.' 13Suddenly there
was with the angel a crowd of heaven's army, singing God's praise.
14'Glory to God in the heights of heaven,' they sang, 'and on earth
peace to mankind, on whom God's favour rests.'*

15When the angels had left them and gone back to heaven, the
shepherds said to each other: 'Come! We must go over to Bethlehem
and see what has happened, and what the Lord has told us about.'
16So they went as fast as they could, and they found Mary and Joseph,
and the baby lying in the manger. 17When they saw him, they told
everyone what they had been told about this child. 18And everyone

*Here some manuscripts have, *and on earth his peace and his favour towards men.*

who heard it was astonished at the shepherds' story. 19Mary treasured
all this in her memory, and wondered in her mind what it all meant.
20So the shepherds went back glorifying and praising God for all that
they had heard and seen, for everything was exactly as they had been
told.

21When the eight days which must precede circumcision had
elapsed, he was named Jesus, the name given him by the angel,
before his mother had conceived him.

22When the days which, according to the law of Moses, must
precede the ceremony of their purification had elapsed, his parents
brought him to Jerusalem to present him to the Lord, 23in accordance
with the regulation in the Lord's law, which states that every first-
born male creature must be regarded as consecrated to the Lord,
24and to make the sacrifice prescribed in the Lord's law, that is, a pair
of doves or two young pigeons.

25There was a man in Jerusalem called Simeon. He meticulously
observed the Law and devoutly reverenced God. He was waiting
for the comforting of Israel, and the Holy Spirit was upon him.
26He had received a special message through the Holy Spirit that death
would not come to him until he had seen the Lord's Messiah. 27Guid-
ed by the Spirit, he went into the Temple precincts. When his parents
brought in the baby Jesus, to carry out the customary ceremonies
of the Law, 28he took him in his arms. He blessed God and said:

29'Now, O Lord, as you promised,
you are giving your servant his release in peace,
30because my eyes have seen the saving power
31which you have prepared for all peoples to see,
32to be a light to bring your revelation to the Gentiles,
and glory to your people Israel.'

33His father and mother were astonished to hear this said about
him. 34Symeon blessed them, and said to Mary his mother: 'As for
this child, he is destined to be the cause whereby many in Israel will
fall, and many will rise, and to be a message from God which men will
reject. 35As for you, a sword will pierce your soul. It will be his work
to lay bare the secret thoughts of many a heart.'

36There was a prophetess called Anna, the daughter of Phanuel, a
member of the tribe of Asher. She was far advanced in years. For seven
years after she grew to womanhood she had lived with her husband,

37and now she was a widow of eighty-four years of age. She was never
away from the Temple precincts, and day and night she worshipped
continually with fasting and prayers. 38Just at that moment she came
up. She began to thank God, and to speak about him to all who were
waiting expectantly for the deliverance of Jerusalem.

39When they had discharged all the duties which the Lord's law
prescribes, they returned to Galilee, to their own town of Nazareth.
40The child grew bigger and stronger; he was full of wisdom, and the
grace of God was on him.

41Every year Jesus' parents used to go to Jerusalem for the Festival
of the Passover. 42When he was twelve years old, they went up to the
festival as they usually did. 43They stayed to the very end of the festi-
val, and, when they were on their way back home, the boy Jesus
stayed on in Jerusalem. His parents were not aware that he had done
so. 44They thought that he was in the caravan, and, at the end of the
first day's journey, they began to search for him among their relations
and friends. 45When they did not find him, they turned back to Jerus-
alem, searching for him as they went. 46It was three days before they
discovered him in the Temple precincts, sitting in the middle of the
teachers, listening to them, and asking them questions. 47All the
listeners were amazed at his intelligence and at his answers. 48They
were very surprised to see him there. 'Child,' his mother said to him,
'why have you behaved like this to us? Your father and I have been
searching for you, and we have been worried to distraction.' 49'Why
had you to look for me?' he said. 'Didn't you know that I was bound
to be in my Father's house?'

50They did not understand the meaning of what he said. 51So he
went down with them, and came to Nazareth, and he was obedient
to them. His mother stored all these things in her memory and kept
thinking about them, 52And Jesus grew wiser in mind and bigger in
body, and more and more he won the approval of God and of his
fellow men.

Chapter 3

IN the fifteenth year of the reign of Tiberius Caesar, when Pontius
Pilate was governor of Judaea, when Herod was tetrarch of Galilee,
his brother Philip tetrarch of Ituraea and of the district of Trachon-
itis, and Lysanias tetrarch of Abilene, 2in the high priesthood of Annas
and Caiaphas, the word of God came to John, Zacharias' son, when
he was in the desert. 3So he went all over the Jordan valley, proclaim-
ing a baptism which was a sign of the repentance which leads to the
forgiveness of sins. 4It was all as scripture said it would be in the book
of the words of the prophet Isaiah:

> 'The voice of one shouting in the wilderness,
> Get ready the road by which the Lord will come,
> straighten the paths by which he will travel.
> 5Every ravine will be filled in,
> every mountain and hill will be levelled;
> the twisted paths will be made into straight ways,
> and the rough tracks into smooth roads,
> 6and all men shall see the saving power of God.'

7John's message to the crowds who came out to be baptized by him
was: 'Brood of vipers! Who put it into your heads to flee from the
coming wrath? 8Prove the sincerity of your repentance by your life
and conduct. Don't begin to say to yourselves: "We have Abraham
as our father." For I tell you that God can produce children for
Abraham from these stones. 9Even now the axe is poised at the root
of the trees. Every tree which does not produce good fruit is going to
be cut down and flung into the fire.'

10The crowds kept asking: 'What does this mean that we must do?'
11'If a man has two shirts,' he answered, 'he must share with the man
who has none, and the man who has food must do the same.' 12The
tax-collectors came to be baptized. 'Teacher,' they said to him, 'what
ought we to do?' 13'Exact no more than the rate fixed,' he said to
them. 14The soldiers too asked him: 'What ought we to do?' 'Treat no
man with violence,' he said to them. 'Never be a blackmailer. Be
content with your pay.'

15When the people were in a state of expectancy, and when they

were all debating in their minds whether John could be the Messiah,
16John said to them all: 'I baptize you with water, but the One who is
stronger than I is coming. I am not fit to untie the strap of his sandals.
He will baptize you with the Holy Spirit and with fire. 17He is going
to winnow the chaff from the corn. He will cleanse every speck
of rubbish from his threshing-floor, and gather the corn into his
granary, but he will burn the chaff with fire that nothing can put
out.'

18So, then, appealing to the people with these and many another
plea, John announced the Good News to them. 19But, when Herod
the tetrarch was reproved by him for his conduct in the matter of
Herodias, his brother's wife, and for all the other wicked things he
had done, 20in addition to all his other crimes, he shut up John in
prison.

21When all the people had been baptized, Jesus too was baptized,
and, while he was praying, heaven was opened, 22and the Holy Spirit
in bodily form came down like a dove on him, and there came a voice
from heaven: 'You are my Son, the Beloved and Only One, on whom
my favour rests.'*

23When Jesus entered upon his ministry, he was about thirty years
of age. He was the son, so it was believed, of Joseph, the son of Heli,
24the son of Matthat, the son of Levi, the son of Melchi, the son of
Jannai, the son of Joseph, 25the son of Mattathias, the son of Amos,
the son of Nahum, the son of Esli, the son of Naggai, 26the son of
Maath, the son of Mattathias, the son of Semein, the son of Josech,
the son of Joda, 27the son of Joanan, the son of Rhesa, the son of
Zerubbabel, the son of Salathiel, the son of Neri, 28the son of Melchi,
the son of Addi, the son of Cosam, the son of Elmadam, the son of Er,
29the son of Joshua, the son of Eliezer, the son of Jorim, the son of
Matthat, the son of Levi, 30the son of Symeon, the son of Judah, the
son of Joseph, the son of Jonam, the son of Eliakim, 31the son of
Melea, the son of Menna, the son of Mattatha, the son of Nathan, the
son of David, 32the son of Jesse, the son of Obed, the son of Boaz, the
son of Sala, the son of Naasson, 33the son of Aminadab, the son of
Admin, the son of Arni, the son of Esrom, the son of Phares, the son
of Judah, 34the son of Jacob, the son of Isaac, the son of Abraham, the
son of Terah, the son of Nahor, 35the son of Serouch, the son of

*Here some manuscripts have, *You are my Son, the Beloved and Only One. Today I have begotten you.*

Ragau, the son of Phalek, the son of Eber, the son of Sala, 36the son of
Cainam, the son of Arphaxad, the son of Shem, the son of Noah, the
son of Lamech, 37the son of Methuselah, the son of Enoch, the son of
Jared, the son of Maleleel, the son of Cainam, 38the son of Enos, the
son of Seth, the son of Adam, the son of God.

Chapter 4

JESUS came back from the Jordan full of the Holy Spirit. 2For forty
days he was under the direction of the Spirit in the desert, 2and
during all that time he was undergoing the ordeal of temptation by
the Devil. During that time he ate nothing, and at the end of the
period he was attacked by the pangs of hunger. 3The Devil said to
him: 'If you really are the Son of God, tell this stone to become a
loaf of bread.' 4Jesus answered: 'Scripture says, "It takes more than
bread to keep a man alive."' 5The Devil took him up and showed
him in a flash all the kingdoms of the inhabited world. 6The Devil said
to him: 'I will give you control over all these, and I will give you
their splendour, for it has all been handed over to me, and it is mine
to give to anyone I wish. 7If you worship me, all of it will be yours.'
8Jesus answered: 'Scripture says, "You must worship the Lord your
God, and you must serve only him."' 9The Devil took him to Jeru-
salem, and placed him on the highest spire of the Temple. 'If you
really are the Son of God,' he said to him, 'fling yourself down from
here, 10for scripture says, "He will give his angels orders to guard you
through all dangers," and, 11"They will carry you in their arms to
ensure that you never strike your foot against a stone."' 12Jesus
answered: 'It has been said, "You must not try to see how far you can
go with the Lord your God."' 13So when the Devil had exercised his
every tempting wile, he left him until another opportunity of putting
him to the test should come.

14So Jesus returned to Galilee equipped with the power of the
Spirit. The whole countryside was talking about him. 15He went
on teaching in their synagogues, and he was held in high reputation
by all.

16He went to Nazareth, where he had been brought up, and, as his
habit was, he went into the synagogue on the Sabbath. He rose to read
the scripture lesson. 17The roll containing the prophecies of Isaiah

was handed to him. He unrolled the roll and found the passage where
it is written:

> 18'The Spirit of the Lord is upon me,
> because he has anointed me,
> to bring good news to the poor.
> He has sent me to announce to the prisoners
> that they will be liberated,
> and to the blind that they will see again,
> to send away in freedom
> those who have been broken by life,
> 19to announce that the year
> when the favour of God will be shown has come.'

20He rolled up the roll, and handed it back to the officer. He took the
preacher's seat, and the eyes of everyone in the synagogue were
fixed intently on him. 21'Today,' he said to them, 'this passage of
scripture has come true, as you listened to it.'

22They all agreed that the reports that they had heard of him were
true, and they were astonished at the gracious words he spoke.
'Isn't this Joseph's son?' they said. 23He said: 'You are bound to quote
the proverb to me, "Doctor, cure yourself." Do here in your home
country all that we have heard about you doing in Capernaum.'
24He went on: 'This is the truth I tell you, no prophet is accepted in
his own native place. 25You know quite well that it is the fact that
there was many a widow in Israel in Elijah's time, when the sky was
closed for three and a half years, and there was a severe famine all
over the country; 26but to none of them was Elijah sent; he was sent
to a widow in Sarepta in Sidon. 27There was many a leper in Israel in
the time of Elisha; and none of them was cured; but Naaman the
Syrian was.' 28The people in the synagogue were all enraged, when
they heard him speak like this. 29They rose from their seats and
hustled him out of the town. They took him to the brow of the hill
on which their town is built, to hurl him down. 30But he walked
straight through the middle of them, and went on his way.

31So he went down to Capernaum, a town in Galilee. On the
Sabbath he was teaching there, 32and they were astonished at the way
in which he taught, because he spoke like a man who needed no other
authority than his own.

33In the synagogue there was a man who had a spirit of an unclean

demon. This man shrieked at the top of his voice: 34‘Let us alone!
What business have you with us, Jesus of Nazareth. Have you come
to destroy us? I know who you are. You are God’s Holy One.’ 35Jesus
reprimanded the spirit. ‘Silence!’ he said. ‘Come out of him!’ The
demon threw the man into a convulsion right in front of them all,
and then came out of him without doing him any harm. 36Astonish-
ment gripped them. They kept saying to one another: ‘What kind of
way is this to speak? He gives his orders to unclean spirits with
authority and power, and they come out.’ 37The report of what Jesus
had done spread all over the surrounding district.

38Jesus went out of the synagogue, and went into Simon’s house.
Simon’s mother-in-law was in the grip of a major fever. They asked
him to do something for her. 39He stood over her and reprimanded
the fever, and it left her. There and then she got up, and began to
serve them with their meal.

40When the sun was setting, everyone who had friends who were ill
with all kinds of troubles brought them to Jesus, and he laid his hands
on each of them, and cured them. 41Demons too went out of many
people, shouting: ‘You are the Son of God.’ He reprimanded them,
and would not allow them to speak, because they knew that he was
the Messiah.

42At daybreak he left the house and went out to a lonely place. The
crowds kept searching for him, and, when they found him, they tried
to keep him from leaving them. 43‘I must tell the good news of the
Kingdom of God to the other towns too,’ he said to them, ‘because
that is what I was sent to do.’ 44So he continued to proclaim his
message in the synagogues of Judaea.

Chapter 5

JESUS was standing on the shore of the Lake of Gennesaret, and the
crowd were pressing in upon him in their eagerness to hear the
word of God. 2He saw two boats drawn up on the lake-side. The
fishermen had disembarked and were washing their nets. 3He got into
one of the boats, which belonged to Simon, and asked him to push
out a little from the land. He sat down and went on teaching the
crowds from the boat.

4When he had finished speaking, he said to Simon: 'Push out into
the deep water, and let down your nets for a catch.' 5'Master,' Simon
answered, 'we have worked our hardest all night and we have caught
nothing. All the same, if you say so, I will let down the nets.' 6When
they had done so, they caught so many fish in the nets that they were
on the point of breaking. 7They signalled to their partners in the other
boat to come to their help. They came and filled both boats so full
that they were in danger of sinking. 8When Simon Peter saw what
had happened, he threw himself at Jesus' feet. 'Lord,' he said, 'leave
me, for I am a sinful man.' 9The size of the catch of fish they had
taken left Peter and his crew in wondering amazement, 10and James
and John, Zebedee's sons, Peter's partners, were equally astonished.
'Don't be afraid,' Jesus said to Simon. 'From now on it will be men
that you catch.' 11Then they hauled the boats up on to the land, and
left everything, and became his followers.

12When Jesus was in one of the towns, a man who was a mass of
leprosy came and threw himself prostrate in front of him. 'Sir,' he
appealed to Jesus, 'if you want to cure me, you can.' 13Jesus reached
out his hand and touched him. 'I do,' he said. 'Be cured!' There and
then the leprosy left him. 14Jesus gave him orders not to tell anyone.
'But go,' he said, 'and show yourself to the priest, and take him the
offering for your cleansing which Moses prescribed, to prove to them
that you really are cured.' 15But the news about Jesus spread all the
more, and huge crowds gathered to listen to him and to have their
illnesses cured. 16But Jesus withdrew into the lonely places and
remained there in prayer.

17One day, as Jesus was teaching, a group of Pharisees and legal
experts were sitting listening. They had come from every village in
Galilee and from Judaea and from Jerusalem. The Lord's power
made Jesus able to make sick people well. 18A party of men came
carrying on a bed a man who was paralysed. They tried to carry him
in to lay him in front of Jesus. 19They were unable to find any way to
carry him in because of the crowd. So they went up on to the roof,
and they let him down, bed and all, through the tiles, right into the
middle of the crowd, in front of Jesus. 20When Jesus saw their faith,
he said: 'Man, your sins are forgiven you.' 21Then questions began to
arise in the minds of the experts in the Law and of the Pharisees.
'Who is this fellow who is insulting God?' they said. 'Can anyone but
God forgive sins?' 22Jesus was well aware of what was going on in

their minds. 'What are your minds going on about?' he said. 23'Which
is easier, to say, "Your sins are forgiven you," or to say, "Get up and
walk"? 24Just to show you that the Son of Man actually has power to
forgive sins on earth'—he said to the paralysed man—'Get up, I tell
you! Lift your bedding and go home!' 25On the spot the man got up
in front of them all, lifted the mattress on which he had been lying,
and went away home, praising God. 26They were absolutely aston-
ished. They kept on praising God; they were filled with awe. 'We
have seen things beyond belief today,' they said.

27After that, Jesus went out and saw a tax-collector called Levi
sitting in the office where he collected the customs duties. 'Follow
me!' he said to him. 28Levi rose from his seat, left everything, and be-
gan to be his follower. 29Levi gave a big reception for Jesus in his house,
and there was a large crowd of tax-collectors and other guests. 30The
Pharisees and the experts in the Law complained to the disciples:
'Why do you eat and drink with tax-collectors and with people with
whom no respectable Jew would have anything to do?' 31Jesus
answered: 'It is not those who are well who need a doctor, but those
who are ill. 32I did not come to bring an invitation to repent to those
who are good, but to those who are sinners.'

33They said to him: 'John's disciples fast frequently and carefully
observe the prescribed prayers, and so do the disciples of the Pharisees.
But your disciples eat and drink when and what they like.' 34'Obvi-
ously,' Jesus said to them, 'you cannot expect the bridegroom's
closest friends to fast while the bridegroom is with them. 35The time
will come when the bridegroom will be taken away from them.
When that time comes, they will fast.'

36He used an illustration to speak to them. 'No one,' he said,
'tears a piece from a new coat and uses it to patch an old coat. If he
does, he will tear the new coat, and, at the same time, the patch
from the new coat will not match the old coat. 37No one puts new
fermenting wine into old wineskins which have lost their elasticity.
If he does, the new wine will burst the wineskins, and the wine itself
will be spilled, and the wineskins will be ruined too. 38Newly made
wine must be put into new wineskins. 39No one wants to drink new
wine when he has old wine, for he says: "The old is mellow."'

Chapter 6

JESUS was walking through the cornfields on a Sabbath day. His
disciples began to pluck the ears of corn, and to rub them in their
hands and eat them. 2Some of the Pharisees said: 'Why are you doing
what it is not permitted by the Law to do on the Sabbath?' 3'Have you
never read,' Jesus answered, 'what David did when he and his friends
were hungry? 4Don't you know the story of how he went into the
house of God, and took and ate the sacred loaves which are placed
in the presence of God, and which only the priests are permitted to
eat, and how he gave them to his friends as well? 5The Son of Man's
authority,' he said to them, 'extends over the Sabbath.'

6On another Sabbath he went into the synagogue and was teaching
there. There was a man there whose right hand was withered. 7The
experts in the Law and the Pharisees were watching him closely, to
see if he would heal the man on the Sabbath, for they wanted to find
something to use as a charge against him. 8Jesus was well aware of
what was going on in their minds. He said to the man with the
withered hand: 'Get up, and stand where everyone can see you!' The
man stood up. 9'I will put a question to you,' Jesus said to them. 'Is
it permitted on the Sabbath day to help or to hurt, to save life or to
destroy life?' 10His gaze swept round them all. 'Stretch out your hand,'
he said to the man. The man did so, and his hand was restored to
health. 11They were furious, and they began to discuss with each
other what they could do to Jesus.

12At that time Jesus went away to the hillside to pray. He spent the
whole night in prayer to God. 13When day came, he summoned his
disciples, and from them he chose twelve, whom he called apostles;
14Simon, to whom he gave the name Peter, and his brother Andrew,
and James and John, and Philip and Bartholomew, 15and Matthew
and Thomas and James, Alphaeus' son, and Simon who was called the
Nationalist, 16and Judas, James's son, and Judas Iscariot, who became
a traitor.

17He came down with them, and took his stand on a level place.
There were with him a huge crowd of his disciples, and a great mob
of people from all over Judaea, and from Jerusalem, and from the

sea coast of Tyre and Sidon. They had come to listen to him and to
have their illnesses cured. 18Those who were troubled by unclean
spirits were cured. 19The crowd were all trying to touch him, for
power issued from him, and he healed them all.

20Jesus looked up at his disciples and said:

'O the bliss of you who are destitute,
for the Kingdom of God belongs to you!
21O the bliss of you who are hungry in this world,
for you will be satisfied to the full!
O the bliss of you who weep in this world,
for you will laugh!
22Yours is this bliss,
when men will hate you,
and when they will shut the door in your face,
when they will heap insults on you,
when they will banish your very name
as an evil thing,
for the sake of the Son of Man.
23Rejoice when that happens,
and thrill with joy.
You will receive a rich reward in heaven,
for their fathers treated the prophets
in exactly the same way.

24'But tragic is the fate of you who are rich,
for you have received all the comfort you will ever get.
25Tragic is the fate of you who have eaten your fill in this world,
for you will be hungry.
Tragic is the fate of you who laugh in this world,
for you will mourn and weep.
26Tragic is your fate, when everyone sings your praises,
for their fathers treated the false prophets
in exactly the same way.

27'I say to those of you who are listening to me:
Love your enemies.
Be kind to the people who hate you.
28Bless those who curse you.
Pray for those who abuse you.

29 If anyone strikes you on one cheek,
offer him the other to strike as well.
If anyone tries to take your shirt from you,
make no attempt to stop him taking your coat too.
30 If anyone asks you for anything,
give it to him,
and don't demand your possessions back
from anyone who takes them from you.

31 'Treat others as you would wish them to treat you.
32 What credit is it to you,
if you love the people who love you?
Even sinners love the people who love them.
33 What credit is it to you,
if you are kind to the people who are kind to you?
Even sinners are that.
34 What credit is it to you,
if you lend to those
from whom you have every hope of getting your money back?
Even sinners lend to sinners,
when they are sure they will get it back.
35 You must love your enemies;
you must be kind to them;
you must lend without hope of getting anything back.
If you do that,
you will receive a rich reward,
and you will be like the Most High,
for he is kind to the ungrateful and to the mean.
36 You must show yourself merciful,
as your Father is merciful.

37 'Do not make a habit of judging other people,
and you will not be judged yourselves.
Do not make a habit of condemning other people,
and you will not be condemned yourselves.
Forgive, and you will be forgiven.
38 Be generous, and you will find others generous to you.
Good measure, close-packed, and shaken down,
brimming over, will be poured into your lap.
You will get in exactly the same proportion
as you give.'

39Jesus went on to use an illustration. 'Surely,' he said, 'one blind man
cannot lead another blind man. If he tries to, both of them are sure
to fall into a hole in the road.'

40'A scholar is not superior to his teacher;
every well-equipped scholar will be like his teacher.

41'Why do you see the speck of dust
in your brother's eye,
and never notice the plank
that is in your own eye?
42How can you say to your fellow man,
"Brother, let me remove the speck of dust that is in your eye,"
when you don't see the plank in your own eye?
Your trouble is that you completely fail
to practise what you preach.
Begin by removing the plank
out of your own eye,
and then you will be able to see clearly
to remove the speck of dust
in your brother's eye.

43'A fine tree does not produce rotten fruit,
nor, on the other hand, does a rotten tree produce fine fruit.
44You can tell
what kind of tree any tree is
by its fruit.
You can't gather figs from thorn-bushes,
and you can't pluck grapes from a bramble-bush.
45A good man produces good
from his heart's good treasure-house.
An evil man produces evil
from his evil.
A man's words are the overflow
of the thoughts that are in his heart.

46'Why do you call me Lord, Lord
and not do what I tell you?
47I will tell you
what every man who comes to me,
and who listens to my words,
and obeys them, is like.

48He is like a man,
who, in building his house,
dug and excavated,
until he laid the foundations on the rock.
Then when a flood arose,
the river swept down on the house,
but it was powerless to shake it,
because it was well and truly built.
49But a man who has listened to me,
and who has not obeyed my words,
is like a man
who built a house on earth,
without any foundations.
The river swept down upon it,
and it collapsed at once,
and the ruin of that house was complete.'

Chapter 7

WHEN Jesus had finished telling the people what he wanted them
to hear, he went to Capernaum. 2There was a centurion there
whose slave was so ill that there was no hope of his recovery. This
slave meant a great deal to him. 3He heard about Jesus, and sent a
party of Jewish elders to him, with a request that Jesus should come
and save his slave's life. 4They came to Jesus with an urgent appeal.
'He deserves to have you do this for him,' they said, 5'for he loves our
nation, and it was he who built our synagogue for us.' 6Jesus started
out with them, but, when he was not far from the house, the cen-
turion sent some friends with a message to him. 'Don't trouble
yourself, sir,' he said. 'I am not fit to have you come into my house.
7That is why I did not even think myself fit to approach you person-
ally. All I ask you to do is to say the word, and so to answer my prayer
that my servant should be cured. 8I know what it is to be under
authority, and I have soldiers under my command. I am used to say-
ing to one, "Go!" and he goes, and to another, "Come here!" and he
comes, and to my slave, "Do this!" and he does it.' 9Jesus was aston-
ished to hear this. He turned to the crowd which was following him.
'I tell you,' he said, 'not even in Israel have I met a faith like this.'

10When those who had been sent returned to the house, they found
the slave in perfect health.

11Soon afterwards Jesus went into a town called Nain. He was
accompanied by his disciples and a large crowd of people. 12When he
was near the town gate, a dead man was being carried out for burial.
He had been his mother's only son, and she was a widow. A great
crowd of the townspeople were with her. 13The Lord was heart-sorry
for her when he saw her. 'Stop crying,' he said to her. 14Then he
stepped forward, and put his hand on the coffin, and the bearers
halted. 'Young man,' he said, 'I tell you, Rise up!' 15The dead man
sat up and began to talk, and Jesus gave him to his mother. 16They
were all awestruck and praised God. 'A great prophet has emerged
among us,' they said. 'God has come in kindness to his people!' 17The
story of what Jesus had done spread all over Judaea and all over the
surrounding countryside.

18John's disciples brought him news about all that was going on.
19John summoned two of his disciples and sent them to the Lord.
'Are you the One who is to come,' he said, 'or are we to go on waiting
and hoping for someone else?' 20When the men reached Jesus, they
said: 'John the Baptizer has sent us to ask, "Are you the One who is to
come, or are we to go on waiting and hoping for someone else?" '
21At that time Jesus cured many who were ill and suffering and pos-
sessed by evil spirits, and he gave the gift of sight to many who were
blind. 22'Go!' he said, 'and tell John the story of all that you have
seen and heard. Blind men are seeing again; lame men are walking;
lepers are being cleansed; deaf men are hearing; dead men are being
raised to life; poor men are hearing the good news. 23And happy is the
man who does not find himself antagonized by me!'

24When John's messengers had gone away, Jesus spoke to the
crowds about John. 'What did you go out to the desert to see?' he
said. 'Was it to see what you can see any day there—the long grass
swaying in the wind? 25If it was not that, what did you go out to see?
Was it to see a man clothed in dainty and delicate clothes? Those who
are magnificently dressed, and who live in luxury, are in royal palaces.
26If it was not that, what did you go out to see? Was it a prophet?
Yes, indeed it was, I tell you, and more than a prophet. 27This is the
man of whom scripture says:

"Look! I am sending my messenger ahead of you,
and he will go on in advance to prepare your road for you."

28I tell you that among mortal men no greater figure than John has
ever emerged in history. All the same, the least in the Kingdom of
God is greater than he.' 29All the people who heard this, and especially
the tax-collectors, praised God for his goodness, for they had been
baptized by John; 30but the Pharisees and legal experts had frustrated
God's purposes for themselves, because they refused to be baptized by
John.
31Then Jesus went on: 'In view of all this, with what can I compare
the people of today? What are they like? 32They are like children
sitting in the market-place, calling to each other:

"When we played you a happy tune,
  you did not dance;
when we wailed you a sad lament,
  you did not weep."

33For John the Baptizer came living the life of an ascetic, and you
say: "He is demon-possessed." 34The Son of Man came enjoying life
like a normal person, and you say: "A glutton and a drunkard! The
friend of renegade tax-collectors and people with whom no respec-
table Jew would have anything to do." 35And yet wisdom is vindicated
by all her children.'

36One of the Pharisees asked Jesus to have a meal with him. Jesus
went into the Pharisee's house and took his place at table. 37There
was a woman in the town who was a notoriously bad character.
When she heard that Jesus was a guest at a meal in the Pharisee's
house, she took an alabaster phial of perfumed oil, 38and, as Jesus
reclined on his couch, she stood behind him at his feet. She began to
let her tears pour down on his feet, and she wiped them with her hair,
and she kissed his feet, and she poured the perfumed oil over them.
39The Pharisee who had invited Jesus to the meal saw this. 'If this
fellow was really a prophet,' he said to himself, 'he would have known
who and what this woman who is touching him is, for she is a notor-
iously bad character.' 40'Simon,' Jesus said, 'I would like to say some-
thing to you.' 'Go ahead and say it, Teacher,' Simon answered. Jesus
said: 41'There was a creditor who had two people in debt to him.
One owed him twenty-five pounds, the other owed him two pounds
ten shillings. 42When they were unable to settle the debt, he let both
of them off without paying anything. Which of them will love him
more?' 43'I suppose,' Simon answered, 'the one he let off the greater

debt.' 'Your conclusion is correct,' Jesus said. 44Then Jesus turned to
the woman. 'You see this woman?' he said to Simon. 'When I came
into your house, you did not give me any water to wash the dust off
my feet. This woman has drenched my feet with her tears, and has
wiped them with her hair. 45You did not give me any kiss of welcome.
Since I came in, she has not stopped kissing my feet. 46You did not
anoint my head with oil. She has anointed my feet with perfume.
47This is why I tell you that, although she has sinned greatly, her
sins are forgiven, because she loved greatly. He who is forgiven little
loves little.' 48He said to her: 'Your sins are forgiven.' 49'Who is this
who forgives even sins?' his fellow-guests said to themselves. 50Jesus
said to the woman: 'Your faith has saved you. Go, and God bless
you!'

Chapter 8

AFTER this Jesus went through one town and village after another,
preaching, and spreading the Good News of the Kingdom of God.
The Twelve accompanied him, 2and so did a group of women, who
had been cured of evil spirits and of illnesses. There was Mary, known
as Mary from Magdala. Seven demons had come out of her. 3There
was Joanna, the wife of Chuza, one of Herod's financial secretaries.
There was Susanna, and there were many others, who used their
private means to provide for the needs of Jesus and his comrades.

4A great crowd was gathering, and from one town after another
people were coming to him. He used a parable to speak to them.

5'A sower,' he said, 'went out to sow his seed. As he sowed, some
seed fell by the side of the road, and it was trampled on, and the
birds of the sky snapped it up. 6Some seed fell on the rock in pockets
of soil, and it withered as soon as it grew, for it had no moisture.
7Some seed fell in the middle of thorn-bushes, and the bushes, as they
grew along with it, choked the life out of it. 8Some seed fell on good
ground, and grew, and produced a crop a hundred times more than
was sown. If a man has ears to hear,' Jesus went on to say, 'let him
hear.'

9Jesus' disciples asked him what the parable meant. 10'You,' he said,
'have received the privilege of knowing the secrets of the Kingdom of
God, secrets which only a disciple can understand. But to other

people the truth is spoken in parables, so that, although they see,
they may not see, and, although they hear, they may not under-
stand.

11'This is the meaning of the parable. The seed is the word of God.
12The picture of the seed which fell on the side of the road represents
those who hear, and then the devil comes and snatches the word out
of their hearts to stop them from believing and being saved. 13The
picture of the seed which fell on the rock represents those who
enthusiastically welcome the word as soon as they hear it; but these
have no root. Their faith is at the mercy of the moment; and, when
they are involved in any situation which puts their faith to the test,
they quit. 14The picture of the seed which fell among the thorn-
bushes represents those who have heard the word, but who go away
and allow their lives to be all choked up with worries and wealth and
the pleasures of life. The seed never gets a chance to mature.
15The picture of the seed which fell into the good ground represents
those who hear the word with a fine and good heart, and who keep
fast hold of it, and bear fruit through thick and thin.'

16'No one lights a lamp, and then hides it under a bowl or puts it
below the bed. He puts it on a lampstand, so that anyone who comes
in can see its light.

17'There is nothing hidden which will not be brought out into the
open, and there is nothing secret which will not be known and come
out into the open.

18'Be careful how you listen, for to the man who already has, more
will be given; but even what he thinks he has will be taken away from
the man who has not.'

19Jesus' mother and brothers arrived, but they were unable to get
to him because of the crowd. 20A message was brought to him:
'Your mother and your brothers are waiting outside, and they want
to see you.' 21'My mother and my brothers,' he answered, 'are those
who listen to God's word and obey it.'

22One day Jesus embarked on a boat with his disciples. 'Let us cross
over to the other side of the lake,' he said to them. 23So they set sail.
While they were sailing, Jesus fell asleep. A violent squall of wind
swept down on the lake, and they were in serious danger of being
swamped. 24They came and woke Jesus. 'Master, Master,' they said,
'we're drowning.' Jesus awoke and reprimanded the wind and the

boiling surf. They ceased their raging and there was a calm. 25'Where
is your faith?' he said to them. They were awestruck and astonished.
'Who can this be?' they said to each other. 'For he gives his orders to
the winds and the water, and they obey him.'

26They put in at the Gergesene district, which is opposite Galilee.
27When Jesus stepped out of the boat on to the land, a man from the
town who had a demon in him met him. For a long time he had gone
naked, and had stayed, not in a house, but among the tombs. 28When
he saw Jesus, he shrieked, and flung himself down at his feet. 'What
business have you with me, Jesus, Son of the Most High God?' he
shouted at the top of his voice. 'Please don't torture me.' 29Jesus had
ordered the unclean spirit to come out of the man. Many a time the
unclean spirit had seized him, and, although he had been bound with
chains and fetters, and had been kept under guard, he had often
snapped the bonds apart, and had been driven by the demon into
the desert. 30'What is your name?' Jesus asked him. 'A regiment,' he
said, for many demons had got into him. 31The demons pleaded with
Jesus not to order them into the Abyss.

32A herd of pigs was grazing there on the hillside. They pleaded
with him to allow them to go into them. He allowed them to do
as they asked. 33The demons came out of the man and went into the
pigs, and the whole herd stampeded down the cliff into the lake and
were drowned. 34When the herdsmen saw what had happened, they
fled and told the whole story both in the town and all over the
countryside. 35The people came out to see what had actually hap-
pened. They came to Jesus, and found the man out of whom the
demons had gone sitting at Jesus' feet, fully clothed and in his senses,
and they were terrified. 36Those who had seen what had happened
told them the story of how the demon-possessed man had been cured.
37The whole population of the surrounding district of the Gergesenes
asked Jesus to go away, for they were gripped with a great fear. Jesus
got on board the boat and returned to the other side. 38The man out
of whom the demons had gone pleaded to be allowed to stay with
him, but Jesus sent him away. 39'Go back home,' he said, 'and tell
the story of all that God has done for you.' So he went away and
all over the town he proclaimed all that Jesus had done for him.

40When Jesus returned, the crowd welcomed him, for they were all
waiting eagerly for him.

41A man called Jairus, who was president of the synagogue, came

and threw himself at Jesus' feet. He pleaded with Jesus to come to his
house, 42because he had an only daughter of about twelve years of
age, and she was dying. When they were on the way, the crowds were
crushing in on Jesus.
43There was a woman who had a haemorrhage for twelve years.*
Her illness was such that she had never been able to find anyone who
could cure her. 44She came up behind Jesus and touched the tassel of
his cloak, and on the spot the flow of blood was stopped. 45'Who
touched me?' Jesus said. Everyone denied that they had done so.
'Master,' Peter said, 'the crowd are all around you, jostling in on you.'
46'Someone did touch me,' Jesus said, 'for I know that power has gone
out of me.' 47When the woman saw that there was no hope of con-
cealment, she came and flung herself trembling at Jesus' feet, and in
front of everyone told him the reason why she had touched him and
how then and there she had been cured. 48'Daughter,' Jesus said to
her, 'your faith has cured you. Go, and God bless you.'
49While he was still speaking, a man arrived from the president's
house. 'Your daughter is dead,' he said. 'Don't trouble the teacher
any more.' 50When Jesus heard this, he said: 'Don't be afraid! Only
trust, and she will be cured!' 51When he came to the house, he did
not allow anyone to go in with him except Peter and John and
James, and the child's father and mother. 52They were all weeping
and wailing for her. 'Stop this crying!' Jesus said. 'She is not dead. She
is sleeping.' 53They laughed at him, for they knew that she had died.
54Jesus gripped her hand. 'Child,' he said, 'get up!' 55Her breath came
back and then and there she stood up. Jesus ordered that she should
be given something to eat. 56Her parents were astonished, but Jesus
ordered them not to tell anyone what had happened.

Chapter 9

JESUS called together the Twelve, and gave them power and autho-
rity over all demons, and to cure diseases. 2He sent them out to
proclaim the Kingdom of God, and to heal.
3'Take nothing for the road,' he said to them. 'Don't take a staff
or a beggar's knapsack. Don't take any bread or money. Don't have
two shirts. 4Stay in whatever house you first go into until you leave
the place. 5If there are any who refuse to welcome you, as you leave

*Here some manuscripts add, *She had spent her whole living on doctors.*

that town, shake the last speck of its dust from your feet, as if you
were leaving a heathen town, to make them see the seriousness of
what they have done.'
6So they went out and made a tour of the villages, everywhere
spreading the Good News and carrying on their healing work.

7When Herod the tetrarch heard about what was going on, he did
not know what to make of it, because such varying verdicts on Jesus
were circulating. By some it was said that John had come back to life.
8Others held that Elijah had appeared, others that one of the ancient
prophets had come back to life. 9'I beheaded John,' Herod said. 'Who
can this be about whom such reports are circulating?' So he made
efforts to meet Jesus.

10When the disciples returned, they told Jesus the story of all that
they had done. He withdrew to a town called Bethsaida to be alone,
and he took them with him. 11The crowds discovered this and
followed him. He welcomed them, and spoke to them about the
Kingdom of God, and cured those who needed healing.
12When the day was drawing to a close, the Twelve came to him.
'Send the crowd away,' they said. 'Tell them to go to the surrounding
villages and farms to find lodgings and food, for this is a desert place
that we are in.' 13'You must give them something to eat,' he said.
They said: 'All we have is five loaves and two fishes, unless—and you
can't mean that—we are to go and buy food for all these people.'
14For there were about five thousand men there. 'Make them sit down
in groups of fifty,' he said to his disciples. 15They did so, and made
them all sit down. 16Jesus took the five loaves and the two fishes;
he looked up to heaven and said the blessing. Then he broke them
into pieces, and gave them to the disciples to serve to the crowd.
17They all ate until they could eat no more; and when what was left
over was collected, it amounted to twelve basketfuls of broken
pieces.

18When Jesus was alone in prayer, and when his disciples were with
him, he put a question to them. 'Who am I popularly supposed to be?'
he said. 19'John the Baptizer,' they answered. 'But some say that you
are Elijah, others that you are one of the ancient prophets come
back to life.' 20He said to them: 'And you—who do you say that I
am?' Peter answered: 'God's Messiah.' 21He gave them strict orders to
tell this to no one. 22'The Son of Man,' he said, 'must undergo many

sufferings. He must be rejected by the elders and chief priests and
experts in the Law. He must be killed, and raised to life again on the
third day.'

23He said to them all: 'If anyone wishes to walk in my steps, he must
once and for all say No to himself, and he must decide to take up his
cross daily, and he must keep on following me. 24Anyone who wishes
to keep his life safe will lose it; but any man who is prepared to lose
his life for my sake will save it. 25What good will it do a man to gain
the whole world, if he destroys himself and has to forfeit his life?
26If a man is ashamed of me and of my words, the Son of Man will
be ashamed of him, when he comes with the glory of his Father and
of the holy angels. 27I tell you truly, there are some of those who are
standing here who will not experience death until they see the
Kingdom of God.'

28About a week after this conversation Jesus took with him Peter
and James and John, and climbed the mountain to pray. 29While he
was praying, the appearance of his face changed, and his clothes
became as white as a lightning flash. 30Two men came and talked with
him. They were Moses and Elijah. 31They appeared in a vision of glory,
and they talked with Jesus about the way in which his life was destined
to end in Jerusalem. 32Peter and his companions were overcome with
sleep, but, when they were fully awake, they saw the glory of Jesus,
and the two men standing with him. 33As the two men were leaving
Jesus, Peter said to him: 'Master, it is a wonderful thing for us to be
here. Let us make three shelters, one for you, and one for Moses, and
one for Elijah.' He did not really know what he was saying. 34While
he was speaking, a cloud enveloped them. They were awestruck as
they entered the cloud. 35Out of the cloud a voice said: 'This is my
Son, the Chosen One! Listen to him!' 36After the voice had spoken,
they saw that there was no one with Jesus. At that time they said
nothing about this, and did not tell anyone about what they had seen.

37Next day, when they had come down from the mountain, a great
crowd came to meet Jesus. 38'Teacher,' a man in the crowd shouted,
'please look at my son. He is my only son, 39and a spirit seizes him,
and all of a sudden the spirit shrieks and convulses him, and he foams
at the mouth. The spirit hardly ever leaves him, and it is breaking the
boy up. 40I asked your disciples to eject the spirit from him, but they
were quite unable to do so.' 41'This modern generation has so little

faith!' Jesus answered. 'There is a fatal perversity about it! How long
must I be with you and endure you? Bring your son here!' 42When the
boy was coming to Jesus, the spirit tore him and convulsed him.
Jesus spoke to the unclean spirit with stern authority, and cured the
boy, and gave him back to his father. 43They were all astonished at the
greatness of God's power.

While they were still lost in wonder at what he was doing, Jesus
said to his disciples: 44'I want what I am going to say to you really to
sink into your minds. The Son of Man is going to be handed over into
the power of men.' 45They could not understand what he meant
when he spoke like this. His meaning was hidden from them to keep
them from seeing it, and they were afraid to ask him what he meant
by saying this.

46A debate started among the disciples about which of them was
greatest. 47Jesus was well aware of what was going on in their minds.
He picked up a little child, and made him stand beside him. 48He said
to them: 'To welcome this little child in my name is to welcome me;
and to welcome me is to welcome him who sent me. It is the man
who thinks himself least of all who is truly great.'

49'Master,' John said, 'we saw a man ejecting demons by the use of
your name. So we tried to stop him, because he is not a follower of
yours like us.' 50'Don't try to stop him,' Jesus said. 'The man who is
not your opponent is your supporter.'

51When the time for him to be taken back to heaven was approach-
ing, Jesus resolutely set out on the journey to Jerusalem. 52He sent
messengers on ahead. They set out and went into a Samaritan village
with the intention of preparing for Jesus' arrival. 53But the villagers
refused to give him any hospitality, because he was clearly on his way
to Jerusalem. 54When his disciples James and John saw this, they said:
'Master, would you like us to call down fire from heaven and wipe
them out?' 55Jesus turned and sternly reprimanded them.* 56So they
continued their journey to another village.

57As they were going along the road, a man said to Jesus: 'I will
follow you wherever you go.' 58Jesus said to him: 'The foxes have
lairs, and the birds of the sky have nests, but the Son of Man has

*Here some manuscripts add, *You do not know the kind of men you ought to be. The Son of Man did not come to destroy lives but to save them.*

nowhere to lay his head.' 59Jesus said to another man: 'Follow me!'
He said: 'Let me go and bury my father first.' 60Jesus said: 'Let the dead
bury their dead. You must go and spread the news of the Kingdom of
God.' 61Another man said: 'Sir, I will follow you, but let me say good-
bye to my family first.' 62Jesus said to him: 'No one who tries to plough
looking backwards is of any use to the Kingdom of God.'

Chapter 10

THE next thing Jesus did was to appoint seventy others, and to send
them out ahead in twos, into every town and place into which he
himself planned to go. 2'The harvest is great,' he said to them, 'but
there are few workers. You must pray to the Lord of the harvest to
send out workers to gather in his harvest.

3'On your way! I am sending you out like lambs among wolves.
4Don't take a purse, or a beggar's knapsack, or sandals. Don't stop to
greet anyone on the road. 5As soon as you go into a house say to it:
"God bless this household." 6If a man whom God has blessed lives
there, then your blessing will rest on it; but if not, your blessing will
return to you. 7Stay in the same house, sharing the food and the
drink of the family, for the workman deserves his wage. Don't keep
moving your lodging from one house to another. 8In any town you
enter, and in any home which gives you hospitality, eat what is put
before you. 9Heal the sick in it, and tell them: "God's Kingdom is
almost here." 10If you go into any town, and they refuse to welcome
you, go out into its streets and say: 11"We wipe off even the dust of
your town that sticks to our feet, as if this was a heathen town, as a
protest against you. All the same, we want you to realize that God's
Kingdom is almost here." 12On the great day, I tell you, Sodom and
Gomorrah will get off more lightly than that town.'

13'Tragic will be your fate, Chorazin! Tragic will be your fate, Beth-
saida! If the miracles which have been done in you had been done in
Tyre and Sidon, they would long ago have sat in penitence in sack-
cloth and ashes. 14But Tyre and Sidon will get off more lightly at the
judgment than you. 15As for you, Capernaum—do you think that
you are going to be exalted as high as heaven? You will go down to
the depths of hell.'

16'To listen to you is to listen to me; to reject you is to reject me;
to reject me is to reject him who sent me.'

17The seventy returned rejoicing. 'Lord,' they said, 'even the
demons obey us at your name.' 18He said to them: 'I saw Satan fall
like a lightning flash from heaven. 19I have given you power to
trample on snakes and scorpions and to tread down all the power of
the Enemy, and nothing will harm you. 20All the same, do not re-
joice because the spirits obey you; rejoice because your names are
written in heaven.'

21At that time the Holy Spirit made Jesus' heart thrill with joy. 'I
thank you, Father, Lord of heaven and earth,' he said, 'that you have
hidden these things from the wise and the clever and that you have
revealed them to those who are as simple as little children. Yes,
indeed, Father, I thank you that this is what you chose to do. 22All
things have been entrusted to me by my Father, and no one but the
Father knows who the Son is; and no one knows who the Father is
except the Son, and those to whom the Son chooses to make him
known.'

23When they were alone, Jesus turned to his disciples. 'Happy are
the eyes which have seen what you are seeing,' he said. 24'For I tell
you that many a prophet and many a king wished to see the events
that you are seeing, and did not see them, and wished to hear the
words that you are hearing, and did not hear them.'

25A legal expert rose to put a test question to Jesus. 'Teacher,' he
said, 'what must I do to possess the eternal life that God has pro-
mised?' 26'What does the Law prescribe?' Jesus said to him. 'What do
you read there?' 27He answered: 'You must love the Lord your God
with your whole heart and your whole soul and your whole strength
and your whole mind, and, you must love your neighbour as your-
self.' 28'That is the right answer,' Jesus said to him. 'You will have life,
if you do this.'

29The legal expert wished to show just how expert he was. 'Yes,'
he said to Jesus, 'but who is my neighbour?' 30Jesus took up his ques-
tion. 'There was a man,' he said, 'who was on his way down from
Jerusalem to Jericho, when he fell into the hands of brigands. They
stripped him naked, and beat him up, and went away and left him
more dead than alive. 31It so happened that a priest was coming down
the road. When the priest saw him, he passed by on the opposite side

of the road. 32In the same way, a Levite arrived at the spot. He went
and looked at the man, and then passed by on the opposite side of the
road. 33A Samaritan, who was on the road, came to where the man
was lying. He was heart-sorry when he saw the state he was in. 34He
went up to him, and poured oil and wine on his wounds, and ban-
daged them. Then he put the man on his beast, and took him to an
inn, and looked after him. 35Next morning he took out two silver
coins and gave them to the inn-keeper. "Look after him," he said,
"and, if you incur any additional expense, I'll square it up with you
on my way back." 36Which of these three would you say was a neigh-
bour to the man who fell into the hands of the brigands?' 37'The man
who took pity on him,' he said. Jesus said to him: 'You too must go
and do the same.'

38In the course of their journey Jesus went into a village. A woman
called Martha welcomed him into her house. 39She had a sister
called Mary, and Mary sat at the Lord's feet and listened to his talk.
40Martha was so worried about getting a meal ready for them that
she was quite distracted. 'Master,' she came up and said, 'don't you
care that my sister has left me to attend to everything alone? Tell her
to give me a hand.' 41'Martha, Martha,' the Lord answered, 'you are
worried and harassed about putting on a meal with a whole lot of
courses. 42One will do perfectly well. Mary has chosen the best dish,
and it is not going to be taken away from her.'

Chapter 11

JESUS was praying in a certain place, and, when he had finished, one
of his disciples said to him: 'Master, teach us a prayer, as John taught
his disciples.' 2He said to them: 'When you pray, you must say:

"Father,
May your name be held in reverence.
May your Kingdom come.
3Give us each day bread for the coming day.
4And forgive us our sins, as we too forgive
everyone who fails in his duty to us.
And do not submit us to any ordeal of testing."

5'Suppose one of you has a friend,' he said to them, 'and suppose

the friend comes to him in the middle of the night, and says: "Friend,
lend me three loaves, 6because a friend of mine on a journey has
arrived at my house, and I haven't a scrap of food in the house to give
him." 7And suppose the man in the house answers: "Don't bother
me! The door is locked for the night, and my children are in bed with
me. I can't get up and give you anything." 8I tell you, if he will not
get up and give him what he needs for friendship's sake, he will get up
and give him all he needs because of his bare-faced persistence.
9'I tell you:

Keep on asking,
  and you will get;
keep on seeking,
  and you will find;
keep on knocking,
  and the door will be opened for you.
10For everyone who keeps on asking
  gets what he asks for;
he who keeps on seeking
  finds;
if a man keeps on knocking
  the door will be opened.
11If any of you is a father,
and his son asks for a fish,
  is he likely to give him a snake?
12Or, if he asks for an egg,
  is he likely to give him a scorpion?
13If, then, although you are naturally evil and ungenerous,
  you know how to give good gifts to your children,
how much more will the heavenly Father
  give the Holy Spirit to those who ask him?'

14Jesus was ejecting a demon which made a man dumb. When the
demon came out of him, the dumb man spoke, and the crowds were
amazed. 15Some of them said: 'It is with the help of Beelzebul, the
prince of demons, that he ejects the demons.' 16Others, with the idea
of testing him, demanded that he should produce some visible divine
action from heaven. 17He knew what was going on in their minds. So
he said to them: 'Any kingdom which is split against itself is on the
way to being laid waste, and the houses in it collapse on top of each
other. 18If Satan is split against himself, how can his kingdom survive?

And that is the situation, if you say that I eject demons with the help
of Beelzebul. 19If I eject demons with the help of Beelzebul, by
whose help do your sons eject them? Ask them what they think of
this argument of yours. 20But, if it is with the finger of God that I
eject demons, then the Kingdom of God has reached you here and
now.

21'When a strong man guards his homestead fully armed, his
property remains secure and undisturbed. 22But, when a still stronger
man attacks and overcomes him, the stronger man takes away the
armour on which he relied, and shares out the spoils.'

23'If a man is not my ally, he is my enemy, and, if a man is not
helping my work, he is undoing it.'

24'When an unclean spirit goes out of a man, it roams through
waterless places looking for rest, and when it finds none, it says: "I
will go back to the house which used to be mine, and which I left."
25So it comes, and finds it swept and in perfect order. 26Then it goes
and brings back along with it seven other spirits worse than itself,
and they go and make their home there. So the last state of that man
becomes worse than the first.'

27While he was saying this, a woman shouted to him from the
crowd: 'Happy is the womb which bore you, and the breasts you
sucked.' 28But Jesus said: 'True, but rather, happy are those who
listen to the word of God and obey it.'

29When the crowds were coming thronging to him, Jesus said:
'This is an evil generation. The people of today want to see some
visible action of God. The only action of God which will be given to
them is the action of God which was seen in the case of Jonah. 30For,
as Jonah was an act of God to the people of Nineveh, so the Son of
Man will be an act of God to this generation.

31'When the day of judgment comes, the Queen of the South will
rise from the dead at the same time as the people of this generation,
and she will condemn them, for she came from the ends of the
earth to listen to the wisdom of Solomon, and there is a greater event
than Solomon here. 32When the day of judgment comes, the people
of Nineveh will rise again at the same time as the people of this
generation, and they will condemn them, because Nineveh repented
at the preaching of Jonah, and a greater event than Jonah is here.'

33'No one lights a lamp, and puts it into a cellar or under a bowl;

he puts it on the lampstand, so that those who come into the house
may see the light.
34'Your eye is the body's lamp. When your eye is sound and gen-
erous, the whole body is full of light. When it is diseased and grudging,
the whole body is full of darkness. 35Since that is so, you must be on
the watch in case the light in you turns to darkness. 36If then your
whole body is filled with light, without a particle of darkness, it will
be all light, as when a lamp gives you light with its rays.'

37While he was speaking a Pharisee asked him to a meal with him.
Jesus went into the house, and took his place at table. 38The Pharisee
was very surprised to see that Jesus did not go through the prescribed
ritual ceremonial washings before the meal. 39The Lord said to him:
'The fact is that you Pharisees carefully clean the outside of the cup
and plate, but your inner life is full of greed and wickedness. 40This is
an utterly senseless proceeding. Surely the same person made the
outside and the inside too? 41In point of fact, if you give the food that
is inside the dishes as a gift to the poor, then everything will be really
clean as far as you are concerned.

42'Tragic will be the fate of you Pharisees! You meticulously set aside
for God the tenth part of mint and rue and of every vegetable in
your kitchen-garden, while you neglect justice and the love of God.
You ought to have kept the second without neglecting the first.
43'Tragic will be the fate of you Pharisees! You love the front seats
in the synagogue, and you like to be deferentially greeted as you
move through the market-places.
44'Tragic will be your fate! You are like hidden graves which men
walk over without realizing what they are walking on.'
45'Teacher,' one of the legal experts said, 'statements like these are
an arrogant insult to us.' 46Jesus said: 'Tragic will be the fate of you
legal experts too! You lay on men's backs intolerable burdens,
and you yourselves do not lift a finger to help them with their
burdens.
47'Tragic will be your fate! You erect memorials to the prophets
whom your ancestors killed. 48Obviously you agree with the verdicts
and approve of the actions of your ancestors, for they did the killing
and you do the building of the memorials. 49That is why God in his
wisdom said: "I will send prophets and apostles to them, and they will
kill some, and they will persecute others." 50God did this in order that
this generation might become responsible for the murder of all the

prophets since the world was created, 51from the murder of Abel to
the murder of Zacharias, who was killed between the altar and the
house of God. Yes, indeed, I tell you, this generation will be held
responsible for all this.
52'Tragic will be your fate, you legal experts! You have removed
the key which unlocks the door of knowledge. You have not gone in
yourselves, and you have debarred those who are trying to get in.'

53When he left there, the Pharisees began a bitter campaign against
him in which they made repeated attempts to provoke him into
giving them answers on many subjects, 54by setting verbal traps for
him, with the idea of catching him out in any statement he might
make.

Chapter 12

MEANWHILE, when the crowds had gathered in their tens of
thousands, and when there were so many people that they were
trampling on each other, Jesus said certain things which were meant
in the first instance for his disciples. 'Be on your guard,' he said,
'against the evil influence of the Pharisees, which is profession without
practice. 2What is veiled must be unveiled, and what is hidden must
be made known. 3What you have spoken in the dark will be heard in
the full light of day. What you have whispered in the ear in your inner
rooms will be broadcast from the housetops.'

4'I tell you, my friends, do not fear those who can kill the body, but
who are powerless to do anything further. 5I will warn you whom to
fear. Fear the One who has the power first to kill you and then to
throw you into hell. Yes, indeed, I tell you, fear him!'

6'Five sparrows are sold for two farthings, aren't they? Yet not one
of them is forgotten by God. 7So far from being forgotten, the hairs
of your head have all been counted. Don't be afraid. You are more
valuable than a whole collection of sparrows.'

8'If anyone publicly acknowledges his loyalty to me in front of his
fellow men, I tell you, the Son of Man will do the same for him in
front of the angels of God. 9But anyone who disowns me in front of
men will be disowned in front of the angels of God.
10'If anyone speaks a word against the Son of Man, he will be for-

given for it, but if anyone insults the Holy Spirit, he will not be for-
given.'

11'When you are put on trial before the synagogues and the gover-
nors and the civil authorities, do not worry about how to defend
yourselves, or about what to say. 12The Holy Spirit will at the time
teach you what you must say.'

13A man in the crowd said to Jesus: 'Teacher, tell my brother to give
me my share of the estate which has been left to us.' 14'Man,' said Jesus
to him, 'who appointed me a judge or an arbitrator between you and
your brother?' 15He said to them: 'Watch carefully not to let any
kind of greed get a grip of you. It does not follow that, because a man
has a superabundance of possessions, his life is one of the things which
belong to him.'

16He used a parable to explain his meaning. 'The ground of a rich
man,' he said, 'produced an excellent harvest. 17He began to ask
himself: "What am I to do? I have no room to store my crops." 18So
he said: "I know what I'll do. I will pull down my barns and I will
build bigger ones. I will store up all my corn and my possessions in
them. 19And I will tell myself: 'You have enough goods stored up to
last for many a year. Sit back and relax! Eat and drink and enjoy
yourself!' " 20But God said to him: "Fool! This very night you must
hand back your life to God! And then who will get all that you have
saved up for the future?" 21This is what happens to the man who
amasses worldly wealth, but who in God's sight has no riches at all.'

22'That,' said Jesus, 'is why I tell you,
Stop worrying about what you are going to eat
to keep you alive.
Stop worrying about the clothes
you are going to put on your body.
23There is more to life than food,
and more to the body than clothes.
24Look at the ravens,
and learn from them.
They do not sow or reap.
They have no storehouse or barn.
Yet God gives them their food.
How much more valuable you are than the birds!

25 'Can any of you add half a yard to his height
by worrying about it?
26 If you can't do a little thing like that
why worry about the rest of life?
27 Look at the wild lilies and learn from them.
They do not spin or weave.
Yet, I tell you, that not even Solomon in all his splendour
was robed like one of these.
28 You have so little faith!
If God clothes the wild flowers,
which have one brief day,
and which tomorrow are used
to make a fire to heat an oven,
how much more can you depend on him to clothe you?

29 'Don't spend your life
thinking about nothing
but what you are going to eat and drink.
Don't get into a panic about things like that.
30 The people in the world who don't know God
spend their lives thinking about things like that.
Your Father knows that you need these things.
31 So far from being like that,
you must make his Kingdom
the object of all your endeavour,
and you will get these other things as well.
32 You are only a little flock,
but don't be afraid.
It is your Father's decision
to give you the Kingdom.

33 'Sell your possessions,
and give them away in charity.
Get yourselves purses
which will never wear out,
and a treasure in heaven
which will never be exhausted,
for there no thief can get at it,
and no moth can destroy it.
34 Your heart is bound to be
where your treasure is.'

35'Always be ready, stripped for action, with your lamps lit. 36Be
like men who are expectantly waiting for their master's return from
a wedding banquet, and whose aim it is to open the door to him the
instant he arrives and knocks. 37Happy are the servants whom their
master will find awake, when he comes. I tell you he will roll up his
sleeves for action, and will make them sit down like guests, and will
come and serve them himself. 38Happy are they, if he finds them like
that, even if he comes just before midnight or in the early hours of
the morning.

39'It is obvious that if the householder had known at what hour
the thief was going to come, he would not have left his house to be
broken into. 40You too must be ready, because the Son of Man is
going to come at an hour when you do not expect him.'

41'Master,' Peter said to him, 'is this parable meant for us, or for
everyone?' 42The Lord said: 'Suppose there is a dependable and
sensible steward, whom his master puts in charge of his staff, with
instructions to issue them their rations at the right time. 43That ser-
vant is a happy man, if his master, when he comes, finds him en-
gaged on that very task. 44He will certainly put him in charge of all
his property. 45But, if the servant says to himself: "It will be a long
time before my master comes back," and if he begins to beat the
manservants and the maidservants, and to eat and to drink until he
is drunk, 46that servant's master will come on a day when he is not
expecting him. He does not know at what time the master will arrive.
And the master will punish him severely, and will assign to him the
fate of the unbelievers.

47'If a servant knows what his master wants him to do, and if he
makes no preparations and takes no action to do it, he will be beaten
with many strokes of the lash. 48But, if he did not know it, even if he
has been guilty of actions which deserve a beating, he will be given
few strokes of the lash. Great privilege brings great responsibility.
When much is entrusted to a man, still more will be demanded from
him.'

49'I have come to set the world ablaze. What is it that I want?
Would that it were already kindled!

50'I must be plunged into a flood-tide of suffering, and there can
be no relief for me, until I have gone through it to the end.

51'Do you think that the result of my coming will be peace in the
world? Far from it. I tell you, the result of my coming will be to bring

division. 52From now on in one house there will be five people in a
state of division, three against two and two against three. 53They will
be divided father against son and son against father, mother against
daughter and daughter against mother, mother-in-law against
daughter-in-law and daughter-in-law against mother-in-law.'

54He said to the crowds: 'When you see a cloud rising in the west,
you immediately say: "Rain is on the way," and the rain comes.
55When you feel the south wind blowing, you say: "It will be as hot
as an oven," and it is. 56You play at being religious. You know how to
read the weather signs from the appearance of the earth and of the
sky. Why can you not read the signs of the present crisis?'

57'Why can you not decide yourselves what justice demands?
58When you are on the way to the magistrate with your opponent,
do your best to come to terms with him when you are on the road.
If you don't, he may well drag you to the judge. Then the judge may
well hand you over to the court officer. The court officer may well
throw you into prison. 59I tell you, if that happens, you will not be
released until you have paid the last farthing in full.'

Chapter 13

It was at that time that some of the people who were there told
Jesus the story of the Galilaeans whom Pilate had murdered at the
very moment when they were offering their sacrifices. 2Jesus said to
them: 'Do you think that these Galilaeans were worse sinners than
the rest of the Galilaeans, because this happened to them? 3Far from
it, I tell you. But, if you do not repent, you will all suffer the same
fate. 4Or, do you think that the eighteen men who were killed when
the tower of Siloam collapsed on them were worse sinners than the
rest of the inhabitants of Jerusalem? 5Far from it, I tell you. But, if
you do not repent, you will all suffer the same fate.'

6He told them this parable. 'There was a man,' he said, 'who had a
fig tree planted in his vineyard. He went to look for fruit on it, and
found none. 7"For the last three years," he said to the vine-dresser,
"I have been coming and looking for fruit on it, and I have never
found any. Cut it down! Why should it exhaust the fertility of the
soil?" 8"Sir," he answered, "leave it for this one more year, and let me

dig round it and put in manure. 9If it bears fruit next year, well and
good. If it doesn't, you can cut it down." '

10Jesus was teaching in one of the synagogues on the Sabbath.
11There was a woman there who for eighteen years had in her an evil
spirit which caused a weakness in her body. She was bent double, and
she was quite unable to straighten herself. 12When Jesus saw her he
called her forward. 'You are released from your weakness,' he said to
her. 13He laid his hands on her, and then and there her body was
straightened, and she praised God.

14The president of the synagogue was indignant because Jesus had
healed on the Sabbath. 'There are six days on which work ought to
be done,' he said to the crowd. 'Come and be healed on them, not
on the Sabbath.' 15The Lord answered: 'Your religion is no more than
a façade of conventional piety! Is there any of you who does not un-
tether his ox or his ass from its stall on the Sabbath, and take it out to
give it water? 16This woman is a daughter of Abraham. For eighteen
years Satan has fettered her. Is it not right that she should be liberated
from her fetters, Sabbath though it is?' 17His opponents were all
shamed by what he said. But the crowd all rejoiced at all the
glorious things that were done by Jesus.

18'What is the Kingdom of God like,' Jesus said, 'and with what will
I compare it? 19It is like a grain of mustard seed, which a man took
and planted in his kitchen-garden. It grew till it was as big as a tree,
and the birds of the sky nested in its branches.'

20Again he said: 'With what will I compare the Kingdom of God?
21It is like leaven which a woman took and inserted into three pecks
of flour, with the result that it was all leavened.'

22Jesus continued his tour of the towns and villages, teaching and
making his way to Jerusalem. 23'Sir,' a man said to him, 'is salvation
something which will come only to a few?' Jesus said to him: 24'Try
your hardest to enter through the narrow door, because many, I tell
you, will try to get in, and will not be able to. 25Once the house-
holder has got up and locked the door, you will be left standing out-
side, knocking at the door. "Sir," you will say, "open the door for
us." "I don't know where you come from," he will answer. 26Then
you will say: "You shared our meals and you taught in our streets."
27"I don't know where you come from," he will say to you. "Your

actions were the actions of bad men. Get out of my sight.' " 28There
will be tears and agony there, when you will see Abraham and Isaac
and Jacob and all the prophets in the Kingdom of God while you are
banished from it. 29They will come from the east and from the west
and from the north and from the south, and will take their places
as guests in the Kingdom of God. 30And some who are now last will
be first, and some who are now first will be last.'

31At that time a group of Pharisees came to Jesus. 'Get away from
here,' they said, 'because Herod is out to kill you.' 32'Go and tell that
fox,' Jesus said, 'that today and tomorrow I am going to eject demons
and continue my work of healing. It will take me three days to com-
plete my work. 33But today and tomorrow and the next day I must
keep moving on, because it is unthinkable that a prophet should die
anywhere else than in Jerusalem.

34'O Jerusalem, Jerusalem! Killer of the prophets! Stoner of those
who were sent to you by God! How often I have wanted to gather
your children together as a bird gathers her brood under the shelter
of her wings—and you refused! 35God no longer has his home among
you! I tell you, you will not see me, until the day comes when you
will say: "God bless him who comes in the name of the Lord." '

Chapter 14

ONCE on a Sabbath day Jesus went for a meal to the house of one
of the leading Pharisees. They were watching him all the time.
2There was a man with dropsy there right in front of him. 3Jesus
said to the legal experts and to the Pharisees: 'Is it permitted to heal
on the Sabbath, or not?' 4They chose to remain silent. Jesus took the
man and cured him and sent him away. 5Then he said to them: 'If
any of you has a donkey or an ox, and it falls into a well, will he not
pull it out at once, even although it is the Sabbath day?' 6They could
find no answer to this argument.

7Jesus told a parable to the guests, when he saw how they tried to
choose the top seats. 8'When you are invited by someone to a wedding
banquet,' he said, 'don't take the top place, in case someone of higher
standing than you may very well have been invited by your host. 9If
that happens, the host who invited both you and the other man is
sure to come and say: "Give this man your seat." Then you will be
humiliated in front of everyone, and you will have to move to the

very foot of the table. 10Instead of that, when you are invited as a guest,
go and sit at the very foot of the table. Then when the host arrives, he
will say to you: "Friend, move up to a higher place." If that happens,
you will be honoured in front of all your fellow-guests. 11For every-
one who exalts himself will be humbled, and the man who humbles
himself will be exalted.'

12'When you give a lunch or a dinner,' Jesus said to the host,
'don't invite your friends or your brothers or your relations or your
wealthy neighbours, for they are entirely likely to give you a return
invitation, and you will then receive a return payment for your
invitation. 13Instead of that, when you give a reception, invite the
poor, the maimed, the lame, the blind. 14That is the way to happi-
ness, for they cannot repay you. You will get your repayment at the
resurrection of all good men.'

15When one of the guests heard this, he said: 'Happy is the man
who is a guest at the feast in the Kingdom of God.' 16Jesus said to him:
'There was a man who planned to give a big dinner to which he
invited a large number of guests. 17When the dinner was due to begin,
he sent his servants to tell those who had received invitations:
"Come! Everything is now ready." 18They all unanimously began to
make excuses. The first said: "I have bought a farm, and I must go
and see it. Please consider me excused." 19Another said: "I have
bought five pairs of oxen, and I am going to try them out. Please
consider me excused." 20Another said: "I have married a wife, and so
I cannot possibly come." 21The servant came back and reported this
to his master. The master of the house was furious. He said to the
servant: "Hurry out to the streets and the lanes of the town, and
bring in the poor and the maimed and the blind and the lame."
22The servant said: "Your orders have been carried out, and there is
still room for more." 23"Go out into the roads and the hedgerows,"
the master said to the servant, "and bring them in, even if you have
to compel them to come. I want my house full. 24I tell you none of
the invited guests will so much as taste my dinner." '

25The people flocked in their crowds to Jesus. He turned to them
and said: 26'No one who comes to me can be my disciple, unless he
hates his father and mother and wife and children and brothers and
sisters, yes, and himself too. 27No one can be my disciple unless he
carries his cross and follows in my footsteps.

28'If any one of you plans to build a tower, does he not begin by

sitting down, and calculating the cost, to see if he has enough money
to finish it, 29in case, when he has laid the foundations, and then
cannot complete it, everyone who sees the half-finished building
makes a fool of him. 30"This man," they will say, "began to build and
couldn't finish the job." 31Or, if a king is contemplating going to war
with another king, does he not begin by sitting down, and consider-
ing whether with ten thousand men he can face an opponent who is
launching an attack on him with twenty thousand men? 32If he
decides that it cannot be done, long before the other gets to close
quarters, he sends an embassy to ask for terms of peace. 33Just so, any
of you who does not renounce all his possessions cannot be my
disciple.'

34'Salt is good, but if the salt has lost its taste, can anything ever
give it its saltness back? 35It is useless either for spreading on the land
or for throwing on the manure-heap. All you can do with it is to
throw it out. Let him who has ears to hear, hear.'

Chapter 15

ALL the tax-collectors and the people with whom no respectable
Jew would have had anything to do kept coming to Jesus to listen
to his message. 2But the Pharisees and the experts in the Law com-
plained: 'This man welcomes people with whom no respectable Jew
would have anything to do, and actually shares their meals with
them.'

3Jesus told them this parable. 4'If any of you,' he said, 'has a hundred
sheep, and loses one of them, is he not sure to leave the ninety-nine
in the desert, and go and search for the lost one, until he finds it?
5And when he has found it, he lifts it joyfully on to his shoulders,
6and goes home and invites his friends and neighbours to come and
share his joy. "Rejoice with me," he says, "I have found my lost
sheep." 7I tell you that in the same way there will be more joy in
heaven over one sinner who repents than over ninety-nine respect-
able people who do not need to repent.'

8'Or, if any woman has ten silver coins and loses one, is she not
sure to light a lamp and to sweep the house and search carefully until
she finds it? 9And, when she has found it, she invites her friends and

neighbours to share her joy. "Rejoice with me," she says, "I have
found the coin I lost." 10I tell you that in the same way the angels of
God rejoice over one sinner who repents.'

11'There was a man,' Jesus said to them, 'who had two sons. 12The
younger of them said to his father: "Father, give me the share of your
estate which is coming to me anyway." So he divided his whole
estate between them. 13Soon after, the younger son realized the
whole lot into money, and went off to a distant country. There he
squandered his whole fortune in a career of debauchery. 14When he
had run through everything he had, a severe famine fell on that land,
and he was very nearly destitute. 15So he went and took service with
a citizen of that country who sent him out to his farm to herd pigs.
16He longed to satisfy the pangs of his hunger with the carob pods
which the pigs were eating, and no one gave him anything.

17'When he came to his senses, he said to himself: "How many of
my father's hired servants have more food than they can eat, and
here am I, ready to die of starvation! 18I will start out, and go to
my father, and I will say to him: 'Father, I have sinned against God
and against you. 19I am no longer fit to be regarded as your son. Take
me back as one of your hired servants.' " 20So he set out, and went to
his father. His father saw him coming a long way away, and he was
heart-sorry for him. He came running, and threw his arms round his
neck, and kissed him. 21The son said to him: "Father, I have sinned
against God and against you. I am no longer fit to be regarded as
your son." 22But his father said to the servants: "Quick! Bring out the
best robe and dress him in it. Give him a ring to wear on his finger,
and shoes for his feet. 23Bring the specially fattened calf and kill it.
Let us eat and celebrate, 24for this son of mine was dead and has come
to life again; he was lost and has been found." So they began to
celebrate.

25'His elder son was out on the farm. When he came near the house
on his way home, he heard the sound of music and dancing. 26He
called one of the servants, and asked what was going on. 27The
servant said: "Your brother has arrived, and your father has had the
specially fattened calf killed, because he got him back again safe and
sound." 28He was furious and refused to go in. His father came and
pleaded with him to come in. 29"I have worked like a slave for you
for so many years," he said to his father, "and I never disobeyed any
order you gave me, and to me you never gave so much as a kid to

celebrate with my friends. 30But when this son of yours, who squan-
dered your fortune with prostitutes, arrives, you have the specially
fattened calf killed for him." 31"Son," his father said to him, "you are
always with me. All that is mine is yours. 32 But we had to celebrate
and rejoice, because your brother was dead and has come to life
again; he was lost and has been found." '

Chapter 16

'THERE was a wealthy man,' Jesus said to his disciples, 'who em-
ployed a manager to take charge of his whole estate. Allegations
were made to him that this man was mismanaging his property. So
he sent for him. 2"What's this story I'm hearing about you?" he
said. "I want to see your books at once, for you're finished as my
manager." 3The manager said to himself: "What am I going to do now
that my employer is going to dismiss me from my job? I haven't the
strength to dig, and I haven't the nerve to beg. 4I know what I'll do
to make sure that, when I leave my present job, I'll never lack for a
welcome in other people's houses." 5So one by one he invited those
who were in debt to his employer to come and see him. "How much
do you owe my employer?" he asked the first one. 6"A thousand gal-
lons of olive oil," he said. "Here's your bill," the manager said. "Sit
down at once, and alter the figure to five hundred." 7"How much
do you owe?" he went on to say to another. "A thousand bushels
of wheat," he said. "Here's your bill," he said. "Alter the figure to
eight hundred." 8His employer praised the dishonest manager,
because he had acted shrewdly, for, when it comes to practical
business with their contemporaries, worldly men are shrewder than
unworldly men. 9My advice to you is, use your money, however
dishonestly it may have been acquired, to get yourselves friends,
so that, when money is no more, you may find a good home in
eternity.

10'The man who is reliable when very little is involved is just as
reliable when a great deal is involved; and when a man is dishonest
when very little is involved, he will be just as dishonest when a great
deal is involved.

11'If you have not shown yourself reliable in this world's ill-gotten
wealth, who will trust you with the real wealth? 12And, if you have

not shown yourself reliable in dealing with someone else's wealth,
who will give you what is your own?'

13 'No servant can be a slave to two owners, for he will either hate
the one and love the other, or he will be devoted to one and despise
the other. You cannot be the servant of the God of heaven and of
the god of this world's wealth.'

14 The Pharisees were fond of money, and, when they heard all this,
they smiled superciliously. 15 'You are the kind of people,' Jesus said
to them, 'who do your best to acquire a human reputation for good-
ness, but God knows what you are really like, for there is nothing
more loathsome to God than human pride.'

16 'The Law and the Prophets were the supreme revelation up to
the time of John. Then the Good News of the Kingdom of God began
to be proclaimed, and everyone tries to storm his way into it.'

17 'Heaven and earth will cease to be before the smallest part of one
letter of the Law will lose its authority.'

18 'If any man divorces his wife and marries another woman, he
commits adultery; and, if anyone marries a woman who has been
divorced from her husband, he commits adultery.'

19 'There was a wealthy man who dressed in the most expensive
clothes made of the finest linen dyed with costly purple dye, and
whose everyday meals were lavish banquets. 20 And there was a poor
man called Lazarus who was left lying at the gate of the rich man's
house. Lazarus was a mass of ulcerous sores, 21 and he longed to
satisfy his hunger with the scraps which were thrown away from
the rich man's table. He was so helpless that the dogs came and
licked his sores.

22 'The poor man died, and the angels carried him away to the arms
of Abraham. The rich man also died and was buried. 23 He was in
Hades and he was in torment. He looked up, and away in the distance
he saw Abraham with Lazarus in his arms. 24 "Father Abraham," he
shouted, "take pity on me, and send Lazarus to dip the tip of his
finger in water to cool my tongue, for I am in anguish in this flame."
25 "Son," Abraham said, "you must remember that you received your
full share of good things during your lifetime, just as Lazarus did of
hardships in his. Now the tables are turned, and he is in comfort here
and you are in anguish. 26 Besides all this, a great gulf has been fixed

between us and you, so that those who wish to cross from here to you
cannot do so, nor can anyone pass from there to us." 27"Well, then,
father," he said, "I have five brothers. 28Please send him to my
father's house to warn them of the truth, and to make sure that they
do not come to this place of torture as I have done." 29"They have
Moses and the prophets," Abraham answered. "Let them listen to
them." 30"No, father Abraham," he said, "they will not do that, but,
if someone comes to them from the dead, they will repent." 31"If they
refuse to listen to Moses and the prophets," Abraham said, "they will
not be convinced, even if someone should rise from the dead." '

Chapter 17

JESUS said to his disciples: 'It is inevitable that things which make
men sin should come, but tragic is the fate of the man who is
responsible for their coming. 2It would be better for him to have a
millstone hung round his neck, and to be hurled into the sea than to
be responsible for anything which causes one of these little ones to
sin.'

3'Watch what you are doing! If your fellow man wrongs you,
reprimand him, and, if he shows that he is sorry, forgive him. 4If he
wrongs you seven times in one day, and if seven times he turns to you
and says that he is sorry for what he did, you must forgive him.'

5The apostles said to the Lord: 'Give us more faith.' 6The Lord said
to them: 'If you have faith as big as a mustard seed, you would say to
this sycamore tree: "Be torn up by the roots and be planted in the
sea," and it would obey you.'

7'If any of you has a servant who is a ploughman or a shepherd, is
he likely to say to him when he comes in from the fields: "Come
along at once, and sit down at table"? 8Not likely! What he will say is:
"Get ready my dinner. Hitch up your robe, and attend to me while
I eat and drink. You can eat and drink when I have finished." 9Surely
he does not thank his servant for doing what he is told to do? 10It is
just so with you. When you have done everything you have been
told to do, you must still say: "We're nothing special in the way of
servants. We have done no more than our duty." '

11When Jesus was on his way to Jerusalem, he was going through

the borderland between Samaria and Galilee. 12As he was entering a
village, ten lepers met him. They kept their distance 13and shouted:
'Jesus, Master, take pity on us!' 14When he saw them, he said to them:
'Go, and show yourselves to the priests.' While they were on the way,
they were cleansed. 15One of them, when he saw that he was cured,
turned back praising God at the top of his voice. 16He threw himself
down at Jesus' feet in gratitude. And he was a Samaritan. 17Jesus said:
'Were the whole ten not cleansed? Where are the nine?' 18Didn't any-
one come back to give praise to God except this foreigner?' 19'Rise and
go,' he said to him. 'Your faith has cured you.'

20When Jesus was asked by the Pharisees when the Kingdom of God
would come, he answered: 'You cannot see the Kingdom of God
coming by watching for visible signs, 21nor will it be possible to say:
"Look, here it is!" or, "Look, there it is!" For the Kingdom of God is
within you.'

22Jesus said to his disciples: 'The time will come when you will long
to see one of the days of the Son of Man, and you will not see it.
23They will tell you: "Look, here he is! Look, there he is!" Don't go
and run after them. 24The coming of the Son of Man in his time will
be like the lightning flash that lights up the earth from one horizon
to another. 25But before that he must undergo many sufferings, and
he must be rejected by this present generation. 26What happened in
the time of Noah will happen all over again at the time when the
Son of Man comes. 27They were eating, they were drinking, they were
marrying, they were being married, right up to the day when Noah
went into the ark, and the Flood came and wiped them all out. 28In
the same way, what happened in the time of Lot will happen all over
again. They were eating, they were drinking, they were buying, they
were selling, they were planting, they were building. 29And on the
day Lot left Sodom fire and brimstone rained down from heaven and
wiped them all out. 30It will be exactly the same on the day when the
Son of Man appears on the stage of history. 31If on that day a man is
on the housetop, and his goods are in the house, he must not go
down to take them out; and, equally so, if a man is working in the
field, he must not turn back. 32Remember what happened to Lot's
wife. 33If a man tries to keep his life safe, he will lose it, and, if a man
is willing to lose it, he will preserve it alive. 34On that night, I tell
you, there will be two people in one bed; one will be taken and the

other will be left. 35There will be two women grinding corn together;
one will be taken and the other will be left.'* 37'Master,' they asked
him, 'where will this happen?' 'Where the body is,' he said, 'the vul-
tures will gather.'

Chapter 18

JESUS told them a parable to illustrate the truth that they must
always keep on praying, and never lose heart. 2'In a town,' he said,
'there was a judge, who had no reverence for God and no respect for
man. 3There was a widow in that town who kept coming to him and
demanding justice against her opponent. 4For a long time the judge
refused to act. But in the end he said to himself: "Even if I have no
reverence for God and no respect for man, 5I will give this woman
justice, because she keeps pestering me, and I don't want her coming
until she completely wears me out."' 6So the Lord said: 'Listen to
what the unjust judge says! 7And will not God see justice done for his
own chosen ones, who appeal to him night and day? Is he slow to act
for them? 8I tell you, it will not be long before he sees justice done for
them. But when the Son of Man does come, will he find that men on
earth have still not lost their faith?'

9Jesus told the following parable, which was meant for some people
who were so confident of their own goodness that they looked with
contempt on everyone else. 10'Two men went up to the Temple to
pray. One was a Pharisee, the other a tax-collector. 11The Pharisee
stood there and this was his prayer, and it was addressed quite as
much to himself as it was to God: "O God, I thank you that I am not
like other people—rapacious, dishonest, adulterers—or even like this
tax-collector here. 12I fast twice a week. I meticulously set aside for
you a tenth of my income." 13The tax-collector respectfully kept his
distance, and would not even look up to heaven. So far from that, he
beat his breast and said: "God! Have mercy on me, the sinner!" 14I tell
you, he went home far closer to God than the other, for everyone
who exalts himself will be humbled, but, if a man humbles himself,
he will be exalted.'

15They tried to bring even the babies to Jesus for him to touch

*Here some manuscripts insert verse 36, *There will be two men in the field; one will be taken and the other one will be left.*

them. When the disciples saw this, they warned them off. 16But Jesus
called them to him. 'Let the little children come to me,' he said, 'and
don't try to stop them, for it is to such as they are that the Kingdom
of God belongs. 17I tell you truly, if a man does not receive the
Kingdom of God like a little child, he will certainly not get into it.'

18A leading Jew put a question to Jesus. 'Good Master,' he said,
'what am I to do to get this eternal life that God promised?' 19Jesus
said to him: 'Why call me good? No one is good except God. 20You
know the commandments—Do not commit adultery, Do not kill,
Do not steal, Do not tell lies about anyone, Honour your father and
your mother.' 21'I have obeyed these since I was a child,' he said.
22When Jesus heard this, he said to him: 'You still lack one thing.
Sell everything you have; share the proceeds among the poor; and
you will have treasure in heaven. And come! Follow me!' 23When
he heard this, it made him very sad, for he was very rich.

24When Jesus saw how he had reacted, he said: 'With what difficulty
will the wealthy get into the Kingdom of God! 25It is easier for a
camel to go through the eye of a needle than for a rich man to get
into the Kingdom of God.' 26Those who heard this said: 'Then who
can be saved?' 27Jesus said: 'The things which are impossible to men
are possible to God.'

28Peter said: 'We have left our homes and families to become your
followers.' 29'This is the truth I tell you,' Jesus said to them, 'there is
no man who has left a house, or a wife, or brothers, or parents, or
children for the sake of the Kingdom of God, 30who will not receive
them back many times over in this present world, and in the world
which is to come, eternal life.'

31Jesus took the Twelve aside, and said to them: 'We are going up
to Jerusalem, and everything predicted in the writings of the prophets
will happen to the Son of Man. 32He will be handed over to the
Romans, and he will be mocked, and treated with wanton insolence,
and spat on. 33They will first flog him and then kill him, and on the
third day he will rise again.' 34They completely failed to grasp all this.
The significance of this statement was hidden from them, and they
had no idea of the meaning of what he was saying.

35As Jesus was approaching Jericho, a blind man was sitting at the
roadside begging. 36When he heard a crowd passing, he asked what
was happening. 37They told him that Jesus of Nazareth was passing

along the road. 38He shouted: 'Jesus, Son of David! Take pity on me!'
39The people in front sharply told him to be quiet, but he shouted
louder than ever: 'Son of David! Take pity on me!' 40Jesus stopped.
He ordered the man to be brought to him. When the man had come
to him he asked him: 41'What do you want me to do for you?' The
man said: 'Master, the only thing I want is to see again!' 42'See again!'
Jesus said to him. 'Your faith has cured you!' 43Immediately his sight
returned, and he followed Jesus praising God, and, when the people
saw it, they all gave praise to God.

Chapter 19

JESUS entered Jericho, and was on his way through it. 2There was
a man called Zacchaeus there. He was the chief tax-collector for the
district, and a wealthy man. 3He was trying to see Jesus, but he could
not because of the crowd, for he was a little man. 4So he ran on ahead
and climbed up into a sycamore tree to see him, for he was to pass
that way. 5When Jesus came to the spot, he looked up and said:
'Zacchaeus, hurry up and come down, because I must stay at your
house today.' 6Zacchaeus hurried down and gladly welcomed Jesus.
7When they saw this, they began to complain that Jesus had gone to
be the guest of a man with whom no respectable Jew would have had
anything to do. 8But Zacchaeus stood there and said to the Lord: 'Sir,
I am going to give half of my belongings to the poor, and, if I have
swindled anyone out of anything, I am going to give him back four
times as much.' 9Jesus said to him: 'Today salvation has come to this
house, for this man too is a son of Abraham. 10The Son of Man came
to search for and to rescue the lost.'

11While they were listening to this, Jesus went on to tell them a
parable, which was particularly appropriate, because he was nearing
Jerusalem, and they thought that the Kingdom of God was going to
appear there and then.

12'There was a nobleman,' he said to them, 'who went away to a
distant land, there to receive a kingdom for himself, and then to
return. 13He sent for ten of his servants, and gave each of them a sum
of five pounds. "Trade with this," he said to them, "until I come
back." 14But his citizens hated him, and sent an embassy on his heels,
to say that they refused to have him as their king. 15He received the

kingdom and returned. Then he ordered the servants to whom he
had given the money to be summoned to his presence, to find out
what profit each had made in his trading.

16‘The first came. “Sir,” he said, “your five pounds have produced
another fifty.” “Well done!” he said. “You arc a good servant! Because
you have shown yourself trustworthy in a very small matter, you are
hereby put in charge of ten towns.” 18The second came. “Sir,” he
said, “your five pounds have made other twenty-five pounds.” 19The
master said to him also: “You too are put in charge of five towns.”
20Another came. “Sir,” he said, “here is your five pounds. I kept them
stored away, wrapped in a cloth, 21because I was afraid of you, because
you are a hard man, and you have a habit of appropriating the re-
wards of a business into which you did not put any money, and of
letting someone else do the work, and then taking the profits.”
22His master said to him: “You are a thoroughly bad servant! You
have pronounced your own condemnation. Were you not well
aware that I am a hard man, and that it is my habit to appropriate the
rewards of a business into which I did not put any money, and to let
someone else do the work, and then to take the profit? 23Why then
did you not give my money to the bankers? If you had done that, I
would have got it back with interest when I came home.” 24So he said
to the attendants: “Take the five pounds from him, and give them to
the man who has fifty pounds.” 25“Sir,” they said, “he already has
fifty pounds.” 26“I tell you,” the master said, “if a man has much, he
will be given more. If a man has nothing, he will lose even what he
has. 27As for these enemies of mine who refused to have me as their
king, bring them here and execute them in my presence.” ’

28After Jesus had said this, he went on ahead on his way to Jeru-
salem. 29When he was near Bethphage and Bethany, at the hill called
Olivet, he sent on two of his disciples. 30‘Go into the village opposite,’
he said, ‘and, as you enter it, you will find a tethered colt, which no
one has ever ridden. Untie it, and bring it to me. 31And if anyone
asks you: “Why are you untying it?” this is what you will say: “The
Master needs it.” ’ 32Those who had been sent on went away and
found everything just as Jesus had told them. 33As they were untying
the colt, its owners said to them: ‘Why are you untying the colt?’
34They said: ‘Because the Master needs it.’

35So they brought it to Jesus. They threw their cloaks on the colt,
and mounted Jesus on it. 36As he rode, they spread their cloaks on

the road. 37By this time he was nearing the descent from the Hill of
Olives. The whole crowd of the disciples began joyfully to shout their
praises to God for all the miracles they had seen:

38'God bless the king who comes in the name of the Lord!
Peace in heaven, and glory in the heights of heaven!'

39Some of the Pharisees in the crowd said to him: 'Teacher, repri-
mand your disciples.' 40'I tell you,' Jesus answered, 'if they remain
silent, the stones will break into a shout.'

41When he came in sight of the city, he wept over it. 42'If only,'
he said, 'you would realize on this day, which should be your greatest
day, the things which would bring you real prosperity—but the
tragedy is that you are incapable of seeing them. 43The time will come
when your enemies will build a mound from which to attack you,
and will encircle you and hem you in on every side. 44They will level
the city to the ground, and you and your children in it. They will not
leave one stone standing on another in you, because you did not
recognize the time when God came to visit you.'

45Jesus went into the Temple precincts and proceeded to drive out
those who were selling. 46'Scripture says,' he said to them, ' "My
house shall be a house of prayer," but you have made it a brigands'
den.'

47He continued to teach in the Temple daily, and the chief priests
and the experts in the Law and the leaders of the people tried to find
some way to kill him, 48but they could discover no way of doing so,
for the people all hung upon his words.

Chapter 20

ONE day, when Jesus was teaching the people in the Temple pre-
cincts, and when he was telling them the Good News, the chief
priests and the experts in the Law came up to him along with the
elders. 2'Tell us,' they said, 'what right have you to act as you do, and
who is it who gave you the right to do so?' 3'I too will ask you a
question,' Jesus answered. 'Tell me, 4was the source of the baptism
which John administered divine or human?' 5They discussed it with
each other. 'If,' they said, 'we say, "Divine," he will say: "Why did
you not believe in him?" 6But, if we say, "Human," the people will all

stone us, for they are convinced that John was a prophet.' 7So they
answered that they did not know the source of John's baptism. 8So
Jesus said: 'No more am I going to tell you what right I have to act as I
do.'

9Jesus told the people this parable. 'A man planted a vineyard,' he
said, 'and let it out to tenants, and went abroad for some considerable
time. 10At the appropriate time of year he sent a servant to the
tenants so that they might give him his due share of the crop. But the
tenants beat him up and sent him away empty-handed. 11He went
on to send another servant, but they beat him up too, and shame-
fully maltreated him, and sent him away empty-handed. 12He went
on to send a third servant, but they wounded him and threw him
out. 13"What am I to do?" the owner of the vineyard said. "I will send
my beloved and only son. It may be that they will treat him with
respect." 14But, when the tenants saw the son, they discussed the
situation with each other. "This is the heir," they said. "Let us kill
him, and then the estate will pass into our hands." 15So they threw
him out of the vineyard and killed him. What then will the owner
of the vineyard do to them? 16He will come and wipe out these
tenants, and will give the vineyard to others.' 'God forbid!' they said,
when they heard this. 17Jesus looked at them. 'What, then,' he said,
'is the meaning of this passage of scripture:

"The stone which the builders rejected,
this has become the headstone of the corner"?

18Anyone who falls against this stone will be shattered to pieces, and
it will crush anyone it falls on.'

19At that time the experts in the Law and the chief priests tried to
find some way to seize Jesus, but they were afraid of the people, for
they were well aware that it was against them that he had directed this
parable.

20They kept Jesus under close observation. They sent spies who
pretended to be genuinely concerned about the right thing to do.
The idea was to seize on what he said, and so to find a reason for
handing him over to the power and authority of the governor.
21So they put a question to him. 'Teacher,' they said, 'we know that
you speak and teach rightly and that man-made prestige means noth-
ing to you, but that you really do teach the life that God wishes us to
live. 22Is it right for us to pay tax to Caesar, or not?' 23Jesus under-

stood their villainy. 24'Show me a shilling,' he said. 'Whose portrait
and whose inscription is on it?' 'Caesar's,' they said. 25'If that is so,'
he said, 'pay to Caesar what belongs to Caesar, and to God what
belongs to God.' 26They were powerless publicly to seize on what he
said. They were so astonished at his answer that they were reduced to
silence.

27Some of the Sadducees, who deny that there is any resurrection,
approached Jesus. They put a question to him. 28'Teacher,' they said,
'Moses prescribed a regulation for us, that, if a man's married brother
dies, and dies childless, his brother should marry his wife, and should
raise a family for his brother. 29Well then, there were seven brothers.
The first married and died childless. 30So did the second, 31and the
third married her too. In the same way the whole seven died, and
left no children. 32The woman afterwards died too. 33Now, of which
of these will the woman be the wife at the resurrection, for the seven
had her as wife?' 34'In this world,' Jesus said to them, 'people marry
and are married, 35but those who are judged fit to enter the other
world and to share in the resurrection of the dead neither marry nor
are married. 36Nor can they die any more, for they are like angels,
and they are real sons of God, because they are resurrection sons.
37That the dead are in fact raised Moses himself has shown in the
passage about the bush, when he speaks of the Lord as the God of
Abraham and the God of Isaac and the God of Jacob. 38God is not
the God of the dead but of the living. For him they are all alive.'
39Some of the experts in the Law answered: 'Teacher, that was an
excellent answer,' 40for they no longer dared to ask him any more
questions.

41Jesus said to them: 'How can it be said that the Messiah is David's
son? 42David himself says in the Book of Psalms:

"The Lord said to my Lord,
Sit on my right hand,
43until I give you the victory over your enemies."

44So then David calls him Lord, and how can he be his son?'

45While all the people were listening, Jesus said to his disciples:
46'Beware of the experts in the Law, for they like to walk about in
long flowing robes, and they love to be deferentially greeted, as they
move through the market-places. They like the front seats in the

synagogue, and the top places at banquets. 47They greedily extract
the last penny from credulous widows, and with their long prayers
they try to give an impression of exceptional piety. They will receive
all the heavier a sentence.'

Chapter 21

JESUS looked up and saw the wealthy people putting their gifts
into the Temple treasury. 2He saw a poor widow putting in two
little copper coins which were together worth half a farthing. 3'I tell
you truly,' he said, 'this poor widow has put in more than all the
others put together. 4They all have more than they need, and it is
out of their surplus that they have put in their gifts, but she has not
enough for her needs, and out of her want she has put in everything
she has to live on.'

5When some of them were talking about the Temple, and how it
was adorned with lovely stones and gifts, Jesus said: 6'These sights
you are gazing at—the time will come when not one stone will be
left standing on another, and when every building here will be
utterly demolished.' 7'Teacher,' they said, 'when will these events
take place, and what will be the sign when they are going to
happen?'

8Jesus said: 'Be careful that you are not misled, for many will
come claiming that they are my representatives. They will say: "I am
he." They will say: "The crucial moment is near." Do not follow
them.

9'When you hear of wars and revolutions, don't get into a panic,
for these events must happen first, but the end will not come im-
mediately.' 10Then Jesus went on to say: 'Nation will attack nation,
and kingdom will attack kingdom. 11There will be great earth-
quakes, and here and there there will be outbreaks of famine and
pestilence; there will be terrifying things and great portents in
the sky.

12'Before all this happens, they will attack you and persecute you.
They will hand you over to the synagogues, and put you in prison.
You will be brought before kings and governors because of your con-
nection with me. 13This will be an opportunity for you to show the
world what you believe. 14Make up your minds not to worry before-

hand what you are going to say in your defence. 15For I will give you
an ability to speak, and a wisdom which none of your opponents will
be able to resist or to refute.

16'You will be betrayed by parents and brothers and relations and
friends. Some of you will be killed. 17You will be universally hated
because of your connection with me. 18But not a hair of your head
will be ultimately lost. 19If you see things through to the end, you
will win your souls.

20'When you see Jerusalem encircled by armies, then you must
realize that the time of her desolation is near. 21At that time those
who are in Judaea must flee to the hills; those who are in the city
must get out; and those in the country districts must not go into it.
22For these are the days in which the vengeance of God will come,
so that everything the scriptures say will come true.

23'It will be a tragic time for those who are carrying children in
the womb, or feeding them at the breast, for all over the land there
will be terrible suffering, and God's wrath will descend on the people.
24They will fall by the edge of the sword; they will be carried away
captive to all countries; and Jerusalem will be trampled upon by the
Gentiles; and this will last until the time allotted to the Gentiles runs
its course.

25'There will be portents in the sun and in the moon and in the
stars, and on earth the nations will not know where to turn, be-
wildered by the roar of the sea and the waves, 26while men will be
fainting from fear, and for the thought of what is going to happen to
the world, for the heavenly bodies will be shaken. 27Then they will
see the Son of Man coming on a cloud with great power and glory.
28When these things begin to happen, lift up your heads, for your
deliverance is near.'

29Jesus used an illustration. 'Look at the fig tree,' he said, 'or indeed
at any tree. 30Whenever you see the trees putting on their leaves, you
do not need anyone to tell you that summer is near. 31So, whenever
you see these events happening, you must realize that the Kingdom
of God is near. 32I tell you truly that these things will certainly hap-
pen within the life-time of this generation. 33Heaven and earth will
cease to be, but my words will never cease to be.

34'Be careful not to let your minds be dulled by dissipation and
drunkenness and the worries of making a living, in case that day
suddenly closes on you like a trap, 35for it will come on everyone all
over the world. 36Watch sleeplessly, and never stop praying that you

may be strong enough to come through all that is going to happen,
and to stand erect in the presence of the Son of Man.'

37During the day Jesus continued to preach in the Temple, and at
night he left the city, and slept in the open air on the hill called
Olivet; 38and early in the morning all the people came to listen to him
in the Temple.

Chapter 22

THE Festival of Unleavened Bread, which is called the Passover,
was just about to begin, 2and the chief priests and the experts in
the Law were trying to find some way to kill Jesus. But it was not easy
to find one, for they were afraid of the people.

3Satan entered into Judas, who is called Iscariot, who was one of the
Twelve, 4and Judas went and discussed with the chief priests and the
officers of the Temple police how he could deliver Jesus into their
hands. 5They were delighted with his proposal, and they agreed to
pay him for his services. 6So he came to an agreement with them, and
he began to look for a good opportunity to deliver him into their
hands, when the crowd was not there.

7The first day of the Festival of Unleavened Bread came, the day on
which the Passover lamb had to be killed and sacrificed. 8Jesus sent off
Peter and John. 'Go,' he said, 'and make all the necessary preparations
for us to eat the Passover.' 9'Where do you wish us to make the
preparations?' they asked. 10'When you have gone into the city,' he
said, 'you will meet a man carrying an earthenware water-jug.
Follow him to the house he goes into. 11You must say to the house-
holder: "The Teacher says to you, Where is the guest room, where I
am to eat the Passover with my disciples?" 12He will show you a big
upstairs room, with the couches spread with rugs. There make all
the necessary preparation.' 13They went off, and found everything
exactly as Jesus had told them, and they made all the necessary pre-
parations for the Passover.

14When the time came, Jesus took his place at the table with the
apostles. 15'I have longed with all my heart,' he said to them, 'to eat
this Passover meal with you, before I suffer, 16for I tell you that I will

not eat it again, until it finds its fulfilment in the banquet of the
Kingdom of God.'

17A cup was handed to him, and he gave thanks to God for it.
'Take this,' he said, 'and share it among yourselves. 18I tell you that
from now on I will not drink of the fruit of the vine, until the King-
dom comes.'

19He took a loaf, and, when he had thanked God for it, he broke it
into pieces, and gave it to them. 'This means my body,' he said,
'which is given for your sake.* Do this so that you will remember
me.' 20In the same way, after the meal he took the cup and said: 'This
cup stands for the new relationship between man and God made
possible at the cost of my life-blood, which is being shed for your
sake.

21'But the traitor's hand is with me at this very table, 22for the Son
of Man takes the road he is destined to take, but tragic is the fate
of that man by whom the Son of Man is being betrayed.' 23They
began to ask each other which of them it could be who was going to
do this.

24They began to quarrel about which of them should be regarded
as the most important. 25'The kings of the Gentiles,' Jesus said to
them, 'lord it over their subjects. It is those who are in a position of
authority who receive the title of benefactor. 26But things must be
very different with you. With you the man who is greatest must
behave like the youngest, and the leader must be like a servant.
27Who would you say is greater? The guest or the servant? Obviously,
the guest. But it is as a servant that I am with you.

28'You are the men who have stood by me, when I was under
attack. 29My Father assigned the royal power to me, and I assign to
you 30the privilege of eating and drinking at my table in my Kingdom,
and you will be enthroned as the judges of the twelve tribes of
Israel.

31'Simon, Simon, Satan has claimed the right to put the loyalty of
all of you through the mill; 32but for you yourself I have prayed that
yours may not fail. And, when you have found the way back, you
must help your brothers to stand fast.' 33'Master,' Peter said to him,
'I am prepared to go to prison and to death with you.' 34'I tell you,

*Some manuscripts omit the words from here to the end of verse 20.

Peter,' Jesus said, 'before the cock crows today you will three times
disown me.'

35Jesus said to them: 'When I sent you out with no purse, and with
no knapsack, and with no sandals, did you lack for anything?' 'For
nothing,' they said. 36'Things have changed now,' he said to them. 'If
you have a purse, you must bring it, and a knapsack too; if you have
no sword, you must sell your coat and buy one. 37For, I tell you, the
passage of scripture which says: "He was reckoned among the
criminals" must come true in what is going to happen to me. Yes,
what was foretold of me is working itself out to its appointed
end.' 38'Master,' they said, 'here are two swords.' 'It is enough,' he
said.

39Jesus went out to the Hill of Olives, as he was in the habit of
doing, and his disciples accompanied him. 40When he reached the
place, he said to them: 'You must pray not to have to face the ordeal
of temptation.' 41He himself withdrew a stone's throw from them.
He knelt and prayed. 42'Father,' he said, 'if it be your will, save me
from having to go through this bitter ordeal. But, not my will but
yours be done.' 43An angel from heaven appeared to him, giving
him strength. 44He was in an agony of mind, and prayed more
intensely. As his sweat dripped on the ground, it was like drops of
blood.* 45He rose from prayer, and came to his disciples. He found
them sleeping, exhausted by sorrow. 46'Why are you sleeping?' he
said to them. 'Up and pray that you may not have to face the ordeal
of temptation!'

47Just as he was saying this, a crowd arrived on the scene, with the
man called Judas, one of the Twelve, at the head of them. He went up
to Jesus to kiss him. 48'Judas,' Jesus said to him, 'are you going to
betray the Son of Man with a kiss?' 49When Jesus' comrades saw what
was going to happen, they said: 'Master, shall we use our swords?'
50And one of them struck the High Priest's servant, and cut off his
right ear. 51'Let them have their way,' Jesus said. And he touched the
ear and healed him.

52Jesus said to the chief priests and the officers of the Temple police
and to the elders who had come to arrest him: 'Have you come out
with swords and cudgels, as if you were out to arrest a brigand? 53I
was with you daily in the Temple precincts, and you made no

*Some manuscripts omit verses 43 and 44

attempt to lay a hand on me. But this is your hour, and the power of
darkness is in control.'

54They arrested him and took him away. They brought him into
the High Priest's house, and Peter was following at a distance. 55They
kindled a fire in the middle of the courtyard, and were sitting round it.
Peter was sitting in the middle of them. 56One of the maidservants saw
him sitting in the light of the fire. She stared intently at him. 'This
man too was with him,' she said. 57Peter denied it. 'Woman,' he said,
'I do not know him.' 58Shortly afterwards another man saw him.
'You too,' he said, 'are one of them.' 'Man,' said Peter, 'I am not.'
59About an hour had passed when another man insisted: 'Quite
certainly this fellow was with him. Indeed he was, for he is a Gali-
laean.' 60'Man,' said Peter, 'I don't know what you're talking about.'
At that very moment, while he was still speaking, the cock crew.
61And the Lord turned and looked straight at Peter, and Peter remem-
bered what the Lord had said to him, and how he had said: 'Before
the cock crows today you will three times disown me.' 62He went out
and wept bitterly.

63The guards who had Jesus in custody flogged him and made him
the victim of their horseplay. 64They blindfolded him, and kept asking
him: 'Prophesy! Who is it who hit you?' 65And they heaped many
another insult on him.

66When day came, the council of the elders assembled with the
chief priests and the experts in the Law, and they took him away to
their Sanhedrin. 67'Tell us,' they said to him, 'are you the Messiah?'
He said to them: 'You will not believe any statement I make, 68and
you will not answer any question I ask. 69But from now on the Son of
Man will be seated at the right hand of Almighty God.' 70'Are you
then the Son of God?' they all said. 'It is you who say so,' he said to
them. 71'What further evidence do we need?' they said. 'We have all
the evidence we need from his own lips.'

Chapter 23

THEY rose in a body and took Jesus to Pilate. 2They began to make
their accusations against him. 'We found this man,' they said,
'attempting to stir up political trouble in our nation, and trying to
stop people paying their taxes to the Emperor, and claiming that he
is the Messiah, a king.' 3Pilate asked Jesus: 'Are you the King of the
Jews?' 'If you like to put it so,' Jesus answered. 4Pilate said to the chief
priests and to the crowds: 'As far as I can see, there is no crime with
which this man can be charged.' 5But they insisted: 'He is a trouble-
maker. He has been spreading his propaganda all over Judaea. He
started in Galilee and now he has reached here.' 6When Pilate heard
this, he asked: 'Is this man a Galilaean?' 7When he found out that
Jesus was under the jurisdiction of Herod, he referred his case to him,
for he too was in Jerusalem at that time.

8Herod was greatly delighted to see Jesus, for he had long wished
to see him because of the reports he had heard about him, and he
hoped to see some visible demonstration of divine power performed
by him. 9He cross-examined Jesus at some length, but Jesus did not
answer him. 10The chief priests and the experts in the Law were
present, and continued strenuously to make their allegations against
Jesus. 11Herod and his troops treated Jesus with contempt, and made
a mockery of him. They arrayed him in a brilliantly-coloured robe,
and sent him back to Pilate. 12On that day Herod and Pilate became
friends with each other again, for previously they had been estranged
from each other.

13Pilate sent for the chief priests and the members of the Sanhedrin
and the people. 14'You brought this man to me,' he said, 'on the
charge of inciting the people to revolution. I have examined him in
your presence, and, so far as I can see, he is not guilty of the charges
you are bringing against him. 15And further, Herod did not regard
him as guilty either, for he referred his case back to me. He is re-
sponsible for no action which merits the death penalty. 16I therefore
propose to flog him and release him.'* 18But the whole mob kept
shrieking in unison: 'Away with this man! Release us Barabbas!' 19Bar-
abbas was a man who had been imprisoned on the charge of being

*Here some manuscripts insert verse 17, *At the festival he was obliged to release one prisoner for them.*

implicated in a rebellion which had arisen in the city, and of murder.
20Pilate again addressed them, for he wished to release Jesus. 21But
they shouted back at him: 'Crucify, crucify him!' 22For the third
time Pilate said to them: 'Why? What crime has he committed? So far
as I can see, he has done nothing to deserve the death penalty.
I therefore propose to flog him and to release him.' 23But they in-
sistently shouted their demand that Jesus should be crucified, and
their shouts got them their way. 24Pilate gave his decision that they
should get what they wanted. 25So he released the man they asked for,
the man who had been imprisoned for sedition and murder, and he
handed over Jesus to them to do what they liked with him.

26As they were taking Jesus away, they seized a Cyrenian called
Simon, who was coming in from the country, and they compelled
him to walk behind Jesus, carrying the cross. 27A huge crowd of
people followed him, with many women among them, who in their
sorrow beat their breasts and wailed their laments. 28Jesus turned to
them. 'Daughters of Jerusalem,' he said, 'do not weep for me. Weep
for yourselves and for your children, 29for the time is coming when
they will say: "Happy are those who could never have a child, and the
wombs that never bore a child, and the breasts at which no child ever
fed." 30When that time comes, they will say to the mountains: "Fall
on us!" and to the hills: "Hide us!" 31For if they do these things in the
spring-time, what will they do when winter comes?' 32Two other men
who were criminals, were led out to be put to death with him.

33When they came to the place called the Skull, they crucified him
there with the criminals, one on his right, and the other on his left.
34Jesus said: 'Father, forgive them, for they do not know what they
are doing.' They shared his clothes between them by drawing lots for
them.

35The people stood looking on, and the Jewish leaders sneered at
him. 'He saved others,' they said, 'let him save himself, if he really is
God's Messiah, the Chosen One!' 36The soldiers too made a mockery
of him by coming to him and offering him their bitter wine. 37'If you
really are the King of the Jews,' they said to him, 'save yourself!'
38Above his head there was a placard: 'This is the King of the Jews.'

39One of the criminals who had been crucified kept hurling insults
at Jesus. 'Are you not the Messiah?' he said. 'Save yourself and us!'
40The other sternly reprimanded him. 'Have you no reverence for

God?' he said. 'You have been sentenced to the same punishment as
he has been, 41and we with justice, for we are getting what we deserve
for our misdeeds, but he has committed no crime. 42Jesus,' he said,
'remember me when you come into your Kingdom.' 43Jesus said to
him: 'Very certainly you will be with me in Paradise today.'

44By this time it was about twelve o'clock midday, and darkness
came over the whole land until three o'clock in the afternoon, 45for
the sun was in eclipse. The curtain of the Temple which veiled the
Holy of Holies was ripped down the middle. 46Jesus shouted at the top
of his voice. Then he said: 'Father, into your hands I entrust my spirit.'
When he had said this, he died.

47When the company commander saw what had happened, he
praised God. 'This was an innocent man indeed,' he said. 48When
the crowds who had come to watch the spectacle saw what had
happened, they all went away beating their breasts. 49All Jesus'
friends were standing at a distance, and the women who came with
him from Galilee were looking on.

50There was a man called Joseph, who was a member of the San-
hedrin, a kindly man and a strict observer of the Law. 51He had not
been in agreement with the policy and action of the Sanhedrin. He
came from Arimathaea, a Judaean town, and he was eagerly waiting
for the Kingdom of God. 52He went to Pilate and asked for Jesus'
body. 53He took it down from the cross, and wrapped it in linen, and
laid him in a tomb hewn out of the rock, in which no one had ever
yet been laid.

54It was Friday evening, the preparation for the Sabbath, and the
Sabbath lamps were just beginning to be lit. 55The women who had
come with Jesus from Galilee followed Joseph, and saw the tomb, and
watched how his body had been laid in it. 56They went home and
prepared spices and perfumes for Jesus' body. They rested during the
Sabbath as the commandment ordered.

Chapter 24

VERY early on Sunday morning they went to the tomb with the
spices which they had prepared. 2They found the stone rolled
away from the tomb. 3They went into it, but they could not find
the Lord Jesus' body. 4While they were quite at a loss what to make

of this, suddenly two men appeared to them in dazzling clothes.
5They were so terrified that they could not even look up. 'Why are
you searching among the dead for him who is alive?' the men said
to them. 6'He is not here! He has risen! Remember how, when he was
still with you in Galilee, he told you 7that the Son of Man had to be
delivered into the power of sinful men, and how he had to be cruci-
fied, and how he had to rise again on the third day.' 8They remem-
bered what Jesus had said. 9They returned from the tomb, and told
the eleven and all the others all that had happened. 10Mary from
Magdala and Joanna and Mary, the mother of James, were there, and,
along with the other women who were with them, they tried to tell
the apostles all about this. 11To them the story sounded like sheer
nonsense, and they refused to believe them. 12Peter went running to
the tomb. He stooped down and looked in, and there was nothing
there to be seen but the linen grave-clothes. He went back home,
astonished at what had happened.

13On that same day two of them were on their way to a village
called Emmaus, about eight miles from Jerusalem. 14They were
talking to each other about all that had happened. 15While they were
talking about it and discussing it, Jesus himself came up to them, and
began to walk along the road with them. 16But although they saw
him, they were prevented from recognizing him. 17'What are you
spending your walk arguing about?' he said to them. They halted
and their faces showed the bitterness of their hearts. 18One of them,
called Cleopas, answered: 'Are you the only visitor to Jerusalem who
has not heard of the recent events there?' 19'What events?' he said.
'What happened,' they said, 'to Jesus of Nazareth who was a prophet
and it was obvious to all, God knows, with what power he could
speak and act, 20and how our chief priests and leaders handed him
over to be condemned to death, and how they crucified him. 21It was
our hope that it was he who would liberate Israel. But it did not work
out that way, and, to add to it all, it is now three days since all this
happened. 22It is true that some women who belong to our circle
brought us the most astonishing news. They had gone to the tomb
early in the morning, 23and they were unable to find his body, and
they came back with a story that they had seen a vision of angels, who
told them that he was alive. 24Some of our friends did go to the tomb,
and found it empty, as the women had said, but they did not see
Jesus.' 25'You are so wilfully blind to the truth!' he said to them. 'You

are so slow to believe all that the prophets have said! 26Surely the
Messiah had to go through all these sufferings before entering into
his glory?' 27And he began from Moses and went down through all
the prophets explaining to them all the references in the scriptures to
himself.

28They were nearly at the village to which they were going. He
made as though he was going farther on. 29But they pressed him.
'Stay with us,' they said. 'It is evening now, and by this time it is late
in the day.' So he went in to stay with them. 30As he sat at table with
them, he took the loaf, and said the blessing, and broke it in pieces,
and gave it to them. 31Suddenly they saw! And they recognized him,
and he vanished from their sight.

32They said to each other: 'Were our hearts not strangely warmed
as he was talking with us on the road, when he was explaining the
meaning of scripture to us?' 33And there and then they started out
and went back to Jerusalem, and found the eleven and their friends
all gathered together, 34and talking about how the Lord had really
risen, and how he had appeared to Simon. 35They told them the story
of all that had happened on the road, and how they had recognized
him, when he broke the loaf.

36While they were still telling this story, Jesus stood among them.
'God's blessing be on you,' he said to them. 37They were startled and
terrified, for they thought that it was a ghost that they were seeing.
38'Why are you in such a state of alarm?' he said to them. 'Why do
you let doubts invade your minds? 39Look at my hands and feet! See!
It is I! Handle me, and see for yourselves, for a ghost does not have
flesh and blood, and you see that I have.' 40After he had said this, he
showed them his hands and his feet. 41While they still thought that
it was too good to be true, and while they were still in a state of be-
wildered astonishment, he said to them: 'Have you any food here?'
42They gave him a piece of cooked fish, 43and he took it and ate it
while they watched him.

44He said to them: 'While I was with you my message to you was
that everything written about me in the Law of Moses and in the
Prophets and in the Psalms must come true.' 45He explained every-
thing to them, so that they were able to understand the scriptures.
46'This is what scripture says,' he said, 'that the Messiah must suffer
and must rise from the dead on the third day, 47and that repentance
which leads to the forgiveness of sins must be proclaimed to all

nations in his name. 'And,' he said, 'you must begin from Jerusalem.
48It is you who must tell the world about all this. 49I am going to
send you the gift my Father promised you, and you must wait in
this city until you are clothed with power from on high.'

50He led them out as far as Bethany, and he lifted up his hands and
blessed them. 51While he was blessing them, he parted from them,
and was taken up to heaven, 52as they knelt in worship. They went
joyfully back to Jerusalem, 53and they spent all their time in the
Temple, praising God.

Introduction to Acts

THE Book of Acts might be called the second volume of Luke's Gospel. Both books were written by the same man and both books were written to the same man, to Theophilus.

Acts is one of the supremely important books of the New Testament, because without it we would know almost nothing about the history of the early days of the Church. Apart from what we can piece together and deduce from the New Testament letters, Acts is our only source of information about the first age of the Church.

It is misleading to call Acts *The Acts of the Apostles*. Apart from Paul, the only apostles who appear in it are Peter, James and John, and of these three only Peter does any speaking. It would be better to call it *Acts of Apostolic Men*, and not to regard it as a consecutive history, but rather as the opening of a series of windows, through which we catch meaningful and significant glimpses into the life of the early Church.

An historian's sources are all-important. In the early part of Acts Luke had a Jerusalem source (1-5; 15.1-16.5); a Caesarean source (8.26-40; 9.31-10.48); an Antiochene source (11.19-30; 12.25-14.28). But in the later parts of Acts a very interesting fact meets us. In the narrative there are stretches in which it is, 'They did this,' and, 'They did that.' But there are certain sections where it is, 'We did this,' and 'We did that' (16.9-18; 20.4-16; 21. 1-18; 27.1-28.6). On these occasions Luke must have been present. Very likely he kept a travel diary, and these are extracts from it. In these places we have the best of all evidence—an eye-witness account.

In Acts Luke has certain objects.

i. He gives us the story of the expansion of Christianity. The disciples are told that they are to be witnesses in Jerusalem, Judaea, Samaria and to the ends of the earth (1.8). The story of Acts tells how Christianity went out in ever-widening circles, until it reached Rome, the capital of the world.

ii. He wishes to commend Christianity to the Roman government in days when persecution was threatening. So he goes out of his way to tell how fair and just the Roman magistrates always were to the Christians, and how again and again they stated that they saw no harm in Christianity (16.35-40; 18.14; 19.37; 23.29; 25.25). Acts is a defence of Christianity to the Roman government.

iii. He wishes to tell us of the unity of the Church, and of how Jew and Gentile learned to live together in a common fellowship with Christ. So in chapter 15 he shows us the decision of the Church that there should be no difference between Jew and Gentile.

iv. He wishes to tell us that the prime mover in this miraculous expansion was the Holy Spirit (2). He begins with the coming of the Spirit at Pentecost. He goes on to show us Stephen as a man of the Spirit (6.3). It is the Spirit who moves Peter to accept Cornelius (11.12); who makes Philip approach the Ethiopian eunuch (8.29); who instructs the Church at Antioch to send Paul and Barnabas out on their journeyings for Christ (13.2). In Acts every great man and every great movement in the Church is inspired and upheld by the Holy Spirit.

Acts tells us of the miracle of the expansion of the Church, and shows us that it was the Spirit who made that miracle possible.

ACTS
of Apostolic Men

Chapter 1

MY DEAR Theophilus, I have already written you a full account
of the life and teaching of Jesus 2up to the time when he was
taken up into heaven, after he had given his instructions through the
Holy Spirit to the apostles whom he had chosen.
3After all that he had gone through, he proved to them on many
occasions that he was still alive, for, during a period of forty days, he
made himself visible to them, and talked to them about the Kingdom
of God. 4While he was still sharing their daily life with them, he gave
them orders not to leave Jerusalem, but to wait for the Father's
promised gift, of which he had already spoken to them. 5'John,' he
said, 'baptized you with water, but very soon you will be baptized with
the Holy Spirit.'

6Once when they were all together, they asked him: 'Are you
going to restore the royal power to Israel at this present time?' 7'You
are not permitted,' he said, 'to know how long things will last or the
date when they will happen. These things are solely in the Father's
control. 8Apart altogether from that, when the Holy Spirit has come
upon you, you will receive power, and you will tell the story of me
in Jerusalem, and all over Judaea, and in Samaria, and all over the
world.' 9After he had said this, he was taken up before their very eyes,
and a cloud received him, and he passed from their sight.
10While they were still gazing up into the sky, as he went away, two
men dressed in white appeared to them. 11'Men of Galilee,' they said,
'why are you standing here looking up into the sky? This Jesus, who
has been taken away from you up into heaven like this, will come
again in the same way as you have seen him going into heaven.'

12They then returned to Jerusalem from the hill called Olivet,
which is near Jerusalem, as far away as the Law allows a man to walk

on the Sabbath. 13When they came in, they went up to the upper
room, which was their headquarters. Peter and John and James and
Andrew, Philip and Thomas, Bartholomew and Matthew, James,
Alphaeus' son, and Simon the Nationalist, and Judas, James's son,
were there. 14These all spent all their time together in prayer with the
women, and with Mary, Jesus' mother, and with his brothers.

15At that time Peter rose when all the Christian brothers were
there—the assembled company numbered about one hundred and
twenty persons. 16'Brothers,' he said, 'the passage of scripture, in
which the Holy Spirit long ago foretold through the mouth of David
how Judas would offer himself as guide to those who arrested Jesus,
had to be fulfilled, 17for he was reckoned as one of our number, and
he received his allotted share in our work. 18He bought a piece of
ground with the pay his villainy had earned for him, but he fell
violently on his face, and his body burst open, so that all his entrails
poured out. 19This became public knowledge to all who lived in
Jerusalem, and that is why they called that piece of ground Akel-
dama in their own language, a word which means the Bloody Field.
20Well, then, in the Psalms it stands written:

> "Let his habitation become desolate,
> and let there be no one to stay in it,"

and,

> "Let another take his office."

21So, then, of the men who accompanied us, during all the time that
the Lord Jesus came in and went out among us, 22from the beginning
of his ministry, when he was baptized by John, right up to the day
when he was taken up and left us—one of these men must be ap-
pointed as a witness of his resurrection along with us.'

23So they put forward two, Joseph who was called Barsabbas and
whose surname was Justus, and Matthias. 24So they prayed. 'Lord,'
they said, 'you know the hearts of all men. Show us which of these
two you have chosen 25to take his place in this service, and to become
one of our apostolic company, which Judas left to go the way which
he had chosen for himself.' 26So they cast lots for them, and the lot
fell on Matthias, and he was elected to office with the eleven apostles.

Chapter 2

THE disciples were all passing the day of Pentecost together. 2All of
a sudden a sound came from the sky like a blast of violent wind,
and it filled the whole house where they were sitting. 3There appeared
to them what looked like tongues of fire, which divided themselves
up, and settled on each one of them. 4They were all filled with the
Holy Spirit, and began to speak in other languages, as the Spirit
enabled them to speak.

5There were Jews staying in Jerusalem, devout men who had come
from every nation under the sun. 6When they heard the sound of
this, they came in their crowds. They were bewildered, because each
of them was hearing the disciples speaking in his own language.
7They were astonished and amazed. 'Aren't all these men who are
speaking Galilaeans?' they said. 8'How then is it that each one of us
hears them speaking in the language we have spoken since we were
born? 9Parthians and Medes and Elamites, those whose homes are in
Mesopotamia, Judaea and Cappadocia, Pontus and Asia, 10Phrygia and
Pamphylia, Egypt and the Cyrenian parts of Libya, visitors from
Rome, 11Jews and converts to Judaism, Cretans and Arabians, we are
hearing them telling of God's great deeds in our own languages.'
12They were all astonished, and completely at a loss what to make of
it. 'What is the meaning of this?' they said to each other. 13Others
treated the whole affair as a jest. 'They are full of new wine,' they
said.

14Peter stood up with the eleven and addressed them in a voice that
all could hear. 'Men of Judaea,' he said, 'and all you whose homes are
in Jerusalem, understand this and listen to what I have to say. 15These
men are not, as you suggest, drunk, for it is only nine o'clock in the
morning. 16So far from that, this is what the prophet Joel spoke
of:

17"In the last days, God says,
I will pour out a share of my Spirit on all mankind.
Your sons and your daughters will become prophets,
your young men will see visions,
and your old men will dream dreams.

18In those days I will pour out a share of my Spirit
on my slave men and my slave girls,
and they will become prophets.
19I will show wonders in the sky above,
and visible demonstrations of my divine power on the earth below,
blood and fire and a mist of smoke.
20The sun will be turned into darkness,
and the moon into blood,
before the great day of the Lord comes in all its splendour.
21And it shall be that everyone who calls on the name of the Lord
will be saved."

22'Men of Israel, listen to what I have to say. Jesus of Nazareth was
a man attested to you by God by miracles and deeds which were
amazing demonstrations of divine power in action. God was acting
through him, and you saw it, and this is a fact of which you your-
selves are well aware. 23In the prearranged plan and knowledge of
God this man was handed over to you, and you killed him, by having
him crucified by heathen men, who had no knowledge of the Law of
God. 24But God loosed the pangs of death, and brought him back to
life again, for it was impossible that he should remain under death's
control. 25For David says of him:

"I saw the Lord always before me,
for he is at my right hand, and therefore I cannot be shaken.
26Therefore my heart was glad, and my tongue rejoiced,
and my life was passed in hope,
27because you will not abandon my soul to the land of the dead,
nor will you allow your Holy One to experience death's decay.
28You have made known to me the paths that lead to life.
You will fill me with gladness, and you will give me your presence."

29'Brothers, as far as the patriarch David is concerned, I can say to
you with no fear of contradiction that he both died and was buried.
His tomb is here to this day. 30Because he was a prophet, and because
he knew that God had given his sworn promise that one of his de-
scendants should sit on his throne, 31he foresaw the resurrection of
the Messiah, and it was about him that he spoke, because in point of
fact the Messiah was not abandoned to the land of the dead, nor did
his flesh experience death's decay. 32That God resurrected this Jesus
is a fact of which we have personal knowledge. 33Now that he has

been exalted to the right hand of God, and now that he has received
from the Father the Holy Spirit, whom he had promised, he has given
this demonstration of the Spirit, which you are now both seeing and
hearing.
34 'David did not ascend into the heavens, but he says:

> "The Lord said to my Lord, Sit at my right hand
> 35 until I make your enemies a footstool for your feet."

36 So then the whole house of Israel must realize for sure that God has
made this Jesus whom you crucified both Lord and Messiah.'

37 When they heard this, it pierced their very hearts. 'Brothers,' they
said to Peter and to the rest of the apostles, 'what are we to do?'
38 'You must repent here and now,' Peter said to them, 'and you must,
each one of you, be baptized in the name of Jesus Christ. Then your
sins will be forgiven, and you will receive the free gift of the Holy
Spirit. 39 For the promise is to you and to your children, and to all
who are a long way away. It is to anyone whom the Lord our God
invites.'
40 Peter laid the facts about Jesus before them at length. 'Save your-
selves from the perverse age in which you live,' he urgently appealed
to them. 41 So those who accepted his message were baptized, and on
that day their numbers received an addition of about three thousand
people.

42 They spent all their time in listening to the apostles as they
taught, and in fellowship, and in breaking bread, and in prayers. 43 A
sense of awe was in the hearts of all, and many wonderful demonstra-
tions of God's power in action were given through the apostles. 44 All
those who had come to believe remained together, and had every-
thing in common. 45 It was their custom to sell their goods and
possessions, and to share out the proceeds among them, as any might
need. 46 Day by day they spent their time in worshipping in the Temple
together, and in breaking bread in each other's houses, and they ate
their share of the food with glad and generous hearts. 47 They were
always praising God, and everyone liked them. The Lord added to
their number those who were daily being saved.

Chapter 3

PETER and John were on their way up to the Temple at the hour of
prayer, at three o'clock in the afternoon. 2A man who had been
born lame was being carried in. He was laid every day at the gate of
the Temple called the Beautiful Gate, to beg for alms from the
people who were going into the Temple. 3When he saw Peter and John
about to enter the Temple, he asked to be given alms. 4Peter looked
intently at him, and so did John. 'Look at us,' Peter said. 5He gave
them all his attention, in the expectation of getting something from
them. 6'I haven't got any silver or gold,' Peter said, 'but I give you
what I have. In the name of Jesus of Nazareth—walk!' 7He gripped
him by the right hand and lifted him up. His feet and ankles were im-
mediately strengthened. 8He jumped up and stood and walked about,
and went into the Temple with them, walking and jumping and
praising God. 9Everyone saw him walking and praising God, 10and
they recognized him as the man who sat begging at the Beautiful Gate
of the Temple. They were amazed and astonished at what had hap-
pened to him. 11The man was holding on to Peter and John. All the
people came running to them in astonishment, to the portico called
Solomon's Portico.

12When Peter saw this, he said to the people: 'Men of Israel, what is
there in this to surprise you so much? Why are you staring at us, as if
it was by our own power or piety that we had made him walk?
13The God of Abraham and of Isaac and of Jacob, the God of our
ancestors, has in this event glorified his servant Jesus, whom you
handed over to Pilate, and whom you repudiated, when Pilate's
judgment was that he should be released. 14You repudiated the Holy
and Just One, and asked as a favour for the release of a man who
was a murderer. 15You killed the man who blazed the way that leads
to life, but God brought him back to life, a fact which we can person-
ally guarantee. 16It is the name of Jesus and faith in that name which
have given strength to this man whom you see and know. It is the
faith which this name awakens that has given him perfect health as
all of you can see. 17And now, brothers, I know that it was in ignor-
ance that you acted, as did your rulers. 18But this was God's way of
fulfilling everything which he foretold through the prophets that the

Messiah should suffer. 19So then repent and turn to God, if you want
the record of your sins to be blotted out, 20if you want to enjoy
times of refreshing sent by the Lord, and if you want him to send
the Messiah, whom he has already appointed—I mean Jesus. 21Heaven
must receive him until the time of that restoration of all things of
which God spoke long ago through his dedicated prophets. 22Moses
said: "The Lord your God will send into the world for you a prophet
from your own people, as he sent me. You must listen to everything
that he says to you. 23Every living creature who refuses to listen to
that prophet will be exterminated from the people of God." 24The
whole succession of the prophets, who spoke from Samuel onwards,
have proclaimed the coming of this present time. 25You are the de-
scendants of the prophets and the children of the covenant, which
God made with your ancestors, when he said to Abraham: "Blessing
will come to all the families on earth through your descendants."
26When God sent his servant into the world, he sent him to you first,
to bring you this blessing by making each one of you abandon his
wicked ways.'

Chapter 4

WHILE Peter and John were speaking to the people, the priests and
the chief of the Temple police and the Sadducees came up.
2They were annoyed because the disciples were setting themselves up
as teachers of the people, and because they were proclaiming that the
resurrection of the dead had happened in Jesus. 3So they seized them
and placed them under arrest, for by that time it was evening, intend-
ing to deal with them the next day. 4Many of those who had heard
Peter's sermon became believers, to the number of about five thous-
and men.

5On the next day there was a meeting in Jerusalem of their leaders
and of the elders and the experts in the Law. 6Annas the High Priest,
and Caiaphas and John and Alexander, and the whole high-priestly
clan were there. 7They called the disciples forward and asked them:
'By what power, or by the use of what name, did you do this?' 8Then
Peter, filled with the Holy Spirit, said to them: 'Leaders of the people
and elders, 9if we today are under examination in regard to the help
that was given to a sick man, if the point at issue is by whose agency

this man has been restored to health and strength, 10we are bound to
inform you and the whole people of Israel that this was done by the
name of Jesus Christ of Nazareth. You crucified him: God brought
him back to life, and it is through him that this man stands before
you completely cured. 11This Jesus is

"the stone which was contemptuously rejected by you builders,
the stone which has become the stone which holds
the whole building together."

12In no one else is there salvation. His is the only name in all the
world, given to mankind, by which you must be saved.'
13When they saw the fearlessness of Peter and John, and when they
realized that they were men who had no education and no expert
knowledge, they were astonished, and they recognized them as hav-
ing been among the supporters of Jesus. 14When they saw the man
standing with them completely cured, they had no answer.
15They told them to leave the Sanhedrin and to wait outside. They
then discussed the problem in private. 16'What are we to do with these
men?' they said. 'It is quite clear to everyone who lives in Jerusalem
that they have been the means of a very remarkable demonstration
of the power of God in action. This is a fact which it is not possible for
us to deny. 17To prevent this affair influencing more and more of the
people, the best thing that we can do is to warn them that the con-
sequences for them will be very serious, if they do not agree never
again to speak to anyone in the name of this person Jesus.' 18So they
called them in, and they forbade them absolutely to speak or teach
in the name of Jesus. 19Peter and John answered them: 'You must
judge for yourselves whether it is right in God's sight to pay more
attention to your instructions than to God's, 20 for it is not possible
for us to stop speaking about what we have seen and heard.' 21When
they had warned them further of the consequences of disobedience,
they let them go, for they could find no way to punish them because
of the people. They were all praising God for what had happened,
22for the man to whom the divine demonstration of healing had
happened was more than forty years old.

23When they were released, they went to their own people, and told
them all that the chief priests and the elders had said. 24When they
heard the story, they joined in united prayer to God. 'Lord,' they said,
'you who made heaven and earth and the sea and everything in

them, 25you who said through the Holy Spirit in the words of our
ancestor David your servant:

> "Why did the nations rage,
> and the peoples form their futile plans?
> 26The monarchs of earth rose up,
> and the leaders banded themselves together
> against the Lord and against his Anointed One."

27It is true that in this very city Herod and Pontius Pilate united with
the Gentiles and the peoples of Israel against your holy servant Jesus,
whom you anointed as Messiah, 28to do to him all that your power
and purpose had already decided should be done. 29And now, O Lord,
in this present situation, look at their threats, and grant to your
servants fearlessly and freely to speak your word, 30and act yourself
to heal and to cause wonderful demonstrations of your power to
happen through the name of your holy servant Jesus.'

31When they had prayed, the place in which they were assembled
was shaken, and they were all filled with the Holy Spirit, and they
freely and fearlessly spoke God's word.

32The whole body of those who had placed their faith in Jesus was
united in heart and soul. None of them claimed that anything he
possessed was his own; they had everything in common. 33The
apostles powerfully asserted their personal knowledge of the fact of
the resurrection of the Lord Jesus. They were greatly respected by
everyone. 34In their fellowship no one was in need. All who possessed
estates and houses sold them, and brought the proceeds of the sales,
35and handed them over to the apostles, and it was shared out to
each of them as anyone might require.

36Joseph, who had been given the name Barnabas by the apostles
(the name means son of comfort), who was a Levite and a Cypriot by
race, 37had a piece of ground. He sold it, and brought the money, and
handed it over to the apostles.

Chapter 5

A MAN called Ananias with his wife Sapphira sold a piece of property.
2He took part of the proceeds and handed it to the apostles, 2but,
with his wife's connivance, he retained a certain amount of the
purchase price. 3'Ananias,' Peter said, 'why have you allowed Satan
to persuade you to lie to the Holy Spirit by retaining a part of the
price of your piece of land? 4While it remained unsold, did it not re-
main your own? And, when it was sold, were you not absolutely free
to do what you liked with the proceeds? What put it into your head
to do this? It is not to men that you have told a lie, but to God.'
5While Ananias was listening to what Peter was saying, he collapsed
and died. Everyone who was listening was terrified. 6The young
men rose and wrapped up his body and carried him out and buried
him.

7About three hours afterwards his wife came in, quite unaware of
what had happened. 8'Tell me,' Peter said to her, 'was it for so much
that you sold the piece of land?' 'Yes,' she said, 'for so much.' 9Peter
said to her: 'Why did the two of you come to an agreement to see
what the Spirit of the Lord would let you away with? Look, you can
hear at the door the footsteps of those who buried your husband, and
they will carry you out too.' 10There and then she collapsed at his
feet and died. When the young men came in, they found her dead,
and carried her out, and buried her beside her husband. 11The whole
Church and all who heard about this were terrified.

12Wonderful demonstrations of the power of God in action were
publicly performed by the disciples. Their common meeting place
was in Solomon's portico. 13None of the others had the courage to
attach themselves to them, but the people regarded them with the
greatest respect. 14Believers in the Lord were increasingly added to
their number, both men and women in crowds. 15So much was this
the case that they carried the sick on to the streets, and laid them
on beds and stretchers, so that even Peter's shadow, as he passed
along, might fall on some of them. 16The crowd came from the
towns around Jerusalem as well, bringing the sick and those who
were troubled by unclean spirits, and they were all cured.

17The High Priest and his supporters, that is, the party of the

Sadducees, were consumed with envy, 18and they proceeded to arrest
the apostles. They committed them to the public prison. 19But
during the night an angel of the Lord opened the prison doors and
brought them out. 20'Go and take your stand in the Temple,' he said
to them, 'and tell the people all about this new life.' 21When they had
heard this, they went into the Temple soon after dawn and pro-
ceeded to teach. When the High Priest and his supporters arrived,
they summoned a meeting of the Sanhedrin, that is, of the whole
Jewish senate. They sent orders to the prison for them to be brought.
22The Temple police arrived and found that they were not in the
prison. They returned and told their story. 23'We found the prison
perfectly securely locked, and the guards standing at the doors,' they
said, 'but, when we opened the doors, we found no one inside.'
24When the chief of the Temple police and the chief priests heard this
report, they were at a loss to know what had happened to them.
25Someone arrived with the news: 'The men you put in prison are
standing in the Temple teaching the people.' 26Then the chief of
the Temple police went with his officers and brought them. They
used no force, for they were afraid that if they did so they would be
stoned by the people.

27So they brought them in and placed them before the Sanhedrin.
28'Did we not strictly order you,' the High Priest demanded, 'not to
teach in this name? And you have filled Jerusalem with your teaching,
and you are out to fasten the responsibility for this man's death on
us.' 29Peter and the apostles answered: 'We must obey God rather
than men. 30You murdered Jesus by hanging him on a cross, but
the God of our fathers brought him back to life. 31God has exalted
him to a place on his right hand as Leader and Saviour, and through
him he offers repentance to Israel and forgiveness for their sins.
32We can personally guarantee the truth of these statements, and
so can the Holy Spirit, whom God has given to those who obey
him.'

33When they heard this, they were infuriated and wanted to kill
them. 34But one of the Pharisees, called Gamaliel, a universally
honoured teacher of the Law, rose in the Sanhedrin. He gave orders
for the men to be removed from the Sanhedrin for a little. 35'Men of
Israel,' he said to them, 'think carefully what you are going to do in
the case of these men. 36Before this, Theudas appeared on the scene
with a claim to be someone, and about four hundred men attached

themselves to him. He was killed, and all who accepted his claims
were dispersed, and the whole affair came to nothing. 37After him
Judas the Galilaean appeared on the scene at the time of the census,
and persuaded some of the people to revolt to him. He too was
wiped out, and all who accepted his claims were scattered. 38In the
present situation my advice to you is, drop the case against these men
and let them go, because, if what they are planning and doing is of
no more than human origin, it will come to nothing. 39But, if its
origin is from God, nothing you can do will destroy them. You
must be very careful not to turn out to be the opponents of God.'
40They accepted his advice. They called in the apostles and had them
flogged, and ordered them not to speak in the name of Jesus, and let
them go.

41They left the Sanhedrin rejoicing that they had been reckoned
worthy to be ill-treated for the Name. 42All day in the Temple and
from house to house they never stopped teaching, and telling the
good news that Jesus was the Messiah.

Chapter 6

At that time, when the number of the disciples was continually
growing, there arose a complaint on the part of the Greek-speak-
ing Jews from overseas against the Hebrew-speaking Jews of Palestine.
They alleged that their widows were being passed over in the daily
distribution of food. 2The Twelve summoned the body of the dis-
ciples. 'It is not right,' they said, 'that we should abandon the preach-
ing of God's word to spend our time serving food at tables. 3You,
brothers, must select from your number seven men of good reputa-
tion, spiritually-minded men with practical ability as well, and we
will put them in charge of this duty. 4This will leave us free to con-
centrate on prayer and on the task of preaching.' 5This suggestion
commended itself to the general body of the congregation. They
selected Stephen, a man full of faith and of the Holy Spirit, and
Philip, and Prochorus, and Nicanor, and Timon, and Parmenas,
and Nicolaus, a convert to Judaism who came from Antioch. 6They
brought them to the apostles, who prayed and laid their hands on
them.

7The word of God was spreading widely, and the number of the

disciples in Jerusalem continued to be greatly increased; and a great
many of the priests were accepting the faith.

8Stephen, full of grace and power, publicly gave wonderful demon-
strations of the power of God in action. 9Some members of the
Synagogue of the Freedmen, as it is called, and of the Cyrenians and
Alexandrians, and of those from Cilicia and Asia proceeded to enter
into debate with Stephen. 10They were quite unable to put up any
defence against the inspired wisdom with which he spoke.

11They then in an underhand way put forward men to say: 'We
heard him making blasphemous statements against Moses and against
God.' 12They incited the people and the elders and the experts in the
Law to action, and they attacked and seized him, and brought him
into the Sanhedrin. 13They produced lying witnesses to say: 'This
fellow never stops making statements calculated to decry the Holy
Place and the Law. 14For we heard him say that this Jesus of Nazareth
will destroy this place and will radically alter the customs which
Moses handed down to us.' 15All those who were sitting in the San-
hedrin looked intently at Stephen, and his face looked to them like
the face of an angel.

Chapter 7

THE high priest said to him: 'Is this so?' 2'Brothers and fathers,'
Stephen said, 'give me a hearing. The God of glory appeared to
our father Abraham while he was in Mesopotamia, before he came to
live in Charran. 3He said to him: "Leave your country and your kin-
dred, and go into the country which I will show you." 4At that time
he left the country of the Chaldaeans and settled in Charran. After
the death of his father, God removed him from there into the
country in which you now live. 5But at that stage he did not give him
possession of even one foot of it, but he did promise to give him and
his descendants after him possession of it, although at the time he
had no child.

6'What God said to him was this. He told him that his descendants
would be aliens in a land which belonged to others, and that for
four hundred years they would be enslaved and ill-treated there.
7"But," God said, "my judgment will come upon that nation to
whom they will be enslaved, and they will afterwards leave that

country, and will worship me in this place." 8And God gave Abraham
the covenant, of which circumcision is the mark. Thus when Abra-
ham had a son Isaac he circumcised him when he was eight days old,
and Isaac became the father of Jacob, and Jacob became the father of
the twelve patriarchs.

9'The patriarchs were jealous of Joseph, and sold him into Egypt.
But God was with him 10and rescued him from all his troubles. God
enabled him by his wisdom to win the approval of Pharaoh, king of
Egypt. Pharaoh appointed him governor over the whole of Egypt,
and over all his affairs. 11There was a famine over the whole of
Egypt and Canaan. There was great distress, and our fathers could
find no food. 12When Jacob heard that there was grain to be had in
Egypt, he sent our fathers on a first expedition there. 13On their
second visit Joseph told his brothers who he was, and Joseph's family
became known to Pharaoh. 14Joseph sent and invited Jacob his father
and the whole clan—about seventy-five persons—to leave their
homes and to come to Egypt. 15So Jacob came down to Egypt, and he
died there and so did our fathers. 16Their bodies were taken back to
Shechem, and laid in the tomb which Abraham had bought for a
sum of silver from the family of Emmor in Shechem.

17'When the time was approaching for the fulfilment of the promise
which God had made to Abraham, the number of the people had
grown and increased in Egypt. 18This went on until there came to the
throne another Egyptian king who had never heard of Joseph.
19This king began a subtle persecution of our nation. He compelled
our fathers to expose their children, so that the children would never
live to grow up. 20It was at that time that Moses was born. He was a
child of quite exceptional beauty. For three months he was brought
up in his father's house. 21Then, when he had to be exposed, Pharaoh's
daughter adopted him, and brought him up as her own son. 22Moses
was educated in all the wisdom of the Egyptians, and he was able both
in speech and in action.

23'When he was forty years old, the idea came to him to visit his
fellow-countrymen, the sons of Israel. 24He went to the help of one
of them, whom he saw being unjustly treated. He stood up for the
rights of the ill-used man, and struck the Egyptian. 25He thought that
his fellow-countrymen would understand that God was going to
rescue them through him. But they did not understand. 26The next
day he came upon two of them fighting with each other, and tried to

stop them quarrelling. "Men," he said to them, "you are fellow-
countrymen. What's the point of injuring each other?" 27But the
man who was injuring his neighbour pushed him away. "Who," he
said, "appointed you as a ruler or judge over us? 28Do you want to
murder me in the way you murdered the Egyptian yesterday?"
29When he heard this, Moses fled. He went into exile in the country of
Midian, and there he became the father of two sons.

30'When forty years had passed, when he was in the desert of Mount
Sinai, an angel appeared to him in a flame of fire in a bush. 31When
Moses saw this, he was amazed at the sight. When he went up to look
at it, God's voice came to him: 32"I am the God of your fathers, the
God of Abraham, of Isaac, and of Jacob." Moses, shaking with fear,
did not dare to look. 33"Remove your sandals from your feet," the
Lord said to him, "for the place on which you are standing is holy
ground. 34I have seen the ill-treatment which my people are receiving
in Egypt, and I have heard their groans, and I have come down to
rescue them. Come now! I am going to send you to Egypt." 35It was
this very Moses whom they had rejected. It was to him they said:
"Who appointed you a ruler or a judge?" It was this man whom
God sent to be their leader and liberator, through the angel who
appeared to him in the bush. 36It was he who led them out, after
providing wonderful demonstrations of the power of God in action
in the country of Egypt and at the Red Sea and in the desert for forty
years. 37It was this Moses who said to the Israelites: "God will raise up
a prophet from your own fellow-countrymen, as he raised me up."
38He it was who, on the day on which the people assembled in the
desert, acted as intermediary between the angel who talked with him
on Mount Sinai and our fathers. He received living words to give to
us, 39but your fathers refused to obey him. Instead of that they
rejected him, and their hearts turned back to Egypt. 40They said to
Aaron: "Make us gods who will lead us on our journeyings, for,
as for this Moses who brought us out of the country of Egypt, we do
not know what has happened to him."

41'At that time they made a calf, and offered sacrifice to that idol,
and held high revelry to celebrate what their hands had made. 42So
God turned from them, and abandoned them to the worship of the
host of the sky, as it stands written in the book of the prophets:

"Did you bring sacrifice and offerings to me
in the wilderness for forty years, O house of Israel?

43Was it not the moving shrine of Moloch you took with you,
and the star of the god Rephan,
the images that you manufactured to worship?
Therefore, I will send you into exile beyond Babylon."

44'It was the Tent of Witness that our fathers had with them in the
desert. It was constructed as he who spoke to Moses ordered, follow-
ing the pattern which Moses had seen. 45It was this Tent of Witness
which our fathers brought in with Joshua, when they took possession
of the territories of the nations whom God drove out before our
fathers, and which they handed down from generation to generation
right down to the time of David. 46David was dear to God, and he
asked to be allowed to provide a dwelling-place for the God of Jacob.
47But it was Solomon who built a house for him. 48But the Most
High does not live in man-made houses. As the prophet says:

49"Heaven is my throne,
and earth is a footstool for my feet.
What kind of house will you build for me? says the Lord,
or what is the place where I am to rest?
50Is it not my hand which has made everything?"'

51'Stubborn men that you are, with hearts and ears no better than
the uncircumcised heathen, you are always resisting the Holy Spirit.
As your fathers did so, so do you. 52Was there a prophet whom your
fathers did not persecute? They killed those who told in advance
about the coming of the Just One. And now you have betrayed and
murdered him, 53and you are the people who received the Law,
transmitted to you by angels—and you have not obeyed it!'

54Stephen's speech so infuriated them that they gnashed their teeth
at him. 55But he, filled with the Holy Spirit, gazed up into heaven,
and saw the glory of God, and Jesus standing at God's right hand.
56'I see the heavens standing open,' he said, 'and the Son of Man
standing at God's right hand.'

57At this they shrieked and shut their ears and rushed at him in a
body. 58They threw him out of the city, and stoned him. The wit-
nesses left their clothes in charge of a young man called Saul. 59So
they stoned Stephen, and, as they did so, he prayed: 'Lord Jesus,
receive my spirit!' 60Then he knelt down, and said in a voice that all
could hear: 'Lord, do not hold this sin against them.' When he had
said this, he fell asleep in death.

Chapter 8

SAUL thoroughly approved of Stephen's murder.
At that time a savage outbreak of persecution against the Jerus-
alem church began. With the exception of the apostles, they were all
dispersed all over Judaea and Samaria. 2Devout men took away
Stephen's body and buried it, and paid it the last tribute of mourning.
3Saul began a merciless attack upon the church. He went from house
to house, seizing both men and women, and committing them to
prison.

4Those who were dispersed went all over the country, bringing the
message of the Good News. 5Philip went down to a town in Samaria
and proclaimed the Messiah to them. 6The crowds as one man listened
eagerly to what Philip was saying, when they heard his words, and
saw the demonstrations of divine power in action which he was
performing. 7Unclean spirits came out of many who were possessed
by them, shrieking as they came out, and many who were paralysed
and lame were cured. 8There was great joy in that city.

9There was in that town a man called Simon, who, before Philip
arrived, had astonished the people of Samaria with his displays of
magic. He claimed to be someone great. 10Everyone of every age
and class listened eagerly to him. 'This man,' they said, 'is the power
of God which is called "The Great".' 11They listened eagerly to him,
because for some considerable time he had been astonishing them
with his magic. 12Both men and women were baptized, when they
took the decision to believe the Good News which Philip was bringing
them about the Kingdom of God, and about Jesus Christ.

13Simon himself took the decision to believe, and, after he had
been baptized, he was constantly in Philip's company. He was aston-
ished as he watched things happening which were great demonstra-
tions of the power of God in action.

14When the apostles in Jerusalem heard that Samaria had welcomed
the message of God, they despatched Peter and John to them. 15They
came down, and prayed for them to receive the Holy Spirit. 16As yet
the Holy Spirit had not descended on any of them. They had so far
been baptized only in the name of the Lord Jesus. 17Then they laid
their hands on them, and they received the Holy Spirit.

18When Simon saw that the Holy Spirit was given through the lay-

ing on of the apostles' hands, he offered them money. 19'Give me too
this gift,' he said, 'so that anyone on whom I lay my hands may
receive the Holy Spirit.' 20Peter said to him: 'May both you and your
money perish together, because you thought you could buy for
money the gift God gives freely. 21This is a matter in which you have
no share or part, for your heart is not right in God's sight. 22Repent
of this wickedness of yours. Pray to God to forgive you, if it is possible,
that such an idea ever entered your mind. 23It is plain to me that you
are no better than the slave of wickedness, on the way to tasting the
bitterness like gall which godless worship brings.' 24'It is you who
must pray to the Lord for me,' Simon answered, 'so that none of the
things you have spoken of may happen to me.'

25So when they had spoken the message of the Lord, and when they
had demonstrated its truth by powerful arguments, they started out
back to Jerusalem, and on the way they brought the Good News to
many Samaritan villages.

26An angel of the Lord spoke to Philip. 'Up,' he said, 'and go south
on the road which goes down from Jerusalem to Gaza.' (This is the
desert road.) 27So he set out. There was an Ethiopian, a eunuch, a
minister of state of Candace, the Ethiopian queen, her chancellor of
the exchequer, who had come to worship at Jerusalem, 28and who was
now on his way home. He was sitting in his carriage, reading the
prophet Isaiah. 29The Spirit said to Philip: 'Go and join the carriage.'
30So Philip ran up, and heard him reading the prophet Isaiah aloud.
'Do you understand what you are reading?' he said. 31'How can I
understand,' he said, 'without someone to be my guide?' He invited
Philip to get in and sit with him. 32This was the passage of scripture
which he was reading:

'He was led like a sheep to be slaughtered,
and, like a lamb, voiceless when its fleece is being cut,
he did not open his mouth.
33He was humiliated and he received no justice.
Who shall describe the family from which he came,
for his life is taken away from the earth?'

34The eunuch said to Philip: 'Tell me, please, who is the prophet
speaking about? Is it about himself or about someone else?' 35Then
Philip began to speak. Starting from this passage of scripture, he told
him the Good News about Jesus. 36As they were going along the road,

they came to some water. 'Here is water,' the eunuch said. 'Is there
any reason why I should not be baptized?'* 38He ordered the carriage
to halt. Philip and the eunuch both went down into the water, and
Philip baptized him.

39When they came up out of the water, the Spirit of the Lord
seized Philip, and he was gone from the eunuch's sight. The eunuch
continued his journey rejoicing. 40Philip arrived in Azotus. He made
a tour of all the towns, spreading the Good News, until he reached
Caesarea.

Chapter 9

SAUL, still in a frenzy of murderous threats against the disciples of
the Lord, went to the High Priest, 2and asked for an official author-
ization to go to Damascus to the synagogues there. His purpose was
to bring as prisoners to Jerusalem any adherents of the Way whom he
might find there, men and women alike.

3On his journey he had reached the outskirts of Damascus, when
all of a sudden a blaze of light from the sky flashed around him. 4He
threw himself to the ground. He heard a voice saying to him: 'Saul,
Saul, why are you persecuting me?' 5'Who are you, Lord?' he said.
The speaker answered: 'I am Jesus, and it is I whom you are persecut-
ing. 6But get up, and go into the town, and you will be told what you
must do.' 7His fellow-travellers stood speechless, for they heard the
voice, but saw no one. 8Saul got up from the ground, but, when he
opened his eyes, he was unable to see anything. So they took his
hand, and led him into Damascus. 9For three days he was unable to
see, and he ate and drank nothing.

10In Damascus there was a disciple named Ananias. 'Ananias,' the
Lord said to him in a vision. 'Here I am, Lord,' he said. 11'Get up,' the
Lord said to him, 'and go to the street called Straight, and ask at
Judas' house for a man from Tarsus, called Saul. He is praying, 12and
in a vision he has seen a man called Ananias coming and laying his
hands on him, to give him back his sight.' 13'Lord,' said Ananias, 'the
harm this man has done to God's people in Jerusalem is common
talk. 14And I have heard too that he has arrived here authorized by

*Here some manuscripts insert verse 37, '*If you believe with your whole heart,' Philip said, 'it can be done.' 'I believe,' he answered, 'that Jesus Christ is the Son of God.*'

the chief priests to arrest all who call on your name.' 15'Go,' the Lord
said to him, 'because I have specially chosen this man to be my
instrument to tell heathen nations and kings and the sons of Israel
about me, 16for I will show him all that he must suffer for my sake.'
17Ananias went off, and went into that house, and laid his hands
upon him. 'Brother Saul,' he said, 'the Lord—Jesus who appeared to
you on the road as you were on your way here has sent me—to enable
you to recover your sight, and so that you may be filled with the
Holy Spirit.' 18Thereupon a substance like scales fell from Saul's eyes,
and he recovered his sight, and got up, and was baptized. 19When he
had taken some food, his strength returned.

Saul remained with the disciples at Damascus for some time. 20He
immediately preached Jesus in the synagogues. 'This,' his message
was, 'is the Son of God.' 21His hearers listened with astonishment.
'Isn't this the man,' they said, 'who in Jerusalem carried on a merciless
campaign against those who call on this name? And wasn't the very
purpose for which he came here to bring them as prisoners to the
chief priests?' 22But Saul preached with increasing power and be-
wildered the Jews who lived in Damascus by proving that Jesus is the
Messiah.

23After some considerable time, the Jews formed a plot to murder
him. 24But Saul got to know about their plot. They were watching
the town gates night and day in order to murder him. 25But his dis-
ciples took him during the night and lowered him in a basket down
over the wall.

26When he arrived in Jerusalem, he tried to attach himself to the
disciples. But they were afraid of him, because they did not really
believe that he was a disciple. 27Barnabas took him, and brought him
to the apostles, and told them the whole story of how Saul had seen
the Lord on the road, and of how the Lord had spoken to him, and
of how in Damascus he had freely and fearlessly preached in the name
of Jesus. 28So he became an accepted member of the community at
Jerusalem, 29and he preached freely and fearlessly in the name of the
Lord. He talked to the Greek-speaking Jews, and debated with them.
They tried to murder him. 30But his fellow-Christians got news of
the plot, and brought him down to Caesarea, and sent him off to
Tarsus.

31So the church enjoyed peace all over Judaea and Galilee and

Samaria, and continued to be built up, and to live in the fear of the
Lord. Through the encouragement of the Holy Spirit the church
continued to grow.

32During his travels amongst them all, Peter came down to God's
people who lived at Lydda. 33There he came upon a man called
Aeneas who had been bed-ridden for eight years. He was paralysed.
34'Aeneas,' Peter said to him, 'Jesus Christ is curing you. Get up, and
make your own bed.' There and then he got up. 35Everyone who
lived at Lydda and Sharon saw him, and they turned to the Lord.

36At Joppa there was a disciple called Tabitha, a name which
means Dorcas, that is, Gazelle. She was constantly engaged in doing
good works and in acts of charity. 37It so happened that at that time
she fell ill and died. They washed her body, and laid it in an upper
room. 38Since Lydda was near Joppa, the disciples had heard that
Peter was there. So they sent two men with an invitation to come to
them. 'Please include us in your travels,' they said, 'and don't delay.'
39Peter started out and went with them. When he arrived, they took
him up into the upper room. All the widows stood there beside him
weeping, and showing him the tunics and cloaks Dorcas used to
make when she was with them. 40Peter put them all outside. He knelt
and prayed. Then he turned to the dead woman and said: 'Tabitha,
get up!' She opened her eyes, and saw Peter, and sat up. 41He gave her
his hand and helped her to stand. Then he called in God's people and
the widows, and presented her to them alive. 42What had happened
became known all over Joppa, and many believed in the Lord. 43Peter
stayed in Joppa for some considerable time with Simon, a tanner.

Chapter 10

IN Caesarea there was a man called Cornelius, who was a company
commander in the Roman army in what was called the Italian
battalion. 2He was a devout man and reverenced God, and so did all
his household. He was generous in public acts of charity, and constant
in private prayer to God.

3In a vision, about three o'clock in the afternoon, he clearly saw an
angel of God coming down to him, and saying: 'Cornelius!' 4He
gazed at the angel in awe. 'What is it, sir?' he said. The angel said to

him: 'Your prayers and your acts of charity have gone up to God, and
they have made God think very specially about you. 5And now you
must send men to Joppa, and you must bring here a man Simon, who
is called Peter. 6He is staying as a guest with a man Simon, a tanner,
whose house is on the sea-shore.' 7When the angel who spoke to him
had gone away, Cornelius called two of his servants and a devout
soldier, who was one of his personal attendants. 8He told them the
whole story, and sent them off to Joppa.

9On the next day, while they were on their way, and when they
were nearing the town, Peter went up on to the flat roof of the house
to pray. It was about twelve o'clock midday. 10He became hungry and
wanted something to eat. While food was being prepared for him, he
fell into a trance, 11in which he saw heaven standing open, and an
object like a large sheet coming down. It was let down by the four
corners, until it rested on the ground. 12On it there were all the
four-footed animals, all the reptiles that creep on the ground and all
the birds which fly in the sky. 13He heard a voice. 'Up, Peter!' it said,
'Kill and eat!' 14'Certainly not!' Peter said. 'I have never eaten any-
thing which is defiled and unclean.' 15A second time he heard a voice.
'You must not regard as defiled what God has cleansed,' it said to him.
16This happened three times, and immediately afterwards the sheet
was taken back up into heaven.

17While Peter was quite at a loss to understand what the vision he
had seen could mean, the men who had been sent by Cornelius had
enquired their way to Simon's house, and stood at the gate. 18They
called out to ask if Simon called Peter was staying as a guest there.
19While Peter was thinking about the vision, the Spirit said to him:
'Three men are here asking for you. 20Go down, and don't hesitate
to go with them, because it is I who have sent them.'

21Peter came down. 'I am the man you are looking for,' he said to
the men. 'What brought you here?' 22They said: 'Cornelius, a com-
pany commander, a good man and a man who reverences God, and
who is held in high reputation by the whole Jewish nation, was in-
structed by a holy angel to send for you to come to his house, and to
listen to what you have to say.' 23Peter invited them in as his guests.
The next day he left with them, and some of the members of the
congregation at Joppa accompanied him.

24On the following day they entered Caesarea. Cornelius was ex-
pecting them, and had invited his relations and his closest friends to
join him. 25When Peter was about to go into his house, Cornelius

came to meet him and knelt at his feet, and worshipped him. 26Peter
lifted him up. 'Get up!' he said. 'I too am a man.' 27So Peter went into
the house in conversation with him, and found a large gathering of
people there.

28'You are well aware,' Peter said, 'that it is against the Law for a
Jew to have any contact with a foreigner, or to visit him in his house.
But God has shown me that I must not regard any human being as
defiled or unclean. 29That is why I came without any objection when
you sent for me. Tell me, then, what was your reason for sending for
me?' 30'Four days ago, exactly to this very hour,' said Cornelius, 'I was
praying in my house at three o'clock in the afternoon, when a man
in shining clothes stood in front of me. 31"Cornelius," he said, "your
prayer has been heard, and your acts of charity have not gone un-
noticed by God. 32Send, then, to Joppa, and invite Simon, called Peter,
to come to you. He is a guest in the house of Simon a tanner, who
lives in a house on the sea-shore." 33So without delay I sent for you,
and I am very grateful to you for coming. So now we are all here in
God's presence to listen to everything that you have been instructed
by the Lord to say.' 34Peter began to speak. 'I am truly convinced,' he
said, 'that there is no favouritism with God, 35but that he is ready to
receive any man in any nation who reverences him and who does
what is right. 36You know the message that God sent to the people of
Israel, when he sent the Good News of peace with himself through
Jesus Christ—and Jesus is Lord of all. 37You know what happened all
over Judaea. You know how it all began in Galilee, after the baptism
which John proclaimed. 38You know about Jesus of Nazareth, and
how God anointed him with the Holy Spirit and with power, and
how he went about helping everyone, and curing all those who were
under the tyranny of the devil, because God was with him. 39We are
eye-witnesses of all that he did in Judaea and in Jerusalem. You know
how they killed him by hanging him on a cross. 40On the third day
God brought him back to life again, in such a way that he was plainly
and unmistakably seen, 41not by the whole people, but by witnesses
who had been already chosen by God, seen, I mean, by us. We actually
shared meals with him after he had come back to life again. 42He gave
us orders to preach to the people, and to convince them that it is he
who has been destined to be the judge of the living and of the dead.
43All the prophets are witnesses to him, and to the fact that everyone
who believes in him receives forgiveness of sins through him.'

44While Peter was still speaking, the Holy Spirit descended on all

who had been listening to what he was saying. 45The Jewish believers
who had come with Peter were all amazed, because the gift of the
Spirit had been given so freely and generously to people who were not
Jews, 46for they heard them speaking with tongues and praising God.
Then Peter said: 47'Can anyone forbid water to be brought, and can
anyone try to stop these people being baptized? They have received
the Holy Spirit, just as we have done.' 48He gave orders for them to be
baptized in the name of Jesus Christ. Then they asked him to wait
with them for some days.

Chapter 11

THE apostles and the members of the Christian community in
Judaea heard that people who were not Jews had received the
message of God. 2When Peter came up to Jerusalem, the Jewish
Christians questioned his action. 3'You went into the homes of men
who are uncircumcised heathens,' they said, 'and shared meals with
them.'

4Peter began at the beginning, and told them the whole story step
by step. 5'I was praying in the town of Joppa,' he said, 'when in a
trance I saw a vision. I saw an object like a large sheet coming down.
It was being let down by the four corners, and it came right down to
me. 6I looked at it closely and tried to make out what it was. I saw on
it the four-footed animals that walk on the ground, the wild beasts
and the reptiles and the birds of the sky. 7I heard a voice. "Up, Peter!"
it said. "Kill and eat!" 8"Certainly not, sir," I said, "because no defiled
or unclean food has ever entered my mouth." 9The voice spoke a
second time from heaven. "You must not regard as defiled," it said,
"what God has cleansed." 10This happened three times, and then
everything was drawn up again into heaven.

11'At that very moment three men arrived at the house where we
were. They had been sent from Caesarea to me. 12The Spirit told me
not to hesitate to go with them. These six members of the congre-
gation came with me, and we went into the man's house. 13He told
us the story of how he had seen the angel standing in his house, and
how the angel had said to him: "Send to Joppa, and bring here Simon
called Peter. 14He will tell you how you and the members of your
household will be saved." 15No sooner had I begun to speak than the
Holy Spirit descended upon them, as he did on us too at the begin-

ning. 16I remembered how the Lord had said: "John baptized with
water, but you will be baptized with the Holy Spirit." 17If then God
gave them, when they believed in the Lord Jesus Christ, the same gift
as he gave to us, when we first believed, who was I to try to hinder
God? Could I thwart him?'

18When they heard this story, they at once abandoned their op-
position and praised God. 'We can only believe,' they said, 'that God
has given to the Gentiles too the repentance which is the way to life.'

19Those who had been dispersed because of the trouble which
resulted from the case of Stephen penetrated as far as Phoenicia and
Cyprus and Antioch, but they preached the word to no one except to
Jews. 20But there were some of them, men who came from Cyprus
and Cyrene, who arrived in Antioch and who preached there to the
Greeks as well, telling them the Good News of the Lord Jesus. 21The
Lord was their ally, and a large number believed and turned to the
Lord.

22News of what they were doing reached the ears of the congrega-
tion in Jerusalem. So they despatched Barnabas to Antioch. 23When
he arrived and saw God's grace in action, he was glad, and he urged
them all to remain resolutely loyal to the Lord, 24for he was a good
man, full of the Holy Spirit and of faith. The Lord's followers were
increased in crowds. 25Barnabas went to Tarsus to look for Saul.
26When he had found him, he brought him to Antioch. For a whole
year they were the guests of the church there, and they gave in-
struction to crowds of people. It was in Antioch that the disciples were
first called Christians.

27During that time prophets came down from Jerusalem to
Antioch. 28One of them, called Agabus, rose and foretold through
the Spirit that there was going to be a severe famine all over the in-
habited world. This happened in the time of Claudius. 29The disciples
resolved to send help to the Christian community in Jerusalem, each
making the contribution he could afford. 30This they did, and they
sent their contributions to the elders through Barnabas and Saul.

Chapter 12

At that time Herod launched a violent attack on certain members
of the church. 2He beheaded James, John's brother. 3When he
saw that this was a policy which delighted the Jews, he went on to
arrest Peter. (It was during the Festival of Unleavened Bread.) 4He
seized Peter and put him into prison. He handed him over to four
squads of soldiers, each with four men in it, to guard him, for it was
his intention to put him on public trial after the Passover Festival.

5So Peter was closely guarded in prison, but all the time the church
was earnestly praying to God for him. 6On the night before Herod
was going to bring him into court, Peter, fettered with two chains,
was sleeping between two soldiers, and the guards, stationed in front
of the door, were keeping watch over the prison. 7An angel of the
Lord appeared, and a light shone in the building. The angel touched
Peter's side, and wakened him. 'Quick!' he said. 'Up!' His fetters fell
from his hands. 8'Fasten your belt,' the angel said, 'and put on your
sandals.' Peter did so. 'Put on your coat,' the angel said, 'and follow
me.'

9So he went out and followed him. He did not realize that what
was being done by the angel was really happening; he thought that
he was seeing a vision. 10They passed through the first and second
guards, and came to the iron gate which led into the city. All by itself
it opened for them. They went out, and they went one street farther,
and then suddenly the angel left him.

11When Peter came to his senses, he said: 'Now I know for certain
that the Lord sent his angel and rescued me from what Herod was
going to do to me, and from what the Jewish people hoped would
happen.' 12When he realized what had happened, he made his way
to the house of Mary, the mother of John, who was called Mark.
Many had gathered there, and were praying. 13Peter knocked at the
door of the gateway, and a maidservant called Rhoda came to answer
his knock. 14She recognized Peter's voice, and she was so overcome
with joy that, instead of opening the gate, she ran in with the news
that Peter was standing at the gate. 15'You're raving,' they said to her.
She insisted that he was there. 'It is his angel,' they said. 16Peter went
on knocking. When they opened the door, they were astonished to
see him. 17He signed to them with his hand to be quiet, and he told

them the story of how the Lord had brought him out of prison.
'Take the news to James and to the members of the church,' he said
to them. And he went out, and went to another place.

18When day came there was consternation among the soldiers.
They could not think what had happened to Peter. 19When Herod
had ordered a search to be made for Peter, and had failed to find him,
he examined the guards, and ordered them to be executed. Herod
then left Judaea, and went down to Caesarea, and stayed some time
there.

20Herod was angry with the people of Tyre and Sidon. They came
to him in a body, and, when they had gained the support of Blastus,
the king's chamberlain, they sued for peace, for their country de-
pended for its food supplies on the king's country. 21A day was fixed,
and on it Herod put on his royal robes, and took his seat on the bench
in his court, and made an oration to them. 22'It is the voice of a god,
and not of a man,' the people kept shouting. 23There and then an
angel of the Lord struck him, because he did not give the glory to God;
and he was eaten by worms and died.

24The word of the Lord flourished increasingly. 25Barnabas and Saul
completed their mission and then returned from Jerusalem. They
brought with them John, who was called Mark.

Chapter 13

In the congregation at Antioch there was a group of prophets and
teachers. There were Barnabas and Simeon, who was called Niger,
and Lucius who came from Cyrene, and Manaen, who as a boy
had been brought up with Herod the tetrarch, and Saul. 2When they
were worshipping the Lord and fasting, the Holy Spirit said: 'Come!
I want you to assign Barnabas and Saul to the special task to which I
have summoned them.' 3When they had fasted and prayed, they laid
their hands on them and sent them.

4After they had been given their marching orders by the Holy Spirit,
they went down to Seleucia, and from there they sailed to Cyprus.
5When they arrived in Salamis, they proclaimed the message of God
in the Jewish synagogues. They had John with them as their helper.
6They made a tour of the whole island as far as Paphos. There they
met a Jew who was a religious impostor and a practising sorcerer. His

name was Bar-Jesus. 7He enjoyed the patronage of Sergius Paulus, the
proconsul, an intelligent man. Sergius Paulus invited Barnabas and
Saul to visit him, for he was eager to hear the message of God. 8Elymas
the sorcerer—this is the translation of his name—did everything pos-
sible to obstruct them, and did his best to sidetrack the proconsul's
interest in the faith. 9But Saul, whose other name is Paul, was filled
with the Holy Spirit, and looked steadily at him. 10'You utter fraud!'
he said. 'You complete villain! You son of the devil! You enemy of
all goodness! Will you not stop trying to make men lose the way
to God? 11Now the Lord has struck! For a time you will be blind, and
you will not be able to see the light of the sun.' There and then a
mist and a darkness fell upon him, and he went about looking for
people to lead him by the hand. 12When the proconsul saw what
had happened, he decided to accept the Christian faith, for he was
astonished at the teaching of the Lord.

13Paul and his friends set sail from Paphos, and arrived at Perga
in Pamphylia. John left them, and went back to Jerusalem. 14They
went across country from Perga and reached Pisidian Antioch. On
the Sabbath day they went into the synagogue, and took their seats.
15After the reading of the Law and the Prophets the synagogue
officials sent them an invitation. 'Brothers,' they said, 'if you have any
message of exhortation for the people, please give it.'

16So Paul rose, and with a gesture of his hand he said: 'Men of Israel,
and you who, although you are not Jews, reverence God, give me a
hearing. 17The God of this people Israel chose our fathers. During
their stay as aliens in Egypt he raised the people to greatness. He
demonstrated his power by leading them out of Egypt, 18and for some
forty years he supported them in the desert. 19He destroyed seven
nations in the country of Canaan, and then gave them possession of
that country for a period of four hundred and fifty years. 20Following
that, he gave them judges down to the time of the prophet Samuel.
21They then asked for a king, and God gave them Saul, Kish's son.
He belonged to the tribe of Benjamin, and he reigned for forty years.
22Then God deposed him, and made David their king. He showed his
opinion of David's character when he said: "I have found David the
son of Jesse to be a man after my own heart, a man who will do all
that I want him to do."

23'It is one of this man's descendants whom God, as he promised,
has made saviour for Israel—I mean Jesus. 24Before he came, John
called upon the whole people of Israel to be baptized as a sign of their

penitence. 25 When John was nearing the end of his career, he said:
"What do you suppose me to be? I am not he. But after me there is
someone coming whose shoe laces I am not fit to untie." 26 Brothers
—I speak both to those of you who are directly descended from
Abraham and to those of you who, although you are not Jews, share
our worship of God—it is to us that this message of salvation has
been sent.

27 'The citizens of Jerusalem and their leaders failed to recognize
him, and they failed to understand what the prophets said, although
the books of the prophets are read to them every Sabbath; but by
condemning him to death they fulfilled these very prophecies.
28 Though they could find no charge to justify his death, they asked
Pilate to have him killed. 29 When they had finished doing everything
to him that scripture said had to be done, they took him down from
the cross, and laid his body in a tomb. 30 But God brought him back
to life again. 31 Over a period of some considerable time he appeared
to those who came up from Galilee to Jerusalem with him, and they
can supply first-hand evidence to the people that this is so. 32 We
bring to you the Good News that God has made the promise that he
gave to our ancestors 33 come true for our children, by bringing Jesus
back to life, as it stands written in the second psalm:

> "You are my son,
> today I have begotten you."

34 As for the fact that he did bring him back to life again, never again
to return to death's decay, this is what he says:

> "I will give you the blessings of David holy and certain."

35 That is why in another passage he says:

> "You will not allow your holy one to experience death's decay."

36 David served the will of God in his own day and generation, and
slept the sleep of death, and went to join his ancestors. He thus did
actually experience death's decay. 37 But he whom God brought back
to life again never experienced death's decay. 38 Brothers, we want
you to know that forgiveness of sins is offered to you through this man,
39 and that everyone who believes in him is acquitted from everything
for which the Law of Moses could never gain acquittal. 40 You must
be very careful to see to it that what the prophet spoke about does
not happen to you:

41"Look, you scoffers, wonder and perish!
For in your days I will do something,
Something you will never believe,
even if someone tells you of it." '

42As they were leaving the synagogue, the congregation urged them
to come and talk about these things to them again on the next
Sabbath. 43When the congregation was dispersed, many of the Jews
and many of the Gentiles, who had been converted to Judaism and
who worshipped with them, accompanied Paul and Barnabas, who
continued to talk to them and to try to persuade them to commit
themselves to the grace of God.

44On the next Sabbath almost the whole population of the town
gathered to listen to the message of the Lord. 45The Jews were con-
sumed with jealousy when they saw the crowds. They contradicted
everything that Paul said, but it was invective rather than argument
that they used. 46Paul and Barnabas did not mince their words. 'We
were bound to give you the first opportunity to hear God's message,'
they said. 'But, since you rejected it, and since by so doing you stand
self-condemned as not fit to receive eternal life, we turn to the
Gentiles. 47This is what God has instructed us to do:

"I have made you a light for the Gentiles,
So that through you salvation may be brought
to the ends of the earth." '

48When the Gentiles heard this, they were glad, and they praised
the Lord for the message he had sent; and all who were destined for
eternal life became believers. 49The message of the Lord spread all
over the countryside.

50But the Jews exerted their influence on pious and aristocratic
women and on the leading men of the town, and thus instigated
persecution against Paul and Barnabas, and they ejected them from
their district. 51They shook the last speck of dust from their shoes,
to show them that they regarded them as godless heathens, and went
to Iconium; 52and the disciples were filled with the joy of the Holy
Spirit.

Chapter 14

IN Iconium they went in the same way into the Jewish synagogue,
and they spoke with such effect that a large number of both the Jews
and the Greeks believed. 2The Jews who refused to believe incited the
Gentiles, and deliberately poisoned their minds against the members
of the Christian community. 3They spent some considerable time
there, speaking fearlessly with complete confidence in the Lord, who
confirmed the message of his grace by enabling them to perform
wonderful demonstrations of the divine power in action.
4The population of the town was split in two. Some sided with the
Jews and some with the apostles. 5But, when they became aware that
there was a move afoot both of the Jews and of the Gentiles and their
leaders savagely to attack and to stone them, 6they made their escape
to the Lycaonian towns of Lystra and Derbe and the surround-
ing country. 7There they continued to tell the story of the Good
News.

8In Lystra there was a man whose feet were helpless. He had been a
cripple since he was born and had never walked. 9He listened to Paul
speaking. Paul looked intently at him, and saw that he had faith to be
cured. 10He said to him in a commanding voice: 'Get up, and stand
erect on your feet!' The man jumped up and began to walk.
11When the crowds saw what Paul had done, they shouted in the
Lycaonian language: 'The gods have taken human form, and have
come down to us.' 12They called Barnabas Zeus, and Paul Hermes,
because he was the chief speaker. 13The priest of Zeus, whose temple
was just outside the town gates, brought bulls and garlands to the
gates, for he and the people wanted to offer sacrifice. 14When the
apostles Barnabas and Paul heard what was going on, they ripped
their clothes in distress, and rushed into the crowd. 15'Men,' they
shouted, 'why are you doing this? We too are men with feelings
exactly the same as yours, and we are bringing you the Good News
which invites you to turn from these futile things to a God who is
alive, the God who made the sky and the earth and the sea, and
everything in them. 16In past ages he allowed all the nations to go
their own way. 17And yet he did not leave himself with nothing to
point men to himself. He showed his kindness to you by giving you

rains from the sky, and the seasons, each with its crops, and by satisfy-
ing your hearts with food and joy.' 18Even though they said this, they
could hardly stop the crowds sacrificing to them.

19A group of Jews arrived from Antioch and Iconium, and they so
worked on the crowds that they stoned Paul, and dragged him out of
the town, thinking that he was dead. 20But, when the disciples were
standing in a circle round him, he got up and went into the town.
The next day he left for Derbe with Barnabas.

21After they had told the Good News to that town, and had made
many disciples, they returned to Lystra and to Iconium and to
Antioch. 22In each place they fortified the souls of the disciples, and
urged them to stand fast in the faith. 'Through many trials,' they said,
'we must find our way into the Kingdom of God.' 23When they had
appointed elders for them in each congregation, and when they had
prayed and fasted, they committed them to the Lord in whom they
had believed. 24So they went through Pisidia, and came to Pamphylia.
25When they had preached their message in Perga, they reached the
coast at Attaleia. 26From there they sailed to Antioch, where they had
been commended to the grace of God for the task which they had
now completed. 27When they arrived there, they called a meeting of
the congregation, and told them the story of all that God had done
along with them, and how he had opened the door of faith to the
Gentiles. 28They spent a long time with the disciples.

Chapter 15

A GROUP of men came down from Judaea, and tried to teach the
members of the Christian community that, if they were not
circumcised, as the Mosaic practice demanded, it was not possible
for them to be saved. 2Paul and Barnabas strongly differed from them
and hotly debated with them. It was decided that Paul and Barnabas
and some others of them should go up to meet the apostles and
elders in Jerusalem to discuss the whole question with them. 3When
they had been sent on their way by the congregation, they went
through Phoenicia and Samaria, telling the story of the conversion
of the Gentiles as they went, and all the members of the Christian
communities were delighted to hear it.

4When they arrived in Jerusalem, they were welcomed by the

congregation and the apostles and the elders, and they told them the
news of all that God had done in company with them.
5Some men who had accepted the faith, and who belonged to the
party of the Pharisees, rose and said that the Gentiles must be cir-
cumcised, and that they must enjoin them to observe the Law of
Moses. 6The apostles and the elders held a meeting to examine the
whole matter. 7After a long debate Peter rose. 'Brothers,' he said to
them, 'you are aware that in the very early days of our faith it was
God's choice that I should be the means whereby the Gentiles heard
the message of the Gospel, and accepted it. 8And God, who knows the
hearts of all, signified his approval by giving them the Holy Spirit,
exactly as he gave him to us too. 9He made no distinction between
them and us, for it was by faith that he purified their hearts. 10Why,
then, are you trying to make God change his mind, by insisting that
the disciples should submit to a yoke which neither we nor our fathers
were able to bear? 11Surely the fact is that we believe that it is through
the grace of the Lord Jesus Christ that we were saved, just as they
have been.'
12At this the whole assembly fell silent. They proceeded to listen to
Barnabas and Paul recounting the story of all the wonderful demon-
strations of divine power that God had shown among the Gentiles
through them.
13When they had finished speaking, James said: 'Brothers, give me
a hearing. 14Simeon has related to you the story of the first occasion
when God demonstrated his care for the Gentiles, and his intention
to take from them a people for himself. 15And this is precisely what
the prophets said would happen. You remember the passage:

16"After this I will return,
and I will rebuild the fallen dwelling of David.
I will rebuild the ruins,
and I will set it up again,
17in order that the rest of mankind may seek the Lord,
and all the Gentiles who are called by my name,
18says the Lord who has made these things known long since." '

19'It is therefore my considered judgment that we should not lay un-
necessary burdens on the Gentiles who turn to God, 20but that we
should instruct them to have nothing to do with anything which
has been polluted by contact with idols, and to have nothing to do
with unchastity, and not to use as food the flesh of animals which

have been killed by strangling, and from which the blood has not
been properly drained away.* 21 If anyone still personally wants to
observe the Law he can do so, for from ancient times there have been
those in every town who proclaimed the Law of Moses, and it is still
read in the synagogues every Sabbath.'

22 Then the apostles and the elders, together with the whole congre-
gation, decided to choose men to represent them, and to send them
to Antioch with Paul and Barnabas. It was Judas, called Barsabbas, and
Silas, leading men in the Christian community, whom they chose.
23 They gave them this written message to take with them: 'As brothers
to brothers, we the apostles and elders send our greetings to those in
Antioch and Syria and Cilicia who have come into the church from
the Gentiles. 24 Since we heard that some people from us have dis-
turbed you and have unsettled your minds with their statements,
although they were not acting under instructions from us, 25 after
we had held a meeting, we decided to choose men and to send them
to you, with our beloved Barnabas and Paul, 26 who are men who have
risked their lives for the sake of our Lord Jesus Christ. 27 So we have
sent Judas and Silas, and they will tell you by word of mouth the
same things as are in this letter.

28 'The Holy Spirit and we have decided to lay no further burden on
you other than these necessary things—29 that you must have nothing
to do with meat which has formed part of a sacrifice to an idol, that
you must not use as food the flesh of animals from which the blood
has not been properly drained away, and which have been killed by
being strangled, and that you must have nothing to do with un-
chastity. If you carefully guard against these things, you will do well.
Farewell!'

30 When they had been sent on their way, they went down to
Antioch. There they called a meeting of the congregation, and
delivered the letter to them. 31 When they had read the letter, they
rejoiced in the encouragement it gave them. 32 Judas and Silas, for
they themselves were prophets, said much to encourage the Christian
community, and to settle them more firmly in the faith. 33 When
they had stayed for some time, the community sent them back to
those who had sent them, with every good wish for their welfare.

Both here and at verse 29 there are variations in the text. Some manuscripts omit, *that you must have nothing to do with unchastity*. Some omit, *which have been killed by being strangled*. Some add after *unchastity*, *and not to do to others anything they would not wish them to do to themselves*.

35But Paul and Barnabas stayed on in Antioch, teaching and telling
along with many others the Good News of the message of the Lord.

36Some time later, Paul said to Barnabas: 'Let us go back and visit
the Christian communities in every town in which we proclaimed the
message of the Lord, and let us see how things are going with them.'
37Barnabas wished to take John, called Mark, with them as well.
38But Paul did not think it wise to take with them the man who had
been a deserter in Pamphylia, and who had not gone with them to
the work. 39There was such a sharp difference of opinion between
them that they parted company, and Barnabas took Mark and
sailed to Cyprus, 40while Paul chose Silas and went off, after he had
been committed to the Lord's grace by the Christian community.
41He made a tour of Syria and Cilicia, strengthening the congre-
gations as he went.

Chapter 16

PAUL reached Derbe and Lystra. There was a disciple called Timothy
there. He was the son of a Jewess who was a Christian, but his
father was a Greek. 2He was well spoken of by the members of the
Christian community in Lystra and Iconium. 3Paul wanted him to
come away with him. So he took him and circumcised him, so as not
to prejudice his work among the Jews of those parts, for they all
knew that his father had been a Greek.

4On their way through the towns, they passed on to them the
decisions which had been reached by the apostles and elders in
Jerusalem, and told them to observe them. 5So day by day the congre-
gations were strengthened in the faith, and increased in number
more and more.

6They made a tour of the Phrygian and Galatian district, because
they had been prevented by the Holy Spirit from telling the message
in Asia. 7When they reached the borders of Mysia, they tried to
make their way into Bithynia, but the Spirit of Jesus did not allow
them to do so. 8So they skirted Mysia, and came down to the sea-
coast at Troas.

9During the night a vision appeared to Paul. The vision was of a man
from Macedonia, standing there pleading with him. 'Come over into

Macedonia and help us,' the man said. 10 When Paul had seen the
vision, we immediately looked for some means of getting to Mace-
donia, for we concluded that God had called us to tell them the
Good News. 11 So we set sail from Troas, and had a straight run to
Samothrace. On the next day we reached Neapolis. 12 From there we
went on to Philippi, the leading town of that district of Macedonia,
and a Roman colony. We spent some days in this town.

13 On the Sabbath we went out through the town gate along the
river bank, where we expected to find a place where the Jews met for
prayer. When we reached it, we sat down and began to talk to the
women who had come to the meeting. 14 There was a woman called
Lydia there. She was a dealer in purple dye, and she came from the
town of Thyatira. Although she was a Gentile, she was a worshipper
of God. She listened, because the Lord had opened her heart, and
awakened her interest in what Paul had to say. 15 When she and all her
household had been baptized, she urged them: 'If you are really con-
vinced that I am a loyal follower of the Lord, come to my house and
stay with me.' And she would take no refusal.

16 As we were on our way to the place of prayer, a little slave-
girl, who was regarded as being inspired by the spirit of Apollo, met
us. Her owners made a handsome profit out of her fortune-telling.
17 She kept following Paul and us and shouting: 'These men are the
servants of the Most High God, and they are proclaiming to us the
way of salvation.' 18 She kept on doing this for many days. Paul could
stand it no longer. He turned and said to the spirit: 'In the name
of the Lord Jesus Christ I order you to come out of her.' There and
then it came out of her.

19 When her owners saw that their hope of profit was gone, they
seized Paul and Silas, and forcibly led them to the city square to the
town officials. 20 They brought them to the magistrates. 'These men,'
they said, 'who are Jews, are disturbing our town. 21 They are trying
to propagate ways of life which it is quite wrong for us who are
Romans to accept or to practise.' 22 The mob joined in attacking them.
The magistrates forcibly stripped them, and ordered them to be
flogged. 23 When they had given them a severe beating, they threw
them into prison, with strict orders to the gaoler to keep them
securely. 24 Since he had received such an order, he flung them into
the inner prison, and fastened their feet in the stocks.

25About midnight Paul and Silas were praying and singing hymns to
God. The prisoners were listening to them. 26Suddenly there was so
violent an earthquake that the foundations of the prison were shaken.
Immediately all the doors burst open, and the fetters of all the
prisoners were loosened from the wall.

27When the gaoler awoke, and saw the doors standing open, he
drew his sword and was about to commit suicide, for he thought that
his prisoners had escaped. 28'Don't injure yourself,' Paul shouted to
him. 'We are all here.' 29The gaoler called for lights and rushed in,
shaking in every limb. He threw himself down at the feet of Paul and
Silas. 30He brought them out and said: 'Sirs, what must I do to be
saved?' 31They said: 'Commit yourself to the Lord Jesus Christ, and
you and your family will be saved.' 32They told the message of the
Lord to him and to his whole household.

33There and then, although it was in the middle of the night, he
took them in and bathed the weals the flogging had left on them. He
and all his family were at once baptized, 34and he took them into his
house and provided them with a meal. He rejoiced, and so did all his
family, that he had become a believer in God.

35When day came, the magistrates sent their attendants to say:
'Let these men go!' 36The gaoler reported this message to Paul. 'The
magistrates,' he said, 'have sent orders for your release. So now, come
out, and go on your way, and all good things go with you!' 37But
Paul said to him: 'They publicly flogged us without a trial, and they
flung us into prison—and we are Roman citizens! And now are they
going to put us out and hush the business up? They are not going to
get away with that! Tell them to come themselves and take us out!'
38The attendants reported to the magistrates what Paul had said. The
magistrates were terrified when they heard that they were Roman
citizens. 39So they came and apologized to them, and took them out,
and requested them to leave the town. 40When they had left the
prison, they went to Lydia's house, and, when they had seen the
members of the Christian community, and had spoken encourag-
ingly to them, they left.

Chapter 17

WHEN they had taken the road through Amphipolis and Apol-
lonia, they arrived in Thessalonica, where there was a Jewish
synagogue. 2As he always did, Paul went into the synagogue, and for
three Sabbaths he argued with them on the basis of scripture, 3ex-
pounding the scriptures and citing passages as evidence that the
Messiah had to suffer and come back to life again after he had died.
'This Jesus of whom I am telling you is the Messiah,' he said. 4Some
of them were convinced and attached themselves to Paul and Silas,
including many of the Greeks, who, without becoming Jews, at-
tended the synagogue to worship God, and the wives of many of the
leading men in the community.

5The Jews bitterly resented the success of Paul and Silas. They got
hold of some rascally street-corner idlers, and organized them into a
mob, and attempted to set the city in an uproar. They attacked
Jason's house. They were looking for Paul and Silas, to bring them
before the public assembly of the people. 6When they were unable to
find them, they dragged Jason and some of the members of the
Christian community to the magistrates. 'The men,' they shouted,
'who are reducing the whole civilized order of things to chaos, have
arrived here too, 7and Jason has received them as his guests. Their
conduct is in flat contradiction of the decrees of Caesar, for they are
declaring that someone else called Jesus is king.' 8The crowd and the
magistrates were disturbed when they heard this, 9and they bound
over Jason and the others to keep the peace, and let them go.

10The members of the Christian community immediately sent
Paul and Silas away to Beroea under cover of night. When they
arrived there, they made their way to the Jewish synagogue. 11The
Jews there were more generous in their sympathies than those in
Thessalonica. They listened eagerly to the Christian message, and
they examined the scriptures every day, to find out if what Paul was
saying was really true. 12Many of the Jews took the decision to believe,
and so did a considerable number of wealthy Greek women, and men
too. 13When the Thessalonian Jews learned that the message of God
had been proclaimed by Paul in Beroea too, they came there also, and
proceeded to incite the crowds to riot and disorder. 14The Christian

community immediately sent Paul off on the road to the sea-coast.
Silas and Timothy remained there in Beroea. 15 Paul's escort convoyed
him as far as Athens. They left him after he had given them instruc-
tions to Silas and Timothy to join him as soon as possible.

16 While Paul was waiting for them in Athens, the sight of the city
in the grip of idol-worship angered him. 17 In the synagogue he carried
on an argument with the Jews and with the Gentiles, who, without
becoming Jews, attended the synagogue to worship God. And every
day he talked in the city square with those whom he happened to
meet.

18 Some of the Epicurean and Stoic philosophers encountered him.
Some of them said: 'What can this fellow with his ill-digested scraps
of knowledge mean?' Others said: 'He seems to be a preacher of
foreign divinities.' This was because Paul was telling the good news
of Jesus and the resurrection. 19 They took him and brought him to
the Court of the Areopagus. 'May we know,' they said, 'what this
new and strange teaching of yours is all about? 20 Some of the things
you are trying to introduce sound very strange to us. We would
like to know what they mean.' 21 The Athenians and the foreigners
who live in Athens spend all their time in nothing other than in
talking about and listening to whatever is the latest novelty.

22 Paul took his stand in the middle of the Court of the Areopagus.
'Men of Athens,' he said, 'I cannot help seeing that generally speaking
you tend to be a very religious people. 23 As I was walking through the
city, and as I was looking at the objects of your worship, in addition
to all the other things, I came on an altar inscribed: "To an Unknown
God." I have come to tell you about that which you worship without
knowing what you are worshipping.

24 'The God who made the world and everything that is in it is the
Lord of heaven and earth. He does not have his home in man-made
temples, 25 nor can he be served by human hands, as if he stood in
need of anything that men could give him. It is he who gives to all
men life and breath and all things. 26 He created every nation of man-
kind of one common stock, and gave them their homes all over the
world. He fixed the appointed periods of every nation's rise and fall,
and settled the boundaries within which they were to live. 27 He
created them to seek God, with the hope that they might grope after
him in the shadows of their ignorance, and find him—and indeed
he is close to each one of us. 28 "In him we live and move and are," as

even some of your own poets have said, "We are his children."
29Since we are the children of God, we ought not to think that the
Deity is like an image of gold or silver or stone, fashioned by human
art and design. 30God shut his eyes to the folly of those times when
men knew no better. But now he is issuing his orders to all men
everywhere to repent, 31because he has fixed a day on which his
righteous judgment will come upon the world, through a man
whom he has destined for that task. He has provided proof to all men
that this is so by bringing this man Jesus back to life when he was dead.'

32When they heard of the resurrection of dead men, some laughed
the whole matter out of court. But some said: 'We would like you to
talk to us again about this.' 33With the discussion at this stage Paul
left the court.

34There were some who attached themselves to him, and who
decided to become believers. Among them were Dionysius, a member
of the Court of the Areopagus, and a woman called Damaris, and
others along with them.

Chapter 18

AFTER that Paul left Athens and went to Corinth. 2There he made
the acquaintance of a Jew called Aquila. Aquila's family belonged
to Pontus, but he had newly arrived from Italy with Priscilla, his
wife. They had had to leave Italy, because Claudius had issued an
order that all Jews must remove themselves from Rome. Paul went to
visit them. 3Because he was of the same trade as they were, he stayed
with them, and worked with them, for they were leather-workers
by trade.

4He argued the case for Christianity every Sabbath in the synagogue,
and tried to convince both Jews and Greeks. 5When Silas and Timothy
came down from Macedonia, Paul began to devote himself entirely to
preaching, insisting to the Jews that the Messiah was Jesus. 6When
they opposed him with invective rather than with reason, he shook
out his clothes at them, as a Jew might shake the polluted dust from
his clothes, when he left a heathen town. 'The responsibility for your
fate is your own,' he said to them. 'No blame attaches to me. From now
on I will go to the Gentiles.' 7So he changed his lodging, and went to
stay in the house of a man called Titius Justus, a worshipper of God,
though not a Jew. This man's house was next door to the synagogue.

8Crispus, the president of the synagogue, became a believer in the
Lord with his whole household. Many of the Corinthians who
listened to Paul became believers and were baptized. 9During the
night the Lord said to Paul in a vision: 'Don't be afraid! Go on speak-
ing, and don't stop! 10For I am with you, and no one will try to harm
you, because there are many people in this city who belong to me.'
11Paul settled among them for a year and six months, engaged in the
work of instructing them in the message of God.

12When Gallio was proconsul of Achaia, the Jews made a con-
certed attack on Paul, and brought him to Gallio's court of justice.
13'This man,' they said, 'is trying to persuade people to worship God
in a way that is illegal.' 14When Paul was going to speak, Gallio
said to the Jews: 'If, you Jews, this was a matter of crime or of fraud, it
would be reasonable for me to agree to give you a hearing. 15But, if
this is a matter of debates about words, and about names, and about
your own law, you must deal with it yourselves. I have no desire to
give judgment on such things.' 16He forcibly ejected them from his
court. 17They all took Sosthenes, the president of the synagogue, and
beat him up in full view of Gallio's judgment seat. But Gallio was not
concerned with things like that.

18Paul stayed on for some considerable time longer. Then he said
goodbye to the members of the Christian community, and sailed
away to Syria, accompanied by Priscilla and Aquila. At Cenchreae he
had his hair cut off, because he had taken the Nazirite vow. 19When
they reached Ephesus, he left them and went by himself into the
synagogue, and debated with the Jews. 20When they asked him to
stay longer, he refused, 21but, when he had said goodbye to them, he
said: 'God willing, I will come back again to you.' So he sailed away
from Ephesus. 22He arrived in Caesarea, and from there went up to
Jerusalem, and greeted the congregation there. Then he went down
to Antioch. 23After spending some time there, he went on a tour of
the various places in the Galatian territory and in Phrygia, strengthen-
ing all the disciples as he went.

24A Jew, called Apollos, who was a native of Alexandria, arrived in
Ephesus. He was a man of culture, and able to make very effective use
of the scriptures. 25He had received instruction in the Way of the
Lord. He was filled with enthusiasm, and in his speaking and teaching
he gave an accurate account of the story of Jesus. But the only bap-

tism he knew was John's. 26He began to speak freely and fearlessly in
the synagogue. When Aquila and Priscilla had heard him speaking,
they took him and gave him a more accurate account of the Way of
God. 27When he wished to cross over to Achaea, the Christian com-
munity encouraged him to do so, and wrote to the disciples there to
give him a welcome. When he arrived, he was of great assistance to
those who through the grace of God had become believers, 28for he
strenuously out-argued the Jews in public debate, by proving through
the use of the scriptures that the Messiah is Jesus.

Chapter 19

WHILE Apollos was in Corinth, Paul went to Ephesus by way of the
inland route. There he met a group of disciples. 2He asked them
if they had received the Holy Spirit, when they became believers. 'No,'
they said. 'We have not even heard that there is a Holy Spirit.' 3'What
kind of baptism did you receive?' he said. 'John's baptism,' they said.
4Paul said: 'John's baptism was a baptism which was a sign of re-
pentance. It was in the One who was coming after him that he told
the people to believe, that is, in Jesus.' 5When they heard this, they
were baptized in the name of the Lord Jesus. 6When Paul laid his
hands on them, the Holy Spirit came upon them, and they began to
speak with tongues and to prophesy. 7In all there were about twelve
of these men.

8Paul went into the synagogue, and for three months he freely and
fearlessly debated about the Kingdom of God, and tried to persuade
men to accept it. 9When some in their obstinate refusal to believe
resorted to slanderous statements about the Way in the presence of
the whole congregation, Paul left them, and withdrew the disciples
with him, and carried on the debate daily in the lecture hall of
Tyrannus. 10This went on for two years, with the result that everyone
who lived in the province of Asia, both Jews and Greeks, heard the
message of the Lord. 11Through the hands of Paul, God performed
extraordinary miracles, 12so that sweat-bands or towels which had
been in contact with Paul's skin were taken away to those who were
ill, and their illnesses left them, and the evil spirits went out of them.

13Some of the itinerant Jewish exorcists ventured to pronounce the
name of the Lord Jesus over those who had evil spirits. 'I charge you

by the Jesus whom Paul preaches,' was their formula. 14There were
seven sons of a Jewish high priest called Scaeva who were doing this.
15But the evil spirit answered them: 'I know who Jesus is, and I under-
stand who Paul is—but who are you?' 16The man in whom the evil
spirit was jumped on them, and mastered and overpowered them all.
The result was that they fled from that house naked and wounded.

17When this became known to all the Jews and Greeks who lived
in Ephesus, they were terrified, and the name of the Lord Jesus came
to be regarded as something quite extraordinary. 18Many of them
accepted the Christian faith and came and confessed the error of
their ways, and revealed the secrets of their spells. 19Many of those
who practised sorcery brought their books and publicly burned them.
When they reckoned up the value of them, they found it came to
more than two thousand pounds.

20So the word of the Lord was powerfully increased and was
mightily effective.

21After all this had happened, Paul under the guidance of the Spirit
formed a plan to make a tour of Macedonia and Achaea, and then to
go on to Jerusalem. 'After I have been there,' he said, 'I must see
Rome too.' 22He sent two of his helpers, Timothy and Erastus, to
Macedonia, while he himself stayed on in Asia for some time.

23At that time the Way was involved in a violent commotion.
24There was a man called Demetrius, a silversmith, who made silver
models of the temple of Artemis, and who thereby provided very
considerable profit for the craftsmen. 25He called a meeting of the
craftsmen and of all who were similarly employed. 'Men,' he said to
them, 'you well know that our financial prosperity depends on this
business. 26You have the evidence of your eyes and ears that, not only
in Ephesus, but practically all over Asia, this fellow Paul has per-
suaded a great many people to change their ideas altogether, for he
says that the gods which are manufactured by hand are not gods at all.
27Not only is there a risk that our business is going to fall into dis-
repute, but there is also a danger that the temple of the great goddess
Artemis may come to be regarded as of no importance, and that she
whom Asia and the whole civilized world worships will be despoiled
of her majesty.' 28When they heard this they were furiously angry.
'Great is Artemis of the Ephesians!' they kept shouting.

29Confusion spread all over the city. They seized Gaius and Aris-
tarchus, fellow-travellers of Paul from Macedonia, and dragged them

along with them, as they rushed like one man to the city theatre.
30Paul wished to go into the crowd, but the disciples would not allow
him. 31Some of the Asiarchs, who were friendly with him, sent and
urged him not to risk going into the theatre. 32Some kept shouting
one thing, and others another, for the meeting was in complete con-
fusion, and the majority of them did not know why they had met.

33Some of the crowd conjectured that Alexander must be the ring-
leader of the trouble, for the Jews were pushing him forward. Alex-
ander wanted to speak to the people in his own defence, so he gestured
to the crowd to be silent. 34When they realized that he was a Jew, the
crowd roared like one man, and for about two hours they shouted
continuously: 'Great is Artemis of the Ephesians!'

35When the city secretary had succeeded in quietening the mob, he
said: 'Men of Ephesus, who is not well aware that the city of Ephesus
is warden of the temple of the great Artemis, and of the sacred image
which fell from heaven? 36No one can deny that this is so. You must
therefore keep calm and do nothing reckless. 37You have brought
these men here, although they are guilty neither of sacrilege nor of
blasphemy against our goddess. 38If Demetrius and his fellow-crafts-
men have a complaint against anyone, assizes are held, and there are
proconsuls. Let the parties to the dispute bring charges against each
other. 39If you have any further claim to make, the matter must be
settled in a legally constituted assembly of the people. 40In point
of fact we run the very real danger of being charged with rioting
because of today's proceedings, for there is no legitimate reason that
we can offer for this uproar.' 41With these words he dismissed the
assembly.

Chapter 20

WHEN the uproar had subsided, Paul sent for the disciples, and,
after he had spoken encouragingly to them, he said goodbye to
them, and left to go to Macedonia. 2He made a tour of those parts,
and gave the people there many an encouraging talk. Then he went
to Greece. 3When he had been there for three months, the Jews
hatched a plot against him, just when he was on the point of sailing
for Syria. He, therefore, decided to return through Macedonia.
4Sopater of Beroea the son of Pyrrhus, accompanied him, and so
did Aristarchus and Secundus of Thessalonica, Gaius of Derbe, and

Timothy, and Tychicus and Trophimus of Asia. 5They went on ahead,
and waited at Troas for us. 6We sailed from Philippi, after the Passover
week was finished, and five days later we caught up with them at
Troas, where we spent a week.

7On the Saturday evening we met for our common meal. Paul,
who was due to leave the next day, began to talk to them, and pro-
longed his talk till midnight. 8There were many lamps in the upper
room in which we were meeting. 9A young man, Eutychus, was sit-
ting in the window-seat. As Paul went on talking, he grew sleepier
and sleepier. Completely overcome by sleep, he fell from the third
storey to the ground below, and was picked up dead. 10Paul went
down and took him in his arms, and lay on top of him. 'Stop this
uproar,' he said. 'His life is still in him.' 11Paul went back upstairs,
and shared in the common meal with them. He talked long with
them until the dawn came, and then he left. 12They took the boy
away alive, and they were greatly relieved.

13We went on ahead to the ship, and set sail for Assos. We were to
take Paul on board there. That was the arrangement he had made, for
he intended to travel on foot. 14When he met us at Assos, we took him
on board, and proceeded to Mitylene. 15Next day we sailed from there
and arrived off Chios. The following day we crossed to Samos, and
on the day after that we reached Miletus, 16for Paul had decided not
to put in at Ephesus. He did not wish to be delayed in Asia, for he
was hurrying to reach Jerusalem, if possible, in time for the day of
Pentecost.

17From Miletus Paul sent to Ephesus, and asked the elders of the
congregation there to come to see him. 18When they arrived, he said
to them: 'You yourselves well know the kind of life I lived all the time
I lived amongst you from the day I first set foot in Asia. 19You know
how I served the Lord with all humility and with tears, amidst all the
trials I had to endure because of the plots of the Jews. 20You know
that I did not shrink from telling you all that was for your good, and
from teaching you publicly and in your own homes. 21You know
that to Jews and Greeks I continually insisted on the necessity of the
repentance which turns to God and on faith in our Lord Jesus. 22Now
I am going to Jerusalem, because the Spirit will not let me do any-
thing else. What will happen to me there, I do not know. 23I only
know that, as I go from town to town, the Holy Spirit leaves me in
no doubt that imprisonment and troubles are waiting for me there.

24 But I do not reckon my life of any importance, nor do I regard it as
precious to myself, so long as I can finish my course, and complete
the task which the Lord Jesus gave me to do for him, the task of
bearing my personal witness that the Good News of the grace of God
is true.

25 'And now I know that none of you, amongst whom I went about
preaching the Kingdom, will ever see me again. 26 I want to go on
record as saying to you today that I am responsible for the death of
no man's soul, 27 for I never shrank from telling you the whole pur-
pose of God. 28 Be careful about your own spiritual life, and care for
the flock in which the Holy Spirit has appointed you as guardians.
Make it your aim to be the shepherds of the church of God, which
he has bought for himself at the price of the blood of his own One.

29 'I know that after I am gone fierce wolves will get in among you,
and will not spare the flock. 30 I know that from your own members
men will emerge who will preach a perverted version of the truth in
an attempt to seduce the disciples from their loyalty, and to per-
suade them to follow them. 31 That is why you must be sleeplessly on
the watch. That is why you must remember that night and day for
three years I never stopped giving each one of you with tears the
advice which kept you right.

32 'Now I commit you to God and to the message of his grace, that
message which is able to build you up, and to give you a share in the
blessedness of all who have been consecrated to him. 33 I had no desire
to possess any man's money or finery. 34 You yourselves know that
these hands of mine worked for my own needs, and the needs of my
companions. 35 I have always shown you that we must work like this
to help those who are weak. We must always remember the words of
the Lord Jesus and never forget that it was he who said: "It is a happier
thing to give than to get." '

36 After Paul had said all this, he knelt down with them all and
prayed. 37 They all wept bitterly, and flung their arms round him, and
kissed him lovingly again and again. 38 What grieved them most of all
was that he had told them that they would never see him again.
They escorted him to the ship.

Chapter 21

WHEN we had torn ourselves away from them and set sail, we
made a straight run to Cos. The next day we reached Rhodes,
and from there we sailed to Patara. 2There we found a ship about to
make the crossing to Phoenicia. We went on board and set sail. 3We
sighted Cyprus, and left it on our port beam. We sailed on to Syria,
and put in at Tyre, for there the ship was to discharge her cargo.
4We sought out the local disciples, and stayed there for a week. They
told Paul through the Holy Spirit not to proceed with his journey to
Jerusalem. 5When we had come to the end of our time there, we
left to continue our journey. All of them, with their wives and chil-
dren, escorted us outside the town. We knelt down on the beach,
and prayed, and said goodbye to each other. 6Then we went on
board the ship, and they returned to their homes. 7When we had
completed our voyage from Tyre, and had reached Ptolemais, we
greeted the Christian community there, and stayed with them for
one day. 8We left on the next day, and arrived at Caesarea. We went
into Philip the Evangelist's house—he was one of the Seven—and
stayed with him. 9He had four unmarried daughters, who were
prophetesses.

10While we were staying there for several days, a prophet called
Agabus came down from Judaea. 11He came to us and took Paul's
belt, and tied up his own hands and feet with it. 'The message of the
Holy Spirit,' he said, 'is that this is the way in which the Jews in
Jerusalem will bind the man to whom this belt belongs, and will
hand him over to the Gentiles.' 12When we heard this, both we and
the local people pleaded with Paul not to go up to Jerusalem. 13Paul
answered: 'What do you mean by going on like this, weeping and
trying to crush the courage out of my heart? I am ready, not only to
be imprisoned, but even to die in Jerusalem for the sake of the Lord
Jesus.' 14When he would not be persuaded, there was nothing left for
us to say but: 'The Lord's will be done.'

15At the end of our time in Caesarea, after we had made all the
necessary preparations for the journey, we set out on the road up to
Jerusalem. 16Some of the disciples from Caesarea came with us, and
they took us to Mnason, a native of Cyprus, and one of the very

first disciples, in whose house hospitality was to be provided for us.
17 When we arrived in Jerusalem, the Christian community gladly
welcomed us. 18 On the next day Paul took us with him to pay a visit
to James. All the elders were also present. 19 When he had greeted
them, Paul gave them a detailed account of all that God had done
among the Gentiles through his ministry. 20 They praised God, when
they had heard the story. 'Brother,' they said to Paul, 'you see how
many thousands of Jews have accepted the Christian faith, and all of
them remain devoted adherents of the Law. 21 Rumours have reached
them that you teach all the Jews who live in Gentile communities to
desert their loyalty to Moses, and that you tell them not to circumcise
their children, and not to follow their ancestral customs. 22 What are
we to do about this? They will, of course, all hear that you have
arrived in Jerusalem. 23 We have a suggestion to make which you
would do well to act on.

'We have four men here who have put themselves under a volun-
tary vow. 24 Take these men. Join them in their ritual purifications.
Accept financial responsibility for their expenses. Then they will be
able to embark on their vow by having their heads shaved. Then
everyone will realize that the rumours they have heard about you
have no foundation in fact, but that, so far from that, you yourself
keep the Law, and guide your conduct by it. 25 As for the Gentiles who
have become believers, we have already issued our decision that they
must have nothing to do with meat that has formed part of the
sacrifice to an idol, that they must have nothing to do with meat
from which the blood has not been properly drained away, that they
must have nothing to do with meat from animals which have been
killed by strangling, and that they must have nothing to do with un-
chastity.'

26 Paul took the men, and on the next day, after he had undergone
ritual purification with them, he went into the Temple to give notice
of the date when the period of purification would be completed,
and when the necessary sacrifice could be offered for each of them.
27 When the week's period, which purification required, was almost
completed, the Asian Jews saw Paul in the Temple precincts. They
incited the mob to riot and seized Paul. 28 'Men of Israel,' they shouted,
'help! This is the man whose teaching is everywhere directed against
God's people and against the Law and against this place. And, what is
more, he has brought Greeks into the sacred precincts, and has
defiled this holy place.' 29 They made this charge because they had

previously seen Trophimus, the Ephesian, in Paul's company in the
city, and they thought that Paul had brought him into the sacred
precincts.
30The whole city was seething with excitement. There was a con-
certed rush of the people, and they seized Paul and dragged him out
of the Temple precincts. Immediately the gates were shut. 31While
they were trying to murder Paul, a report reached the officer com-
manding the company of soldiers on garrison duty that the whole of
Jerusalem was in an uproar.
32He immediately took soldiers and centurions, and rushed down
to them. When the mob saw the officer and the soldiers, they stopped
beating Paul. 33The commander came up and seized him, and ordered
him to be bound with two chains. 'Who is he?' he asked. 'And what
has he done?' 34Some of the mob shouted one thing and some
another. When he could not discover what the facts were because of
the disturbance, he ordered Paul to be taken into the barracks.
35When Paul reached the steps, he had actually to be carried by the
soldiers because of the violence of the mob, 36for the mass of the
people followed, screaming: 'Kill him!'
37Just as Paul was going to be taken into the barracks, he said to the
commander: 'Will you allow me to say something to you?' 'Do you
know Greek?' the commander said. 38'Are you not the Egyptian who
some time ago started a revolt and led the four thousand Assassins out
into the desert?' 39'I am a Jew,' Paul said, 'a native of Tarsus in Cilicia,
a citizen of a most illustrious city. Will you please permit me to speak
to the people?'
40When the commander had given his permission, Paul took his
stand on the steps, and made a gesture to the people with his hand.
They were hushed to silence and Paul addressed them in the Hebrew
language.

Chapter 22

'BROTHERS and fathers,' he said to them, 'give me a hearing, and
give me a chance to defend myself to you.' 2When they heard him
addressing them in the Hebrew language, they were still quieter.
3'I am a Jew,' Paul went on, 'born in Tarsus in Cilicia, but brought up
in this city. I was trained in the school of Gamaliel with all the strict-
ness which our ancestral Law demands. I am as whole-heartedly

devoted to God as any of you here today. 4I was such a persecutor of
the Way that I wished to put its followers to death. I chained and
imprisoned both men and women, 5and that is a fact to which the
High Priest and all the council of the elders can provide evidence. I
received letters of introduction from them to our brother Jews in
Damascus, and I set out there to bring those of the Way who were
there to Jerusalem to be punished.

6'When I was approaching Damascus on my journey, suddenly
about midday a great light from the sky flashed around me. 7I fell to
the ground. I heard a voice. "Saul, Saul," it said to me, "why are you
persecuting me?" 8"Who are you, Lord?" I answered. "I am Jesus the
Nazarene," the voice said to me, "and it is I whom you are persecut-
ing." 9My travelling companions saw the light, but they did not hear
the voice of the speaker. 10"What am I to do, Lord?" I said. "Get up,"
the Lord said to me, "and go into Damascus, and there you will be
told about all you are destined to do." 11I had been blinded by the
brilliance of that light. So, led by the hand by my companions,
I went into Damascus.

12'A certain Ananias, a man who devoutly kept the Law, and who
was highly esteemed by all the Jews who resided in Damascus, 13came
to me. He stood beside me. "Brother Saul," he said, "receive your
sight again!" There and then I recovered my sight, and looked up at
him. 14"The God of our fathers," he said to me, "has appointed you
to know his will, and to see the Just One, and to hear him actually
speaking, 15because you are to be a witness for him to all men of what
you have seen and heard. 16And now, why delay? Up! Call on his
name, be baptized, and wash away your sins!"

17'When I had returned to Jerusalem, and while I was praying in the
Temple precincts, I fell into a trance. 18I saw Jesus and heard him
saying to me: "Hurry! Get out of Jerusalem as fast as you can, for they
will not accept what you affirm about me." 19"Lord," I said, "they
themselves know that I used to go from synagogue to synagogue
imprisoning and flogging those who believe in you. 20They know
that when Stephen, your martyr, was murdered, I was standing
there, and that I fully agreed with his death, and that I was guarding
the clothes of those who killed him." 21"Go!" he said to me, "for I
will send you far away to the Gentiles." '

22Until he said this, they were willing to give him a hearing, but at
these words they shouted: 'Away with him! A creature like this is
not fit to live.' 23They were shrieking, and waving their cloaks, and

throwing dust into the air. 24The commander ordered that Paul
should be taken into the barracks. He gave orders for him to be
cross-examined under the lash, for he wanted to find out why they
shouted at him like that.

25When they were strapping him down, preparatory to flogging
him, Paul said to the centurion who was standing by: 'Have you any
right to flog a man who is a Roman citizen—and to flog him without
a trial?' 26When the centurion heard this, he went and reported it to
the commander. 'What are you going to do?' he said. 'This man is a
Roman citizen.' 27The commander came up. 'Tell me,' he said to Paul,
'are you a Roman citizen?' 'Yes,' said Paul. 28'I had to pay heavily to
obtain this citizenship,' the commander answered. 'I am a citizen by
birth,' said Paul. 29Those who had been about to cross-examine
him stood back at once. The commander was alarmed when he
realized that Paul was a Roman citizen, and that he had put him in
chains.

30On the next day the commander wished to ascertain the real
reason why Paul was accused by the Jews. So he released him from
prison, and ordered the chief priests and the whole Sanhedrin to
assemble. He brought Paul down and confronted him with them.

Chapter 23

PAUL looked steadily at the Sanhedrin. 'Brothers,' he said, 'all my
life I have had a completely clear conscience before God, and I still
have.' 2Ananias the High Priest ordered those who were standing be-
side Paul to hit him on the mouth. 3'God is going to strike you,' Paul
said, 'you white-washed wall! Are you going to sit there in legal
judgment on me, and at the same time quite illegally order me to be
struck?' 4'Are you insulting God's High Priest?' those who were
standing by said to Paul. 5'Brothers,' said Paul, 'I did not know that
he was High Priest, or I would not have spoken like that, for scripture
says: "You must not abuse the ruler of the people." '

6Paul knew that one half of the Sanhedrin were Sadducees and that
the other half were Pharisees. So he shouted for all the Sanhedrin to
hear: 'Brothers, I am a Pharisee, and I come from a line of Pharisees.
What I am on trial for is the hope of the resurrection of the dead.'
7When he said this, there was a violent division between the Pharisees

and the Sadducees, and the meeting was split in two, 8because the
Sadducees say that there is no resurrection, and that there are neither
angels nor spirits, while the Pharisees believe in all three. 9The meet-
ing developed into a shouting match. Some of the experts in the Law,
who belonged to the party of the Pharisees, rose to speak. 'We can
find nothing wrong with this man,' they insisted. 'What if a spirit or
an angel has spoken to him?' 10The dispute grew so violent that the
commander was afraid that they would tear Paul apart. So he
ordered his troops to come down and forcibly to remove Paul from
the meeting, and to take him into the barracks.

11The next night the Lord came and stood beside Paul. 'Courage!'
he said. 'You have declared my story in Jerusalem, and you must
speak for me in Rome too.'

12When day came, the Jews formed a plot. They took a solemn
oath that they would neither eat nor drink, until they had killed Paul.
13More than forty of them were involved in this conspiracy. 14They
went to the chief priests and elders. 'We have taken a solemn oath,'
they said, 'to abstain from all food, until we have killed Paul. 15So
what we want you and the Sanhedrin to do is to inform the com-
mander that you propose to make a fuller investigation into his
case. That will make it necessary for him to bring Paul down to you.
We are prepared to see to it that he will not reach the court alive.'

16Paul's nephew heard of the proposed ambush. He went into the
barracks and told Paul about it. 17Paul called one of the centurions.
'Take this young man to the commander,' he said. 'He has something
to report to him.' 18So the centurion took him to the commander.
'The prisoner Paul,' he said, 'called me and requested me to bring
this young man to you, because he has something to tell you.' 19The
commander took his arm and drew him aside. When they were alone,
he asked him: 'What is it that you have to report to me?' 20'The Jews,'
he said, 'have made an agreement to ask you to bring Paul down to
the Sanhedrin tomorrow, on the grounds that the Sanhedrin is going
to carry out a fuller enquiry into his case. 21You must not allow them
to persuade you to do so, for more than forty of them have taken a
solemn vow neither to eat nor drink, until they have murdered him,
and they are waiting in ambush for him. They are ready now, and they
are only waiting for you to promise to do as they will request.' 22The
commander dismissed the young man with strict orders not to tell
anyone that he had given him this information.

23He called two of his centurions, and said to them: 'Get ready an
infantry force of two hundred men to go to Caesarea, together with
seventy cavalrymen and two hundred spearsmen. Have them stand-
ing by from nine o'clock in the evening onwards.' 24He also instructed
them to provide horses to mount Paul, and to bring him safely to
Felix the governor. 25He then wrote a letter in the following terms:
26'Claudius Lysias to his Excellency, the governor Felix, greetings.
27This man was seized by the Jews and was about to be killed by them.
I intervened with my troops and rescued him, for I learned that he is a
Roman citizen. 28Since I wished to know the reason why they accused
him, I brought him down to their Sanhedrin. 29I discovered that the
accusation related to questions of their own Law, and that he was
accused of nothing which merited death or imprisonment. 30I was
informed that they intended an attempt on this man's life. I therefore
send him to you. I have instructed his accusers to state before you
what they have against him.'

31The soldiers took Paul, as they had been instructed, and brought
him by night to Antipatris. 32On the next day they left the cavalry to
go with him, while they returned to barracks. 33When they reached
Caesarea, they delivered the letter to the governor, and handed Paul
over to him. 34When he had read the letter, he asked Paul what
province he came from. When he learned that he came from Cilicia,
35he said: 'I will deal with your case, whenever your accusers arrive.'
He gave orders that Paul was to be kept under guard in Herod's head-
quarters.

Chapter 24

FIVE days later the High Priest Ananias came down, with a group of
elders and with an advocate called Tertullus. They laid information
against Paul before the governor. 2When Paul had been summoned,
Tertullus began the case for the prosecution. 'Your Excellency Felix,'
he said, 'to you we owe the prolonged peace which we enjoy, and you
in your foresight have initiated a series of reforms for this nation 3of
every kind and in every place, and we welcome all this with all
gratitude. 4I do not want to detain you for any length of time, so I ask
you in your clemency to give us a brief hearing. 5We have found this
man to be a troublesome pest. He is a disruptive influence among all
the Jews all over the world. He is the ring-leader of the Nazarene

party. 6He even tried to desecrate the Temple precincts. We arrested
him,* 8and by examining him yourself you can discover from himself
the facts about all the crimes of which we accuse him.' 9The Jews
joined in the attack, and alleged that these charges were true.

10The governor signed to Paul to speak. 'Since I know,' Paul
answered, 'that you have been the judicial head of this nation for
many years, I confidently embark upon my defence. 11You can easily
check the fact that it is no more than twelve days ago that I went up
to worship in Jerusalem. 12They did not find me arguing with anyone
in the Temple precincts, or collecting a crowd, either in the syna-
gogues or in the city. 13They cannot produce any evidence to support
the charges which they are now bringing against me. 14This I do
admit to you—I do worship the God of our fathers as the Way—they
call it a sect—teaches; but at the same time I accept everything that is
laid down in the Law and written in the prophets, 15and I have the
same hope in God as they themselves accept, I mean that there will
be a resurrection of both good and bad. 16That is why I too always
discipline myself to have a clear conscience before God and men.

17'It is some years since I have been in Jerusalem. I arrived there to
bring gifts to my people, and to offer sacrifices to God. 18It was when
I was engaged in this that they came upon me in the Temple precincts.
I had gone through all the necessary purifications. I was not the
centre of a crowd, and there was no disturbance. The whole trouble
has been caused by some Jews from Asia, 19who ought to be here in
your court to make whatever accusations they have to bring against
me. 20Failing that, these men here ought to state of what crime they
found me guilty when I appeared before the Sanhedrin, 21other
than this one statement which I publicly made, when I was standing
in their meeting: "What I am on trial for in your court today is the
resurrection of the dead." '

22Felix reserved his judgment, for he was very well informed of the
facts about the Way. 'When Lysias the commander comes down,' he
said to them, 'I will investigate your case.' 23He then gave orders to
the centurion that Paul was to be kept in custody and that he was to
be given a certain amount of liberty, and that no one was to stop
his friends from rendering him any service.

*Here certain manuscripts insert verses 6b, 7, 8a. 6b, *It was our intention to try him under our own law.* 7, *but Lysias, the commander arrived and used considerable force to remove him from our hands,* 8a, *and ordered his accusers to appear before you.*

24Some days afterwards Felix came with his wife Drusilla, who was
a Jewess. He sent for Paul, and listened to him talking about faith in
Christ Jesus. 25When Paul was discoursing about goodness and self-
control and the coming judgment, Felix became alarmed. 'Leave me
for the present,' he said. 'When I have time to spare, I will send for
you.' 26He had at the same time hopes that Paul would give him a
bribe. So he sent for him very frequently, and had many conversa-
tions with him. 27At the end of two years Felix was succeeded by
Porcius Festus. Felix left Paul in prison, because he wished to curry
favour with the Jews.

Chapter 25

THREE days after he entered his province Festus went up from
Caesarea to Jerusalem. 2The chief priests and the leading Jews laid
information against Paul, and they pleaded with Festus as 3a special
favour to have Paul sent up to Jerusalem. Their intention was to
ambush him and to murder him on the road. 4Festus' answer was that
Paul was being held at Caesarea, and that he himself intended soon to
leave for there. 5'The best thing your authorities can do,' he said, 'is
to come down with me, and to make their accusations against the
man, if he has committed any crime.'

6He spent no more than eight or ten days with them, and then
went down to Caesarea. On the next day he took his place in his
court, and ordered Paul to be brought in. 7When Paul came in, the
Jews who had come down from Jerusalem surrounded him, and
brought against him many serious charges, which they were quite
unable to substantiate. 8It was Paul's defence that he was guilty of
no crime against the Jewish Law, or against the Temple, or against
Caesar. 9Festus wished to curry favour with the Jews. He therefore
said to Paul: 'Are you willing to go to Jerusalem, and to be tried
before me there on these charges?' 10'It is Caesar's court of justice in
which I am standing,' said Paul, 'and it is precisely there that my case
must be tried. I am entirely innocent of any crime against the Jews, as
you very well know. 11If I am a criminal, and if I have done anything
that merits the death penalty, I have no objections to dying, but, if
there is no substance in these accusations which are being made against
me, then no one can make a free gift of me to the Jews. I appeal to

Caesar.' 12Festus conferred with his council. 'You have appealed to
Caesar,' he said. 'You will go to Caesar.'

13Some days after this, King Agrippa and Berenice arrived in Caes-
area to pay their respects to Festus. 14As they were staying for some
time, Festus consulted the king about Paul's case. 'There is a prisoner
here,' he said, 'who was left behind by Felix. 15When I was in Jerus-
alem, the Jewish chief priests and elders laid information against
him, and demanded his condemnation. 16I replied that it is not the
Roman custom to hand over any accused man, before he has an
opportunity to confront his accusers face to face, and to defend
himself against the charge made against him. 17When they came here,
I did not delay the matter. On the next day I took my place in my
court, and ordered the man to be brought in. 18When his accusers
rose to speak, they charged him with none of the crimes that I had
expected. 19The questions at issue with him were about their own
religion, and about one Jesus who had died, but whom Paul asserted
to be alive. 20I was at a loss to know how to hold an enquiry into
matters like that. I therefore asked him if he was willing to go to
Jerusalem, and to be tried on these charges there. 21But Paul appealed
that he should be kept in custody until the Emperor should decide
his case. I therefore ordered him to be so kept until I could remit his
case to Caesar.' 22'I should like to have a personal talk with this man,'
Agrippa said to Festus. 'You shall have a talk with him tomorrow,'
said Festus.

23On the next day Agrippa and Berenice arrived in full state, and
went into the audience hall with the top-ranking army officers and
the most prominent citizens of the town. At the order of Festus, Paul
was brought in. 24Festus said to King Agrippa and to the whole
audience: 'You are looking at the man about whom the whole body
of the Jews petitioned me in Jerusalem and here. They vociferously
insisted that he must not be allowed to live any longer. 25As far as I
could see, he has done nothing to merit the death penalty, but when
he himself appealed to the Emperor, I decided to send him to him.
26I have no definite facts to report in writing about him to my im-
perial master. I have therefore brought him before you all, and espe-
cially before you, King Agrippa, so that a preliminary enquiry may be
held, and so that I may thus have some definite information to include
in my report, 27for it seems unreasonable to me to remit a person to
the Emperor without making it clear what he is charged with.'

Chapter 26

‘YOU have our permission to tell your story,’ Agrippa said to Paul.
Paul stretched out his hand, and began his defence. 2‘I count my-
self fortunate, King Agrippa,’ Paul said, ‘that it is before you that I am
today about to defend myself against all the accusations brought
against me by the Jews. 3I count myself specially fortunate, because
you are an expert in all Jewish customs and questions. I therefore ask
you to give me a patient hearing.
4‘All the Jews well know the kind of life I lived from the days of
my youth, for it was lived amongst my own people and in Jerusalem.
5Their knowledge of me goes back a long way. If they were willing to
do so, they could give evidence that my life was the life of a Pharisee,
lived in obedience to the principles of the strictest sect of our religion.
6And now it is because my hope is that God will keep the promise
which he made to our fathers that I stand here on trial today. 7It is
that very hope which the twelve tribes strive to attain, by worshipping
God with strenuous devotion night and day. It is for cherishing this
hope, your Majesty, that I am accused—and my accusers are Jews!
8Why should you regard it as incredible that God raises the dead?
9‘I was myself convinced that it was my duty to do all that I could
to oppose Jesus the Nazarene. 10This I did in Jerusalem. I shut up many
of God’s people in prison, after I had received authority from the
chief priests to do so. When they were being put to death, I cast my
vote against them. 11I went from synagogue to synagogue punishing
them, and trying to force them to curse the name of Jesus. In my
insane rage I engaged in a campaign of persecution even in cities
outside Palestine.
12‘As part of all this, I was on my way to Damascus with the author-
ity and the commission of the chief priests. 13On the road at midday,
your Majesty, I saw a light from the sky, brighter than the sun, shining
around me and my fellow-travellers. 14We all fell to the ground. I
heard a voice. “Saul, Saul,” the voice said to me in the Hebrew lan-
guage, “Why are you persecuting me? You only hurt yourself by
kicking against the goads.” 15“Who are you, Lord?” I said. The Lord
said: “I am Jesus, and it is I whom you are persecuting. 16Up! Stand on
your feet! I have appeared to you, because I have chosen you to be
my servant, and to tell people the story of the vision of me you have

seen, and of the visions of me you will see. 17I will rescue you from
the people and from the Gentiles. It is to the Gentiles that I am going
to send you. 18I want you to open their eyes, so that you will make
them turn from darkness to light, and from the power of Satan to
God, for I want them to receive forgiveness of their sins, and a share
in the blessedness of those who through faith in me have become
God's consecrated people."

19'Therefore, King Agrippa, I did not disobey the heavenly vision,
20but first to those in Damascus, then in Jerusalem, then all over the
country of Judaea, then to the Gentiles, I brought the message to
repent, and to turn to God, and to make their conduct match their
repentance. 21That is why the Jews seized me in the Temple precincts
and tried to murder me. 22God gave me his support. Today I stand
declaring my faith to people from the top to the bottom of society.
I am saying nothing beyond what the prophets and Moses said would
happen—23that the Messiah must suffer, and that, because he was the
first to rise from the dead, he would bring the message of light to the
Jewish people and to the Gentiles.'

24When Paul came to this stage in his defence, Festus shouted:
'You're raving, Paul. All this study is driving you mad.' 25'Festus, your
Excellency,' Paul said, 'I am not raving. So far from that, I am speak-
ing words of truth and sanity. 26King Agrippa knows about these
things, and I do not need to mince my words to him. I do not believe
that any of the things I have been speaking of have escaped his notice.
This thing was not done in a corner. 27King Agrippa, do you accept
the message of the prophets? I know you do.' 28Agrippa said to Paul:
'You think that it won't take you long to make a Christian out of
me.' 29'I could pray to God,' said Paul, 'that, whether it takes a long
time or a short time, not only you but all who are listening to me
today should be made such as I—apart from these chains.'

30The king rose, and so did the governor and Berenice and those
who had been seated with them. 31When they had withdrawn, they
discussed the case with each other. 'There is nothing in this man's
conduct,' they said, 'which merits death or imprisonment.' 32'This
man,' Agrippa said to Festus, 'could well have been released, if he had
not appealed to Caesar.'

Chapter 27

WHEN the verdict that we should sail for Italy was reached, Paul and a group of other prisoners were handed over to a centurion of the Imperial regiment, called Julius. 2We embarked on a ship whose home port was Adramyttium, which was about to make the voyage to the ports on the Asian coast, and set sail. Aristarchus, a Macedonian from Thessalonica, accompanied us. 3Next day we put in at Sidon. Julius treated Paul kindly, and allowed him to visit the friends and to enjoy their hospitality. 4We put to sea from there, and sailed under the lee of Cyprus, because of head-winds. 5We then sailed across the open sea off the coast of Cilicia and Pamphylia, and arrived at Myra in Lycia. 6There the centurion found an Alexandrian ship which was bound for Italy, and put us on board it.

7For many days our passage was slow, and it was with difficulty that we arrived off Cnidus. Since we could make no progress because of the head-wind, we sailed under the lee of Crete, off Salmone. 8We coasted along with difficulty until we came to a place called Fair Havens, which was near the town of Lasea.

9A great deal of time had been lost, and by this time sailing was dangerous, because it was late September and the fast of the Day of Atonement was already over. So Paul warned them. 10'Men,' he said, 'I see that this voyage is going to involve damage and serious loss, not only to the cargo and the ship, but also to our lives.' 11The centurion was influenced more by the captain and the ship-owner than by what Paul said.

12That place was not suitable for wintering in. So the majority favoured a plan to sail on from there, in the hope that it might be possible for them to make Phoenix, and to winter there. Phoenix is a harbour in Crete open to the south-west and north-west winds. 13When a light southerly breeze sprang up, they thought that they had as good as achieved their purpose. So they weighed anchor, and coasted along Crete, keeping inshore. 14Soon after a hurricane-like wind—the wind called the north-easter—rushed down on them, blowing from off the island. 15The ship was caught in the wind. It was impossible to keep her head to it. So we yielded to the wind, and ran before it.

16When we had run under the lee of a little island called Cauda, we

succeeded with difficulty in getting control of the dinghy. 17When
they had hauled it on board, they used their tackle to undergird the
ship. They were afraid they would run on to the Syrtis quicksands,
so they lowered the top-gear and allowed the ship to run.

18We were violently battered by the storm, and on the next day
they began to jettison the cargo. 19On the third day they manhandled
the ship's spare gear overboard. 20For many days the sun and the
stars were invisible, and the storm continued to rage. In the end we
began to abandon all hope that we would ever come through it alive.

21When they had gone without food for a long time, Paul gathered
them round. 'Men,' he said, 'you should have listened to me, and you
should not have sailed from Crete. Then your only profit from the
voyage would not have been this damage and loss. 22But, even as
things are, take my advice, and keep your hearts up. Not one of you
will lose his life. The only thing that will be lost is the ship. 23For
tonight there stood by me an angel of the God to whom I belong and
whom I worship. 24"Don't be afraid, Paul," he said. "You must stand
before Caesar, and God has given you the lives of all your companions
on this voyage." 25Keep your hearts up, men! For I trust in God that
everything will turn out exactly as I have been told. 26But we have to
be cast ashore on an island.'

27It was the fourteenth night, and we were drifting helplessly
across the Sea of Adria. It was about midnight when the sailors sus-
pected that land was approaching. 28They took soundings, and found
a depth of twenty fathoms. A little farther on they took soundings
again, and found a depth of fifteen fathoms. 29They were afraid of
piling up on a rocky coast. So they let go four anchors from the
stern, and prayed for daylight.

30The sailors were attempting to get out from the ship. They had
actually begun to let the dinghy down into the sea, on the excuse that
they were going to lay out anchors from the bow. 31'Unless these
men stay in the ship,' Paul said to the centurion, 'you cannot hope to
survive.' 32The soldiers then cut the ropes of the dinghy, and let it
fall away.

33Just before daybreak Paul urged them all to take some food. 'For
fourteen days,' he said, 'you have been in constant suspense without
food, and have eaten nothing. 34I strongly advise you to take some
food. This is essential, if you are going to survive. For I assure you that
not a hair of anyone's head will be lost.' 35When he had said this, he
took a loaf, and gave thanks to God in front of them all, and broke it

in pieces, and began to eat. 36This put fresh heart into them, and they
took some food. 37All together there were two hundred and seventy-
six of us on board the ship. 38When they had eaten all they wanted,
they lightened the ship by jettisoning the cargo of grain into the sea.

39When day broke, they did not recognize the land. They noticed
a bay with a sandy beach, and they planned, if possible, to run the
ship ashore there. 40They slipped the anchors, and let them fall into
the sea. At the same time they unleashed the lashings of the steering-
paddles. They hoisted the foresail to the wind, and made for the
beach. 41They struck a spit of land, and beached the ship. The bow
stuck fast and remained immovable. The stern began to break up
under the pounding of the waves. 42It was the soldiers' plan to kill the
prisoners, in case any of them should swim away and make their
escape. 43But the centurion put a stop to that, because he wished to
save Paul's life. He ordered those who could swim to jump over-
board and to make for the land. 44The rest he ordered to make for
the shore, some on planks, and some on parts of the ship. And thus
it was that they all reached the land in safety.

Chapter 28

WHEN we had safely reached the land, we learned that the island
was called Malta. 2The natives showed us quite extraordinary
kindness. It had begun to rain and it was cold; so they lit a bonfire and
brought us to it.

3Paul had twisted together a bundle of sticks and laid it on the fire.
Because of the heat a viper came out, and fastened on his hand. 4When
the natives saw the beast hanging from his hand, they said to each
other: 'This man must be a murderer. He escaped from the sea, but
justice has not let him live.' 5Paul shook the beast off into the fire,
and was none the worse of it. 6They were expecting him to proceed to
swell up, or suddenly to drop dead. They watched him for a long time.
When they saw that nothing out of the way was happening to him,
they changed their minds, and began to say that he was a god.

7In the nearby countryside there were estates which belonged to
the chief magistrate of the island. His name was Publius. He welcomed
us, and entertained us hospitably for three days. 8It so happened that
Publius' father was lying ill with recurrent attacks of fever and with

dysentery. Paul went to visit him. He prayed and laid his hands on
him and cured him. 9When this happened, the other people in the
island who were ill came too, and were cured. 10The result was that
they heaped honours upon us, and, when we sailed, they put on
board everything we could need.

11After three months we set sail in a ship which had wintered in the
island. She was an Alexandrian ship, and she had the Heavenly Twins
as her figurehead. 12We put in at Syracuse, and stayed there for three
days. 13From there we sailed round and reached Rhegium. The day
after, a south wind blew, and two days' sailing took us to Puteoli.
14There we met some members of the Christian community, and at
their urgent invitation we stayed with them for a week. And so we
came to Rome.

15The members of the Christian community had heard about us,
and they came to meet us as far as the Forum of Appius and the
Three Taverns. When Paul saw them, he thanked God, and was
greatly encouraged. 16When we got to Rome, Paul was allowed to
live by himself, with a soldier to guard him.

17Three days after this Paul invited the leaders of the local Jews to
come to see him. When they were all there, he said to them: 'Brothers,
although I had done nothing hostile to the Jewish nation and nothing
to contravene our ancestral customs, I was handed over to the
Romans in Jerusalem. 18When the Romans had examined me, they
wished to release me, because there were no grounds in my life and
conduct for a charge involving the death penalty. 19When the Jews
objected to my release, I could not do anything else but appeal to
Caesar—not that I had any accusation to make against my nation. 20It
is because I stand for the hope which all Israel shares that I am wear-
ing this chain, and that is why I have requested to see you and to talk
to you.' 21'We,' they said to him, 'have received no letters from
Judaea about you, and no member of the Jewish community who
arrived here has brought any report or rumour that you have been
involved in anything criminal. 22We think it only right to hear from
yourself what your views are. The only thing we do know about this
sect is that there is universal opposition to it.'

23They fixed a day with him, and they came to him in his lodging
in still greater numbers. From morning to night he expounded the
Kingdom of God to them, supporting his statements with vigorous

arguments, and trying to persuade them to accept Jesus by citing
passages from the Law of Moses and from the prophets. 24Some of
them were convinced by what he said; others refused to accept it.
25They were far from being in agreement with each other. Before they
left, Paul said one thing more. 'The Holy Spirit,' he said, 'well said to
your fathers through the prophet Isaiah:

> 26"Go to this people and say:
> you will certainly hear,
> but you will certainly not understand
> the meaning of what you hear;
> you will certainly see,
> but you will certainly not perceive
> the meaning of what you see.
> 27The mind of this people has become lazily shut,
> and their ears have become hard of hearing,
> and they have deliberately obscured their own sight,
> lest at any time they should see with their eyes,
> and hear with their ears,
> and understand with their minds,
> and turn and find their cure in me."

28I want you to know that the saving power of God has been sent to
the Gentiles. They will listen.'*

30Paul stayed there for two whole years at his own expense. He wel-
comed everyone who came to see him. 31All the time he continued
to proclaim the Kingdom of God, and to teach the facts about the
Lord Jesus Christ, completely freely and fearlessly, and there was no
attempt to stop him.

*Here some manuscripts insert verse 29, *After he had said this, the Jews went away, hotly debating with each other.*

Introduction to John

TRADITION is unanimous that John's Gospel was the last Gospel to be written. Its date is about A.D. 100. Since it is so much later than the other Gospels, it is different in character. By the time it was written three things were happening. First, Christians were studying the records of the life of Jesus closely and with scholarly care. Second, Christianity had gone out far beyond Judaism into the wider world. Third, heresies had begun to arise, and the meaning of the Christian faith had to be stated and restated. John's Gospel has three aims corresponding to these three factors in the situation.

i. John's Gospel was written partly with an historical aim. It was written to supply certain gaps in the narrative of the other three. For instance, John's Gospel tells us of a ministry of Jesus in Jerusalem before his main ministry in Galilee, and his return to Jerusalem for the last days.

ii. John's Gospel was written partly with an apologetic aim. All the other Gospels had arisen within Judaism and necessarily used Jewish categories of thought. But John's Gospel was most likely written in Ephesus, and was written for Greeks. Must then, as one scholar has put it, these Greeks be routed, or even detoured, into Christianity via Judaism? To meet this situation John finds the idea of Jesus as The Word. The Greek word is *Logos*. *Logos* has two meanings, which no one English word can express. *Logos* means *word*, and *Logos* means *mind*. A word is the expression of a thought. Therefore, Jesus is the expression of the thought of God. Or, to take the other meaning, in Jesus we see the mind of God. John says to us: 'If you want to see what God is thinking, if you want to see how God feels to men, and how God thinks of men, look at Jesus. In Jesus the mind of God became a person.'

iii. John's Gospel was written partly with a theological aim. There is a very old tradition about how John's Gospel came to be written. It was, so the story runs, suggested to John that before he died, he should write what he remembered of Jesus, for he must by that time have been a very old man. So it was decided that John should write and that all the others should review it. For seventy years these men had lived under the guidance of the Holy Spirit. So we may think of them sitting down and saying: 'Do you remember how Jesus said?'

'Yes,' another would say, 'and now we know what he meant.' And there would be written down the word and the Spirit-guided interpretation of it. One famous ancient verdict called John's Gospel *the spiritual Gospel.* It is interested not only in the events of Jesus' life, but even more in the meaning of them. It is interested not only in what Jesus said, but also in the meaning and interpretation of what he said. A famous scholar described John's Gospel as 'what Jesus becomes to a man who has known him long.' In it Jesus is still speaking, and the promise that the Spirit would take of Jesus' things and declare them to those who love him (16.14) has come true.

JOHN'S VERSION
of the Story of the Good News

Chapter 1

WHEN the world began, the Word was already there. The Word was
with God, and the nature of the Word was the same as the nature
of God. 2The Word was there in the beginning with God. 3It was
through the agency of the Word that everything else came into being.
Without the Word not one single thing came into being. 4As for the
whole creation, the Word was the life principle in it, and that life was
the light of men. 5The light continues to shine in the darkness, and
the darkness has never extinguished it.

6On to the stage of history there came a man sent from God. His
name was John. 7The purpose of his coming was to declare the truth,
and the truth he declared was about the light. The aim of his declara-
tion was to persuade all men to believe. 8He himself was not the light.
His only function was to tell men about the light. 9The real light, the
light which enlightens every man, was just about to come into the
world. 10He was in the world, and, although it was through him that
the world came into being, the world failed to recognize him. 11It
was to his own home that he came, but his own people refused to
receive him. 12But to all who did receive him he gave the privilege of
becoming God's children. That privilege was given to those who do
believe that he really is what he is. 13They were born, not by the
common processes of physical birth, not as the consequence of some
moment of sexual passion, not as a result of any man's desire. Their
birth came from God. 14The Word became a human person, and lived
awhile among us. With our own eyes we saw his glory. It was the glory
which an only son receives from his father, and he was full of grace
and truth. 15John told all men who he was. His prophetic proclama-
tion was: 'This is he of whom I said, "He follows me in time, but he
ranks ahead of me, for he existed before I was born." '

16This was his message, because out of the Word's complete per-
fection we have all received, and to us there has come wave upon wave
of grace. 17For it was through Moses that the Law was given, but it is
through Jesus Christ that grace and truth have come. 18No one has
ever seen God as he is. It is the Unique One, the Divine One, he who is
nearest the heart of the Father, who has disclosed to us the mystery
of God.

19This is how John declared the truth. When the Jews of Jerusalem
sent priests and Levites to ask him who he was, 20his answer was
definite and positive. 'I am not the Messiah,' he openly declared. 21So
they asked him: 'What are you then? Are you Elijah?' 'I am not,' he
said. 'Are you the promised prophet?' 'No,' he said. 22'Who are you?'
they said. 'We want to take back an answer to those who sent us.
What have you to say about yourself?' 23He said:

'I am the voice of one shouting in the wilderness,
"Straighten the road by which the Lord will come,"

as the prophet Isaiah said.' 24Some of the deputation were Pharisees.
25'Why, then,' they asked him, 'are you baptizing, if you are neither
the Messiah, nor Elijah, nor the promised prophet?' 26'It is with water
I baptize,' John answered. 'Although you are not aware of it, there
stands among you 27the One who is to come after me. I am not fit to
untie the strap of his sandal.' 28This incident happened in Bethany
on the far side of the Jordan, where John was baptizing.

29Next day John saw Jesus coming towards him. 'Look!' he said.
'The Lamb of God, the One who takes away the sin of the world! 30It
was of him I said, "A man is coming after me who ranks before me,
for he existed before I was born." 31I myself did not know him, but the
very reason why I have come baptizing with water is that he might be
made plain for all Israel to see. 32I saw the Spirit,' John declared,
'coming down like a dove from heaven and settling on him. 33I my-
self did not know him. But it was he who sent me to baptize with
water who said to me: "He on whom you shall see the Spirit coming
down and settling is he who is to baptize with the Holy Spirit." 34I
have seen it myself, and I now declare that this is the Son of God.'

35Next day, when John was again standing with two of his disciples,
36he saw Jesus walking past. 'Look!' he said. 'The Lamb of God!'
37When the two disciples heard him say this, they followed Jesus.
38Jesus turned and saw them following him. 'What are you looking

for?' he said. 'Rabbi,' they said to him—the translation of the word
Rabbi is Teacher—'where are you staying?' 39'Come and see,' he said
to them. They came and they saw where he was staying, and they
stayed with him for the rest of that day. It was about four o'clock in
the afternoon when they met him.

40Andrew, Simon Peter's brother, was one of the two disciples who
had heard what John said, and who had followed Jesus. 41The first
thing he did was to find his brother Simon. 'We have found the
Messiah,' he said to him. (The translation of the word Messiah is
Christ.) 42He brought him to Jesus. Jesus looked at him. 'You are
Simon, John's son,' he said. 'You will be called Cephas.' (Peter is the
translation of Cephas.)

43Next day Jesus intended to leave for Galilee. He met Philip and
said to him: 'Follow me!' 44Philip came from Bethsaida, the town
from which Andrew and Peter came. 45Philip met Nathanael. 'We
have found the person about whom Moses wrote in the Law and
whom the prophets foretold,' he said. 'He is Jesus, the son of Joseph,
from Nazareth.' 46'Can anything good come from Nazareth?' Nath-
anael said. 'Come and see,' said Philip. 47When Jesus saw Nathanael
approaching, he said: 'Here is a real Israelite! A man who is genuine all
through!' 48'How do you know me?' Nathanael said. 'I saw you,'
Jesus said, 'at your quiet time under the fig-tree, before Philip spoke
to you.' 49'Rabbi,' answered Nathanael, 'you are the Son of God! You
are the King of Israel!' 50'Do you believe in me because I said that I
saw you under the fig-tree?' Jesus answered. 'You will see greater
things than that. 51This is the truth I tell you—you will see heaven
standing wide open, and the angels of God ascending and descending
on the Son of Man.'

Chapter 2

Two days after this there was a wedding at Cana in Galilee. Jesus'
mother was there, 2and Jesus too was invited to the wedding with
his disciples. 3When the wine ran short, Jesus' mother said to him:
'They have no wine.' 4'You must not try to tell me what to do,' Jesus
said. 'My time has not yet come.' 5'Do whatever he tells you to do,'
his mother said to the servants. 6Six stone water-jars were standing
there, as the Jewish ceremonial customs of purification required, each

of them with a capacity of twenty or thirty gallons of water. 7'Fill the
jars with water,' Jesus said to them. They filled them up to the brim.
8'Now,' said Jesus to them, 'draw some out and take it to the master of
ceremonies.' They did so. 9The master of ceremonies tasted the water
which had become wine. He did not know where it had come from,
although the servants who had drawn the water knew. He called the
bridegroom. 10'Everyone,' he said to him, 'lays on the good wine first,
and then, when the guests have had quite a lot to drink, the not so
good wine. You have kept the good wine until now.'

11Jesus gave this first demonstration of the power of God in action
at Cana in Galilee, and so displayed his glory, and his disciples believed
in him.

12After this Jesus went down to Capernaum with his mother and
his brothers and his disciples, and they stayed there for a few days.

13The Jewish Passover Festival was shortly to be observed. So Jesus
went up to Jerusalem. 14In the Temple precincts he found the sellers
of oxen and sheep and pigeons, and the money-changers sitting at
their tables. 15He made a whip out of pieces of cord, and he drove
them all out of the Temple precincts, and the sheep and the oxen
along with them. He scattered the coins of the money-changers and
upset their tables. 16He said to the pigeon sellers: 'Take these out of
here! Stop turning my Father's house into a shop!' 17His disciples
remembered that scripture says: 'Zeal for your house will consume
me.' 18'What proof can you give us of your right to act like this?' the
Jews said to him. 19'Destroy this Temple,' Jesus answered, 'and in
three days I will raise it from the ruins.' 20'It took forty-six years to
build this Temple,' the Jews said, 'and are you going to raise it from
the ruins in three days?' 21But Jesus was speaking of the temple of his
body. 22So when he was raised from the dead, his disciples remem-
bered that he had said this, and they believed the scripture, and
realized that what he had said was true.

23When Jesus was in Jerusalem at the Festival of the Passover, many
believed in him, for they saw that his actions were visible demonstra-
tions of the power of God. 24But he did not entrust himself to them,
25for he knew all men. He did not need anyone to tell him about
human nature, because he was well aware what it is like.

Chapter 3

THERE was a man called Nicodemus, who belonged to the school
of the Pharisees, and who was a member of the Sanhedrin. 2This
man came to Jesus at night. 'Rabbi,' he said to him, 'we know that you
are a teacher who has come from God, for no one could do things
which are so obviously demonstrations of divine power, unless God
was with him.' 3'I tell you,' said Jesus, 'and it is true, that unless a man
is born again from above, he can have no experience of the Kingdom
of God.' 4'How can a man be born when he is old? It is obviously
impossible for a man to enter his mother's womb a second time, and
to be born all over again,' Nicodemus said to him. 5'I tell you,' Jesus
answered, 'and it is true, unless a man is born of water and the Spirit,
he cannot become a member of the Kingdom of God. 6Physical birth
can only beget a physical creature; but spiritual birth begets a spiritual
creature. 7You must not be surprised that I said to you that you must
all be born again from above. 8The wind blows where it wills, and you
hear the sound of it, but you do not know where it comes from and
where it is going. And there is the same invisible and unpredictable
power in everyone who undergoes this spiritual rebirth.' 9'How can
this happen?' Nicodemus answered. 10'Are you the famous teacher of
the famous Israel,' Jesus said to him, 'and yet you do not understand
this? 11I tell you, and it is true, we speak of that of which we have
knowledge; we declare the truth of what we have seen; and you refuse
to accept our word for it. 12If you do not believe when I have spoken
to you about the familiar things of earth, how will you believe if I tell
you about the strange things of heaven? 13There is only one person
who has gone up to heaven, and he is the person who came down
from heaven, I mean, the Son of Man who comes from heaven.'

14Just as Moses lifted high the serpent in the wilderness, so the Son
of Man must be lifted high, 15so that everyone who believes in him
may have eternal life. 16For God loved the world so much that he
gave his only Son, so that everyone who believes in him should have
not destruction but eternal life. 17God did not send his Son into the
world to judge the world; he sent him so that through him the
world should be saved. 18There is no judgment for the man who
believes in him; but if anyone does not believe in him, he already
stands condemned, because he has refused to believe in God's only

Son. 19The fact which really judges men is that the light came into
the world, and they loved the darkness rather than the light, because
their deeds were evil. 20If a man's conduct is bad he hates the light,
and refuses to come into the light, for he does not want his actions to
be openly convicted. 21But if a man's conduct is dictated by the truth,
he willingly comes into the light, for by so doing he will make it clear
to everyone that his conduct has its inspiration in God.

22After this Jesus went into the territory of Judaea with his disciples,
and there he spent some time with them baptizing. 23John too was
baptizing at Aenon near Salim, because there was plenty of water
there. A continuous stream of people flocked out to him to be bap-
tized, 24for John had not yet been put into prison. 25A discussion
about ceremonial purification arose between John's disciples and a
Jew. 26They came to John and said to him: 'Rabbi, the man in whose
greatness you publicly declared your belief, when you met him on the
far side of the Jordan, is here baptizing, and the people are all going to
him.' 27'A man can only receive what God gives him,' John answered.
28'You yourselves can witness to the fact that I said that I am not
the Messiah. You can bear witness to the fact that what I did say was
that I have been sent on ahead of him. 29It is the bridegroom who has
the bride. The bridegroom's friend, who is there to support him and
to carry out his orders, is very glad when he hears the voice of the
bridegroom. That is what joy means to me, and I have it in full. 30He
must go on from strength to strength; I must fade out of the picture.'

31He who comes from above is above all others. If a man has his
origin in this world, he belongs to this world, and what he has to say
has no other authority than that of this world. He who comes from
heaven is above all others. 32He declares what he has actually seen
and heard, and yet no one accepts what he declares. 33If a man accepts
his declaration, he sets his seal on his conviction that God is absol-
utely to be relied upon, 34for the messenger of God brings the mes-
sage of God, for God gives him no meagre share of his Spirit. 35The
Father loves the Son, and has put everything under his control. 36To
believe in the Son is to enjoy the experience of eternal life; to refuse
to believe in the Son is to deprive oneself of the experience of life.
More, it is to become the object of the wrath of God.

Chapter 4

When Jesus learned that the Pharisees had heard a report that he was making more disciples and baptizing more converts than John—2although Jesus himself was not in the habit of baptizing at all; it was his disciples who did so—3he left Judaea and went back again to Galilee. 4It was necessary for him to take the road that led through Samaria.

5He came to a town in Samaria called Sychar, near the piece of land which Jacob had given to his son Joseph. 6Jacob's spring was there. Jesus, tired out by his journey, was sitting just as he was beside the spring. It was about twelve o'clock midday.

7A woman from Samaria came to draw water. Jesus said to her: 'Give me a drink of water.' 8His disciples had gone away into the town to buy food. 9The Samaritan woman said to him: 'How can you, a Jew, ask a drink of water from me, a Samaritan woman?' (No Jew would drink out of a cup that a Samaritan had used.) 10Jesus answered: 'If you knew what God's free gift is, and if you realized who it is who is asking you for a drink of water, it is you who would have asked him, and he would have given you living water.' 11'Sir,' the woman said to him, 'you have nothing to draw water with and the well is deep. Where are you going to get this living water from? 12Surely you are not greater than our ancestor Jacob, who gave us this well, and who himself drank from it with his sons and his cattle.' 13'If anyone drinks from this water he will be thirsty again,' Jesus answered, 14'but once a man has drunk the water which I will give him, he will never be thirsty again. The water which I will give him will become a spring of water inside him, always welling up to give him eternal life.' 15'Sir,' the woman said to him, 'give me this water so that I will not be thirsty, and so that I will not need to come all this way to draw water.'

16'Go,' Jesus said to her, 'and tell your husband to come, and come back here.' 17'I haven't got a husband,' the woman said. Jesus said to her: 'You are perfectly right to say that you have no husband. 18You have had five husbands and the man you are now living with is not your husband. You told the truth this time.' 19'Sir,' the woman said to him, 'I see that you are a prophet. 20Our ancestors worshipped on this hill, but you say that Jerusalem is the place where everyone

ought to worship.' 21'Believe me,' Jesus said to her, 'a day is coming
when you will worship the Father neither on this hill nor in Jerus-
alem. 22You are worshipping in ignorance; we are worshipping in
knowledge; for salvation comes from the Jews. 23But a day is coming
—it is here—when the true worshippers will offer the Father a truly
spiritual worship, for such are the worshippers whom the Father is
looking for. 24God is a spiritual being, and his worshippers must offer
him a truly spiritual worship.' 25The woman said to him: 'I know that
the Messiah (who is called Christ) is coming. When he comes he will
tell us everything.' 26Jesus said to her: 'I am the Messiah, I who am
speaking to you.'

27At this Jesus' disciples came up. They were astonished to find
Jesus in conversation with a woman, but none of them asked him
what he wanted with her or why he was talking to her. 28As for the
woman, she left her water-jar and went off into the town. 29'Come,'
she said to the people there, 'and see a man who has told me every-
thing I ever did. Can this be the Messiah?' 30They went out of the town
and started out to see Jesus.

31Meanwhile his disciples were urging him: 'Rabbi, eat something.'
32'I have food of which you know nothing,' he said to them. 33'Surely
someone hasn't brought him something to eat?' the disciples said to
each other. 34Jesus said to them: 'My food is to do the will of him who
sent me, and to finish what he gave me to do. 35Do you not say:
"There are still four months before the harvest comes"? Open your
eyes and look at the fields, I tell you, and you will see that they are
white for the harvesting. 36Already the harvester is receiving his
wages; already he is gathering a crop destined for eternal life, so that
the sower and the harvester may rejoice together. 37Here is a situation
in which the saying is true—one sows and another harvests. 38I sent
you to reap a crop for which you did not toil. Others have toiled, and
you have entered into the result of their toil.'

39Many of the Samaritans from that town believed in Jesus, because
the woman affirmed that he had told her everything she had done.
40So the Samaritans came and asked him to stay with them, and he
did stay there for two days. 41Far more believed when they heard him
for themselves. 42'We no longer believe because of your story', they
said to the woman. 'We have heard him for ourselves and we know
that this really is the Saviour of the world.'

43After staying there for two days Jesus left for Galilee, 44for Jesus

himself declared that no prophet is honoured in his own native place.
45When he arrived in Galilee, the Galilaeans welcomed him, for they
had seen all that he had done in Jerusalem at the time of the festival,
for they too had gone to the festival.

46Jesus went back again to Cana in Galilee, the place where he had
turned the water into wine. There was in Capernaum an official of
the imperial government whose son was ill. 47When this man heard
that Jesus had arrived in Galilee from Judaea he left home and went
to Jesus, and asked him to come down and cure his son, for the son
was at the point of death. 48'Unless you see visible and astonishing
displays of the power of God in action,' Jesus said to him, 'you will
never believe.' 49'Sir,' the official said to him, 'come down before my
boy dies.' 50'Get on your way,' Jesus said to him. 'Your son will live.'
The man believed what Jesus said to him, and set off. 51While he was
still on the way down his servants met him with the news that his
son was alive. 52He asked them what time it was when he had shown
signs of betterment. 'Yesterday,' they told him, 'at one o'clock in the
afternoon, the fever left him.' 53Then the father realized that that was
the very time at which Jesus had said to him that his son would live.
And he and his whole household believed.

54This was Jesus' second demonstration of the power of God in
action, after he had come back to Galilee from Judaea.

Chapter 5

AFTER this Jesus went up to Jerusalem to observe one of the Jewish
festivals. 2There is in Jerusalem, beside the Sheep Gate, a bath
which in Hebrew is called Bethzatha. It has five porches 3in which
there used to lie a crowd of ailing people, people who were blind and
lame and whose limbs were paralysed.* 5There was a man there
who had been ill continuously for thirty-eight years. 6Jesus saw him
lying there. He knew that he had been ill for a long time now. 'Do
you want to be cured?' he said to him. 7'Sir,' the sick man answered,

*Here some manuscripts insert verse 4, *They were waiting for the famous movement of the water, for from time to time an angel of the Lord would come down, and the water in the bath was disturbed, and whoever was the first to step into the bath after the water had been disturbed was cured of whatever disease he was suffering from.*

'I have no one to put me into the bath when the water has been dis-
turbed. While I am on my way to the water, someone else always
gets down before me.' 8Jesus said to him: 'Get up! Lift your mat! And
walk!' 9There and then the man was cured. He lifted his mat and
began to walk.
That day was the Sabbath. 10The Jews said to the man who had been
cured: 'It is the Sabbath, and you have no right to be carrying your
mat.' 11He answered: 'It was the man who cured me who told me to
lift my mat and walk.' 12'Who is this man who told you to lift your
mat and walk?' they asked him. 13The man who had been cured did
not know who Jesus was, for the place was crowded, and Jesus had
slipped away.
14Afterwards Jesus met him in the Temple precincts. 'You have
been cured,' he said to him. 'From now on stop sinning in case some-
thing worse happens to you.' 15The man went away and told the Jews
that it was Jesus who had cured him. 16It was because Jesus habitually
acted like this on the Sabbath that the Jews tried to prosecute him.
17Jesus answered: 'My Father goes on with his work until now, and I
go on with mine.' 18It was because Jesus not only habitually broke the
Sabbath, but because he also kept speaking of God as his own father,
thus putting himself on an equality with God, that the Jews tried all
the harder to kill him.

19Jesus said to them: 'I tell you, and it is true, the Son cannot do
anything on his own initiative; he can only do what he sees the
Father doing, for whatever the Father does, the Son does too. 20For
the Father loves the Son, and shows him all that he himself is doing;
and he will show him even greater deeds than these, to fill you with
wonder. 21As the Father raises the dead and gives them life, so the Son
gives life to those to whom he wishes. 22The Father does not pass
judgment on anyone, but he has given all judgment to the Son, 23so
that the Son may be universally honoured in the same way as the
Father is honoured. Not to honour the Son is not to honour the
Father who sent him. 24I tell you, and it is true, if a man listens to my
message and believes in him who sent me, he already has eternal life.
He is no longer on the way to judgment; he has already crossed the
boundary between death and life.
25'I tell you, and it is true, that a time is coming—it has come—
when the dead will hear the voice of God's Son, and, if they listen,
they will live. 26As the Father himself is the source of life, so he has

given the Son power to be the source of life. 27He has given him
authority to execute judgment, because he is the Son of Man. 28Do
not be surprised at this, for a time is coming when all who are buried
in the tombs will hear his voice, 29and they will come out. For those
who have lived well, their resurrection will mean life, and for those
who have lived badly, their resurrection will mean judgment. 30I can
do nothing on my own initiative. As I hear from God, so I judge, and
my judgment is just, because my only aim is not to do my own will
but to do the will of him who sent me. 31If I make claims on my own
behalf, my claims need not be valid. 32But it is another who affirms
my claims, and I know that what he says about me is true. 33You sent
to John, and John was a witness to the truth. 34I do not need any
human being to give evidence in support of my claims. The message
I bring you has as its aim your salvation. 35John was a burning and a
shining lamp, and for a time you were willing to rejoice in his light.
36But I can produce greater evidence in support of my claims than the
evidence of John. The deeds which my Father gave me power to do,
these very deeds which I am now doing, these are my evidence that
the Father has sent me. 37The Father who sent me has himself given
evidence on my behalf. You have never heard his voice, nor have you
ever seen his form. 38You do not possess his word dwelling in you,
because you refuse to accept him whom he sent. 39You carefully study
the scriptures, because you think that in them you have eternal life,
and it is these very scriptures which provide you with evidence about
me, 40and yet you refuse to come to me to find life.

41'I am not interested in human glory. 42I know that you have not
the love of God in your lives. 43I have come as the representative of
my Father, and you refuse to receive me. But if someone else comes
as the representative of no one but himself, you will receive him.
44How can you believe, when all you are interested in is the human
glory you get from each other, and when you are quite indifferent
to the glory which comes from the only God? 45Do not think that it is
I who will be your accuser to my Father. Moses is your accuser, Moses
in whom you place your trust! 46If you believed in Moses, you would
believe in me, for it was about me that he wrote. 47 If you do not be-
lieve what he wrote, there is no possibility that you will believe what
I say.'

Chapter 6

AFTER this Jesus went away across the Lake of Galilee (or Tiberias).
2Everywhere he went a great crowd went with him, because they
recognized the power of God in action in what he did for the sick.
3Jesus went into the hill country and he was sitting there with his
disciples. 4It was very near the date of the Passover, the famous
Jewish festival. 5Jesus looked up and saw a large crowd of people
arriving. 'Where are we going to buy bread for these people to eat?' he
said to Philip. 6He said this as a test of Philip, for he himself knew
what he was going to do. 7Philip answered: 'A year's wages would not
buy enough bread for each of them to get a little.' 8One of his disciples,
Andrew, Simon Peter's brother, said to him: 9'There's a small boy here
who has five barley loaves and two little fishes. But what use is that
for a crowd like this?' 10Jesus said: 'Get the people to sit down.' There
was plenty of grass in the place. So the men sat down, about five
thousand of them. 11Jesus took the loaves. He thanked God for them,
and shared them out to the people as they lay on the grass. He did the
same with the fishes, and they all got as much as they wanted. 12When
the people had eaten their fill, he said to the disciples: 'Collect the
pieces that are left over. We mustn't waste anything.' 13So they
collected them, and filled twelve baskets with the pieces of the five
barley loaves which were left over after the people had eaten.

14When the people saw this demonstration of divine power that
Jesus had given, they said: 'This must be the Prophet who is to come
into the world!' 15Jesus knew that they were just on the point of
coming and trying forcibly to make him king. So he withdrew again
alone into the hill country.

16When evening came, his disciples went down to the lake, 17and
embarked on a boat, and started out across the lake to Capernaum.
By this time it was already dark and Jesus had not yet arrived. 18The sea
was rising because a gale was blowing. 19When they had rowed three
or four miles, they saw Jesus walking on the lake, and approaching
the boat, and fear gripped them. 20'It is I,' he said. 'Don't be afraid!'
21They wanted to take him on board the boat, but immediately the
boat was at the land for which they were making.

22On the next day, the crowd who had remained on the far side of
the lake realized that there had only been one boat there, and that

Jesus had not got into the boat with his disciples, but that his disciples
had gone off alone. 23Other little boats from Tiberias approached the
place where they had eaten the bread, when the Lord had given
thanks. 24So when the crowd saw that neither Jesus nor his disciples
were there, they boarded the little boats and went to Capernaum to
look for Jesus. 25When they found him on the other side of the lake,
they said to him: 'Rabbi, when did you get here?'

26'I tell you,' said Jesus, 'and it is true, you are not looking for me
because you recognized the power of God in action, but because you
ate your fill of the loaves. 27Do not work for the food which does not
last; work for the food which lasts for ever and which gives eternal
life, the food which the Son of Man will give to you, for it is he whom
the Father, God, has marked out as his own.' 28'What are we to do,'
they said to him, 'to do what God requires?' 29'What God requires,'
Jesus answered, 'is that you should believe in him whom he has sent.'
30'What visible proof are you going to give to us,' they said to him,
'that we may see it and believe in you? What are you going to do?
31Our fathers ate manna in the desert. As it stands written: "He gave
them bread from heaven to eat."' 32'I tell you,' Jesus said to them,
'and it is true, it was not Moses who gave you the bread from heaven;
it is my Father who is giving you the real bread from heaven. 33For
God's bread is he who comes down from heaven and gives life to the
world.' 34'Sir,' they said to him, 'give us now and always this bread.'
35'I am the bread of life,' Jesus said to them. 'If anyone comes to me,
he will never be hungry, and, if anyone believes in me, he will never
be thirsty. 36But, I have told you, though you have seen me, you do
not believe. 37All that the Father gives to me will come to me; and I
will not reject anyone who comes to me, 38because I have come down
from heaven, not to do my will, but to do the will of him who sent
me.

39'It is the will of him who sent me that of all that he has given me
I should not lose a single one; it is his will that I should raise up every
one of them on the last day. 40It is the will of the Father that anyone
who sees the Son and believes in him should have eternal life, and I
will raise him up on the last day.'

41A buzz of critical comment rose from the Jews because Jesus said:
'I am the bread of life which came down from heaven.' 42'Isn't this
Jesus, Joseph's son?' they said. 'Don't we know his father and mother?
How can he say, as he said just now, that he has come down from
heaven?' 43 Jesus said: 'Stop your whispering campaign of complaint.

44It is impossible for any man to come to me, unless the Father, who
sent me, draws him. But, if he does come, I will raise him up on the
last day.

45'It stands written in the prophets: "All will be taught by God." If
a man listens to the Father and learns from him, he will come to me.
46Not that anyone has seen the Father. The only one to have seen the
Father is he who has come from the presence of God; he has
seen the Father. 47I tell you, and it is true, to believe is to have eternal
life. 48I am the bread of life. 49Your ancestors ate the manna in the
desert—but they died. 50This is the bread which comes down from
heaven, and it has come, so that if anyone eats it, he will not die.
51I am the living bread which came down from heaven. To eat this
bread is to live for ever. The bread which I will give you is my flesh,
given for the life of the world.'

52The Jews began to argue violently with each other. 'How is it
possible for this man to give us his flesh to eat?' they said. 53'I tell you,'
Jesus said to them, 'and it is true, unless you eat the flesh of the Son of
Man and drink his blood, you have no life in you. 54But if anyone eats
my flesh and drinks my blood, he possesses eternal life, and I will
raise him up at the last day. 55My flesh is the real food, and my blood
is the real drink. 56If anyone eats my flesh and drinks my blood, he
remains in me and I in him. 57It is the living Father who sent me, and
it is through the Father I live; and he who eats me will live through
me. 58This is the bread which came down from heaven. It is not like
the bread which your ancestors ate, for, although they all ate it, they
died. To eat this bread is to live for ever.'

59This is the substance of the teaching Jesus gave in the synagogue
at Capernaum. 60Many of his disciples who had been listening said:
'This is a very difficult message. Who can listen to this?' 61Jesus was
well aware of the buzz of puzzled conversation that was going on
among his disciples. 'Does this shock you?' he said to them. 62'What
if you were to see the Son of Man ascending to where he formerly
was? 63It is the spirit which gives life; the flesh is of no help. The words
I have spoken to you are spirit and life. 64But there are some of you
who do not believe.' Jesus said this for he knew from the beginning
who did not believe, and he knew who it was who was going to
betray him. 65'It is for this reason,' he said, 'that I told you that it is
impossible for anyone to come to me, unless it was given to him to
do so by the Father.'

66From that time on many of his disciples turned back and no
longer remained with him. 67'Do you too want to go away?' Jesus
said to the Twelve. 68'Master,' Simon Peter answered, 'who could we
go to? You have the words of eternal life, 69and we are convinced and
sure that you are God's Holy One.' 70Jesus answered: 'Did I not
choose you, the twelve of you, and one of you is a devil?' 71He meant
Judas, Simon Iscariot's son, for he—one of the Twelve—was going to
betray him.

Chapter 7

AFTER that, Jesus moved about in Galilee. He was unwilling to do
so in Judaea, because the Jews were trying to find a way to kill
him.
2The Jewish Festival of Tabernacles was due soon to be celebrated.
3So Jesus' brothers said to him: 'Leave here and go to Judaea, to
give your disciples too a chance to see you in action. 4No one acts
secretively, if he wishes to focus public attention on himself. If you do
these things, make up your mind to show yourself to the world.'
5His brothers took this line, because not even they believed in him.
6'My time has not yet arrived,' Jesus said to them. 'Your time is any
time. 7It is impossible for the world to hate you, but it does hate me,
because I am a witness to the evil of its deeds. 8Go up to the festival
yourselves. I am not yet going up to this festival because my time has
not yet fully come.' 9He said this to them, and stayed on in Galilee.
10When his brothers had gone up to the festival, then he too went
up, not publicly, but secretly. 11The Jews were looking for him at the
festival. 'Where is this man everyone is talking about?' they kept
saying. 12The crowds were buzzing with talk about him. Some of them
said: 'He is a good man.' Others said: 'No! On the contrary! He is
leading the crowd astray.' 13But no one spoke about him openly for
fear of the Jews.
14When the festival was already half finished, Jesus went into the
Temple, and began to teach. 15'Where,' said the Jews in astonishment,
'does this man get this knowledge, when he has never been a college
student?' 16'My teaching,' Jesus said, 'is not my own; it comes from
him who sent me. 17Anyone who is willing to do his will, will know
whether this teaching comes from God, or whether I am speaking
only on my own authority. 18The man who speaks with no authority

beyond himself is seeking his own personal glory. It is the man who
seeks the glory of him who sent him who speaks the truth. There is no
wickedness in him. 19Didn't Moses give you the Law? Yet none of
you perfectly obeys the Law. Why are you trying to kill me?' 20'You're
demon-possessed,' the crowd answered. 'Who is trying to kill you?'
21'I performed one miracle on the Sabbath,' Jesus said, 'and you are
all shocked. 22Now Moses gave you circumcision—not that circum-
cision started with Moses; it started with the patriarchs—and you
circumcise a man on the Sabbath. 23If a man can be circumcised on
the Sabbath without breaking the Law of Moses, how can you be
angry with me, because I gave a whole man his health on the
Sabbath day? 24Don't judge by externals; let your judgment be really
just.'

25Some of the people of Jerusalem said: 'Isn't this the man they are
trying to kill? 26And here he is speaking boldly and openly and
nobody says anything to stop him. Is it possible that the government
has actual knowledge that this is the Messiah? 27But he can't be,
because we know where this man comes from, but when the Messiah
comes, no one is to know where he comes from.' 28As he was teaching
in the Temple precincts, Jesus said in a voice that all could hear:
'You know me, and you know where I came from. I did not come on
my own initiative. It is the one who is the source of truth who sent
me—and you do not know him. 29I know him, because I come from
him, and it was he who sent me.' 30They would have liked to seize
him, but no one laid a hand upon him, because his hour had not yet
come.

31Many of the crowd believed in him. 'When the Messiah comes,'
they said, 'surely he will not provide greater demonstrations of the
power of God in action than this man has done?' 32The Pharisees
heard the crowd buzzing with talk like this about Jesus. So the chief
priests and Pharisees sent officers to arrest him. 33'I am to be
with you a little longer,' Jesus said, 'before I go back to him who sent
me. 34You will search for me, you will not find me, and you cannot
come where I am to be.' 35The Jews said to each other: 'Where is he
going to go that we will not be able to find him? Can he be going to
the Jews who are scattered throughout the Greek world, to teach the
Greeks? 36What can he mean when he says that we will search for him
and not be able to find him, and that it will be impossible for us to
come where he is to be?'

37On the last day of the festival, the great day, Jesus took his stand,
and said for all to hear: 'If anyone is thirsty, let him come to me, and
let him drink. 38If a man believes in me—as the scripture says—
rivers of living water shall flow from within him.' 39In saying this, he
was speaking about the Spirit, whom those who believed in him were
going to receive, for as yet there was no such thing as the Spirit, for
Jesus had not yet been glorified.

40When they heard these words, some of the crowd said: 'This really
is the promised Prophet.' 41'This is the Messiah,' others said. 'But
surely,' others said, 'the Messiah does not come from Galilee? 42Does
the scripture not say that the Messiah is to be a descendant of David,
and is to come from Bethlehem where David was?' 43The crowd were
split in their attitude to him. 44Some of them wished to arrest him,
but no one laid a hand on him.

45So the officers went back to the chief priests and Pharisees, who
said to them: 'Why haven't you brought him?' 46'No one ever spoke
as this man speaks,' the servants answered. 47'Have you too been led
astray?' the Pharisees answered. 48'Has any member of the Sanhedrin
believed in him, or any of the Pharisees? 49As for the mob who neither
know nor want to know the Law, they are bound for hell anyway.'
50Nicodemus, who had come to Jesus before, and who was one of
them, said to them: 51'Does our Law condemn any man without giv-
ing him a hearing, and without investigating his actions?' 52'Are you
too from Galilee?' they answered. 'Examine the scriptures and you
will see that no prophet emerges from Galilee.'

53They all went home.

Chapter 8

But Jesus went to the Hill of Olives.
2Early in the morning he went back to the Temple precincts,
and the people all flocked to him. He sat down and began to teach
them. 3The experts in the Law and the Pharisees brought to him a
woman arrested for adultery. They placed her in the centre of the
crowd. 4'Teacher,' they said to him, 'this woman was arrested in
the very act of adultery. 5Moses laid it down in the Law for us that
the penalty in such cases is stoning. What do you say?' 6They
intended this as a test question, for they wished to have grounds

on which to formulate a charge against him. Jesus stooped down
and wrote with his finger on the ground. 7When they continued
to question him, he straightened himself. 'If there is anyone here
who is sinless,' he said, 'let him start the stoning!' 8And he again
stooped down and wrote on the ground. 9When they heard this,
beginning from the oldest, they began to leave one by one, and
Jesus was left alone with the woman standing there. 10Jesus
straightened himself. 'Where are they?' he said. 'Has no one con-
demned you?' 11'No one, sir,' she said. 'I don't condemn you
either,' Jesus said. 'Go and from now on stop sinning.'*

12Jesus again spoke to them. 'I am the light of the world.' he said. 'To
follow me is to walk, not in the dark, but to be in possession of the
light of life.' 13'You make claims about yourself,' the Pharisees said to
him, 'and your claims are not true.' 14'Even if I do make claims
about myself,' Jesus answered, 'my claims are true, because I know
where I came from and where I am going to. You do not know where
I came from or where I am going to. 15You pass judgment on purely
human standards. I do not pass judgment on anyone. 16But, if I do
pass judgment, my verdict is true, because I am not alone, but I and
the Father who sent me combine to judge. 17It is written in your Law
that the evidence of two men is true. 18It is I who make claims for
myself, and the Father who sent me makes the same claims for me.'
19'Where is your father?' they said to him. 'You do not know either
me or my Father,' Jesus answered. 'To know me is to know my
Father too.'

20He said this in the Treasury, when he was teaching in the Temple
precincts; and no one arrested him for his hour had not yet come.

21Jesus went on to say to them: 'I am going away, and you will try
to find me, and you will die in your sin. It is impossible for you to go
where I am going.' 22'Is he going to kill himself?' the Jews said. 'Is this
what he means when he says that it is impossible for us to go where
he is going?' 23'You belong to the world below,' he said to them. 'I
belong to the world above. You belong to this world; I do not belong
to this world. 24I told you that you will die in your sins, for, if you do
not believe that I am who I am, you will die in your sins.' 25'Who are
you?' they said to him. 'What I have told you from the beginning,'

* The best and most ancient manuscripts of the New Testament do not contain this story.

Jesus said to them. 26'I have many things to say about you, and many
judgments to pass on you; but he who sent me speaks nothing but
the truth, and I tell the world what he told me.' 27They did not
realize that he was speaking to them about the Father. 28'When you
lift high the Son of Man,' Jesus said to them, 'then you will realize that
I am who I am, and that nothing I do has its source in myself, but I say
what the Father taught me to say. 29He who sent me is with me. He
has not left me alone, because I always do what pleases him.' 30While
he was saying this many believed in him.

31Jesus said to the Jews who had believed in him: 'If you make my
message the fixed centre of your life, you really are my disciples, 32and
you will know the truth, and the truth will liberate you.' 33'We are
Abraham's descendants,' they answered, 'and we have never been
slaves to anyone. How can you say that we will be liberated?' 34'I tell
you,' Jesus answered, 'and it is true, if a man's actions are sinful, he is
the slave of sin. 35The slave has no permanent home in the house; the
son has a permanent home in the house. 36If the Son gives you free-
dom, it will be real freedom. 37I am well aware that you are Abra-
ham's descendants. For all that, you are trying to kill me, because you
are incapable of receiving my message. 38It is what I have seen in my
Father's presence that I tell you about. You ought to obey the message
that has come to you from the Father.' 39'Abraham is our father,' they
answered. 'If you are Abraham's children,' Jesus said to them, 'you
ought to act like Abraham. 40As it is, you are doing your best to kill
me, a man who has told you the truth, the truth that God told me.
That is not the way in which Abraham acted. 41You must act as your
father acted.' They said to him: 'We were not born as the result of any
adulterous union. We have one Father—God.' 42'If God was your
father, you would have loved me,' Jesus said to them. 'It is from God
I am, and it is from God I come. It is not on my own initiative
that I have come, I came because he sent me. 43Why can't you
understand what I say? It is because you are incapable of hearing
my message.

44'The devil is your father, and you wish to identify your actions
with the Desires of your father. He was a murderer from the begin-
ning. He did not take his stand on the truth, because the truth is not
in him. It is characteristic of him to tell lies, because he is a liar and the
father of falsehood. 45The very fact that I speak the truth keeps you
from believing in me. 46Which of you can prove me guilty of sin? If
I speak the truth, why do you not believe me? 47If a man's life has its

source in God, he will listen to God's words. It is because the source
of your life is not in God that you do not listen to me.'
48 The Jews answered: 'Are we not perfectly right to say that you are
a Samaritan and that you are devil-possessed?' 49 'I have no devil,'
Jesus answered. 'I honour my Father, and you dishonour me. 50 I do
not seek my own glory. There is One who does seek it—and he is
judge. 51 I tell you, and it is true, anyone who obeys my message will
never experience death.' 52 'Now we know that you are devil-pos-
sessed,' the Jews said to him. 'Abraham died, and so did the prophets,
but you say, that anyone who obeys your message will never ex-
perience death. 53 Are you greater than our father Abraham? He died,
and the prophets died. Who do you think you are?' 54 'If I glorify
myself,' Jesus answered, 'my glory means nothing. The Father is the
One who glorifies me, that God who, you claim, is your God. 55 You
do not know him—but I know him. If I say to you that I do not
know him, I will be a liar like you; but I do know him, and I do obey
his word. 56 Abraham your father rejoiced to see my day, and he was
glad when he saw it.' 57 'You are not yet fifty,' the Jews said to him.
'How can you have seen Abraham?' 58 'I tell you,' said Jesus, 'and it is
true, before Abraham came into being, I am.' 59 They picked up stones
to throw at him, but Jesus hid himself, and went out of the Temple
precincts.

Chapter 9

As Jesus was walking along the street, he saw a man who had been
born blind. 2 'Rabbi,' his disciples asked him, 'was it this man's own
sin, or was it the sin of his parents, which was responsible for the fact
that he was born blind?' 3 Jesus answered: 'The reason for this man's
blindness is neither any sin of his own nor of his parents; the reason
is to allow the activity of God to be displayed in him. 4 We must carry
on the work of him who sent me so long as it is day; the night is
coming when it is impossible for any man to work. 5 So long as I re-
main in the world, I am the light of the world.'
6 After saying this, Jesus spat on the ground and made clay with the
spittle, and smeared the man's eyes with the clay. 7 'Go,' he said to him,
'and wash in the Pool of Siloam.' (The word Siloam means sent.)
So he went and washed and came back able to see.
8 The neighbours, and those who recognized him as the beggar they

used to see, said: 'Isn't this the man who used to sit and beg?' 9Some
said: 'It is him.' Others said: 'No! It's someone very like him.' He him-
self said: 'I am the man.' 10'How were you made able to see?' they
asked him. 11The man answered: 'The man called Jesus made clay and
smeared it on my eyes, and told me to go to Siloam and wash. So I
went and washed—and saw!' 12'Where is this man?' they said to him.
'I don't know,' he said.

13They took him to the Pharisees, this man who had once been
blind. 14Now the day on which Jesus had made the clay and had
cured his blindness was the Sabbath. 15The Pharisees too asked him
again how he had come to see. He said to them: 'He put clay on my
eyes, and I washed, and I can see.' 16'This man does not come from
God,' some of the Pharisees said, 'because he does not observe the
Sabbath.' But others said: 'Is it possible for a man who is a bad man to
perform actions like this, for such actions are visible signs of the
power of God at work?' And they differed violently about Jesus.

17They said to the blind man again: 'What have you to say about
him? Do you really claim that he cured your blindness?' 'He is a
prophet,' he said. 18The Jews did not believe that the man had been
blind and that he had been made able to see, until they had called the
parents of the man who had been made able to see, 19and asked them:
'Is this your son, and do you say that he was born blind? How can he
now see?' 20'We know that this is our son,' his parents answered, 'and
we know that he was born blind, 21but how he now sees we do not
know, nor do we know the man who made him able to see. Ask
him! He is no child! He is quite old enough to speak for himself!' 22His
parents took this line because they were frightened of the Jews. For the
Jews had already agreed that anyone who expressed the belief that
Jesus was the Messiah should be excommunicated. 23That is why his
parents said: 'He is not a child! Ask him!'

24They summoned a second time the man who had been born
blind. 'Give God the glory,' they said to him. 'We know that this man
is a bad man.' 25He answered: 'I do not know whether or not he is a
bad man. I do know one thing—I was blind and now I can see.'
26'What did he do to you?' they said to him. 'How did he make you
able to see?' 27'I have already told you,' he said, 'and you didn't listen.
Why do you want to hear the story all over again? Would you too like
to become his disciples?' 28They hurled abuse at him. 'It is you who are
his disciple,' they said. 'We are Moses' disciples. 29We know that God
spoke to Moses, but we have no idea where this man has come from.'

30'Here indeed is an astonishing state of affairs,' the man answered.
'You don't know where he comes from, and he has made me able to
see. 31We know that God does not listen to bad men, but he does
listen to anyone who reverences him and obeys him. 32Since the
world began, it is an unheard-of thing for anyone to make a man born
blind able to see. 33If this man did not come from God, he could not
do anything.' 34'You were born in nothing but sin,' they said to him,
'and do you have the nerve to try to teach us?' And they threw him
out.

35When Jesus heard that they had thrown him out, he sought him
out and said to him: 'Do you believe in the Son of Man?' 36'But who
is he, sir?' the man answered. 'I would like to believe in him.' 37Jesus
said to him: 'You have not only seen him. It is he who is speaking to
you now.' 38'Lord,' he said, 'I believe.' And he knelt in front of him.
39Jesus said: 'It is for judgment that I came into this world, so that
those who do not see may see, and that those who see may become
blind.' 40When some of the Pharisees who were there heard this, they
said: 'Are we included among the blind?' 41'If you were blind,' Jesus
said to them, 'you would not be guilty of any sin; as it is, you claim to
be able to see, and so your sin remains.'

Chapter 10

'I TELL you,' Jesus said, 'and it is true, if anyone does not enter the
sheepfold by the door, but climbs in by some other way, he is a
thief and a brigand. 2If a man is a shepherd of the sheep, he enters
through the door. 3The doorkeeper opens the door to him, and the
sheep recognize his voice, and he calls each of his sheep by its own
name, and leads them out. 4When he brings all his sheep out, he
walks in front of them, and the sheep follow him, because they
recognize his voice. 5They will not follow a stranger; they will run
away from him, because they do not recognize the voice of
strangers.' 6Jesus addressed this parable to them, but they did not
realize what he was saying to them.

7So Jesus spoke again to them. 'I tell you,' he said, 'and it is true, I
am the door of the sheep. 8All who came before me are thieves and
brigands, but the sheep did not listen to them. 9I am the door. If
anyone enters through me, he will go in and out in safety, and will
find pasture. 10The thief comes only to kill and destroy. I have come

that they may have life and overflowing life. 11I am the good shepherd.
The good shepherd is ready to die for the sheep. 12The man who is
working only for pay, the man who is not really a shepherd, and who
is not the real owner of the sheep, leaves the sheep and runs away
when he sees a wolf coming—and the wolf savages the sheep and scat-
ters them—13because he cares for nothing but his pay, and does not
really care what happens to the sheep.

14'I am the good shepherd, and I know my sheep, and they know
me, 15just as the Father knows me, and I know the Father, and I am
ready to die for the sheep. 16I have other sheep which do not belong
to this fold. These too I must bring in. They will hear my voice, and
there will be one flock, one shepherd. 17The reason why the Father
loves me is that I lay down my life so that I may receive it back again.
18So far from anyone forcibly taking it from me, I am laying it down
of my own free will. I have the power to lay it down, and I have the
power to take it back again. This is the command I have received
from my Father.'

19These words caused a further cleavage of opinion among the
Jews. 20Many of them said: 'A demon has made him insane. Why
do you listen to him?' 21Others said: 'These are not the words of
a demon-possessed madman. Can a demon enable the blind to see?'

22It was the Feast of the Dedication. 23It was winter. Jesus was
walking in the Temple precincts in Solomon's Porch. 24The Jews
surrounded him. 'How long are you going to keep us in suspense?'
they demanded. 'Tell us definitely whether or not you are the
Messiah.' 25'I have told you,' Jesus answered, 'and you do not
believe me. My actions as the representative of my Father are my
evidence for my claims. 26But you do not believe, because you are no
sheep of mine. 27My sheep recognize my voice, and I know them.
They follow me, 28and I give them eternal life. So long as the world
lasts, they will never perish, and no one will ever snatch them out
of my keeping. 29It is my Father's power which gave them to me,
and that power is greater than all else. No one can snatch them
out of the Father's keeping. 30I and the Father are one.'

31The Jews picked up stones to stone him. 32Jesus answered: 'You
have seen me do many lovely things, things which had their source in
the Father. Which of them are you stoning me for?' 33The Jews
answered: 'It is not for any lovely action that we are stoning you.

We are stoning you for your blasphemous claims, for you, a man, are
making yourself God.' 34Jesus answered: 'Does it not stand written in
your Law: "I said, you are gods"? 35Scripture then says that those to
whom the message of God came were gods, and scripture cannot be
annulled. 36Can you then accuse me, me whom the Father conse-
crated and sent into the world, of blasphemy, because I said that I am
the Son of God? 37If my actions are not the actions of my Father, then
don't believe in me. 38But, if they are, even if you don't believe in me,
believe in what I do. Then you will know and realize that the Father
is in me, and that I am in the Father.'

39Again they tried to seize him, but he slipped through their
hands. 40Jesus went away again to Transjordan, to the place where
John had first baptized, and remained there. 41Many came to him.
'John himself,' they said, 'did nothing in which the action of God
was visibly displayed, but everything John said about this man was
true.' 42And many believed in him there.

Chapter 11

A MAN called Lazarus was ill. He belonged to Bethany, the village
where Mary and her sister Martha lived. 2It was Mary who
anointed the Lord with perfume, and who wiped his feet with her
hair, whose brother Lazarus was ill. 3The sisters sent a message to
Jesus. 'Master,' they said, 'the man you love is ill.' 4'This illness will
not prove fatal,' Jesus said, when he received the news. 'It is designed
for the glory of God, and it is meant to be the means of bringing
glory to the Son of God.' 5Martha and her sister and Lazarus were
very dear to Jesus.

6Jesus remained for two days in the place where he was, after he
had heard the news that Lazarus was ill. 7He then said to his disciples:
'We must go to Judaea again.' 8'Rabbi,' his disciples said to him, 'how
can you propose to go back there again, when the Jews so short a
time ago tried to stone you?' 9'Aren't there twelve hours in the day?'
Jesus answered. 'If a man walks in the day-time, he does not stumble,
because he sees this world's light. 10But if a man walks in the night-
time, he does stumble, because there is no light in him.'

11After saying this he went on to say to them: 'Our dear friend
Lazarus is asleep, but I am going to him to waken him.' 12'Master,' his
disciples said to him, 'if he is asleep, he will get better.' 13It was about

the death of Lazarus that Jesus had spoken, but they thought that he
was speaking about the slumber of natural sleep. 14Jesus then said to
them plainly: 'Lazarus is dead, 15and for your sakes I am glad that I
wasn't there, because this has all happened to strengthen your faith.
But we must go to him.' 16Thomas, who was called the Twin, said to
his fellow-disciples: 'We've got to go too, to die with him.'

17So Jesus went, and found that by this time Lazarus had been in
his tomb for four days. 18Bethany was near Jerusalem, about two
miles away. 19Many of the Jews had come to Martha and Mary, to
comfort them in their grief for their brother's death. 20When Martha
heard that Jesus was coming, she went and met him, but Mary re-
mained sitting in the house. 21'Master,' Martha said to Jesus, 'if you
had been here, my brother would not have died. 22But, even as things
are, I know that God will give you anything you ask him for.' 23'Your
brother will rise again,' Jesus said to her. 24Martha said to him: 'I
know that he will rise at the resurrection of the dead on the last day.'
25'I am the resurrection and the life,' Jesus said to her. 'In death
to believe in me is to live again. In life, for any man, to believe in
me is never to die. Do you believe this?' 27'Master,' she said to him,
'I do. I am sure that you are the Messiah, the Son of God, the One
who is to come into the world.'

28When she had said this, she went and called her sister Mary. She
said to her, without letting anyone else know: 'The Teacher is here,
and wants you to come.' 29When Mary heard this, she rose quickly
and went to Jesus. 30Jesus had not yet entered the village. He was still
in the place where Martha had met him. 31When the Jews, who were
with her in the house, and who were trying to comfort her, saw that
Mary had risen quickly and had gone out, they followed her, think-
ing that she was going to the tomb to weep there. 32Mary came to the
place where Jesus was. When she saw him, she threw herself down at
his feet. 'Master,' she said, 'if you had been here, my brother would
not have died.' 33When Jesus saw her, and the Jews who had come
with her, weeping, he was deeply and visibly moved, and distressed in
spirit. 34'Where have you buried him?' he said. 'Sir,' they said to him,
'come and see.' 35Jesus burst into tears. 36'Look how he loved him!'
the Jews said. 37Some of them said: 'Is it not possible that this man,
who made the blind man see, could have stopped Lazarus dying too?'
38Jesus was visibly moved again. He came to the tomb. It was a cave,
and a stone had been placed at the mouth of it. 39'Take the stone
away!' Jesus said. Martha, the dead man's sister, said to him: 'His body

has the stench of death, for it has been in the tomb for four days.'
40Jesus said to her: 'Didn't I tell you that, if you have faith, you will
see the glory of God?' 41They removed the stone. Jesus looked up and
said: 'Father, I thank you that you have heard me. 42I know that you
always hear me. But it is for the sake of this crowd here I spoke. I
want them to believe that you have sent me.' 43When he had said
this, Jesus shouted: 'Lazarus, come out!' 44The dead man came out,
wrapped around hand and foot in the grave-clothes, and with a towel
wrapped round his face. 'Free him from the wrappings,' Jesus said,
'and let him go.' 45Many of the Jews, who had come to visit Mary, and
who had seen what Jesus did, there and then believed in him. 46But
some of them went off to the Pharisees, and told them what Jesus had
done.

47The chief priests and Pharisees assembled the Sanhedrin. 'What
are we to do?' they said. 'This man's actions frequently have all the
marks of divine action. 48If we leave him alone to go on like this,
everyone will believe in him, and the Romans will come and destroy
our Temple, and it will be the end of religious and political freedom.'
49One of them, Caiaphas, the High Priest for that year, said to them:
'You haven't grasped the seriousness of the situation. 50You do not
see that the only reasonable conclusion is that it is better for our
interests for one man to die for the people than for the whole nation
to be wiped out.' 51He did not really think this out for himself. He
said it because he was the High Priest for that year, and so unwittingly
prophesied that Jesus was to die for the nation, 52and not for the
nation only, but in order that the children of God, who were scat-
tered all over the world, should be gathered into one.

53From then on they planned to kill Jesus. 54So Jesus no longer
moved publicly amongst the Jews. He left them and went away to a
district near the desert, to a town called Ephraim, and stayed there
with his disciples.

55The Jewish Passover Festival was near, and people came up in
large numbers from the countryside to Jerusalem before the Passover
to make themselves ceremonially clean. 56As they stood about in the
Temple precincts talking to each other, they kept looking for Jesus.
'What do you think?' they said. 'Surely he is not likely to come to the
festival?' 57For the chief priests and Pharisees had issued instructions
that, if anyone knew where Jesus was, he should give information
which might lead to his arrest.

Chapter 12

Six days before the Passover Jesus went to Bethany. Lazarus, whom
he had raised from the dead, stayed there. 2They gave him a dinner
there, at which Martha served the guests, and Lazarus was one of
those who sat at table with him. 3Mary took a pound of pure and very
expensive nard perfume, and anointed Jesus' feet with it, and wiped
his feet with her hair. The house was filled with the scent of the
perfume.

4Judas Iscariot, one of Jesus' disciples, the man who was going to
betray him, said: 'Perfume like this would cost a year's wages for a
working man. 5Why wasn't it sold, and the proceeds given to the
poor?' 6It was not because the poor meant anything to him that he
said this, but because he was a thief, for he had charge of the money-
box, and he pilfered from what was deposited in it. 7'Let her alone,'
Jesus said. 'Let her observe the last rites now in anticipation of the
day when my body will be buried. 8You have the poor with you
always, but you do not have me always.'

9The Jews knew that he was there, and they came in their crowds.
They came, not only because of Jesus, but also to see Lazarus, whom
Jesus had raised from the dead. 10The chief priests decided to kill
Lazarus, 11for because of him many of the Jews were abandoning
Judaism and beginning to believe in Jesus.

12The next day, when the thronging crowds who had come to the
festival heard that Jesus was coming to Jerusalem, 13they took palm
branches and went out to meet him. They kept shouting:

> 'Send your salvation!
> Blessings on him who comes in the name of the Lord,
> on him who is the King of Israel!'

14Jesus found a young donkey and mounted it, just as it stands writ-
ten:

> 15'Have no fear, daughter of Sion!
> Your King is coming,
> mounted on an ass's colt.'

16His disciples did not at the time understand the meaning of these

events, but, when Jesus was glorified, then they remembered that
these things had been written about him and had been done to him.
17The crowd, who were with Jesus when he had called Lazarus from
the tomb and raised him from the dead, told the story of what
he had done. 18It was because they had heard that he had given
this visible demonstration of divine power in action that the crowd
came to meet him. 19The Pharisees said to each other: 'It is plain to
see that nothing is any good. All the world has felt his fatal attraction.'

20There were some Greeks amongst those who came up to worship
at the festival. 21They approached Philip, who came from Bethsaida
in Galilee, with a request. 'Sir,' they said to him, 'we wish to see
Jesus.' 22Philip went and told Andrew, and Andrew and Philip came
and told Jesus.

23Jesus said: 'The time has come for the Son of Man to be glorified.
24I tell you, and it is true, if a grain of corn does not fall into the
ground and die, it remains alone. But if it dies, it produces a large crop.
25To love your life is to lose it; to hate your life in this world is to keep
it, and the end will be eternal life. 26If anyone wishes to serve me, he
must follow me, and where I am, my servant will be too. The Father
will honour anyone who becomes my servant.

27'I am in distress of soul just now. What am I to say? Am I to say:
"Father, save me from this hour"? But no! It is for this purpose that
I have come to this hour. 28Father, glorify your name.' A voice came
from heaven: 'I have glorified it already, and I will glorify it again.'
29When the crowd who were standing by heard this, they said that it
was the noise of thunder. 'An angel spoke to him,' others said.
30Jesus answered: 'It was not for my sake that this voice came, but for
yours. 31The time for the judging of this world has come. The prince
of this world will now be banished. 32As for me, when I am lifted up
from the earth, I will draw all men to me.' 33He said this as an indication
of the kind of death he was going to die. 34The crowd answered:
'Our information from the Law is that the Messiah is to remain as long
as time lasts. How can you say that the Son of Man must be lifted up?
Who is this Son of Man?'

35Jesus said to them: 'It is only for a little while longer that the light
is to be with you. Get on your way while you have the light so that
darkness may not come down upon you. When a man walks in the
dark, he cannot see where he is going. 36While you have the light,

believe in the light, that you may become sons of light.' After he
had said this, Jesus went away and hid himself from them.

37Although the actions of Jesus had been so visibly filled with
divine power, they did not believe in him. 38Their unbelief was the
fulfilment of the word which the prophet Isaiah spoke:

'Lord, who has believed our report?
And to whom has the arm of the Lord been revealed?'

39It was impossible for them to believe for the reason given by Isaiah
in another passage:

40'He has blinded their eyes;
He has made them impervious to all appeal,
In case they should see with their eyes,
and understand with their heart, and turn,
and I should heal them.'

41It was because he saw Jesus' glory that Isaiah said this. It was about
him he spoke. 42In spite of this, many of the national leaders did take
the decision to believe in him, but because of the Pharisees, they did
not openly affirm their faith, for they did not wish to find themselves
barred from the synagogue. 43They were more concerned with their
popular reputation than with the honour which only God can give.
44Jesus said for all to hear: 'To believe in me is to believe, not in me,
but in him who sent me; 45and to see me is to see him who sent me.
46I have come as light into the world, and therefore to believe in me
is no longer to remain in darkness. 47If anyone listens to my words
and does not obey them, it is not I who am his judge. It was not to
judge the world that I came, but to save it. 48If anyone regards me
as of no account, and if anyone does not accept my message, he has
his judge. The word I have spoken will be his judge on the last day.
49For I did not speak out of my own authority; it was the Father who
sent me who gave me a command what to speak and what to say.
50And I know that his command is eternal life. When I speak, I repeat
what the Father has said to me.'

Chapter 13

BEFORE the Passover, Jesus knew that the time had come for him to
leave this world and to go to the Father. He had always loved his
own in this world, and now he gave them a proof of his love, beyond
which love could not go.
2The evening meal was in progress. The Devil had already put the
decision to betray Jesus into the heart of Judas Iscariot, Simon's son.
3Jesus knew that God had handed all things over to him, and that he
had come from God, and was returning to God. 4He therefore rose
from the meal, and stripped off his clothes, and took a towel and
fastened it round his waist. 5He then put water into a ewer, and began
to wash his disciples' feet, and to wipe them with the towel which he
had round his waist.
6He came to Simon Peter. 'Master,' Simon Peter said to him, 'are
you going to wash my feet?' 7'At the moment you do not understand
what I am doing,' Jesus answered, 'but, when you look back, you will
realize the meaning of it.' 8'You will never wash my feet,' Peter said to
him. 'If I do not wash you,' Jesus answered, 'you can never be my
partner.' 9'Don't stop at my feet,' Simon Peter said to him. 'Wash my
hands and my head too!' 10Jesus said: 'If a man has been bathed, when
he comes in off the street, all that he needs washed is his feet. The
whole of him is clean. And you are clean—but not everyone of you.'
11He knew who was betraying him. That is why he said that not all
of them were clean. 12When he had washed their feet, he put on his
clothes again, and returned to his place at table. 'Do you understand
what I have done to you?' he said to them. 13'You address me as
Teacher and Master, and you are right to do so, for so I am. 14If I the
Master and the Teacher have washed your feet, then you too ought
to wash each other's feet, 15for I have given you an example to teach
you to treat others as I have treated you. 16I tell you, and it is true, the
servant is not superior to his master, nor is the messenger superior to
the person who sent him. 17If you know that this is true, you are
happy if you act as if it was true.
18'I am not speaking about you all. I know the men whom I have
chosen. The passage of scripture must come true: "He who eats my
bread has lashed out at me with his heel." 19I am telling you of this
before it happens, so that when it does happen, you may believe that

I am who I am. 20I tell you, and it is true, to receive anyone whom I
send is to receive me, and to receive me is to receive him who sent
me.'
21When Jesus had said this, he was in deep distress in spirit. 'I tell
you, and it is true,' he solemnly said, 'that one of you will betray me.'
22His disciples looked at each other, for they had no idea whom he
meant. 23One of his disciples, the disciple who was specially dear to
Jesus, was reclining on Jesus' right, so that his head was leaning against
Jesus' shoulder. 24Simon Peter signed to him. 'Ask him who he is
talking about,' he said. 25So then, leaning close to Jesus as he was, he
said to him: 'Master, who is it?' 26Jesus answered: 'It is the one for
whom I will dip the bread in the dish and give it to him.' So he dipped
the bread in the dish, and gave it to Judas, Simon Iscariot's son. 27It was
after he had received the bread that Satan entered into him. Jesus said
to him: 'Do what you are going to do, and do it quickly.' 28None of
those who were present at the table knew why Jesus said this to him.
29Since Judas had charge of the common purse, some of them
thought that Jesus was telling him to buy the things they needed for
the festival, or to see to the customary Passover gift for the poor.
30Immediately after Judas had received the bread, he went out. It
was night.
31After Judas had gone out, Jesus said: 'Now the Son of Man has
been glorified, and God has been glorified in him; 32and God will
glorify himself in him, and will glorify him here and now. 33Dear
children, I will not be with you much longer now. You will look for
me, and, as I said to the Jews I now say to you too, you cannot come
where I am going. 34I give you a new commandment—to love each
other. As I have loved you, you too must love each other. 35It is by
your love for each other that all will recognize that you are my
disciples.'
36'Master,' Simon Peter said to him, 'where are you going?' 'It is not
possible for you now to follow me where I am going,' Jesus answered,
'but afterwards you will follow.' 37'Master,' Peter said to him, 'why
can't I follow you now? I will die for you.' 38'So you will die for me?'
Jesus answered. 'I tell you, and it is true, before the cock crows, you
will disown me three times.'

Chapter 14

'DON'T let your heart be distressed. Keep on believing in God, and
keep on believing in me. 2There are many rooms in my Father's
house. If there weren't, would I have told you that I am going to get
ready a place for you? 3If I go and get ready a place for you, I will come
back again, and I will take you with me, so that you too may be where
I am. 4You know the way to where I am going.' 5'Master,' Thomas
said to him, 'when we don't know where you're going, how can we
possibly know the way?' 6Jesus said to him: 'I am the true and living
way. The only way for anyone to come to the Father is through me.
7To know me is to know the Father. From now on you do know him
and you have seen him.' 8'Master,' Philip said to him, 'show us the
Father, and we will be content.' 9'Have I been with you all this time,
Philip,' Jesus said to him, 'and have you still not realized who I am?
To have seen me is to have seen the Father. How can you say: "Show
us the Father"? 10Do you not believe that I am in the Father, and that
the Father is in me? I myself am not the source and origin of what I
say to you. The Father lives in me and acts through me. 11You must
believe me when I say that I am in the Father and that the Father is in
me. If you do not believe me because of what I say, you must believe
me because of what I do. 12I tell you, and it is true, if anyone believes
in me he will not only do what I am doing, he will do even greater
things, because I am going to the Father. 13I will do whatever you ask
in my name, so that the Father may be glorified in the Son. 14I will
do anything you ask me in my name.

15'If you love me, you will obey my commands. 16I will ask the
Father, and he will give you another Helper to be with you for ever,
17I mean the Spirit of truth. It is impossible for the world to receive
him, because it neither sees nor knows him. You know him because
he stays with you, and is in you. 18I will not leave you to face life all
alone. I am coming to you. 19Very soon the world will no longer see
me, but you will see me. Because I live, you too will live. 20When that
time comes, you will know that I am in my Father, and that you are
in me and that I am in you.

21'To know my commands and to obey them is really to love me.
If anyone loves me, he will be loved by my Father, and I too will love
him, and I will show myself clearly to him.' 22Judas—not Iscariot—

said to him: 'Master, why is it that you are going to show yourself to
us, but not to the world?' 23Jesus answered: 'Anyone who loves me
will obey what I say; and my Father will love him, and we will come
and make our home with him. 24If a man does not love me, he does
not obey what I say. The message I have brought to you is not mine;
it comes from the Father who sent me.

25'I have told you this while I am still with you. 26But the Helper,
the Holy Spirit, whom my Father will send in my place, will teach
you everything, and will remind you of all that I said to you.

27'My last gift to you is peace. It is my own peace that I give to you.
My gift is not a gift the world can ever give. Don't let your heart be
distressed, and don't let it lose its courage. 28You have heard me tell-
ing you that I am going away and that I am coming back to you. If
you really loved me, you would be glad that I am going to my Father,
for the Father is greater than I.

29'I have told you this now before it happens, so that, when it does
happen, you may not lose your faith. 30I am not going to talk very
much more to you. The prince of this world is coming, but he has no
hold over me. 31It has all got to happen to make the world realize that
I love the Father, and that I do exactly what he has instructed me to
do. Up! We must go!'

Chapter 15

'I AM the real vine,' Jesus said, 'and my Father is the vine-dresser.
2Any branch in me which bears no fruit, he removes, and any
branch which bears fruit, he purifies, to make it bear more fruit. 3You
are already purified through the message which I brought to you. 4It
is essential that you should remain in me, and I in you. No branch
can bear fruit in isolation by itself; it must remain in the vine. Just so,
neither can you, unless you remain in me. 5I am the vine; you are the
branches. If anyone remains in me, and I in him, he bears much fruit,
because apart from me it is impossible for you to do anything. 6If
anyone does not remain in me, he is thrown out like a withered
branch. Branches like that are collected and thrown into the fire to
be burned. 7If you remain in me, and if my words remain in you, ask
anything you wish, and it will be done for you.

8'The only way in which you can bring glory to my Father is to
bear much fruit, and to show yourselves to be my disciples. 9My love

for you is the same as the Father's love for me. Remain in my love.
10To obey my commands is to remain in my love, just as I have
obeyed my Father's commands, and remain in his love. 11I have
spoken like this to you so that I may find my joy in you, and so that
your joy may be complete.

12'It is my command that your love for each other should be the
same as my love for you. 13The greatest love that a man can have is
to give his life for his friends. 14To be my friends you must do what
I command you. 15I am no longer going to call you servants. A servant
does not know what his master is doing. I have called you friends,
because I have told you everything which my Father told me.'

16'It was not you who chose me; it was I who chose you. I have
appointed you to go and bear fruit, fruit that will be permanent, so
that my Father may give you anything you ask in my name. 17My
command to you is to love each other. 18When you experience the
world's hatred, you must realize that it hated me before it hated you.
19If you had belonged to the world, the world would have loved its
own. The very reason that the world hates you is that you do not
belong to the world, but that I have picked you out of the world.
20Remember what I said to you. The servant is not superior to his
master. If they have persecuted me, they will persecute you too.
They will respond to your message in the same way as they responded
to mine. 21They will do all these things to you because of your con-
nection with me, because they do not know him who sent me.'

22'If I had not come and spoken to them, they would not be guilty
of sin. As it is, they have no excuse for their sin. 23To hate me is to
hate my Father too. 24If they had not seen me act in a way in which
no one else ever acted, they would not be guilty of sin. As it is, they
have seen and hated both me and the Father. 25But all this happened
that the saying written in their Law might come true: "They have
hated me without a cause."'

26'When the Helper, whom I will send to you from the Father,
comes, I mean the Spirit of truth, who comes from the Father, he will
be a witness for me. 27And you too must be witnesses for me, because
you have been with me from the beginning.'

Chapter 16

'I HAVE told you all these things so that, when they happen, your
faith will not collapse. 2They will banish you from the synagogues.
More—the time is coming when to kill you will be regarded as an act
of sacred service to God. 3They will treat you like this because they
did not know either the Father or me. 4I have told you these things so
that, when the time comes for them to happen, you may remember
that I had already told you about them. I did not talk like this to you
at first, because I was still with you, 5but now I am going back to him
who sent me, and none of you asks me where I am going.

6'But because I have talked like this to you, your heart is filled with
distress. 7But I am telling you the truth—it is to your advantage that
I should go away, for I must go away before the Helper will come to
you. If I do go away, I will send him to you. 8When he comes, he will
convict the world of its own sin, and he will convince the world of
my righteousness and of the certainty of judgment. 9He will compel
the world to see that not to believe in me is sin. 10He will compel
them to see that the fact that I am going to the Father and passing
beyond your sight is the proof of my righteousness. 11He will compel
the world to see that judgment has come, because the prince of this
world stands condemned.

12'There is still much that I have to say to you, but at present it
would be too much for you to bear. 13When he has come, I mean the
Spirit of truth, he will guide you into all the truth. It will not be out
of his own knowledge that he will speak; he will speak all that he will
hear from God, and he will tell you about the things which are going
to happen. 14He will glorify me, for everything he will tell you will
have its source in what is mine. 15Everything that belongs to the
Father belongs to me. That is why I said that everything he will tell
you has its source in what is mine.

16'Very soon you will not see me any more, and then again very
soon you will see me.' 17Some of the disciples said to each other:
'What does he mean when he says to us that very soon we will not see
him any more, and that then again very soon we will see him? What
does he mean when he says that he is going away to the Father?
18What does he mean,' they said, 'when he speaks about "very soon"?
We have no idea what he is talking about.'

19Jesus knew that they wanted to ask him what he meant. So he said
to them: 'Are you asking each other what I meant, because I said that
very soon you will not see me, and that then again very soon you will
see me? 20I tell you, and it is true, you will weep and you will lament
like mourners at a funeral, but the world will be glad. You will be in
distress, but your distress will turn to joy. 21When a woman is having
a baby, she is in distress because her time has come. But, as soon as the
baby is born, she does not remember the pain any more in her joy
that a man child has been born into the world. 22Just so, you for the
present are in distress. But I will see you again, and your heart will
rejoice, and no one is going to take your joy from you. 23When that
time comes, you will not ask me for anything. I tell you, and it is
true, the Father will give you anything you ask for in my name. 24Up
to now you have asked nothing in my name. Keep on asking and you
will keep on receiving, and so your joy will be complete.

25'I have talked to you so far in pictures and in figures of speech.
The time is coming when I will no longer talk to you in pictures and
in figures of speech, but when I will tell you about the Father absol-
utely clearly. 26When that time comes you will take your own re-
quests to the Father in my name. I tell you that I will not ask the
Father to give you an answer. 27I will not need to, because, the
Father himself loves you, because you have loved me, and because
you have believed that I have come from God. 28It was from the
Father I came, when I came into the world. It is to the Father I go,
now that I am leaving the world again.'

29'This is plain speaking now,' the disciples said to him. 'This is not
just a picture and a figure of speech. 30We know now that you know
everything, and that there is no necessity for anyone to ask you
questions. This makes us quite sure that you have come from God.'
31'Do you believe now?' Jesus answered. 32'The time is coming—it has
come—when you will all be scattered to your own homes, and when
you will leave me all alone. But I am not alone, because the Father is
with me. 33I have told you these things that in me you may have all
that makes for true happiness. In the world you are going to have
trouble. But courage! I have conquered the world.'

Chapter 17

WHEN he had said this, Jesus looked up to heaven and said: 'Father,
the time has come. Glorify your Son that the Son may glorify
you, 2 for you have placed all mankind under his authority, so that he
may give eternal life to everyone you have given to him. 3 It is eternal
life to know you, the only real God, and Jesus Christ whom you
sent. 4 I have glorified you on earth by completing the task you gave
me to do. 5 And now, Father, give me in your own presence the glory
which I had with you, before the world came into existence.
6 'I have shown the men whom you took out of the world and
gave to me what you are really like. They belonged to you, and you
gave them to me, and they have obeyed the message which you sent
to them. 7 They now know that all the gifts you have given to me do
come from you, 8 for I have told them what you told me, and
they accepted my message, and they know for certain that I came
from you, and they have accepted it as true that you sent me.
9 'It is for them that I pray. I do not pray for the world; I pray for
those whom you have given me, because they belong to you. 10 All
that I have is yours, and all that you have is mine, and in them I am
glorified. 11 I am no longer in the world, but they are in the world. I
am coming to you. Holy Father, protect them with your personal
protection, as you did me, that they may be one just as we are one.
12 When I was with them, I protected them with your personal pro-
tection, as you did me, and so well did I guard them that the only one
of them who is lost is the man who had to be lost, so that what
scripture foretold might come true.
13 'Now I am coming to you, and I am telling them all this while I
am still in the world that they may have within them that fulness of
joy which only I can give. 14 I brought them your message, and the
world hated them, because they do not belong to the world, just as I
do not belong to the world. 15 I do not ask you to remove them from
the world. What I do ask you to do is to protect them from the evil
one. 16 They do not belong to the world just as I do not belong to
the world. 17 Consecrate them to yourself by the truth. Your word is
truth. 18 I sent them out into the world, just as you sent me into the
world. 19 I consecrate myself to you for their sakes, that they too
may be consecrated by the truth.

20'I do not pray only for my disciples here. I pray too for those who
are to believe in me through their preaching. 21I pray that all of them
may be one. I pray that just as you, Father, are in me and I am in you,
so they too may be in us, for it is this that will make the world believe
that you have sent me. 22I have given them the glory which you gave
me, so that they may be one as we are one, 23I in them and you in me,
that they may be perfectly one, for it is this that will make the world
realize that you sent me, and that you loved them as you loved me.

24'Father, it is my wish for all whom you have given me, that they
should be with me where I am, so that they may see my glory which
you have given me, because you loved me before the creation of the
world. 25Righteous Father, although the world does not know you,
I know you, and these know that you sent me. 26I have told them
what you are like, and I will continue to tell them, so that the love
with which you loved me may be in them, and so that I may be in
them.'

Chapter 18

WHEN he had said this, Jesus went out with his disciples, across the
gulley where the Kedron flows. There was a garden there, and
Jesus went into it with his disciples. 2Judas, who was arranging his
betrayal, knew the place well, for Jesus and his disciples often met
there. 3So Judas obtained a detachment of Roman soldiers, together
with a party of the Temple police, who were supplied to him by the
chief priests and Pharisees, and went there with lanterns and torches
and weapons. 4Jesus was well aware of all that was going to happen to
him. He stepped forward and said to them: 'Who are you looking
for?' 5'Jesus the Nazarene,' they answered. 'I am he,' he said to them.
Judas the traitor was standing there with them. 6When Jesus said to
them: 'I am he,' they stepped back and fell to the ground. 7Jesus asked
them again: 'Who are you looking for?' 'Jesus the Nazarene,' they
said. 8'I told you that I am he,' Jesus answered. 'If it is me you are
looking for, let these men go.' 9He said this so that his own statement
that he had not lost a single one of those whom God had given him
might come true.

10Simon Peter had a sword. He drew it, and struck the High Priest's
servant, and cut off his right ear. The servant's name was Malchus.

11 'Put your sword into its scabbard,' Jesus said to Peter. 'Shall I not
willingly accept whatever the Father sends me, however bitter it may
be?'

12 The company of soldiers and their commander and the Jewish
Temple police seized Jesus, and bound him. 13 They began by taking
him to Annas. Annas was the father-in-law of Caiaphas who in that
year was High Priest. 14 It was Caiaphas who had advised the Jews that
the sensible thing was that one man should die for the people.

15 Simon Peter followed Jesus along with another disciple. That
disciple was personally known to the High Priest. So he went into the
courtyard of the High Priest's house with Jesus, 16 while Peter remained
standing outside at the gate. The other disciple who was personally
known to the High Priest went out and spoke to the maidservant who
was in charge of the door, and brought Peter in. 17 The maidservant
who was in charge of the door said to Peter: 'You too are one of this
man's disciples, aren't you?' 'I am not,' he said. 18 The servants and the
Temple police had made a fire, and were standing beside it warming
themselves, because it was cold. Peter was standing warming himself
with them.

19 The High Priest questioned Jesus about his disciples and about his
teaching. 20 Jesus answered: 'I spoke to the world perfectly openly. I
have always taught in the synagogue and in the Temple precincts,
where all the Jews meet. I have said nothing in secret. 21 Why do you
question me? Ask those who heard me what I said to them. They
know what I said.' 22 When Jesus said this, one of the Temple police
who was standing by gave him a slap across the face. 'How dare you
answer the High Priest like that?' he said. 23 'If there is anything wrong
with what I have said,' Jesus answered, 'you must produce your
evidence to prove that it was wrong. If there is nothing wrong with
what I said, why strike me?' 24 So Annas sent him bound to Caiaphas
the High Priest.

25 Peter was standing warming himself. They said to him: 'You too
are one of his disciples, aren't you?' He denied it. 'I am not,' he said.
26 One of the High Priest's servants, who was a relation of the man
whose ear Peter had cut off, said to him: 'Didn't I see you in the garden
with him?' 27 Peter denied it again. Just then the cock crew.

28 Jesus was then taken from Caiaphas' house to the governor's
headquarters. It was early in the morning. The Jews did not them-

selves enter the governor's headquarters. They did not want to risk
being ceremonially defiled. They wanted to be able to eat the Pass-
over meal. 29So Pilate came out to them. 'What is the charge you are
bringing against this man?' he said. 30'If he had not been a criminal,'
they answered, 'we would not have handed him over to you.' 31'Take
him yourselves,' Pilate said, 'and try him by your own law.' 'We are
not permitted to put anyone to death,' the Jews said to him. 32By
saying this they made it certain that Jesus' statement foretelling how
he would die would come true. 33Pilate went into his headquarters
again. He summoned Jesus. 'Are you the King of the Jews?' he said to
him. 34Jesus answered: 'Are you saying this because you have dis-
covered it yourself, or because other people told you that I am?'
35'Am I a Jew?' Pilate answered. 'It is your own nation and the chief
priests who have handed you over to me. What have you done?'
36'My kingdom does not belong to this world,' Jesus answered. 'If my
kingdom belonged to this world my supporters would have been
putting up a struggle to stop me being handed over to the Jews. The
plain fact is that my kingdom does not belong to this realm of things.'
37'So you are a king?' Pilate said to him. Jesus said: 'It is you who are
calling me a king. The reason why I was born, and the reason why I
came into the world, is to declare the truth. If a man is a child of the
truth, he listens to what I have to say.' 38'What is truth?' Pilate said to
him. After he had said this, he again went out to the Jews. 'There is
nothing of which I can find this man guilty,' he said to them. 39'You
have a custom that at the Passover time I should release one prisoner
as a favour to you. Do you wish me to release the King of the Jews?'
40They shrieked: 'Not this man, but Barabbas!' Barabbas was a brigand.

Chapter 19

PILATE then took Jesus and had him flogged. 2The soldiers twisted
some thorny twigs into a crown and put it on his head. They
dressed him in a purple robe. 3They kept coming up to him and say-
ing: 'Hail! King of the Jews!' Repeatedly they slapped him across the
face. 4Pilate came out again. 'Look!' he said to them. 'I am bringing
him out to you, because I want you to know that there is nothing
of which I can find him guilty.' 5So Jesus came out wearing the crown
of thorns and the purple robe. Pilate said to them: 'Here is the man!'
6When the chief priests and the Temple police saw him, they shrieked:

'Crucify him! Crucify him!' 'Take him and crucify him yourselves,'
Pilate said to them, 'for there is nothing of which I can find him
guilty.' 7'We have a law,' the Jews answered, 'and by the law he ought
to be put to death, because he claimed to be the Son of God.'
8When Pilate heard this he was still more alarmed. 9He went into his
headquarters again and said to Jesus: 'Where do you come from?'
Jesus refused to answer him. 10'You will not speak to me?' Pilate said.
'Are you not aware that it is in my power to release you, and in my
power to have you crucified?' 11'You would have no power over me at
all,' Jesus answered, 'if it had not been given to you from above. For
that reason the man who betrayed me is guilty of a greater sin than
you are.'

12From then on Pilate tried everything to release Jesus. But the
Jews kept shrieking: 'If you release this man, you are no friend of
Caesar. Anyone who sets himself up as a king is in opposition to
Caesar.' 13When Pilate heard this, he brought Jesus out. He took his
place upon his official judgment seat, on the place called the Pave-
ment—in Hebrew it is called Gabbatha. 14It was the day before the
Passover, and it was about twelve o'clock midday. 'Here is your king!'
he said to the Jews. 15They shrieked: 'Away with him! Away with
him! Crucify him!' 'Am I to crucify your king?' Pilate said to them.
'Caesar is the only king we have!' the chief priests answered. 16Then
Pilate handed Jesus over to them to be crucified.

17So they took Jesus, and he went away carrying his cross for him-
self, to the place called the Place of a Skull, the Hebrew name of
which is Golgotha. 18They crucified him there, and along with him
they crucified two others, one on each side and Jesus between them.

19Pilate had an inscription written and fixed to the cross. The
writing ran: 'Jesus the Nazarene, the King of the Jews.' 20Many of the
Jews read this inscription, because the place where Jesus was crucified
was near the city, and it was written in Hebrew and in Latin and in
Greek. 21The Jewish chief priests said to Pilate: 'Don't write, "The
King of the Jews." "Write, He claimed to be the King of the
Jews."' 22Pilate answered: 'What I have written, I have written.'

23When the soldiers had crucified Jesus, they took his clothes, and
divided them into four parts, one part for each soldier. They kept his
tunic separate. The tunic was seamless, woven from top to bottom in
one piece. 24'We mustn't tear it,' they said. 'It will be better to draw

lots to decide who is to get it.' This they did, so that the passage of
scripture might come true:

> 'They divided my clothes amongst them,
> and they cast lots for my raiment.'

This is what the soldiers did.

25Jesus' mother, his mother's sister, Mary the wife of Cleopas, and
Mary from Magdala were standing beside the cross. 26When Jesus saw
his mother with the disciple who was specially dear to him standing
beside her, he said to his mother: 'Look! Your son!' 27Then he said to
the disciple: 'Look! Your mother!' From then on the disciple took her
into his own home.

28After that, since he knew that everything was now completed
and done, Jesus said: 'I am thirsty,' so that the words of scripture
might come true. 29A jar of bitter wine was standing there. So they
put a sponge soaked in bitter wine on a spear and lifted it to his mouth.
30When he had received the bitter wine, Jesus said: 'Finished!' He
bowed his head and surrendered his life to God.

31Since it was the day before the Passover, the Jews asked Pilate to
have the legs of the crucified men broken, and their bodies removed,
to prevent their bodies remaining on their crosses during the Sabbath,
for that Sabbath was a specially great day. 32So the soldiers came and
broke the legs of the first man, and of the other man who had been
crucified with Jesus. 33But, when they came to Jesus, they saw that
he was already dead. So they did not break his legs. 34But one of the
soldiers pierced his side with a spear, and water and blood immediately
issued from it.

35The man who actually saw this happen is a witness to it and his
evidence is true (God knows that he is telling the truth), for his aim
is that you too may believe. 36This happened that the passage of
scripture should come true: 'Not one of his bones shall be broken.'
37And again, another passage of scripture says: 'They shall look
on him whom they have pierced.'

38After this, Joseph of Arimathaea asked Pilate for permission to
remove Jesus' body. He was a disciple of Jesus, but in secret, because
he was afraid of the Jews. Pilate gave him permission. So he came
and took Jesus' body away. 39Nicodemus, who had first come to Jesus
at night, came too. He brought with him about a hundred pounds of

a mixture of myrrh and aloes. 40They took Jesus' body, and wrapped
it in strips of linen cloth with the spices, for this is the customary
Jewish method of burial.

41There was a garden at the place where Jesus was crucified, and in
the garden there was a new tomb, in which no one had ever been
laid. 42So, because it was for the Jews the evening of the preparation
for the Sabbath, and because the tomb was close at hand, they laid
Jesus there.

Chapter 20

ON Sunday Mary from Magdala went to the tomb so early in the
morning that it was still dark. When she saw that the stone had
been removed from the tomb, 2she went running to Simon Peter
and to the other disciple, the disciple who was specially dear to Jesus.
'They have taken away the Master from the tomb,' she said, 'and we
don't know where they have put him.' 3Peter and the other disciple
set out on the way to the tomb. 4They both began to run. The other
disciple ran on ahead, faster than Peter, and reached the tomb first.
5He stooped down and looked in, and saw the linen grave-clothes
lying there, but he did not go in. 6Simon Peter arrived after him,
and went into the tomb. He saw the linen grave-clothes lying there,
7and he saw the towel, which had been round Jesus' head, lying not
with the other grave-clothes, but still in its folds, separately in a
place all by itself. 8Then the other disciple, who had arrived at the
tomb first, went in, and when he saw the inside of the tomb he was
convinced. 9As yet they did not understand that scripture said that
Jesus had to rise from the dead. 10So the disciples went back home.

11But Mary stood beside the tomb, outside it, crying. In the midst of
her tears she stooped down, and looked into the tomb. 12She saw two
angels dressed in white, sitting one at the head, and one at the feet of
the place where the body of Jesus had lain. 13'Why are you crying?'
they said to her. 'They have taken away my Master,' she said, 'and I
don't know where they have put him.' 14When she had said this, she
turned round, and saw Jesus standing there, but she did not know it
was Jesus. 15'Why are you crying?' Jesus said to her. 'Who are you look-
ing for?' She thought that he was the gardener. 'Sir,' she said, 'if you
have removed him, tell me where you have put him, and I will take

him away.' 16Jesus said to her: 'Mary!' She turned and said to him in
Hebrew: 'Rabbouni!' which means, 'Teacher!' 17'You must not cling
to me,' Jesus said to her, 'for I have not yet gone up to the Father. Go
to my brothers and tell them that I am going to my Father and your
Father, to my God and your God.' 18Mary from Magdala went with
the news to the disciples. 'I have seen the Lord!' she said, and she told
them what he had said to her.

19On the evening of the same day, the Sunday, when the doors of
the room, where the disciples were, were locked because of their fear
of the Jews, Jesus came and stood among them. 'God's blessing be on
you!' he said to them. 20When he had said this, he showed them his
hands and his side. When the disciples saw the Lord, they were glad.
21Jesus said to them again: 'God's blessing be on you! I am sending
you as the Father sent me.' 22When he had said this, he breathed on
them. 'Receive the Holy Spirit,' he said. 23'If you forgive anyone's sins,
they are forgiven. If you retain anyone's sins, they stand retained.'

24Thomas, one of the Twelve, who was called the Twin, was not
with them when Jesus came. 25The other disciples said to him: 'We
have seen the Lord!' 'Unless I see the mark of the nails in his hands,'
he said, 'unless I put my finger in the mark of the nails, and unless I
put my hand into his side, I refuse to believe it.' 26A week later the
disciples were indoors together again, and Thomas was with them.
When the doors were locked, Jesus came and stood among them.
'God's blessing be on you!' he said. 27Then he said to Thomas: 'Look
at my hands! Put your finger here! Take your hand, and put it into my
side! Stop being unbelieving, and believe!' 28Thomas answered: 'My
Lord and my God!' 29Jesus said to him: 'Do you believe, because you
have seen me? Blessed are those who have believed, although they
have never seen me!'

30Jesus did many other things in the presence of his disciples in
which the power of God was demonstrated in action, but they are
not written in this book. 31This book was written to make you believe
that Jesus is the Messiah, the Son of God, and that your belief may
bring you life through his name.

Chapter 21

AFTER this Jesus again showed himself to the disciples on the shore
of the Lake of Tiberias. This is the story of how he did so.
2Simon Peter, and Thomas, who is called the Twin, and Nathanael
from Cana in Galilee, and Zebedee's sons, and other two of his
disciples were together. 3'I am going to the fishing,' Simon Peter
said to them. 'We are coming with you too,' they said. They went
away and embarked on the boat, and that night they caught nothing.
4Just as the day was breaking, Jesus stood on the beach, but the
disciples did not know that it was Jesus. 5'Lads,' Jesus said to them,
'have you caught any fish?' 'No,' they answered. 6'Cast your net on
the right-hand side of the boat,' he said to them, 'and you will find
some.' So they cast the net, and now they could not haul it in, because
there were so many fish in it. 7The disciple who was specially dear to
Jesus said to Peter: 'It is the Lord!' When Simon Peter heard him say
that it was the Lord, he threw on his tunic, for he was stripped for
work, and jumped into the sea. 8The others followed in the boat—
they were no great distance from land, only about a hundred yards
away—dragging the net filled with fish. 9When they disembarked on
the land, they saw a charcoal fire laid, with fish cooking on it, and a
loaf. 10'Bring some of the fish you have just caught,' Jesus said to
them. 11Simon Peter got on board, and dragged the net to land, full
of big fish, one hundred and fifty-three of them; and, although there
were so many of them, the net was not broken.
12'Come and have breakfast,' Jesus said to them. None of the
disciples dared to ask him who he was, for they knew that it was the
Lord. 13Jesus went and took the loaf, and gave it to them, and the fish
too. 14This was the third time that Jesus appeared to his disciples,
after he had been raised from the dead.

15When they had breakfasted, Jesus said to Simon Peter: 'Simon,
son of John, do you love me more than these others do?' 'Yes, indeed,
Lord,' Peter said to him, 'you know that I love you.' 'Feed my lambs,'
Jesus said to him. 16Jesus said to him a second time: 'Simon, son of
John, do you love me?' 'Yes, indeed, Lord,' Peter said to him, 'you
know that I love you.' 'Be a shepherd to my sheep,' Jesus said to him.
17Jesus said to him a third time: 'Simon, son of John, do you love me?'

Peter was vexed that Jesus said to him a third time: 'Do you love
me?' 'Lord,' he said to Jesus, 'you know everything. You do know that
I love you.' 'Feed my sheep,' Jesus said to him.*

18'I tell you, and it is true,' Jesus went on to say to Peter, 'when you
were young, you tucked up your robe for action, and went where you
chose. But when you are old, you will stretch wide your arms, and
someone else will bind you, and carry you to a place not of your own
choosing.' 19Jesus said this to indicate the kind of death by which
Peter would glorify God. When he had said this, he said to him:
'Follow me!'

20Peter turned and saw following them the disciple who was
specially dear to Jesus, the disciple who had been sitting next to Jesus
at the evening meal with his head on Jesus' shoulder, and who had
asked: 'Lord, who is it who is going to betray you?' 21When Peter
saw him, he said to Jesus: 'Lord, what is going to happen to this man?'
22'If it should be my will that he should survive until I come,' Jesus
said to him, 'what has that got to do with you? All that concerns you
is to follow me.' 23The Christian community got to know about
this saying, and they took it to mean that that man would not die.
But Jesus did not say to him that he would not die. What he said
was: 'If it should be my will that he should survive until I come, what
has that got to do with you?'

24It is this disciple who guarantees the truth of these facts, and who
has written the story of them, and we know that his evidence is true.
25Jesus did many other things, so many that, if a detailed account of
them were written down, I do not think that the world itself would be
able to hold the books that would have to be written.

* Verses 13-17: In the Greek of this passage two different words are used for 'to love'. It is almost certain that there is no difference in meaning between them, but if a difference in meaning is to be expressed the passage may be translated as follows:

15When they had breakfasted, Jesus said to Simon Peter: 'Simon, son of John, do
you love me more than these others do?' 'Yes, indeed, Lord,' Peter said to him,
'you know that you are dear to me.' 'Feed my lambs,' Jesus said to him. 16Jesus
said to him a second time: 'Simon, son of John, do you love me?' 'Yes, indeed,
Lord,' Peter said to him, 'you know that you are dear to me.' 'Be a shepherd to
my sheep,' Jesus said to him. 17Jesus said to him a third time: 'Simon, son of John,
am I dear to you?' Peter was vexed that Jesus said to him the third time: 'Am I
dear to you?' 'Lord,' he said to Jesus, 'you know everything. You do know that
you are dear to me.' 'Feed my sheep,' Jesus said to him.

On Translating the New Testament

On Translating the New Testament

WHAT need is there for still another translation of the New Testament? This is a question which may well be asked. But there are at least two answers to it.

F. C. Grant has truly said: 'Biblical translation is an endless process.'[1] And he also says: 'If a translation is to be any good, it must be addressed to the times in which it is written.'[2] This necessarily means that there is a sense in which a translation begins to go out of date on the day when it is completed, for language is never static, but always on the move.

The second reason for the production of new translations is that in the nature of things perfection in translation is impossible. However carefully wrought a translation is, it can never perfectly express the thought and convey the impression of the original. The translators of the Authorised Version said of themselves and of their work: 'Neither did we disdain to revise that which we had done, and to bring back to the anvil that which we had hammered.'[3] However much the thing is revised, and however often it is brought back to the anvil, the perfection of the marriage of one language to another must remain for ever elusive.

A heavy responsibility is laid on any translator, for he deliberately takes it upon himself to be the medium through which the ancient writer reaches the modern reader; and, when the ancient book is the book which is the foundation document of the Christian faith, the responsibility becomes even heavier. That responsibility has never been better expressed than by John Purvey, John Wycliffe's successor, in his 'General Prologue' written in 1395 or 1396:

> 'A translator hath great need to study well the sense both before and after, and then also he hath need to live a clean life and be full devout in prayers, and have not his wit occupied about worldly things, that the Holy Spirit, author of all wisdom and knowledge and truth, dress him for his work and suffer him not to err. By this manner, with good living and great travail, men

[1] F. C. Grant, *Translating the Bible*, p. 97.
[2] F. C. Grant, *Translating the Bible*, p. 133.
[3] *The Authorised Version*, 'The Translators to the Reader'.

can come to true and clear translating, and true understanding of holy writ, seem it never so hard at the beginning. God grant us all grace to know well and to keep well holy writ, and to suffer joyfully some pain for it at the last.'[1]

John Purvey knew that a man must know more than languages, if he is to be an adequate translator, and of that truth a translator must ever be humbly mindful.

If the spirit of the translator was long ago described by John Purvey, the aim of the translator was equally well described by John Wycliffe in his preface to the *Harmony of the Gospels*:

'I beseech and with all my heart pray them that read this work, that for me they pray the mercy of God, that I may fulfil what is set in the drawing of this book; and that he at whose suggestion I this work began, and they that read this work, and all Christian men with me, through doing of that which is written in this book, may come together to that bliss that shall never end.'[2]

In the end the translator's aim is that those who read his translation should know Christ more clearly and follow him more nearly and love him more dearly.

In the early days of translation the desire of the ordinary people to know the Scripture was there. It is Foxe's witness that in 1520 multitudes were tasting and following the sweetness of God's word, that they were sitting up all night to read or to hear it, that some 'gave five marks, some more, some less for a book; some gave a load of hay for a few chapters of St. James or of St. Paul in English.' He speaks of 'their travails, their earnest seekings, their burning zeal, their readings, their watchings, their sweet assemblies.'[3] And it was the determination of the early translators to meet this need. As John Foxe tells in his *Book of Martyrs*, Tyndale said to a learned man: 'If God spare my life, ere many years I will cause a boy that driveth the plough shall know more of the Scriptures than thou dost.'[4] And as Erasmus said in the preface to his Greek New Testament of 1516:

'I totally disagree with those who are unwilling that the Holy

[1] Quoted thus in F. F. Bruce, *The English Bible*, p. 20; in the original spelling in *History of the English Bible*, B. F. Westcott, 3rd edn., rev. Aldis Wright, p. 16.

[2] Quoted B. F. Westcott, *History of the English Bible*, p. 16.

[3] Quoted B. F. Westcott, *History of the English Bible*, p. 20.

[4] Quoted F. F. Bruce, *The English Bible*, p. 29.

Scriptures, translated into the common tongue, should be read by the unlearned. Christ desires his mysteries to be published abroad as widely as possible. I could wish that even all women should read the Gospel and St. Paul's Epistles, and I would that they were translated into all the languages of all Christian people, that they might be read and known not merely by the Scots and Irish but even by the Turks and Saracens. I wish that the farm workers might sing parts of them at the plough, that the weaver might hum them at the shuttle, and that the traveller might beguile the weariness of the way by reciting them.'[1]

In the ancient days the aim of the translator was to satisfy the hunger of the hearts of men; and it may be the aim of the modern translator, not so much to satisfy that hunger, as to awaken it.

The spirit of the translator, the aim of the translator and the need of translation are clear. The problem is the method of translation.

It is clear that translation to be of any value must be far more than the substitution of a word in one language for a word in another language. Translation done like that ends up by being in no language at all, and anyone who translates like that can produce something of which he does not even begin to understand the meaning. Words have been changed from one language into another, but in the process the meaning has been lost. F. C. Grant cites an example of this word-by-word translation of Luke 20.1,2:

'And it became in one of the days teaching of him the people in the temple and evangelizing they stood up the high priests and the scribes with the presbyters and they said saying against him, They tell us in such authority these things you do. . . .'

In that passage each Greek word has its English equivalent correctly given from the dictionary point of view, but the result is intolerable. In many cases the famous Bohn library of translations followed this literal method, and F. C. Grant quotes the verdict of the Philadelphia bookseller William H. Allen on it. He described it in a catalogue as 'a fairly intelligible translation, provided you use the Greek as a pony, (that is, as a crib).'[2] It is precisely that kind of translation which has ruined the classics for so many schoolboys.

Simply to turn a word in one language into a word in another

Quoted F. F. Bruce, *The English Bible*, p. 29.
F. C. Grant, *Translating the Bible*, pp. 131, 135.

language is certainly not to translate in any intelligible sense of the term. What is probably 'the most literal translation ever made'[1] is the Bible of Robert Young, famous for the *Analytical Concordance to the Bible*. It was first published in 1862. Two short extracts from it will show what it is like:

> 'Already also the axe to the root of the trees is laid, every tree, therefore, not bringing forth good fruit is cut down, and into the fire cast.' (Luke 3.9)
>
> 'And the thing they kept to themselves, questioning together what that is—to rise from the dead.' (Mark 9.10)

This is completely literal translation, but, whatever it is, it is not English.

Certain essentials of a translation may be laid down. 'It should be perfectly intelligible in itself without reference to the Greek.' It ought to be 'idiomatic and interesting, not only to the scholar, but to the unlearned reader.' 'The translation should retain as far as possible the characteristic qualities of the ancient writer . . .; or the best part of him will be lost to the English reader. It should read as an original work and should also be the most faithful transcript which can be made of the language from which the translation is taken, consistently with the first requirement of all, that it be English.'[2]

Here we have the basis of the principles of New Testament translation. The Greek of the New Testament is not classical Greek; it is not even very good Greek. Gilbert Murray wrote to Sybil Thorndike: 'Read St. John's Gospel; it's bad Greek, but it will open a door for you.'[3] The Greek of the New Testament is not the Greek which the cultured people of the time either wrote or spoke; it is the Greek of the man in the street. It is in what is called *koinē* Greek, common Greek, the simplified, non-literary, colloquial Greek, which, following the conquests of Alexander the Great, had become the *lingua franca* of the ancient world. It finds its best illustrations, not in the literary works contemporary with it, because the literary people were still trying to write classical Greek, but in the papyrus letters of the ordinary men and women of the time, letters which never got into

[1] H. Pope, *English Versions of the Bible*, pp. 544, 545.

[2] These quotations are from the preface to the second edition (1875) of Benjamin Jowett's translation of the Dialogues of Plato, and are quoted in F. C. Grant, *Translating the Bible*, pp. 136, 131, 136.

[3] Gilbert Murray, *An Unfinished Autobiography*, p. 174.

books, but which have been dug up from the dust-heaps of Egypt. It has in fact been said that, apart from its religious value, the New Testament is one of the most important linguistic books in the world, for in it alone do we find the Greek which the men and women of the first century spoke on the street and in their homes. It is therefore a simple fact that anything which makes the New Testament sound stately and dignified and archaic, or even beautiful, in style gives precisely the wrong impression of what it originally was. It spoke the common language which all men spoke and understood. It is not slang, and to make it sound like slang is bad translation; but it is colloquial and to make it sound like ordinary speech is good translation. Its *-eths*, and its *-ests*, and its *thou*'s and its *thee*'s were perfectly right in 1611, because then people did speak like that. They now give the New Testament an archaism which produces precisely the opposite effect to that which it first had. It is of interest to note that *The Gospels: A New Translation*, by Andrew Norton, published in Boston in 1855, was apparently the first modern translation to use the normal *you* for the archaic *thou*.[1]

One of the strangest facts in the history of translation is how long it has taken for this principle to become accepted, and even yet it is still by no means fully accepted. In 1888 a certain Ernest Bilton published an experimental translation entitled *The Four Gospels, translated into Modern English from the Authorised and Revised Versions*. He found it necessary to explain in his preface that he had no desire 'to bring ridicule on the Gospel by thus translating it into the language of everyday life.'[2] No true translation of the New Testament can be made so long as the dominating desire is for beauty of literary style rather than plain and challenging lucidity of meaning.

The problem of the translator is to find a way to the production of such a translation. Basically, there are two kinds of translation. 'Two alternatives present themselves at once, the literal and the literary method of translation.'[3] To put it in another way, the one method sets out to reproduce one word by another, even, if possible, maintaining the order of the words in the original, with no attempt at all to write English style; the other method is more concerned with the sense than with the form, and seeks to make a translation which reads like original English, and not like a translation at all. F. F. Bruce

[1] H. Pope, *English Versions of the Bible*, p. 546.
[2] H. Pope, *English Versions of the Bible*, p. 587.
[3] Ronald A. Knox, *On Englishing the Bible*, p. 3.

quotes C. J. Cadoux: 'There are two ideals in translation, associated respectively with the Universities of Oxford and Cambridge. While the Oxford method aims at conveying the sense in free and idiomatic English without much regard for the exact wording of the original, the Cambridge method aims at translating the words and nuances of the original as literally as possible, provided that no actual violence is done to English usage.'[1]

John Purvey was well aware of this difference in method even in the fourteenth century. In his 'Preface' he writes:

> 'First, be it known that the best translating out of Latin into English [it was the Vulgate from which he was translating] is to translate after the sentence [by 'sentence' he means 'sense' or 'meaning,' not 'sentence' in the sense of a group of words] and not only after the words, so that the sentence be as open [that is, clear or plain], or opener, in English as in Latin, and go not far from the letter; and, if the letter may not be followed in the translating, let the sentence ever be whole and open, for the words ought to serve to the intent and sentence, or else the words be superfluous or false.'[2]

It was not the words, but the sense, which Purvey was concerned to transmit.

Long before Purvey, Jerome himself had been well aware of this choice in translation. Jerome solved his problem in the same way as Purvey—but with one all-important difference and exception. In his letter to Sunnia and Fretela, Jerome wrote that the task of a good translator 'consists in rendering idiomatic expressions of one language into the modes of expression peculiar to the other.' Elsewhere, in some of his prefaces, he emphasizes that he does not translate word for word, but sense for sense.[3]

Letter 57 sets out Jerome's normal theory of translation. 'I render sense for sense, and not word for word.' Jerome quotes the words of Cicero in Cicero's introduction to his translation into Latin of the two speeches *On the Crown*, originally delivered by Aeschines and Demosthenes. 'I have rendered them, not as a translator, but as an

[1] *The Bible in Ancient and English Versions*, ed. H. W. Robinson, p. 251; quoted F. F. Bruce, *The English Bible*, p. 142.

[2] Quoted F. F. Bruce, *The English Bible*, pp. 19, 20.

[3] Jerome, *Letters* 106.3.3; quoted W. Schwarz, *Principles and Problems of Biblical Translation*, p. 34.

orator, keeping the sense but altering the form, by adapting both the metaphors and the words to suit our idiom. I have not deemed it necessary to render word for word, but I have reproduced the general style and emphasis. I have not supposed myself bound to pay the words out one by one to the reader, but only to give him an equivalent in value.' 'In making it [the translation] I have utilised all the excellences of the originals, I mean the sentiments, the forms of expression and the arrangement of the topics, while I have followed the actual wording only so far as I could do so without offending our notions of taste. If all that I have written is not to be found in the Greek, I have at any rate striven to make it correspond with it.' Jerome goes on to quote Horace's advice in the *Art of Poetry*:

> 'And care not thou with over anxious thought
> To render word for word.'[1]

Jerome refuses to identify 'fidelity in transcription' with what he calls 'pestilent minuteness'. A word, he says, in any language has its own meaning, and another language may not possess any equivalent, and so the translator may have 'to make a circuit to reach his goal'. Each language has its own inbred characteristics, and any attempt to translate them literally will merely sound uncouth. For example, to render Homer word for word into Latin prose would make 'the most eloquent of poets sound inarticulate'. 'A literal translation from one language into another obscures the sense.' 'My version of the Life of Antony always preserves the sense, although it does not invariably keep the words of the original. Leave others to catch at syllables and letters; do you for your part look for the meaning.'[2] But—and this is for Jerome the important point—there is one case in which he does not use this method of translation. 'For myself I not only admit but freely proclaim that in translating from the Greek, *except in the case of Holy Scriptures where even the order of words is a mystery*, I render sense for sense and not word for word.'[3]

It was this second principle of translation which won the day in the translation of the Revised Version, in which the New Testament was completed in 1881 and the Old Testament in 1885. Especially in the New Testament, under the influence of the great J. B. Lightfoot, a

[1] Horace, *Ars Poetica*, 133.
[2] All the quotations are from *Letter* 57, in the translation of W. H. Freemantle in the *Select Library of the Nicene and Post-Nicene Fathers*, pp. 112-19.
[3] Jerome, *Letters*, 57.5.

principle of 'faithfulness' was followed in which even the order of the Greek words was kept, which, as F. C. Grant comments, resulted in 'an absurd and unidiomatic order of the English words', and in a version from which the spark of life has flown.[1] This method produced a version of 'almost pedantic accuracy and precision', 'a schoolmasters' translation', an excellent crib for the student studying for an examination, but totally inadequate to replace the Authorised Version either for public worship or private devotion.[2]

It has become increasingly clear that literalism is not translation. What then is to be done? Let us look first at Luther's views on translation.[3] We may begin with a saying of Augustine. Augustine was defending the Septuagint, the Greek Version of the Hebrew Old Testament, against the attacks of Jerome, who strongly criticized the omissions from and the additions to the Hebrew text which the Septuagint contains. He declared that these additions and omissions go to prove that 'no human servitude to words was at work, which the translator ought to have, but rather a divine power which filled and ruled the translators' minds.'[4] In translation there are therefore two things at work—the requisite linguistic knowledge and the requisite inspiration of the Holy Spirit. With this Luther would have wholly agreed. He writes in the *Encomium Eloquentiae*:

> 'I have not the mistaken view that the holy can be penetrated through the industry of human talent. There is something in the holy that nobody can ever see, unless it is shown to him by God: and Christ cannot be known to us without the Holy Spirit teaching us. . . . But, apart from prophecy, the meaning of the words must be known in which, as in a shrine, the divine mysteries are hidden. For what is the use of reciting in a magic way words that have not been understood? Is it not like telling a story to a deaf person?'[5]

There must be freedom. 'Figures of speech and the liveliness of sentences and arguments can be rendered in a free translation only.' Only thus can the translator transmit 'the spirit of the author'. So, for

[1] F. C. Grant, *Translating the Bible*, pp. 92, 93.
[2] F. F. Bruce, *The English Bible*, p. 142.
[3] Luther's views are well described in W. Schwarz, *Principles and Problems of Biblical Translation*, pp. 167-212, especially pp. 210, 211.
[4] Augustine, *The City of God*, 18.42,43.
[5] Quoted W. Schwarz, *Principles and Problems of Biblical Translation*, p. 195.

instance, Luther says that, if the angel had spoken to Mary in German, he would have used the appropriate form of address; and this and this only is the correct translation, whatever the original words may be.[1]

So Luther held that words are only the signs for the real things. 'Languages themselves do not make a theologian, but they are of assistance, for it is necessary to know the subject matter before it can be expressed through languages.' 'It is not enough to know the grammar, but one must pay attention to the sense: for the knowledge of the subject matter brings out the meaning of the words.'[2]

Schwarz outlines Luther's translational practice in difficult passages.[3] 'Grammar is necessary for declension, conjugation and construction of sentences, but in speech the meaning and subject matter must be considered, not the grammar, for the grammar shall not rule over the meaning.' So when Luther came upon a difficult passage, he asked first whether it referred to 'grace' or 'law', to 'God's anger' or to the 'remission of sins'. He then related the passage both to its context and to Christ. And only after that did he begin to enquire into the grammar of the sentence. It may be said that Luther established the meaning before he translated. 'A real translation,' he said, 'is the application of sayings in a foreign language to one's own language.'[4] The principle is translation by meaning and not by words; it is not what the author says, but what he means, which is important—and it is precisely for this reason that the translator requires the help of the Holy Spirit, however accomplished a linguist or grammarian he may be.

We shall now look at the principles of another translator, who expresses this point of view better than any other translator. Ronald Knox in his *On Englishing the Bible* quotes as the most illuminating advice for the translator a passage from a lecture by Hilaire Belloc, given at the Taylorian in Oxford in 1931:

> 'Transmute boldly: render the sense by the corresponding sense without troubling over the verbal difficulties in your way. Where such rendering of sense by corresponding sense involves considerable amplification, do not hesitate to amplify for fear of being verbose. . . . Sometimes, even, a whole passage must be transmuted, a whole paragraph thrown into a new form, if we would justly render the sense of the original; and the rule should

[1] Quoted W. Schwarz, pp. 205, 207. [2] Quoted W. Schwarz, p. 210.
[3] W. Schwarz, p. 211. [4] W. Schwarz, p. 206.

> stand that, after having grasped as exactly as possible all that the original stands for, with the proportion between its various parts, the distinction between what is emphasized and what is left on a lower plane, we should say to ourselves, not "How shall I make this foreigner talk English?" but "What would an Englishman have said to express the same?" *That* is translation. *That* is the very essence of the art: the resurrection of an alien thing in a native body; not the dressing of it up in native clothes but the giving to it of native flesh and blood.'[1]

The essence of the matter is not so much *translation* as *transmutation*. This involves certain things.

First, as Knox has it: 'You cannot be a translator without being, to some extent, an interpreter.'[2] So, for instance, F. C. Grant can say of Jowett's translation of the Dialogues of Plato that the work is not only a translation; it is really 'a superb interpretation of Plato'.[3] However impossible it may be to achieve it, the aim of the translator must be to produce a translation which can stand by itself, and which needs no commentary to make it intelligible.

Second, this will necessarily involve what is known as paraphrase. Knox writes: 'The translator, let me suggest in passing, must never be frightened by the word "paraphrase"; it is a bogey of the half-educated.'[4] This also means the abandonment of the principle that the same word in Greek must always be translated by the same word in English. This Knox describes as 'the capital heresy among translators'. 'You cannot,' he says, 'quote an exact English equivalent for a French word, as you might quote an exact English equivalent for a French coin.'[5] The translator must be free to use the resources of the English language to transmute the resources of the other language into English.

Third, all this will mean that the translator must accept the risk of putting something of himself into the translation. It was once alleged of Gilbert Murray's translations that sometimes Euripides spoke with the voice of Murray. Murray's answer was: 'It is not a ventriloquist's trick, only a translator's occupational risk.'[6]

[1] R. A. Knox, *On Englishing the Bible*, p. 19.
[2] R. A. Knox, *On Englishing the Bible*, p. 21.
[3] F. C. Grant, *Translating the Bible*, p. 131.
[4] R. A. Knox, *On Englishing the Bible*, p. 12.
[5] R. A. Knox, *On Englishing the Bible*, pp. 10, 11.
[6] Gilbert Murray, *An Unfinished Autobiography*, p. 138.

The translator must feel about what he translates in the same way as the author who originally wrote it felt. He must in some way, not only interpret, but also repeat and share the experience of the author. Here is where the principle and the control of what is usually called paraphrase enters in. My old teacher, W. M. Macgregor, that prince of interpreters of the New Testament, never used to ask for a *translation* of a passage in any examination; he always asked for a *paraphrase*. He insisted that, from the examination point of view, it was possible to translate a passage of the New Testament without having any idea of what it meant, but that to make a paraphrase a student must not only know the meaning of the Greek words, but must also understand the mind and intention of the author.

The most notorious example of paraphrase in the rendering of the Greek New Testament into English is in the translation of E. Harwood, published in 1768.[1] The work's description of itself on its title page is an example of its style: *A Liberal Translation of the New Testament: being an Attempt to translate the Sacred Writings with the same Freedom, Spirit and Elegance, with which other English Translations from the Greek Classics have lately been executed: The Design and Scope of each Author being strictly and impartially explored, the True Significance and Force of the Original critically observed, and, as much as possible, transfused into our language, and the Whole elucidated and explained upon a new and rational Plan: With Select Notes, Critical and Explanatory. By E. Harwood.* In Harwood's translation 'Our Father which art in heaven; Hallowed be thy name' appears as:

> 'O Thou great governour and parent of universal nature—who manifestest thy glory to the blessed inhabitants of heaven—may all thy rational creatures in all the parts of thy boundless dominion be happy in the knowledge of thy existence and providence, and celebrate thy perfections in a manner most worthy thy nature and perfective of their own!'

Matthew 13.51,52 reads:

> 'After speaking these parables, Jesus said to his disciples—Do you perfectly understand my meaning and intention?—they answered in the affirmative.
>
> He then said to them—every public teacher of Christianity ought to study the precepts and doctrines of it with such sedulous

[1] Harwood's is described in H. Pope, *English Versions of the Bible*, pp. 529, 530, and in F. F. Bruce, *The English Bible*, p. 130.

> application and industry, that he, like a careful and provident master of a large family, may lay up a rich and inexhaustible fund of useful knowledge, and may upon every occasion be always able from a mind replete with wisdom to administer an ample and salutary repast for the consolation and benefit of mankind in every various state and condition.'

Matthew 10.28 appears as:

> 'But let that great Being be the object of your fear, who can involve both soul and body in total and everlasting destruction. Let that great Being, I repeat it, be the object of your constant fear.'

Interestingly, Matthew 26.26 reads:

> 'Take and eat this bread—which I design should represent my own body.'

Harwood's idea is right, but his execution of it is very wrong, and it is wrong for the reason that he never did what Murray did in the case of the Greek dramatists; he never entered into the mind of the New Testament writers to think as they thought and to feel as they felt. Paraphrase is only safe and effective when the mind and heart of the translator are married to the mind and heart of the author.

The demand on the translator is very difficult. Ideally, he should be a master of two languages, the language from which he translates and the language into which he translates. Ideally, his mind should be in perfect unison with the mind of the author whom he seeks to translate, even to the extent of sharing, or at least entering into, the experience of that author. Ideally, he should have the courage always to try to state the meaning of the author without being bound to the 'servitude of words'. The ideal is unattainable—but that is no reason for not trying to attain it.

We have now looked at the general principles of translation. It remains to look at particular passages in which explanation is necessary.

WORDS

We begin by looking at certain passages in which the problem is the precise meaning of words. We cannot in an appendix discuss every word which needs explanation. All we can do is to select certain instances of words which are difficult to translate. Ronald Knox said of his own experience of translating: 'It is not till you sit down to translate the Bible that words begin to haunt you with their evasiveness.' He says of the translator's experience: 'Words are for ever eluding his grasp.'[1] It is sometimes said that it is not difficult to translate words for *things*, because a table or a chair remains a table or a chair in any circumstances; the difficulty, it is said, lies in words which have to do with *ideas*. But this is only partly true. Clothes, money, even furniture may be so very different from those with which we are familiar that our familiar words may convey a quite wrong picture. The problem of translation certainly applies more acutely to words which have to do with ideas, but it does in fact apply to almost any word. We propose therefore to list certain words wherein there lies some special need for comment.

ADULTEROUS: This word occurs in the phrase, 'an evil and *adulterous* generation' (Matthew 16.4). The meaning here is not that of physical and sexual adultery. In the Old Testament there is a series of ideas connected with the relationship of Israel to Yahweh. Yahweh is said to be Israel's husband (e.g. Hosea 2.16). Marriage is necessarily an exclusive relationship. Hence God can be spoken of as a 'jealous' God (e.g. Deuteronomy 4.24). For Israel to have anything to do with any other god is infidelity to her husband. We therefore get in the AV the phrase which speaks of Israel going 'a whoring' after strange gods (e.g. Exodus 34.15; Hosea 9.1). Such conduct is what might be called spiritual adultery. An 'adulterous' generation is therefore not necessarily a generation which is marked by sexual sin, although that may be a mark of the disease. It is rather an *apostate* generation.

AGAIN: In the Nicodemus story we have the phrase 'born again' (AV; 'born anew,' RSV). It occurs in John 3.3,7. The word translated 'again' is *anōthen*. It certainly can mean 'again', as it does in Galatians 4.9. But an even commoner meaning is 'from above'. It is so used, for instance, in Matthew 27.51, where it is said that at the death of Jesus the Temple curtain was ripped 'from top' to bottom. *Anōthen* is therefore a word of two meanings; it means both 'again' and 'from above'. In John 3.3,7 it is entirely likely that we do not need to choose between these two meanings, but that both are meant. There is no

[1] Ronald A. Knox, *On Englishing the Bible*, pp. 11, 28.

one English word which will cover both. The phrase should therefore be translated 'born again from above'.

BAPTIZE: There is normally no difficulty in translating this word, for in almost every case it is used of *baptism*. But there is one case in which the translation of it does present a problem. In Mark 10.38 Jesus asks James and John, after they have made their request for the premier places in his kingdom: 'Can ye be baptized with the baptism that I am baptized with?' In secular Greek the word *baptizein* has many metaphorical meanings. It was not originally a religious or liturgical word. It simply meant to dip something below the surface of a liquid. It is, for instance, used of dipping a garment in dye. It thus acquired most of the meanings which the English word 'submerge' possesses. It can be used of a ship being sunk at sea. To be 'baptized' in wine is to be dead drunk. To be 'baptized' in debts is to be head over ears in debt. A boy, defeated by a cross-examiner's questionings, is said to be 'baptized'—in the English colloquial idiom, sunk. The word therefore means in its metaphorical use to be submerged in any experience, usually a bitter experience. I believe that it is much better to take it in its quite normal Greek metaphorical meaning in this passage. I think that what Jesus said was: 'Can you be submerged in the sea of troubles in which I must be submerged?'

BELOVED: The voice from heaven which Jesus heard called him the 'beloved' Son (Mark 1.11; 9.7). The word is *agapētos*, and at first sight there seems to be no difficulty here, for *agapētos* does mean 'beloved'. This is its normal meaning. But both in secular and in sacred Greek another idea comes into the word. In the Septuagint, the Greek version of the Old Testament, the version which practically all the New Testament writers used, *agapētos* is used to translate the Hebrew word *iachidh* which means 'only'. Isaac in the Hebrew is Abraham's 'only' son (Genesis 22.2,12,16), Jephthah's daughter is his 'only' daughter (Judges 11.34), and yet in both cases the word in the Greek translation, the Septuagint, is *agapētos*. It is entirely natural that an *only* child should be a *beloved* child; but it does mean that *agapētos* has in it, not only the idea of one who is *loved*, but also the idea of one who is *unique*. Since no one English word covers both meanings it is better to translate *agapētos* by the composite phrase 'beloved and only'.

CHRIST: Although the word 'Christ' has come to be used as such, it is not originally a proper name. It is the same word as 'Messiah'.

'Christ' is the Greek, and 'Messiah' is the Hebrew for 'the Anointed One', that is, for the one who is God's King. It is therefore frequently better to translate *Christos* by the title Messiah. It is better to translate Peter's declaration of faith: 'You are the Messiah' (Mark 8.29; Matthew 16.16). It is better to translate Acts 9.22 that Paul was proving that Jesus was the Messiah (cp. Acts 2.36; 17.3).

BROTHER: The word *adelphos*, 'brother', has three main usages in the New Testament. (i) It is used in the family sense, as in Matthew 13.55 where the 'brothers' of Jesus are spoken of. (ii) It is used in address either to individuals (Acts 21.20), or to a group (Acts 15.7). There is no need to alter it in these cases, except to substitute 'brothers' for the archaic 'brethren', which even the RSV retains. (iii) It is used as a description of the members of the Christian Church. Both the AV and the RSV speak consistently of the brethren. So we have: 'The apostles and the brethren who were in Judaea' (Acts 11.1); 'Certain men which came down from Judaea taught the brethren' (Acts 15.1). In almost all these cases it is better to translate *adelphoi* by 'members of the Christian community'. So when Acts 16.2 speaks of Timothy, it is better to translate it: 'He was well spoken of by the members of the Christian community in Lystra and Iconium.'

CENTURION: A Roman centurion was in charge of one hundred men in a legion whose full complement was six thousand men. It is sometimes better to translate it 'company commander'.

CHURCH: The word *ekklēsia* has two uses in the New Testament. (i) It can stand for the whole Church, as when Paul speaks of the Church of the Lord (Acts 20.28). In such cases Church is the correct translation. (ii) It can stand for the particular part of the Church which exists in any local situation, in which case it can be used in the plural as well as in the singular. In this case it is better to translate it 'congregation'. So in Acts 16.5 it is better to translate: 'The congregations were strengthened in the faith.' In Acts 13.1 it is better to speak of the congregation in Antioch. The word 'Church' should be kept for the whole Church, and the word 'congregation' should be used for the Church group in any local situation.

COMFORT: In both the AV and the RSV the second beatitude is translated in almost exactly the same way: 'Blessed are they that mourn: for they shall be comforted' (Matthew 5.4). The word which is translated by the English word 'comfort' is *parakalein*. *Parakalein* is a word with a variety of meanings, and with two of them we are specially concerned in this beatitude. (i) *Parakalein* does mean 'to comfort'. It is the word which is used in the Greek version of Isaiah 40.1: 'Comfort, comfort my people, says your God.' (ii) But *parakalein* also means 'to encourage'. It is used, for instance, of a teacher urging pupils to higher moral endeavour, and it is used of comrades cheering their fellow warriors as they go into battle. Comfort by itself tends to be a sentimental term without the strength which this word has in it. It is better to keep both ideas, and to translate: 'They shall have courage and comfort.'

COMFORTER: The previous note leads directly into this one. The word which the Fourth Gospel uses for the Holy Spirit is *paraklētos*, which has been transliterated into English as 'paraclete', and which the AV translates 'comforter'. *Paraklētos* means 'one who is called in', but although it is passive in form it is very much active in meaning, for the main idea is the purpose for which the person is called in. A *paraklētos* may be a person called in to give medical aid, to give legal counsel, to give evidence for the defence, to cheer and encourage those whose spirit is broken. It can therefore be seen that the function of the *paraklētos* is very much wider than that of being a comforter in sorrow. The use of the word Comforter in fact limits the function of the Holy Spirit. A *paraklētos* is one who makes us able to cope with life. The only word which is wide enough to translate it in all its width is the word 'Helper'.

It is to be noted that the word 'comforter' first came into the English Bible with Wycliffe in 1386. For Wycliffe the word was correct, for at that time comforter was very much nearer in meaning to its derivation, which is the Latin word *fortis*, which means 'brave'. A comforter at that time was one who put courage into you. The idea that Wycliffe attached to the word 'comfort' may be seen from his translation of Ephesians 6.10, which he translates: 'Be ye *comforted* in the Lord.' The word that he here translates 'comfort' is the Greek word *endunamoun*, which has the same root (*dunamis*=power) as we find in the English word dynamite. A comforter in Wycliffe's sense is one who fills us with dynamic power. It can be seen that 'comforter' is one of the AV words which very much needs modernising, if the full greatness of the doctrine of the Holy Spirit is to be understood.

COMPEL: In the Sermon on the Mount the Christian is told that, if anyone 'compels' (RSV 'forces') him to go one mile, he must go two

(Matthew 5.41), and the same word is used when it is said that they 'compelled' Simon of Cyrene to bear the cross of Jesus (Mark 15.21). The verb is *aggareuein*, and it is an unusual word. It is Persian in origin, and had to do with the Persian government postal system. This system worked in stages; and the government always had the right to commandeer horses, and fodder, and lodging to keep the service going. The word then came to be used of any commandeering, or of impressing into service. At the time when the New Testament events were happening Palestine was an occupied country, and any Jew could without notice be compelled to act as a baggage-porter for the Romans for a mile. The word means much more than to force or compel a man to do something; it means to commandeer his services, to impress him into service, and thereby to make him for the moment no better than the slave of his country's conquerors.

COMPASSION: In the AV it is frequently said of Jesus that he was 'moved with compassion' (Matthew 9.36; 14.14; 15.32; 18.27; 20.34; Mark 1.41; 6.34; 8.2; 9.22; Luke 7.13; 10.33; 15.20). The word is *splagchnizesthai*. The word from which this verb comes is *splagchna*, which means the 'bowels'. It is the strongest word for compassion in the Greek language. The meaning can best be expressed by using the phrase 'heart-sorry'.

CUP: To drink the cup is an expression which appears more than once in the Gospels. Jesus asks James and John if they can drink the cup that he has to drink (Matthew 20.22; Mark 10.38), and in Gethsemane he prays, that, if it is possible, he may not have to drink the cup (Matthew 26.39; Mark 14.36; Luke 22.42). The phrase is a Hebrew metaphor for going through a bitter experience, and it is better simply to translate it so.

DOCTRINE: There is room for misunderstanding in the AV use of the word *doctrine*. In seventeenth-century English 'doctrine' had two meanings. (i) It had the meaning which has survived until today, 'that which is taught and believed', a system or body of belief. It does frequently have this meaning in the New Testament Letters, and the Greek behind it is *didaskalia*. (ii) But the AV uses the word doctrine even oftener in the meaning of 'the act of teaching', and the Greek behind it in this case is *didachē*.

We may take two examples. In Matthew 7.28, 29 the AV has it that 'The people were astonished at his doctrine: for he taught them as one having authority and not as the Scribes.' The second half of the passage makes it clear that the listeners were astonished, not so much at *what* Jesus taught as at *the way* in which he taught. The RSV and the NEB both substitute 'teaching' for 'doctrine'. The word teaching remains ambiguous, and it is better to say: 'The crowds were astonished at the way he taught.' The second illustration comes from Acts 2.42, and could in the AV be even more misleading: 'They continued steadfastly in the apostles' doctrine.' In modern English the natural meaning of this would be that they refused to abandon what the apostles had taught them, that they, so to speak, clung fast to orthodox belief. But that is not what the passage means at all. *Didachē* is here 'the act of teaching'. The RSV has: 'They devoted themselves to the apostles' teaching.' The NEB is even clearer: 'They met constantly to hear the apostles teach.' Still clearer is: 'They spent all their time in listening to the apostles as they taught.' It is this second sense that the AV use of 'doctrine' in the Gospels and Acts by far most commonly represents.

EVIL, SINGLE: In the Sermon on the Mount the words 'single' and 'evil' are used in connection with the eye. 'If therefore thine eye be *single* (RSV, 'sound'), thy whole body shall be full of light. But if thine eye be *evil* (RSV, 'not sound'), thy whole body shall be full of darkness' (Matthew 6.22,23). The word for 'single' is *haplous*, and the word for 'evil' is *ponēros*. The translation of the AV and the RSV is perfectly possible. But *haplous* and *ponēros* acquired secondary meanings, especially as applied to the eye. *Haplous* came to mean 'generous', and *ponēros* came to mean 'grudging'. The RSV gives this meaning to *ponēros* in Matthew 20.15 where the AV has: 'Is thine eye evil because I am good?', and where it has: 'Do you begrudge my generosity?' As so often happens in Greek, the two meanings are being combined, and it is better to translate: 'So then, if your eye is sound and generous, your whole body will be full of light; but if your eye is diseased and grudging, your whole body will be full of darkness.'

GOOD: There are two words in Greek for 'good'. There is the word *agathos*, which simply describes the moral quality of an action, and which sometimes can mean 'generous' (cp. Matthew 20.15). There is also the word *kalos*, of which the New Testament writers are very fond. *Kalos* always has in it the idea of beauty; it is in fact the adjective to describe a beautiful person. A person or an action which can be described by the word *kalos* is not only *good*; he or it is also *beautiful*.

It therefore has in it the idea of the goodness which is winsome and attractive. Very often the best translation of it is 'lovely'. So, for instance, Matthew 5.16 is better translated: 'Just so, your light must shine for everyone to see, so that, when they see the lovely things you do, it may make them want to praise your Father who is in heaven.'

GROAN: The word *embrimasthai* is several times used of Jesus in the Gospels, and it presents a problem both of meaning and of translation. It occurs in Matthew 9.30 where the AV has 'straitly charged' and the RSV 'sternly charged'. The same translations are given in Mark 1.43. In Mark 14.5 it is used of the reaction of the spectators to the action of the woman who anointed Jesus with the expensive perfume. There the AV has 'murmured against her', and the RSV 'reproached her'. It occurs, again of Jesus, in John 11.33,38 in the Lazarus story. There the AV translates by 'groan', and the RSV by 'deeply moved'. Basically the word is used of an animal *snorting*. It is therefore used of persons who are almost inarticulate in a moment of some deep emotion either of anger or of sorrow. The translation will therefore depend on the context, but the idea of strong emotion will always need to be retained.

HELL: There are two words in the New Testament which in the AV are both translated 'hell', one of them rightly and the other wrongly.

(i) *Hades* should never be translated 'hell'. It is the land of the dead. In the earlier Jewish belief there was no real belief in immortality or in life after death. All that remained after death was a gray shadowy land in which the shades moved in colourless and strengthless weakness, separated alike from God and from man. Hell gives quite the wrong idea, for in it there was neither penalty nor suffering. The AV wrongly translates Acts 2.27: 'Thou wilt not leave my soul in hell' and the RSV rightly translates it: 'Thou wilt not abandon my soul to Hades.' It is better still to translate it: 'You will not abandon my soul to the land of the dead.' To say that a person is in Hades in Jewish thought was not to say that that person was under punishment in the place reserved for sinners; it is simply to say that he was really and truly dead.

(ii) On the other hand *Gehenna* is properly hell. In e.g. Matthew 5.29 both the AV and the RSV rightly translate it 'hell'. Gehenna was the Valley of Hinnom and was in a ravine outside Jerusalem. It had been notorious as the place where the worship of Moloch went on and where infants were sacrificed in the fire to the fire-god. Josiah had desecrated it (2 Kings 23.10), and it had become the public refuse dump and incinerator of the city of Jerusalem. It was the place in which all that was waste and evil was destroyed. It thus came symbolically to stand for hell, where the wicked are destroyed.

HARDNESS: The phrase 'hardness of heart' occurs several times in the Gospels (Mark 3.5; 6.52; 8.17; John 12.40). The noun for 'hardness' is *pōrōsis*, and the verb 'to harden' is *pōroun*. 'Hardness' as a translation can be a little misleading. The hardness is not the hardness of cruelty or lack of sympathy. It is the hardness of impenetrability. These words can be used of a callus, of hardened skin, which has lost its feeling. They can be used of the new bone formation which knits a fracture and which is harder than bone itself. They can be used of rock or marble which is so hard that no impression can be made upon it. In the New Testament hardness of heart is not the cruelty which we usually associate with the expression hard-hearted; it is the utter impenetrability and insensitiveness into which the truth cannot gain an entry.

HOSANNA: *Hosanna* is the shout of the crowds to Jesus as he entered Jerusalem (Matthew 21.9,15; Mark 11.9,10; John 12.13). The AV, the RSV, and even the NEB, leave the word untranslated, perhaps rightly. If it is to be translated, it presents very real problems. It may be said to have three possible meanings. (i) Literally it means: 'Help, or save, I pray' and comes from Psalm 118.25. (ii) During the Feast of Tabernacles the worshippers carried bunches of palm, myrtle and willow branches on the last day of the Feast. And they were known as *hosannas*. (iii) It was used simply as a shout of greeting and welcome, and as a liturgical exclamation. So in the Gospels it has been suggested, very improbably, that it means: 'Up with your green branches!' It has been suggested that it is simply an untranslatable shout of welcome, in the same category as the usually untranslated word *Hallelujah*. It has been suggested that it is a prayer for safety, and that it does mean something like, 'God save him who comes in the name of the Lord!' We have taken it as a prayer for safety, but it may well be simply an untranslatable shout of welcome and greeting.

HYPOCRITE: The modern translations usually keep the word 'hypocrite', but it at least needs filling out. The key fact about it is that the word *hupokritēs* is the normal Greek word for 'an actor'. 'A hypocrite is a man who is always playing a part. He is pretending to be what he is not; or, he is always conscious of the audience which is looking at him; or, his practice does not match his profession; or, he spends his time erecting a façade of conventional piety, while the thoughts of his heart are very different. The hypocrite is the man who is putting on an act to impress other people.

INHERIT: The word 'inherit' is quite common in the Gospels. For instance, the rich young ruler says to Jesus: 'What must I do to inherit eternal life?' (Mark 10.17). Here the NEB has 'to win'. There is a problem of translation here. In ordinary English to inherit is to enter into possession of something when its previous owner has died, and an inheritance is something that comes to us on the death of its original possessor, who has left it to us. This is not the New Testament sense of the word at all. What it does mean in the New Testament is to enter into possession of that which has been promised by God, with the added implication that, since the promise has been made by God, the fulfilment of the promise is sure. The word 'inherit' should be dropped from translation because of the implications of the death of the testator. It is better to translate thus: 'What am I to do to get this eternal life which God has promised?'

IS: It would not seem that any problem arises in the translation of the word 'is'; but there is a certain problem in one use of the word. There are cases in which 'is' unmistakably means 'stands for' or 'represents' and must be so translated.

This is clear in the interpretation of parables. In Matthew 13.20 and 22 the AV runs: 'But he that received the seed into stony places, the same is he that heareth the word, and anon with joy receiveth it. . . . He also that received seed among the thorns is he that heareth the word; and the care of this world, and the deceitfulness of riches, chokes the word, and he becometh unfruitful.' Apart from modernizing the language the RSV is the same; but the NEB translates: 'The seed sown on rocky ground stands for the man who, on hearing the word, accepts it at once with joy. . . . The seed sown among thistles represents the man who hears the word, but worldly cares and the false glamour of wealth choke it, and it proves barren.' Similarly in Matthew 13.38 the AV has: 'The good seed are the children of the kingdom; but the tares are the children of the wicked one.' Here the RSV has: 'The good seed means the sons of the kingdom; the weeds are the sons of the evil one.' The NEB has: 'The good seed stands for the children of the Kingdom, the darnel for the children of the evil one.' There is no doubt that in these passages the translation 'means', 'stands for', 'represents', is more accurate.

The problem becomes serious in the words of the Last Supper: 'This is my body.' We cannot here enter upon the theological problems involved, but there is certainly no linguistic reason why the 'is' should not be rendered 'means'.

JOT OR TITTLE: In Matthew 5.18 Jesus says that not one 'jot or tittle' shall pass from the Law. The RSV has 'not an iota, not a dot'. The NEB has 'not a letter, not a stroke'. The 'jot' is the Hebrew letter *iodh*; it is the smallest letter in the Hebrew alphabet and is rather like an apostrophe—thus: '. The tittle is what is called the serif. In a capital I, for instance, there are little projecting strokes at the top and bottom of the letter. All the letters which have straight up and down strokes in them have this little projection, as they are commonly printed. Type without these projections is called 'sans serif' type. So the best way to translate is to say that not the smallest letter, and not the smallest part of a letter, will pass from the Law.

LORD: The word for Lord is *kurios*, and it is one of the most difficult words in the New Testament to translate. Its difficulty lies in its enormous range of meaning. (i) It is the normal Greek title of respect, the equivalent of the English word 'sir'. (ii) It means owner. In Luke 19.33 it is used for the owners of the colt. (iii) It is master as opposed to slave, as in Matthew 10.24. (iv) It was the official title of the Roman Emperors. In Acts 25.26, after Paul has appealed to Caesar, Festus complains that he has no firm information to send to his *kurios*, that is, the Emperor, about Paul. (v) It was the normal prefix to the name of any god. So they spoke about the Lord Serapis, or the Lord Apollo. (vi) It was the Septuagint translation of the name Yahweh, the name of God. So then *kurios* can indicate anything from respect to worship.

When *kurios* is used of Jesus in the course of the narrative in the Gospels then it is correctly translated 'Lord', as in Luke 22.61. But when it is used in address to Jesus, the general rule is that it does not mean 'Lord' until after the Resurrection, for it is only then that the lordship of Jesus was truly known. This means that both the AV and the RSV use the word 'Lord' far too often. For instance, in Matthew 15.22 by the Syro-Phoenician woman and in Matthew 17.15 by the father of the epileptic boy, in the AV and the RSV Jesus is called 'Lord'; in the NEB in both cases it is correctly 'sir'. Neither of these people could possibly have known Jesus in the sense which 'Lord' implies. Similarly, in the parables, as in Matthew 25.11, 'Lord' should almost always be 'master'.

To repeat, the general rule is that in narrative *kurios* should be translated 'Lord', but in address to Jesus prior to the Resurrection it should be 'sir' or 'master', for it is only after the Resurrection that respect turns to worship.

MEEK: The third beatitude both in the AV and the RSV is translated: 'Blessed are the meek' (Matthew 5.5). The NEB has: 'Blessed are those of a gentle spirit.' The word in question is the word *praüs*, and the problem is that it is not difficult to define its meaning, but it is almost impossible to find an English word to translate it.

It is a word with two backgrounds. (i) It has a Hebrew background, and it translates the Hebrew word *'anaw*, which describes the humble and submissive man, who accepts in uncomplaining faith and confidence what God sends to him. (ii) It has a Greek background. The Greek ethical writers, especially Aristotle, had a great deal to say about this word. The Greek ethical writers saw virtue as the mean between two extremes, on the one hand the extreme of excess and on the other the extreme of defect. Virtue consisted, as they saw it, of the happy medium. For instance, on the one hand there is recklessness; on the other hand there is cowardice; and in between there is true courage. This word *praüs*, they said, described the man who had the right attitude to anger, the man who was angry neither too much nor too little, the man who was angry at the right time, for the right reason, against the right people and in the right way. Taken solely from the Greek background, the beatitude would say that the blessing is on the man who is always angry at the right time, and never at the wrong time.

The further problem arises that in modern language 'meek' has tended to come down in the world, until it describes a rather colourless and spineless kind of person. Into the translation two things have to be introduced—the idea of humility and the idea of strength of self-control. It is therefore better to take 'meek' as describing those 'whose strength is in their gentleness'. They are gentle, but the gentleness is not the gentleness of weakness but of strength. It is illuminating to remember that in Greek the word could be used to describe a thoroughly trained and domesticated animal, like a well-trained sheepdog.

MURMUR: The word for 'to murmur' is the verb *gogguzein* (John 6.41, 43; 7.12.32). The RSV and the NEB keep the word 'murmur', although both sometimes substitute 'muttering' or 'whispering'. The word is very commonly used in the Old Testament narrative to describe the murmurings of the people, when they were embittered and discontented in their wilderness journeyings (e.g. Numbers 14.27). The word is pronounced '*gonguzein*', and it is an onomatopoetic word. That is to say, it imitates with its sound the phenomenon which it stands for. What it describes is the low, muttered, buzz of talk which comes from a resentful and discontented crowd. It does not so much describe articulate complaint or protest; it rather describes that inarticulate sound which rises from a crowd when they are complaining to each other in half-muttered, half-whispered conversation. So John 6.41 may be translated: 'A buzz of critical comment arose from the Jews.' It is better to translate on these lines than to keep 'murmur'.

MYSTERY: In the New Testament 'mystery' has a specialized meaning. In Matthew 13.11 and Mark 4.11 the disciples are congratulated by Jesus that to them has been given to know the 'mysteries' or 'mystery' of the Kingdom of heaven. Both the RSV and the NEB substitute 'secret'. In religious Greek a *mustērion*, a 'mystery', is not something which as in the English word is complicated and mysterious. It is something which is obscure and unintelligible to the outsider, but crystal-clear to the initiate to whom the inner meaning of it has been revealed. An example of this is the action of the Lord's Supper. To the outsider the sight of people taking a sip of wine and a piece of bread is obscure and, it may be, even slightly ridiculous. To the member of the Church who understands the inner meaning of it, it is the most precious action of the Church's worship. It will therefore often happen that to translate '*mustērion*' by 'mystery' or even by 'secret' will be misleading in English, and the translation has to be filled out. So we may translate Jesus' words: 'You have received the privilege of knowing the meaning of the Kingdom of God, a secret which only a disciple can understand.'

OFFENCE, OFFEND: The words *skandalon* and *skandalizein* present a real problem in translation. The AV consistently and unvaryingly translates them 'offence' and 'offend', which in modern English are not good translations. It will help to see the basic meaning of the words. They are both connected with the word *skandalēthron*, which means 'the bait-stick in a trap'. When an animal stepped on the bait-stick, the trap was sprung and so the animal was caught. The action was the same as that of a modern mousetrap. The word *skandalon* then comes to mean any kind of trap or snare, a pit into which a man may fall, not seeing that the hole in the ground has been lightly and deceptively covered over, or a trip wire set across the path to trip him up.

There are certain cases where this meaning is clear. In Matthew 5.29 Jesus speaks of the right eye 'offending' a person in the AV. The RSV has 'causes you to sin'; the NEB has 'leads you astray', and 'is your undoing'. In Matthew 18.6 there is the condemnation of anyone who 'offends' one of these little ones in the AV. The RSV has 'causes to sin' in the text and 'causes to stumble' in the margin. The NEB has 'is a cause of stumbling to'. In these cases the idea of tripping up, ensnaring, causing to stumble, is clear and not difficult to translate.

There are other cases which are more difficult. In Matthew 13.57 it is said of the unbelieving people of Nazareth in the AV that 'they were offended in him'. The RSV has 'they took offence at him'. The NEB has 'they fell foul of him'. There is a similar instance in Matthew 11.6 where Jesus' message to John is that the man who is not 'offended' in him is blessed. The RSV has 'takes no offence'. The NEB has 'does not find me a stumbling-block'. These translations are correct enough, but they are hardly idiomatic English. In such cases it is better to translate by some such phrase as 'shocked by', or 'antagonized by'. The idea in such cases is that Jesus and his message are so startlingly new that those who see him and hear him are, as it were, tripped up and stumble and are unable to accept and to follow.

POOR: In the AV and the RSV the first beatitude runs: 'Blessed are the poor in spirit, for theirs is the Kingdom of Heaven' (Matthew 5.3). The NEB has: 'How blest are those who know that they are poor'. There is danger of misunderstanding here, unless the word 'poor' is properly understood and translated. Misunderstanding can beget a kind of inverted snobbery in which poverty is identified with spiritual aristocracy and wealth a sign of inferiority. The word 'poor' has a double background. In Greek it is *ptōchos*, which probably comes from a root meaning 'to crouch' or 'to cower', and which means not simply poverty but destitution; it describes not the man who has too little, but the man who has nothing. In Hebrew the word is *'ani*. *'Ani* began by meaning 'poor'; it went on to mean 'downtrodden' and 'despised by men'; and then it went on to describe the man who has no earthly resources and who has therefore put all his trust in God. In the Psalms the poor man is the man who has nothing but his trust in God, and who is therefore dear to God. 'This poor man cried, and the Lord heard him' (Psalm 34.6). The word 'poor' has in it therefore the idea of conscious destitution and absolute trust. It is thus better to translate it 'those who have realized the destitution of their own lives', and, we might add, who have put their whole trust in God.

PEACE: The word 'peace', *eirēnē*, seems simple enough, and yet in modern English it presents a certain problem in translation. The problem is this. In modern English 'peace' has tended to become a negative word, denoting the absence of trouble. Countries may pile up armaments and watch each other suspiciously, and yet, so long as the guns are not firing and the bombs not dropping, we would say that there is peace. So long as people in some society were not actually arguing violently with each other, we might say that there was peace.

This is not the idea behind the word *eirēnē* in Greek or *shalōm* in Hebrew. In both Greek and Hebrew, 'peace' is an intensely positive word. It has two main meanings. (i) It means 'right relationships between man and man', true fellowship, not just polite tolerance. In Matthew 5.9 the translation should be: 'O the bliss of those who make men friends with each other.' (ii) It means 'everything which makes for a man's highest good'. The blessing *Shalōm* or *Salaam* means: 'May God give you every blessing, every good thing!' It is therefore not sufficient to translate: 'Go in peace' (e.g. Mark 5.34), as even the NEB does. It is better to translate quite simply: 'Go, and God bless you!'

The positive side of the word 'peace' must at all times be stressed.

PUBLICAN: This AV word is now quite misleading. The modern translations rightly translate it 'tax-collector' or 'tax-gatherer'. In Greek it is *telōnēs*; the AV translation comes from the Latin form *publicanus*, which means a man concerned with public money or finance.

The contempt in which tax-collectors were held in New Testament times was due to the fact that Rome farmed out the task of tax-collecting. A district was assessed at a certain sum; someone then contracted to produce that sum from the district. He was allowed to keep for himself all that he could extract over and above that sum, and such extortion was not difficult in a situation in which people had no means of knowing how much they were in fact liable to pay.

REWARD: In the Sermon on the Mount, in the passage which deals with those who ostentatiously practise piety to be seen by men, it is said of such people: 'They have their reward' (Matthew 6.2,5,16). The NEB has: 'They have their reward already.' Neither translation is enough. The word in question is *apechein,* and it means 'to receive payment of an account in full'. On an account or bill, when it was settled, the tradesman wrote: *Apechō*—'I have received payment in full.' Those, therefore, who do things to be admired by men, may win men's admiration. They are paid in full. That is 'all the reward they will ever get'.

A similar, and perhaps more difficult, instance of this word occurs in Mark 14.41. At the approach of the traitor Jesus says: '*Apechei.*' The AV and the RSV have: 'It is enough.' The NEB has in the text: 'Enough!' with a marginal note to say that the Greek is obscure and that the phrase could mean: 'The money has been paid,' or, 'The account has been settled.' It is more likely that the reference is to Judas, and that the meaning is: 'He has had his pay!'

RULER: In John 3.1 in the AV and the RSV Nicodemus is called 'a ruler of the Jews'. It is better to say that he was a member of the Sanhedrin, which was the supreme governing body of the Jews, or, as the NEB correctly has it, 'a member of the Jewish Council'.

SAINTS: Especially in the Letters of Paul, 'saints' is the word for the members of the Church. It presents a problem in translation, because the word 'saint', with its connotation of extreme holiness and piety, its stained-glass-window atmosphere, conveys a quite wrong idea. We have it, for instance, in Acts 9.32 where both the AV and the RSV speak of the 'saints' at Lydda. The NEB has 'God's people'.

The word translated 'saint' is *hagios*. This is the word which is also the common word for 'holy'. The basic meaning of this word is 'different' or 'separate'. The Temple is holy, because it is different from other buildings; the Sabbath is holy because it is different from other days; the Scriptures are holy because they are different from other writings. The 'saint' then is a man who is *different*. It is thus better to translate *hagioi*, 'saints', as 'God's consecrated people', for the difference is not a difference which has resulted in perfection, but is still in process of development.

SCRIBES: In the AV and the RSV we frequently meet the 'scribes', *grammateis*. The word 'scribe' is now misleading. The scribes were the experts in the Jewish Law. The Law as stated in the Old Testament consists of great wide general principles; the scribes were the experts who interpreted the general principles to meet particular cases. The Law, for instance, says that no work must be done on the Sabbath. The scribe defines what work is, and says what is and what is not work, what can and what cannot be done. The scribes turned the great principles into what might be called case law. Clearly, their work was unending and of the greatest detail. The NEB sometimes calls them 'doctors of the law'. This is not a good translation, because it has the implication in modern English of an honorary degree conferred by a university. It is better to call them quite simply 'experts in the Law', for that is what they were.

SEA: The older translations, and even the RSV, speak of the Sea of Galilee, although the NEB has 'Lake' (e.g. Matthew 8.24). The so-called Sea of Galilee was no more than thirteen miles at its longest from north to south, and seven miles at its widest from east to west. The word 'sea' therefore conveys an idea of size which is quite misleading. 'Lake'—'loch' in Scots—is a better translation.

SIGN: Very often the miracles of Jesus are called 'signs' (John 2.11). The word is *sēmeion*. 'Signs' is the translation of the AV, the RSV, and even of the NEB. There are three main words for miracles. There is *teras*, which simply means an amazing and astonishing event, and which is never used alone to describe a miracle. There is *dunamis*, which means a deed of power, a, so to speak, dynamic deed. And there is the word *sēmeion*, which means literally 'a sign'. A sign is an event or a deed, which gives an insight into the mind and heart of the person who performs it. It is a window into the personality of the person through whom it is done. A sign is a demonstration of the power of God in action.

SINNER: There is a certain problem in the translation of the word *hamartōlos*. The AV and the RSV both translate it 'sinner'. The tax-collectors and 'sinners' came to hear Jesus (Luke 15.1). Here the

NEB has 'bad characters'. The woman who anointed Jesus' feet (Luke 7.37) is in the AV and the RSV a 'sinner'. The NEB has it that she was 'living an immoral life'. The problem about this word is that it has not got what might be called a standard and definite content. It describes a person from the point of view of the person who uses the word. So then a person will be a *hamartōlos* to a narrow, respectable, conventional person, and that same person would not necessarily be a *hamartōlos* to someone who was more broad-minded and sympathetic and less critical. The word describes not so much a person who is a blatant sinner, but rather a person with whom no respectable person would have anything to do.

TEMPLE: In the Gospels the word 'temple' is used in two senses, representing two different Greek words, and two different areas. (i) There is the word *hieron*, which describes the whole Temple area which was one thousand feet square, and which consisted, moving inwards, of the Court of the Gentiles, the Court of the Women, the Court of the Israelites, and the Court of the Priests. The outer court, the Court of the Gentiles, was an open space into which anyone of any nation might come, but beyond which no Gentile could go. It was surrounded by porticoes and colonnades, the Royal Porch and Solomon's Porch being two of them. In this sense the Temple covered a wide area, and it is here that Jesus is said to teach (e.g. Matthew 21.23). *Hieron* should be translated 'the Temple precincts' rather than the Temple itself. (ii) There is the word *naos*, which means the Temple proper. It was situated at the far end of the Court of the Priests, and was a rather small building, divided into the Holy Place and the Holy of Holies, separated by a curtain. Into it only the High Priest could go, and even he could only enter it on the Day of Atonement, once a year. It was this *naos* that it was said that Jesus claimed he could destroy and rebuild (Matthew 26.61), and it was its dividing curtain that was ripped in two at the death of Jesus (Matthew 27.51). *Naos* is correctly translated 'Temple'. When Jesus is said to be teaching in the Temple, he was not in a building at all, but in the open Court of the Gentiles, or in one of the colonnades around it. *Hieron* should therefore always be translated 'Temple precincts', and *naos* should be translated 'Temple'.

TEMPT: The Greek word *peirazein*, which the AV consistently translates 'tempt', has overtones in it which are not fully covered by that translation. The difficulty lies in this. In modern language, not in seventeenth-century language, the word 'tempt' always has as its primary meaning 'seduction into sin'. There are undoubtedly occasions when this is still the main meaning of the word. But more often *peirazein* is better represented in modern English by the word 'test'. In Genesis 22.1 the AV has it that God did 'tempt' Abraham. It would be intolerable to think of God attempting to seduce Abraham into sin. The correct translation, as the RSV has it, is that God 'tested' Abraham. In the New Testament, in the introduction to the so-called Temptation narrative, we have: 'Then Jesus was led up by the Spirit into the wilderness to be *tempted* by the devil' (Matthew 4.1). Here even the NEB keeps the word 'tempt', and yet, if that word is being used in the seduction-to-sin sense only, then the Holy Spirit has become a partner in the attempt to persuade Jesus to sin. It is far better to say that Jesus was brought into the desert to undergo the ordeal of temptation by the devil. The idea of *testing* has always to be retained. *Peirazein* is used to describe what happens in a situation in which temptation comes to a man, not primarily as a seduction to sin, although that is in it, but rather as a test and an ordeal out of which a man is meant to emerge better and stronger and more able to face and to conquer all that would lead him away from God.

VERILY: The word 'verily', used singly in the Synoptic Gospels, and doubly in John's Gospel, represents a very unusual form in the Greek original. It represents the Hebrew word *Amēn*, which is transliterated into Greek. *Amēn* is quite unusual, perhaps unique, at the beginning of a sentence. It normally comes at the end, as we use it in prayers, and it denotes a solemn affirmation, or it marks the fact that the person who says it solemnly agrees with what has been said, and makes it his own. 'So let it be' would give the sense, as we use it in the English phrase: 'I say Amen to that.' When it is transferred, as in the Gospels, to the beginning of the sentence, it gives the statement a special seriousness, solemnity and weight. If the single initial *Amēn* of the Synoptic Gospels is unusual, the double *Amēn Amēn* of John's Gospel is unique. The AV translates 'verily' and 'verily verily' (e.g. Matthew 5.26; John 3.3). The RSV has 'truly' and 'truly truly'. The NEB has 'I tell you,' and, 'In truth, in very truth I tell you.' The truth is that here we have an un-English form of expression, for which no English form of expression sounds wholly natural. The single 'verily' may be represented by 'I tell you', and the double 'verily' by 'I tell you, and it is true'.

WITNESS: Especially in John's Gospel the word 'witness' frequently occurs. The word is *marturein*. The problem here is that 'witness' in modern English tends to be connected with legal evidence in a court of law. In the New Testament the idea will very often be much better caught by using the idea of solemn affirmation or declaration.

WOE: In Matthew 23.13-29 there is the great series of 'Woe's' directed against the Scribes and the Pharisees (cp. Matthew 11.21; 18.7). The RSV retains 'Woe'; the NEB has 'Alas for you.' The word is *ouai*, and there is one thing to be remembered. As the very sound of the word shows, there is no savage anger here; there is only infinite sorrow at a heart-breaking situation. If these passages are read in a tone of anger, they are misread. 'Tragic will be the fate' is the idea of these passages. The accent of them is far more nearly tears than invective.

WOMAN: One of the most insoluble problems of translation comes from the Greek usage of 'Woman', *gunai* as a form of address. It is used, for instance, by Jesus to his mother in John 2.4 at Cana of Galilee and in John 19.26 on the cross; it is used by Jesus to the woman taken in adultery in John 8.10; and it is used by the angels in the tomb to Mary Magdalene in John 20.13. In modern English to address a person as 'Woman!' would be a sign of serious discourtesy. In Greek there is no discourtesy at all. It was thus that Ulysses addressed his wife Penelope, and it could even perfectly properly be used in addressing a queen.

It is very difficult to get round this. The RSV retains 'Woman', or 'O woman'. The first gives quite the wrong idea, the idea of discourtesy, and the second is quite unnatural. In the instances in which it is used of Mary the NEB has 'Mother', and in the other instances it also avoids it. Many suggestions have been made, such as 'lady', or 'my dear', or even 'madam'. In this case we believe that it is better to omit the word altogether, as there is no real English equivalent for it.

EXPANSION

If a translation is to be readily and immediately intelligible, it is sometimes necessary to expand the original Greek.

The simplest form of expansion is the substitution of a proper name or the like for a pronoun. This kind of expansion has been common ever since the New Testament was arranged in lectionary form. It enabled the reader to make immediately clear what the ensuing paragraph was about. So, for instance, a new paragraph begins at Mark 1.12, and the AV has: 'Immediately the spirit driveth him into the wilderness.' This is expanded into: 'No sooner had Jesus had this experience than the Spirit compelled him to go out into the desert.' Mark 1.16 begins another new paragraph and in the AV reads: 'And passing along the Sea of Galilee he saw Simon and Andrew.' This is expanded into: 'When Jesus was walking along the shore of the Lake of Galilee, he saw Simon and Andrew.' Mark 1.21 begins another new paragraph and in the AV reads: 'And they went into Capernaum.' This is expanded into: 'Jesus and his disciples went into Capernaum.' This kind of expansion needs no comment. It simply enables the hearer, especially when the paragraph is read in public, to identify at once the principal character or characters involved.

It is sometimes necessary to expand, because an unfamiliar picture or custom is in the original. In the AV Matthew 9.17 reads: 'Neither do men put new wine into old bottles; else the bottles break, and the wine runneth out, and the bottles perish; but they put new wine into new bottles, and both are preserved.' The word 'bottle' is here misleading, because it conveys to modern ears the idea of a glass bottle. The meaning is 'wineskins', for it was in the skins of animals that liquids were carried. The point at issue is that the new wine was still fermenting; the fermentation gave off gas; and the expanding gas literally burst the old wineskin because it had no elasticity left. If this is to be intelligible to the modern reader, it must be expanded thus:

> 'No more do people pour new fermenting wine into old wineskins that have lost their elasticity. If they do, the skins burst, and the wine is spilled, and the skins are destroyed. New wine is put into new wineskins, and both are preserved.'

In Matthew 11.7 Jesus asks the crowds concerning John the Baptist: 'What did you go out into the wilderness to see? A reed shaken with the wind?' It would be possible, and even easy, completely to misunderstand this passage. It would be possible for a modern reader to take the phrase 'a reed shaken with the wind' as the description of a wavering and unstable person at the mercy of every breeze that blows. But this is very far from the meaning. In Palestine 'a reed shaken with the wind' would be a phrase to describe the most ordinary and everyday sight, something that no one could help seeing every day in the week, if he went out to the desert. And of course that is precisely what John was not. When the crowds went out to hear John, it was no common phenomenon that they went to see. It is therefore advisable to amplify this, and to translate: 'What did you go out to the desert to see? Was it to see what you can see any day there—the long grass swaying in the wind?'

In the parables, and especially in the Kingdom parables, a very elliptical way of speaking is used. So in Matthew 13.24 the parable begins: 'The Kingdom of heaven is likened unto a man which sowed good seed in his field.' Clearly, the Kingdom is not like the man. What is really meant is: 'What happens in the Kingdom of heaven is like what happened when a man sowed good seed in his field.' In Matthew 13.45 the parable begins: 'Again, the Kingdom of heaven is like unto a merchant-man,' and in Matthew 13.47 the parable begins: 'Again, the Kingdom of heaven is like unto a net.' Again it is clear that the point is not that the Kingdom of heaven is like the merchant-man or the net. Both introductions have to be amplified: 'What happens in the Kingdom of heaven is like what happened to a trader.' 'What happens in the Kingdom of heaven is like what happened when a net was cast into the sea.'

Another kind of amplification is the kind of amplification that is needed in Matthew 16.12: 'Then understood they how that he bade them not beware of the leaven of bread, but of the doctrine of the Pharisees and of the Sadducees.' The point of this lies in the fact that the word 'leaven' was used metaphorically for 'influence', and especially for 'evil influence'. It is therefore advisable to amplify: 'They then understood that he was not speaking to them about leaven in the sense of leaven that is in loaves, but in the sense of the evil influence of the Pharisees and Sadducees.'

Sometimes a play on words has to be in some way explained in English, because it is impossible to transfer a pun from one language to another without explanation. Matthew 16.18 runs: 'And I say also unto thee, That thou art Peter, and upon this rock I will build my Church.' The point here depends on the fact that the word for Peter is *Petros*, and the word for a rock is '*petra*'. There is thus a play on words between 'Peter' and 'rock'. There is no way in which this can be directly represented in English. We therefore have to amplify: 'I tell you, you are Peter—the man whose name means a rock—and on this rock I will erect my Church.'

A simple instance of amplification comes from Matthew 18.2. There the AV runs: 'Jesus called a little child unto him, and set him in the midst of them.' 'In the midst of them' is not modern English, and even if it is changed to 'in the middle of them' it still remains unnatural in English. It is better to change the phrase to the English phrase which naturally describes what was done: 'Jesus called a little child, and made him stand where they could all see him.'

In the parable of the wicked husbandmen the introductory words require explanatory amplification. In the AV they run: 'There was a certain householder, which planted a vineyard, and hedged it round about, and digged a winepress in it, and built a tower' (Matthew 21.33). To the modern reader the phrases about digging a winepress and building a tower are obscure. The winepress was a stone-lined tank-like structure sunk in the ground. The grapes were thrown into it, and then trampled with the feet, and so the juice was extracted. The tower was a watch-tower, from which a sentinel could keep watch for thieves and marauders. It is therefore clearer to amplify: 'There was a householder who planted a vineyard. He surrounded it with a hedge, and dug out a pit in which the juice could be extracted from the grapes, and built a watch-tower.'

In some very few cases the whole New Testament metaphor is obscure because it comes from a society and from activities which are now quite strange. On some few occasions it is in such instances better to go the whole way with Hilaire Belloc's principle, and to ask, not, how can this be put into English, but, how would an Englishman of the middle twentieth century have said it. For instance in the parable of the talents, Matthew 25.24-27 runs:

> 'Then he which had received the one talent came and said, Lord, I knew thee that thou art an hard man, reaping where thou hast not sown, and gathering where thou hast not strawed: and I was afraid, and went and hid thy talent in the earth; lo, there thou hast that is thine. His lord answered and said unto him, Thou wicked and slothful servant, thou knewest that I reap where I sowed not, and gather where I have not strawed: thou oughtest therefore to have put my money to the exchangers, and then at my coming I should have received mine own with usury.'

This passage as it stands is in terms of agricultural practice, which is quite strange to a modern urban man. It is better therefore to modernize the picture:

> 'The man who had been given the two hundred and fifty pounds came up. Sir, he said, I am well aware that you are a shrewd and ruthless business-man. I know that you have a habit of letting someone else do the work and of then taking the profits. I know that you often step in and appropriate the results of some enterprise which you did not initiate. So I went and hid your two hundred and fifty pounds in a hole in the ground, because I was afraid to take the risk of doing anything with it. Here you are! Your money is safe! You lazy good-for-nothing, his master answered. You knew very well that I have a habit of letting other people do the work and of then taking the profits. You knew very well that I often step in and appropriate the results of some enterprise which I did not initiate. That is all the more reason why you ought to have lodged my money with the bankers, and then, when I came home, I would have got my money back with interest.'

It is neither safe nor wise to use this kind of amplification frequently, but in this particular case there is much to be gained by setting the scene in a contemporary background rather than to leave it in a quite unfamiliar series of pictures.

The New Testament is characteristically elliptical, especially in comparisons, and there are occasions when amplification is required, if the thing is to be said as it would be said in natural and idiomatic English. In the AV John 3.8 reads: 'The wind bloweth where it listeth, and thou hearest the sound thereof, but canst not tell whence it cometh, and whither it goeth: so is everyone that is born of the Spirit.' The meaning is better expressed, if we amplify: 'The wind blows where it wills, and you hear the sound of it, but you do not know where it comes from and where it is going. And there is the same invisible and unpredictable power in everyone who undergoes this spiritual rebirth.'

There is the same elliptical characteristic in the introduction of scriptural quotations, especially when prophecy is involved. In the AV of John 19.24 the incident of the sharing out of Jesus' clothes is told, and an Old Testament quotation is introduced. 'They said therefore among themselves, Let us not rend it, but cast lots for it, whose it shall be; that the scripture might be fulfilled, which saith, They parted my raiment among them, and for my vesture they did cast lots.' To turn this into English an addition must be made: 'We mustn't tear it, they said. It will be better to draw lots to see who is to get it. This they did so that the passage of scripture might come true, They divided my clothes amongst each other, and they cast lots for my raiment.'

In the AV Acts 10.9 reads: 'On the morrow, as they went on their journey, and drew nigh unto the city, Peter went up upon the housetop to pray about the sixth hour.' If this is seen in modern terms, a very odd picture emerges, for a man praying on the roof of a modern house would be in a position at once uncomfortable and insecure. But the Palestinian house had a quite flat roof, reached by an outside stair. Since the Palestinian house of the ordinary people had only one room, life was very crowded, and so the flat roof became the place to which people withdrew for quiet and meditation and prayer. It is better for the sake of the correct picture to translate: 'Peter went up on to the flat roof of the house to pray.'

In Acts 18.18 it is said of Paul that he had 'shorn his head at Cenchreae: for he had a vow.' The vow in question, the vow which involved the cutting of the hair, was the Nazirite vow, which is described in Numbers 6. It is better to insert the word 'Nazirite', and to say: 'At Cenchreae he had his hair cut off, because he had taken the Nazirite vow.'

For and *But*: 'For' and 'but' are words which need special treatment under the heading of expansion. Both are used highly elliptically, and they are used with such freedom that it is not possible to lay down any general rules. Each case must be taken by itself. We can do no more than illustrate the kind of treatment these two words need.

We begin with 'for' (*gar*).

In Matthew 2.2 the AV, and the RSV is to all intents and purposes the same, has in the story of the wise men: 'Where is he that is born king of the Jews? For we have seen his star in the east, and are come to worship him.' To make this into natural English we have to expand thus: 'Where is the newly born King of the Jews? We are looking for him, because we have seen his star rise, and we have come to do homage to him.' In Matthew 14.3,4 in the John the Baptist story two of these 'fors' occur side by side in the AV:

> 'Herod said unto his servants, This is John the Baptist; he is risen from the dead; and therefore mighty works do show forth themselves in him. For Herod had laid hold on John and bound him, and put him in prison for Herodias' sake, his brother Philip's wife. For John said unto him, It is not lawful for thee to have her.'

If this is to run as natural English the 'fors' must be expanded as follows:

> 'This is John the Baptizer, Herod said to his servants. He has come back to life. That is why he possesses these miraculous powers. Herod thought this because he had arrested John the Baptizer, and had imprisoned him in chains because of the affair of Herodias, his brother Philip's wife. The trouble had arisen because John had told him that he had no right to marry her.'

Perhaps the most difficult 'for' in the New Testament occurs in Acts 15.21. Acts 15.19-21 runs:

> 'Wherefore my sentence is, that we trouble not them, which from among the Gentiles are turned to God: but that we write unto them, that they abstain from pollutions of idols, and from fornication, and from things strangled and from blood. *For* Moses of old time hath in every city them that preach him, being read in the synagogues every sabbath day.'

On the face of it, the 'for' seems to have no connection at all with what goes before. Something has to be supplied. We suggest that the connection may be expanded as follows:

> '*If anyone still personally wishes to observe the Law he can do so*, for from ancient times there have been those in every town who proclaimed the Law of Moses, and it is still read in the synagogues every Sabbath.'

We now turn to 'but' (*alla*). *Alla* is an adversative, introducing some kind of contrast with what has gone before. The AV generally retains 'but'. But more flexibility is necessary.

In the AV Matthew 15.11 runs: 'Not that which goeth into the mouth defileth a man; but that which cometh out of the mouth, this defileth a man.' It will be better to translate: 'It is not what goes into a man's mouth that defiles him. On the contrary, it is what comes out of a man's mouth that defiles him.'

John 3.36 runs in the AV: 'He that believeth on the Son hath everlasting life: and he that believeth not on the Son shall not see life: but the wrath of God abideth on him.' It will be better to translate: 'To believe in the Son is to enjoy the experience of eternal life; to refuse to believe in the Son is to deprive oneself of the experience of life. More, it is to become the object of the wrath of God.'

John 9.3 runs in the AV: 'Jesus answered, Neither hath this man sinned, nor his parents: but that the works of God should be made manifest in him.' It will be better to translate: 'Jesus answered: The reason for this man's blindness is neither any sin of his own nor of his parents; the reason is to allow the activity of God to be displayed.'

Sometimes the best way to deal with *alla* is to omit it and to represent the antithesis simply by the silent juxtaposition of two sayings. John 14.24 runs in the AV: 'The word which ye hear is not mine, but the Father's which sent me.' It is more effective simply to say: 'The message I have brought to you is not mine; it comes from the Father who sent me.'

Sometimes the use of *alla* is highly elliptical. John 18.28 reads in the AV: 'They themselves went not into the judgment hall, lest they should be defiled; but that they might eat the Passover.' As it stands, that is not English at all. It should be translated: 'The Jews did not themselves enter the governor's headquarters. They did not want to risk being ceremonially defiled. They wanted to be able to eat the Passover meal.' It can be seen that in the case of both *gar* and *alla* flexibility is the first essential.

OMISSIONS

There is one word and there is one phrase in the New Testament, both of which are best dealt with by simple omission. The word is 'Lo!' (*ide* or *idou*: e.g. Matthew 2.9; 3.16,17; 26.47; 28.7; Mark 10.28; Luke 13.16; 15.29; Acts 13.46). The word represents a Hebrew way of speaking, and has no natural equivalent in English, and in the great majority of cases it is better simply to omit it.

The phrase is of the very essence of biblical language; it is the phrase 'it came to pass' (*egeneto*). It occurs 7 times in Matthew, 6 in Mark, 49 times in Luke, not in this sense at all in John, and 15 times in Acts (e.g. Matthew 7.28; 9.10; Mark 2.15; Luke 1.41; 6.1; Acts 4.5; 22.17). To take only one example, the AV reads: 'And it came to pass, when Jesus had ended these sayings the people were astonished at his doctrine' (Matthew 7.28). 'It came to pass' is a characteristically

Hebrew way of introducing a sentence. In English it has no equivalent and should be omitted, as both the RSV and the NEB omit it. It should be translated simply: 'When Jesus finished speaking, the crowds were astonished at the way he taught.'

MANNERS AND CUSTOMS

It sometimes happens that for clarity's sake manners and customs have to be explained, as it were, within the translation. There are certain occasions when that has been done.

In Matthew 1.18-20 there is an outline of the relationship of Mary and Joseph before the birth of Jesus. As it stands in the AV it is puzzling to western ears:

> 'Now the birth of Jesus Christ was on this wise: When as his mother Mary was espoused to Joseph, before they came together, she was found with child of the Holy Ghost. Then Joseph her husband, being a just man, and not willing to make her a publick example, was minded to put her away privily. But while he thought on these things, behold, the angel of the Lord appeared unto him in a dream, saying: Joseph, thou son of David, fear not to take unto thee Mary thy wife: for that which is conceived in her is of the Holy Ghost.'

The difficulty of this passage to modern minds is that in it Mary appears as being engaged to be married to Joseph, and the whole incident takes place before their marriage; and yet at the same time she is described as his wife, and Joseph is shown as contemplating divorce. The explanation is that in Palestine betrothal lasted for one year. It was as legally binding as marriage. During that time the couple were known as husband and wife, and, if the man should die in the period of betrothal, the girl was a widow. Consequently, the relationship could only be dissolved by divorce. To make this situation clear, the passage should be translated as follows:

> 'This was the way in which the birth of Jesus took place. Mary his mother was pledged to be married to Joseph, but, before they became man and wife, it was discovered that she was going to have a child, as a result of the action of the Holy Spirit. Although Joseph her intended husband was a man who strictly kept the Law, he had no desire publicly to humiliate her, so he wished to

divorce her secretly. While he was planning to do this, an angel of the Lord appeared to him in a dream. Joseph, son of David, the angel said, do not hesitate to marry Mary, for it is as a result of the action of the Holy Spirit that she is going to have a child.'

Within the context of Jewish marriage customs the sequence of events is clear.

The AV of Matthew 3.12 has an expression not now intelligible. It says of the Coming One that his fan is in his hand, and that he will thoroughly purge his floor. The RSV substitutes 'winnowing fork' for 'fan', and the NEB has: 'His shovel is ready in his hand.' All these translations are equally obscure to a western reader in the twentieth century. The 'fan' or 'fork' or 'shovel' was a broad-bladed tool with which the grain was tossed into the air, into the wind. The result was that the heavy grain fell back to the ground, and the chaff was blown away. It is better to say quite simply: 'He is going to winnow the chaff from the grain.'

In the AV of Matthew 10.14 we have: 'And whosoever shall not receive you, nor hear your words, when ye depart out of that house or city, shake off the dust of your feet.' Similar phrases occur in Mark 6.11; Acts 13.51; 18.6. The modern translations do not provide anything fresh. At the back of this there is a Jewish custom. When a Jew left a Gentile city, he was enjoined to shake the last speck of its dust off his shoes and clothes, because it was polluted. It is better to explain the custom within the translation: 'If anyone refuses you a welcome or a hearing, as you leave that house or town, shake the last speck of its dust from your feet, as if you were leaving a heathen town.'

Time expressions have to be altered into their modern equivalents. The Jewish day ran from 6 a.m. to 6 p.m. Therefore (e.g. Matthew 20.3-6) the third hour is 9 a.m., the sixth hour is 12 noon, the ninth hour is 3 p.m. and the eleventh hour is 5 p.m. Time was measured in another way during the night. Matthew 14.25 speaks of 'the fourth watch'. The night was divided into four three-hour watches—6 p.m. to 9 p.m., 9 p.m. to 12 midnight, 12 midnight to 3 a.m., 3 a.m. to 6 a.m. 'The fourth watch' may therefore be translated 'about three o'clock in the morning'.

On certain occasions (e.g. Matthew 9.20; 14.35; Mark 6.56) people who wished to be healed are said to touch, or to wish to touch, the 'hem' of Jesus' garment. The RSV has 'fringe' and the NEB 'edge'. This is a reference to the fringes or tassels that a Jew was ordered by the Law to wear on his outer garment (Numbers 15.37-39; Deuteronomy 22.12). 'Tassel' (as the RSV has in the OT passages) is the best translation.

In Matthew 15.5 and Mark 7.11 there is a reference to the statement of the man who says that he is unable to use any of his money to help his parents. In Matthew the AV has: 'It is a gift.' And in Mark it has: 'It is Corban.' This is a reference to a custom whereby a Jew sometimes dedicated all he had to the service of God. This, of course, could be an act of exceptional and even sacrificial piety, although in the passage in question it was only a legal ruse to avoid giving help. It is better to fill out the translation and to say, 'a gift dedicated to God, and usable for no other purpose.'

In the Gospels there are frequent references to money. The various money terms may be tabulated as follows.

SILVER COINAGE

Talent (Matthew 18.24; 25.15,16). The *talent* was not an actual coin but a weight of silver, equivalent in value to £240.

Mina (Luke 19.13,16), translated 'pound' in the AV. The *mina* was equal to one-sixtieth of a *talent* or to one hundred *drachmae*. It was therefore equal to about £4. A five-pound note would be its nearest English equivalent.

Denarius, misleadingly translated 'penny' in the AV; in the RSV the word *denarius* is retained. It was the commonest of coins and is mentioned most frequently (Matthew 18.28; 20.2,9,10,13; 22.19; Mark 6.37; 12.15; 14.5; Luke 7.41; 10.35; 20.24; John 6.7; 12.5). It was a silver coin worth about 9½d.

Drachma (Luke 15.8,9). The AV calls it 'a piece of silver', the RSV 'a silver coin', explaining in the margin that it was a *drachma*. Its value was the same as the *denarius*. Broadly speaking, it was the Greek equivalent of the Roman *denarius*.

Didrachmon (Matthew 17.24). The AV calls it 'tribute money'; the RSV calls it 'half-shekel'. It was worth about 1s. 6d.

Stater (Matthew 17.27, the coin in the fish's mouth). The AV calls it 'a piece of money'; the RSV calls it a 'shekel'. It was worth four *drachmae*, and was therefore the equivalent of about 3s.

COPPER COINAGE

Assarion (Matthew 10.29; Luke 12.6). The AV calls it a 'farthing', and the RSV a 'penny'. It was one-sixteenth of a *denarius*; the nearest English equivalent is halfpenny.

Kodrantes or *Quadrans* (Matthew 5.26; Mark 12.42). The AV calls it a 'farthing' and the RSV a 'penny'. It was one quarter of an *assarion*, and therefore equal to an eighth of a penny.

Lepton (Mark 12.42; Luke 12.59; 21.2; literally, 'the thin one'). The AV calls it a 'mite', and says two made a farthing; the RSV calls it a copper coin and says two made a penny. It was equal to one-eighth of an *assarion*, that is to say one-sixteenth of a penny. It was the 'widow's mite'.

The unsatisfactory thing about this is that, although it is not difficult to assign a modern equivalent in money to these ancient coins, it is far from easy to get an idea of their purchasing power. The purchasing power was many times greater than that of an equivalent sum today. The standard by which to judge is the fact that one *denarius* was the average day's wage for a working man in Palestine in New Testament times. There are sometimes ways in which this can be shown. In the story of the feeding of the five thousand in the AV Mark 6.37 reads: 'Shall we go and buy two hundred pennyworth of bread and give them to eat?' The RSV does no more than substitute two hundred denarii worth for two hundred pennyworth. The NEB goes a little further and has: 'Are we to go and spend twenty pounds on bread to give them a meal?' A better way to get the sense is to translate: 'Are we going to spend a year's wages buying bread to give them a meal?' The same kind of translation can be used in Mark 14.5 and John 12.5.

In Mark 11.16 there is a curious phrase. It is said of Jesus: 'He would not suffer that any man should carry any vessel through the temple.' The Jewish Law laid it down: 'A man may not enter into the temple mount with his staff or his sandal or his wallet, or with the dust upon his feet, nor may he make of it a short bypath.' In the time of Jesus it had become a not uncommon custom for people to use the Temple precincts as a short-cut from the city to the Mount of Olives. The picture will be clear, if we translate: 'He would not allow anyone to use the Temple court as a short-cut between the shops and their houses.'

There are certain occasions when the Jewish position at meals has to be understood before the scene can be properly visualized. The table was a low block. The guest did not sit at table; he reclined on a couch which usually held three people. The guest reclined, leaning on his left elbow to leave his right hand free, with his feet and legs stretched out on the couch behind him. This meant that the person reclining on a guest's right lay with his head almost resting on the guest's shoulder. This is what the AV means when it says (John 13.25; 21.20) that John was lying on Jesus' breast. The RSV has 'close to the breast of Jesus'. The NEB has, 'leaned back close to Jesus'. The picture is so very different from anything that we know that it is best to translate it: 'One of his disciples, the disciple who was specially dear to Jesus, was reclining on Jesus' right, so that his head was leaning against Jesus' shoulder. Simon Peter signed to him. Ask him who he is talking about, he said. So then, leaning close to Jesus as he was, he said to him, Master, who is it?'

It is important to remember the same custom in Luke 7.36-38. There the AV says that Jesus was sitting at table, and then goes on to say that the woman, standing behind him, anointed his feet with the perfume. If the word 'sitting' is used, the picture becomes very strange, for the only place in which the woman could have been is below the table! The picture is of one reclining, not sitting.

SENTENCE SHAPES

No two languages have the same sentence shape. It is therefore sometimes necessary to reshape the Greek sentence in order to turn it into idiomatic English. We can here select only certain examples of this kind of change.

SUBORDINATION

There are cases in which Greek does not subordinate and in which English would subordinate. In the AV John 1.10 reads: 'He was in the world, and the world was made by him, and the world knew him not.' Here English would subordinate the clauses: 'He was in the world, and, although it was through him that the world came into being, the world failed to recognize him.' There are cases in which Greek does subordinate when English would not. In the AV Mark 12.15 reads: 'Bring me a penny, that I may see it.' Here English would say: 'Bring me a shilling, and let me see it.' In the AV John 6.12 reads: 'Gather up the fragments that remain, that nothing be lost.' English would rather say: 'Collect the pieces that are left over. We mustn't waste anything.'

IMPERATIVES

Greek uses the imperative much more freely than English does. In many cases in which Greek uses the imperative English would more naturally use a form with 'must'. In Matthew 5.48 the AV reads: 'Be ye therefore perfect, even as your Father which is in heaven is perfect.' English more naturally says: 'You must be perfect as your heavenly Father is perfect.' In Matthew 10.5 the AV reads: 'Go not into the way of the Gentiles, and into any city of the Samaritans enter ye not: but go rather to the lost sheep of the house of Israel.' It is more natural English to say: 'You must not go off on any road that leads to Gentile territory; you must not go into any Samaritan town; it is rather to the sheep of the family of Israel who have gone lost that you must go.'

VOCATIVES

Greek uses vocatives much more frequently than English does. In fact, modern English hardly uses the vocative with 'O' at all. In the AV Matthew 6.30 reads: 'Wherefore, if God so clothe the grass of the field, which to day is, and to morrow is cast into the oven, shall he not much more clothe you, O ye of little faith?' English would say: 'You have so little faith! If God clothes like that the wild flowers which have one brief day, and which tomorrow are used to make a fire to heat an oven, can you not depend on him far more to clothe you?' In the AV Matthew 14.31 reads: 'O thou of little faith, wherefore didst thou doubt?' English would say: 'You have so little faith! Why did you begin to doubt?'

CLAUSES BEGINNING 'HE THAT', 'WHOEVER', 'EVERYONE', ETC.

Such clauses are very common in the New Testament writers; they are in fact characteristic of the AV. Often, though not invariably, the sentence will read more naturally in English, if an 'if' clause is used instead. In the AV, Mark 4.25 reads: 'For he that hath, to him shall be given; and he that hath not, from him shall be taken even that which he hath.' A more natural English form is: 'For, if a man already has, more will be given to him, and, if a man has not, even that which he has will be taken from him.'

When such sentences and clauses are statements of general principles an even more idiomatic English sentence shape is attainable by the use of the infinitive. In John 12.44,45 the AV reads: 'Jesus cried and said, He that believeth on me, believeth not on me, but on him that sent me. And he that seeth me seeth him that sent me.' It is more characteristically English to translate: 'Jesus said for all to hear: To believe in me is to believe, not in me, but in him who sent me; and to see me is to see him who sent me.' John 6.58 reads in the AV: 'He that eateth of this bread shall live for ever.' It is better translated: 'To eat this bread is to live for ever.' In the AV, John 14.9 reads: 'He that hath seen me hath seen the Father.' More characteristically English is: 'To have seen me is to have seen the Father.'

INVERSION

There is, especially in John's Gospel, an inversion of the normal English order of the sentence. In the AV, John 17.18 reads: 'As thou hast sent me into the world, even so have I also sent them into the world.' The natural English order is: 'I send them out into the world, just as you sent me into the world.' Again John 17.22 reads in the AV: 'And the glory which thou gavest me I have given them.' The natural English order is: 'I have given them the glory which you gave me.'

There remains one point to comment on. I have naturally used 'you' for 'thou' in all human references; but I have used it in divine references too. There are two reasons for this.

First, in the singular the Bible itself uses the same pronoun both for God and man. All through the Bible the address to both man and God is 'thou', as e.g. in the Ten Commandments. Since the singular form 'thou' is no longer used at all, it is natural still to use the same form of the pronoun as it is in modern English.

Second, Jesus called God *Abba* (Mark 14.36), and it is this very name that we too through the Holy Spirit can use to God (Romans 8.15; Galatians 4.6). It may indeed be said that the whole of Christianity is epitomized in this very word. Now this word is the word which a little Jewish child used in the home circle to his parent—and still does. In any ordinary context it would be 'Daddy'. In this word our relationship to God is summed up in all its intimacy; and we must speak to the God to whom we are as close as that in the ordinary language of a child to his father, and not in an archaic Elizabethan language which no one has used in a person-to-person way for centuries.